Bt 7.50

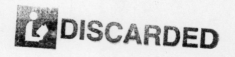

CAVALIER DRAMA

CAVALIER DRAMA

AN HISTORICAL AND CRITICAL SUPPLEMENT TO THE STUDY OF THE ELIZABETHAN AND RESTORATION STAGE

BY

ALFRED HARBAGE

NEW YORK

RUSSELL & RUSSELL · INC

1964

TO
FELIX E. SCHELLING

PREFACE

WHILE preparing biographies of Thomas Killigrew and Sir William Davenant, I found that it encouraged a fresh point of view to deal with material spanning Elizabethan and Restoration dramatic history, and I projected the present book. Facilities for gaining access to manuscripts and rare prints were provided me by a committee of the Board of Graduate Education and Research of the University of Pennsylvania, drawing upon a special research fund. Without the assistance thus rendered, my work could not have been done.

The bibliography originally planned to accompany this study is available elsewhere. Most of the authors treated appear in "Minor Dramatists: 1603-1660," a section in the forthcoming *Cambridge Bibliography of English Literature* with which I have assisted; and the manuscripts are listed in my "Elizabethan and Seventeenth-Century Play Manuscripts," *PMLA*, L (1935), 687-699. Secondary sources of information are indicated in the footnotes (at the end of chapters) with sufficient fullness to insure identification; it may be well to explain, however, that the publications of the *Historical Manuscripts Commission* are numbered according to the system followed in the index volumes of the series.

Of those who have read this study in manuscript, Dr. Joseph Q. Adams of the Folger Shakespeare Library, Professor Allardyce Nicoll of Yale University, and Professor J. S. P. Tatlock of the University of California have been kind enough to communicate with me directly. I wish to thank them for their interest and helpful criticism—without implying that they endorse my views or stand sponsor for the accuracy of my facts. I wish also to acknowledge the courtesies extended to me by the Committee on Research Activities of the Modern Language Association, and by Mr. Donald Goodchild of the American Council of Learned Societies. My generous colleague, Dr. Edgar Potts, has read the proof, and my always helpful wife has prepared the index.

October, 1936.   A. H.

CONTENTS

INTRODUCTION

THE term Cavalier Drama is not so familiar in studies of the English theatre that it needs no apology, yet the term may be properly used. That same class of authors who gave us our Cavalier lyrics wrote also a number of plays, and these plays, although long banished to the realm of half-forgotten things, form an important link in the chain of dramatic history. The purpose of the present book is to discuss the trends in English drama during the Caroline and Commonwealth periods, and the first few years of the Restoration, with a view to illustrating the continuity of an English literary tradition.

That the Commonwealth period, when theatres were outlawed, is not here dismissed as a blank will seem natural enough to students of today. Modern scholars have enabled us to see that the interruption effected by Puritan rule was less complete than used generally to be supposed. Plays were acted during the time of prohibition, by amateurs in private and by professionals in public—furtively as a rule, but sometimes openly and with quasi-official toleration. Plays were more eagerly read than ever before; and new plays were written—by dramatists who had been active before 1642, by others who remained active after 1660, and by others whose total production belongs to this period when once there was supposed to have been no drama.

That neither 1642 nor 1660 is selected as a terminal date will also seem natural. Each was a year of political more than of literary change, and each affected the public performance of plays rather than the English love of plays and inherited aptitude for creating particular kinds. Elizabethan drama did not foresee that, at such and such a time, a Parliamentary resolution would close the theatres, and was not willing to cease evolving after the days of Shakespeare, or the days of Fletcher, merely surviving with diminishing pulse, prepared to expire when that resolution came. By the same token, Restoration drama did not cast its nativity and assume a parcel of self-determined qualities on the day when young Charles debarked from the *Naseby*. Political and literary history are linked, but in no such relation. The wellsprings of drama lie deep in the national culture, a factor more powerful in the end than the spectacular edicts of new political administrations.

What may seem unusual about this book is the lack of emphasis placed upon the popular stage. The explanation lies in the fact that in the mid-seventeenth century the most striking evolution in serious

1

drama was effected, not by professional playwrights, but by the fashionable gentry active in the Caroline court and on the Royal side in the Civil Wars—by the "Cavaliers." When Fletcher died, he was succeeded by no popular playwright with a personal note so novel or so appealing as to set a fashion. Ford in tragedy and Shirley in comedy were original, but they were not immediately influential. Fletcher himself, and Ben Jonson, continued to be imitated in the theatres. Then, in 1633, the Queen of England acted a part in Walter Montague's *The Shepherd's Paradise*, precipitating the "Prynne episode" and inducing a number of courtiers, almost as an expression of loyalty to their Queen, to imitate Montague by writing plays. The courtly usurpation of the stage, so striking after the Restoration, began in the Caroline era. From the time of Montague, Carlell, Suckling, Killigrew, and Cartwright to the time of Stapylton, Digby, Howard, and Orrery scores of plays were written by Cavaliers, some of whom are not commonly known to have written at all. Sometimes the new interest in drama functioned oddly as a social leveller. In 1627 William Davenant, son of a taverner, was a common playwright, while Thomas Killigrew, son of a Vice Chamberlain, was Page of Honor to the King; but in 1660 Killigrew was a playhouse manager, with Davenant—now *Sir* William Davenant—as his professional rival.

Montague and his followers were able, because of the special character of their circle, to work a new variation upon tragicomedy. Courtly predilections, clearly evident as early as the time of *The Arcadia* and *Euphues,* but held in abeyance so long as drama was mainly the property of the London populace, now found expression in plays, together with fads more recently acquired from D'Urfé and the *précieuses.* Like *Tamburlaine, The Spanish Tragedy, Every Man in his Humor,* and *Philaster,* Walter Montague's "pastoral" may be considered as a fashion-setting play. The manner of *The Shepherd's Paradise* was modified by the more heroical tendencies of Carlell and other courtiers, so that a composite inspiration went into the making of typical plays of the Cavalier mode. The mode culminated, or so it may be argued, in the heroic plays of John Dryden. That the plays of Montague and Carlell are inferior in quality should not confuse the issue, for plays need not be good in order to set a fashion.

Nearly all Cavalier plays are inferior in quality, and the historian's penalty for dealing with a body of literature which Time has justly submerged is self-evident. Cavalier plays are often so similar in theme that it is hard to describe them in such a way as to distinguish one from another, and their artistic weakness is so manifest that it is hard to concede the point with play after play without subjecting all to a monotonous drizzle of sarcasm. It is equally hard to convey impressions of merit in certain plays without seeming totally to have lost one's sense of proportion. Depressed by the knowledge that he is dealing constantly with the trivial, the historian must draw comfort from the truism that a body of material, unimportant in each detail, may be important in the aggregate.

Apart from their significance as a stage in the evolution of English drama, the plays to be discussed have an undeniable interest as social history. Although we are here largely concerned with the problem of literary continuity, we are also concerned with Cavalier drama itself— with its kind, with its quality or lack of quality, and with the lives, the character, and the background of those who produced it. The interest of the reader will normally be focussed elsewhere, and he will see in the plays described the last withered blossoms of Elizabethan drama, or the first green buds of Restoration drama, according to his point of view, but it is to be hoped that he will see something else as well. These plays deserve, for a smiling while at least, attention for their own sake. The Cavalier is known by his scintillant lyrics of love and laughter, by his repute as a roisterer and scapegrace, and to some by the records of his social and religious bigotry; but he is revealed here upon a new and almost unsuspected side. These plays furnish insight into a generation, faded, exotic, and absurd though they often are.

The material of the book has been arranged with a view to the convenience of two different classes of readers. In Part I are brought together such conclusions concerning trends as may be of fairly general interest. In Part II is a detailed description of the body of material upon which these conclusions are based. Cavalier plays will never receive the minute scholarly attention which Elizabethan plays have received and which Restoration plays are now receiving. They are, and will remain, the most rarely read and least known of all our earlier English drama, if for no other reason than that many of them exist only in manuscript or in rare and inaccessible early editions. Even the specialist need not feel called upon to read all of these plays. Since the survey in Part II is intended as a substitute for, rather than as a guide to, reading, it has been made, regretfully, encyclopedic: it is filled with biographical data, synopses, and quotations, as well as evaluations. In deprecation one can only say, that it is intended for reference, and that the index is complete.

PART ONE
TRENDS

I

THE COURT INVADES THE DRAMA

WHEN Elizabethan drama was taking shape, the court and the courtiers helped to fashion the mould. Then the theatre of the populace outstripped all else, and except in the schools, the Quality ceased to traffic with an art sullied by the professional dexterity of the sons of Kentish and Warwickshire yeomen. The heyday of drama had passed, and the body of Shakespeare had lain by the banks of the Avon a decade, before courtly hands began to reach again for the puppet strings. They could do little harm now, as in the interim they could have done little good, and the effects produced were divertingly fantastic. These effects were important too, for the prestige of Westminster was still potent enough to send a new current into the stream of our dramatic development.

It was a gesture from the throne that made the court invade the drama. Caroline royalty wished to *participate* in plays, yearning from Stuart illusions in life toward their microcosm on the stage. At least this is one explanation for the renewal of courtly intimacy with the mimic art; there are others less intangible. For their effects to be calculated, the novel features of Caroline dramatic patronage must be recognized; a glance must be spared at the royal attitude during preceding reigns.

Queen Elizabeth had patronized the drama officially. She had permitted it to flourish. For this we should be grateful, but we should not mistake her rôle. Elizabeth was not in reality like that tutelary deity in the red wig who presides benignantly at the Shakespeare festivals of women's colleges. She was further still from the imaginative conception in Clemence Dane's *Will Shakespeare*—a woman holding the threads of destiny in the lives of Marlowe and his Stratford rival, and pondering, with queenly intensity, how the latter must prevail since his is a richer poetic gift for the world. The conjunction of a great drama and a great queen seems to demand a link between the two closer than their being products alike of a great age. Even historians of the drama are a little misleading in this matter. Enthusiasts, they are apt to appropriate the Queen.

The inspiration playwrights took from Elizabeth was generated within; her personal condescensions to their offerings were few, her patronage regally aloof. She permitted herself to be amused by plays, selected, censored, and supervised by her office of the revels, but she was a cold spectator, easily displeased and morbidly quick to take offense. The records preserve but few comments on the many plays that she saw, and usually these are in the vein of her remark to De Silva concerning *Juno and Diana,* "This is all against me."¹ We have no right to expect of her elaborate critiques, or to charge her with lack of appreciation; contemporary appreciation was loud in no quarter and is now scarcely audible. Native drama was not taken to be literature; plays filled the idle hours; trivial in the lives of subjects, how trivial indeed in the life of their great monarch. We shall look in vain for a sign that it was otherwise. Elizabeth, passive as a spectator, is inconceivable as a participant. Peele touched the limits of propriety when he concluded his *Arraignment of Paris* by denying Até's golden apple to Venus herself and presenting it to the fairer Eliza on her throne, thus conscripting her for his cast. Previously it had been matter for remark when a sonnet praising her beauty had been received from a performer with her own queenly hands. Reputedly unconventional, she felt her majesty and kept her royal state; knowledge that an English queen would one day act in a play would have stunned her sense of propriety; nor would she have relished more the thought that an English king would one day supply fables to playmakers. There is a legend that *The Merry Wives of Windsor* was written because Elizabeth wished to see Falstaff in love. Let us believe it, then let us savor it as the Queen's sole intimacy with the drama of her day. May games, archery contests, country dances, plays: Elizabeth was the patron of all diversions—viewed from an eminence.

King James had a relish for plays more demonstrative than Elizabeth's, but he too was content to let them spawn naturally among his subjects, and after a few early generosities to the players, his routine payments of ten pounds per court performance became his only effective liaison with the stage. These court performances he required constantly. "What do you tell me of the fashion?" he replied to his Lords when they demurred at a play on Christmas; "I will make it a fashion."² Since his wife and children could each order the players to court, performances at some seasons occurred almost nightly. Yet little remains to show that one kind of play was preferred before another, save that most should be "new," or that any interest was taken in the men who wrote them. The best of Shakespeare, new minted and made current by his own men, must have been acted at Whitehall, often to be received there with amiable indifference, like dinner music now. James had, truly, a favorite play—not *Lear* or *The Tempest,* not even one of the

spiced romances or wicked comedies of Fletcher, but George Ruggles'
Ignoramus, a broad lampoon. This delighted him so vastly that he
returned to Cambridge to see it again. As a rule, even at the universities, James did not exert himself to be a gracious spectator; he showed
a discouraging tendency to sleep or to leave early. His response to
Barten Holiday's *Technogamia or the Marriage of the Arts* is preserved
by a contemporary wit:

> At Christ Church Marriage, done before the king,
> Lest that those mates should want an offering,
> The king himself did offer; What I pray?
> He offer'd twice or thrice to go away.[3]

James' was a blunt nature, and that simian gravity with which he contemplated his own kingly divinity and the prerogative of his bishops
relaxed into boisterousness, not into the subtle enjoyments of a Mæcenas. He had his literary protégés and his personal ambitions, but
these were in the sphere of piety and pedantry.

Queen Anne showed more initiative than her husband in directing
the pleasures of Whitehall; she frequently, like James on occasion,
danced in court masques; and although her connection with regular
drama is only that of a constant spectator, to a certain popular dramatist she gave steady employment and became the *raison d'être* of one
section of his dramatic works. Ben Jonson's best masques were created
on Anne's commissions for entertainments which she herself planned
and organized. She even at times suggested the subject matter, and if
Jonson was not being simply complimentary in his foreword to the
Masque of Queens, the capital idea of the antimasque originated with
her. Had Anne's interest as a participant extended beyond the masque
and had she been surrounded by a more sympathetic court, the movement we shall trace might have received an earlier impetus. As it is, no
courtly clique of writers responded to the activities of the Queen;
owing to her curious lack of prestige these only contributed to her
reputation of frivolity. When Anne died and left James a widower,
court entertainment tended to center about Buckingham; but the
efforts of Buckingham and his circle found their plane in buffoonery
and the dance; they have scarcely any literary implications.

It was several years after King Charles had ascended the throne that
royal interest in the drama assumed its first true note of intimacy. The
actors were being called to court with greater frequency than ever, and
there are signs that they were received with greater cordiality. Sir Henry
Herbert, his Majesty's Master of the Revels, began to note that certain
plays were "well likte," that the "kinge and queene were very well pleasd

with my service."[4] When Davenant's *Wits* was presented in 1634, Herbert observed that "the kinge commended the language, but dislikt the plott and characters."[5] Characters, plot, language: distinguished and weighed by the King—here is refined criticism! Previously Charles had gone over the manuscript of this play and softened the rigors of censorship by restoring such expressions as *faith, death,* and *slight,* judged by him to be "asseverations only, and no oathes."[6] One can picture neither Elizabeth nor James thus reviewing a playbook. An even closer contact between king and dramatic text is recorded in this same year when *The Gamester* was presented at court, "made by Sherley out of a plot of the king's." Observe too the latter's paternal pride; he "sayd it was the best play he had seen for seven years."[7] Charles must also have supplied the plot of *The Passionate Lovers.* In the epilogue to Part I, he is addressed by Carlell, the author:

> If what hath been presented to your sense
> You do approve, thank your own influence;
> Which moving in the story that you told
> Infus'd new heat into a brain grown cold . . .

Nor were the King's dealings with drama of only one kind. He bore the expense so that Mayne's *City Match* might be acted at Blackfriars.[8] Cartwright planned to destroy the manuscript of *The Siege,* but upon Charles' intervention it was revised and published.[9] These are but isolated examples of a type of patronage that has no recorded counter-part in earlier reigns.

Yet Cavalier drama sprang not from the patronage of the King, but from that of the Queen, Henrietta Maria of Bourbon. Despite the influence upon him of his mother's delight in masques, in which she had encouraged him to appear when a boy, and of Buckingham's fondness for merry making and the dance, Charles would never have been won so completely by the stage had it not been for the example of the French Princess. With this charming lady we shall dwell until the end of the chapter.

Henrietta Maria is best known as a moving spirit in a discredited cause, as the religious zealot and political bigot, the irreconcilable helping to ruin her husband with wrong-headed schemes. But this is not the person with whom we are to deal. In her personal character, especially in her youth, Henrietta was amiable enough. She was lovely of person, sprightly, kind—even tender, and although imperious from the first, of sufficient magnetism to enlist almost at once a following in the English court. Her prestige was great; a love of festive toys and tinsel which in Anne of Denmark had seemed childish frivolity was dignified in "Queen Mary," daughter of Marie de Medicis and Henry of Navarre.

Consonant with the literary movement she provoked, Henrietta had not a jot of literary taste. But she had literary preferences; these indulged with active enthusiasm produced their spectacular effect. It is symbolic that Charles first glimpsed his future wife performing in a masque with the Queen of France and "as many as made up nineteen fair dancing ladies."[10] One of her earliest pastimes after her arrival in England is just as characteristic. "The Queen," we hear, "is much delighted with the River of the Thames and doth love to walk in the meadows and look upon the haymakers, and will sometimes take a rake and fork and sportingly make hay with them."[11] Less than a year later Henrietta sportingly acted a part in a court play! This in a land where women upon a public stage would for some time yet be thought an obscenity, and where women (and men too for that matter) called in professionals to speak the lines even in court masques.[12] The escapade, far more serious than the whimsy of haymaking, requires a foreword of explanation.

Henrietta's background was different from that of the high-born English of the day. In France the Hôtel de Rambouillet was having a pervasive influence in making literature fashionable; compared with it the Pembroke circle, perhaps its closest English prototype, had been parochial in its effect. Despite the fact that Henrietta was reared in the nucleus of the French court, from which the Marquise de Rambouillet had fastidiously retreated, so prevalent was *préciosité* that D'Urfé's *Astrée* was her favorite book. In the French court itself literature, at least play-acting, was a diversion to be participated in, not left solely to professionals. Throughout Henrietta's childhood, her brother, Louis XIII, would conduct his child court to the apartment of the queen mother and have them act plays. In Héroard's *Journal* occur such typical entries as, "Il [Louis] fait jouer dans sa chambre la tragédie de Emon, tirée de l'Arioste, par ses petits . . .," or "Mené au cabinet de la Reine, il fait jouer une comédie par ses enfants d'honneur . . ."[13] Parts were taken not only by noble children, but by their elders as well; court performances in France before 1625, the year of Henrietta's marriage, were nearly always amateur.[14] As a girl she may have heard De Luynes, the King's favorite, chant the title rôle in *La Délivrance de Renaud,* and before her departure she would have seen the lead in devising court entertainments appropriated by no less a person than Henry of Savoy, Duke of Nemours.[15] She may have seen the King himself take the part of Godfrey of Bouillon in a performance in which Bassompierre, soon to be a weighty ambassador in her cause, gamboled about as a centaur. The *ballet de cour* was conducted with none of the aloofness of the English masque. Amateurs and professionals mingled

in the dance; the king and his peers spoke or chanted lines, and assumed character parts—all this in public. Royalty furnished the tidbit
in spectacular amusement; in carnival time at Le Petit-Bourbon, l'Hotel
de Ville, or the grand salle of the Louvre, the ballet was performed
before thousands of spectators, frequently unruly.[16]

With fresh memories of such revels, with her French attendants still
about her, with her high spirit disinclined to yield to English conventions, Henrietta quite naturally behaved in the fashion of France. During her first Christmas season in England, gossip hummed that her
demoiselles were to perform a French pastoral with herself as a principal actress in it.[17] On February 21, 1626, the play was presented at
Somerset House. A description occurs in the Salvetti correspondence:

> Her Majesty the Queen conducts herself with youthful grace. On the
> day of the carnival, for which Tuesday was set aside, she acted in a
> beautiful pastoral of her own composition, assisted by twelve of her
> ladies whom she had trained since Christmas. The pastoral succeeded
> admirably; not only in the decorations and changes of scenery, but
> also in the acting and recitation of the ladies—Her Majesty surpassing
> all the others. The performance was conducted as privately as possible,
> inasmuch as it is an unusual thing in this country to see the queen
> upon a stage; the audience consequently was limited to a few of the
> nobility, expressly invited, no others being admitted.[18]

This account is gracious, for the point of view is Continental. A
description substantially the same occurs among the Venetian state
papers, but it concludes with a dissonant note; the play "did not give
complete satisfaction, because the English objected to the first part
(attione) being declaimed by the queen."[19] This note grows louder in
native Saxon voices. A queen on a stage "would once have been thought
a strange sight," wrote John Chamberlain grumpily,[20] and there is
scent of brimstone in the words of Henry Manners, "I heare not much
honor of the Quene's maske, for, if they were not all, soome were in
men's apparell."[21] It was a bit hard at first: the Queen of England—an
author, a director, an actress in a play!

The heresy in queenly behavior prevailed, but not at once. Charles
himself was disturbed by such Gallic buoyancy. In June, 1626, we hear
that "the king, passing into the queen's side [of Whitehall] and finding
some Frenchmen, her servants, unreverently curveting and dancing in
her presence, took her by the hand and led her into his lodgings, lock-
ing the door after him, and shutting out all, save the queen . . ."[22]
Most of the French attendants were dismissed, and in August it was
reported that "The extreme formality and outward decorum with
which the queen is now waited on by the English ladies, so contrary to
French custom and familiarity, begins to weary her Majesty, who leads

a very discontented life . . ."[23] But these restrictions were of short duration. The decorum of the English ladies relaxed, and most of the French were permitted to return. Once Buckingham, her rival in the King's affections, had been removed, and early differences over religion, the marriage portion, and the French attendants had been adjusted, the reconciliation between Henrietta and Charles became complete and she gained remarkable ascendency over him. Charles's familiarities with drama date from this ascendency. Basically he was not a frivolous man. In later life, when less swayed by the tastes of his wife, he advised John Denham not to jeopardize his dignity by writing verse, and the starchiness thus revealed would have kept him from jeopardizing his own dignity by appearing in certain types of court masques and by conversing with plays in the manner already described had it not been for the Queen. Once he forbade bowling by the gallants in his Spring Garden because of the disturbance there, but the order was recalled on Henrietta's intercession.[24] She was the true Caroline patroness of pleasure. She dined and diverted ambassadors; Denmark House glittered with festive candles; a House of Delight was erected for her at Greenwich. One year the courtiers had never known a duller Christmas, only one play and no dancing at all, because the Queen "has some little Infirmity, a Bile or some such Thing . . ."[25] On her progresses she rode forth with her family of dwarfs, her bands of musicians, her hunting hounds, her "billiard board!" Theatricals in her private suits continued, and we hear at intervals of her "getting her maids to perform pastorals and comedies and other pleasant diversions."[26] Her complaisance in making sure and doubly sure the Stuart succession kept her frequently confined, but as she awaited successive arrivals, she was happy "with her intertainments and devotions."[27] Her entertainments as well as her devotions helped widen the gap between the English people and the King; one of them drove a wedge between the theatre and the remnant of the staid city audience, made plays conclusively a partisan issue, and begat a new development in English drama.

On September 20, 1632, Mr. Pory wrote to Sir Thomas Puckering, "That which the queen's majesty, some of her ladies, and all her maids of honour are now practising upon, is a pastoral penned by Mr. Walter Montagu, wherein her majesty is pleased to act a part, as well for her recreation as for the exercise of her English."[28] In November it was reported that the play would be performed shortly, the Queen to act publicly "for the gratification and pleasure of the king."[29] But there was some delay, and not until January 3, 1633, do we hear more of the project. This time Mr. Pory becomes waggish: "On Wednesday next, the queen's pastoral is to be acted in the lower court of Denmark

House, and my lord-chamberlain saith that no chambermaid shall enter, unless she will sit cross-legged [a propitious posture at births] on the top of a bulk. No great lady shall be kept out, though she have but mean apparel, and a worse face, and no inferior lady shall be let in, but such as have extreme brave apparel and better faces."[30]

On January 9 then, the play was acted, Walter Montague's *Shepherd's Paradise*, one of the worst in the language, as we shall see later, but epoch-making in its type as well as in the circumstances of its production. Three times normal length, it took seven or eight hours to perform,[31] the Marchioness of Hamilton who played the hero, Basilino, lamenting with cause that her part alone was the length of an ordinary play.[32] One cannot believe that these fragile-brained ladies of the court committed to memory such limitless stretches of opaque prose; one pictures them with script delicately poised in their jewelled hands. Henrietta played the part of Queen Bellesa, selected by the pseudo-shepherds in her *précieuse* republic under the regulation that "the Queen must be aged under thirty, and beauty to be most regarded in the election." Naturally it was adjudged that she "excelled really all others both in acting and singing," and since fear that they could not get in had kept many away, a second performance was planned for Candlemas.[33] If this is the *Queen's masque* referred to by the Venetian ambassador, the later performance took place at Whitehall, Shrove Tuesday, March 5, when "the King gladly took part in the dancing until near daybreak."[34] Unlike the first occasion when the Queen acted, no word of distaste is audible in the court.

Elsewhere it was not so—England was England still. An obituary biography of the Queen mentions "odd expressions [i.e. veiled criticisms] in several popular sermons,"[35] and voices prophesying woe must have sounded in the homes and shops of London where nine in every ten were Puritan in conviction. Suddenly thrust into public view as the concentrate of these fumes of popular aversion was Mr. William Prynne, utter-barrister and pamphleteer of the Society of Lincoln's Inn.

For years Prynne had been bestirring his contentious brains, ransacking the authorities, and siphoning the vials of his wrath in order to write a book that would serve as climax to the long list of Puritan attacks upon the stage. Whether through design or otherwise, a point settled only arbitrarily at his subsequent trial, he chose as the time for launching his leviathan the season of the Queen's acting in *The Shepherd's Paradise*. The book, shaped like a building block, and titled *Histriomastix, the Players Scourge, or, Actors Tragœdie*, ranks with the most obtuse works in English—or more properly in English and Latin, for it sags with quotations from the fathers. There is no need to review it;[36] as we browse in it hoping, sacrilegiously, to learn something of the Elizabethan stage, we marvel that a book so long can tell so little. Shakespeare's plays were printed on better paper than were bibles—very good—but more of Shakespeare and his fellows the scribe will not stoop to say. It is a valiant book and sincere, lethally sincere, but painful, reeking with the perverse delight of the righteous in abusive terms. As ugly as the more scabrous plays of the period, it makes us, even while we frown at the tyranny of Prynne's aggressors, sympathize with their charge: "The booke is his accuser, and the wittness agaynste him, beinge the index of his minde."[37]

Histriomastix no doubt would have attracted no official attention had it not been for a suspicious particularity about certain passages. For instance: ". . . dancing, write they [the fathers aforesaid], (yea even in Queenes themselves, and the very greatest persons, who are commonly most devoted to it) hath beene always scandalous and of ill report amongst the Saints of God . . ."[38] The finger points most steadily in the index, which Prynne had just written and used as a cup for the overflow of his zeal. Under the genial listing *Women-Actors, notorious whores* barks this addendum: "S. Paul prohibits women to speak publikely in the church . . . And dare then any Christian women be so more then whorishly impudent, as to act, to speake publikely on a Stage (perchance in mans apparell, and cut haire, here proved sinfull and abominable) in the presence of sundry men and women? . . . O let such presidents of impudency, of impiety be never heard of or suffred among Christians." "It is observable," wrote a correspondent on January 28, "that his book was published the day after the Queen's pastoral at Somerset House."[39]

Subsequently we hear that Prynne is up before the High Commission Court and Star Chamber, our informant quoting from the passage on women-actors, "which words it is thought by some, will cost him his ears, or heavily punished and deeply fined."[40] A preliminary hearing was held at once, and the author, not yearning for martyrdom at the time, lustily proclaimed that his book had been written and even published before the performance of the Queen's play.[41] This defense could easily have been confounded by mention of the fact that the Queen had acted with her maids as early as 1626, on which occasion we may recall, "if they were not all, soome were in men's apparell." But the prosecution preferred to skirt lightly over the identification of Henrietta with "Women-actors," and at the final trial in the Star Chamber, which followed in February, 1634, they persisted in alluding delicately to the Queen's "dancing." There is no doubt, though, for what Prynne was judged. It was a group near to the Queen who thrust home the attack. Let the culprit be found guilty of lese majesty pleaded Sir John Finch, her attorney-general; and as judgment was passed, Henry Jermyn, her favorite, was conspicuously severe, and the Earl of Dorset, her Lord Chamberlain, suggested resourcefully that the victim's nose might be split.[42] The actual punishment decided upon, and inflicted by May, was as follows: the accused to be debarred, to be expelled from Lincoln's Inn, to forfeit his Oxford degree, to pay £5000 fine, to remain in prison at the King's pleasure, finally to stand in the stocks while the state executioner branded S. L. (Seditious Libeller) on his cheeks and cut off his ears.[43] Poor Prynne! He had dedicated his magnum opus to the masters of the bench of Lincoln's Inn, proud that his was the most sober of the Inns of Court. But Lincoln's Inn carried out its part in his punishment by posting him as the utterer of "personall aspersions and contumelies of her Matie" and expelling him with gusto![44]

The man had his sympathizers, thousands of them, somber and mute. He suffered again later with more popular Puritans, when the observant Sir Kenelm Digby wrote, "The king and Queen will be in London on Thursday to assist at the Duke's marriage; but I believe there will not be so great a flocking of the people to see it, as was this last week to accompany Mr. Prynne and Mr. Burton's pilgrimage to their stations in the country, nor be kept with such veneration as the Puritans keep the bloody sponges and handkerchiefs that did the hangman service in the cutting of their ears."[45] Had it not been for the weight of opinion behind him Prynne would not have suffered so cruelly. The throne had reacted in vicious self-vindication; and it proceeded now to embrace its pleasures in the teeth of a moral rebellion.

Playwrights, naturally charmed at the way royalty and the drama had stood together in the breach, were quick in discharging salvos in the ears of the enemy. Shirley satirically dedicated his next published drama, *Bird in a Cage,* to Prynne, and returned to the attack in verses before Ford's *Love's Sacrifice.* Heywood, himself a pious man, rebuked the defiler of his craft on three separate occasions.[46] Later, Mayne in his *City Match* and Cartwright in his prologue to *The Royal Slave* kept the feud alive, the latter with an unequivocal reference to "late damn'd books," while a dozen other plays of the period, either by caricatures in the cast or direct allusions, persisted in gibbeting the Player's Scourge.

But a Star Chamber conviction and a chorus from the dramatists were not the only public demonstrations on the royal side. In this feud involving *The Shepherd's Paradise* and *Histriomastix* must be mentioned a third title, ironically *The Triumph of Peace*. Charles seemed to crave reassurance; the attack had emanated, after all, from the Inns of Court and toward them he beckoned. In ample time before the Star Chamber deliberations, "there came a desire from the King"[47] that the gentlemen of the Inns should show themselves at court; and in the very month of the trial they did so—with a masque "that far exceeded in bravery" any that they had given before Prynne's time.[48] Nothing was left to chance; the committee representing the four Inns numbered such present and future notables as Sir John Finch, Attorney-General Noy, Edward Hyde, John Selden, and Bulstrode Whitelocke; James Shirley, most popular dramatist of the day, wrote the libretto; Inigo Jones designed the scenery; Simon Ives and William Lawes composed the music. On the afternoon of February 2, 1634,[49] the festivities began with a parade from Ely House, Holborn, down Chancery Lane to Whitehall, where the royal family, breathless with delight, bade the marchers twice circle the tilt-yard. Here was gaiety triumphant in the face of Prynne and all Puritans. Behind Marshal Darrel (of the pamphleteer's own Inn!) and his twenty torch-bearers rode the hundred handsomest men of the four Inns, gloriously clad, perfectly mounted, and attended by three hundred pages and lackeys. Then for contrast came a troop of beggars on decrepit nags. There followed troops of song birds, of caricatured monopolists, of owls. Interspersed were bands of English, Scotch, French, Italian, and German musicians, forty lutes playing in unison, to furnish one of the greatest musical demonstrations England had known. Finally came gorgeous chariots bearing the masquers, their silks and satins ruddy in the light of flambeaux. "Their shew through the streets was glorious," wrote Sir Henry Herbert, "and in the nature of a triumph."[50]

The Triumph of Peace itself was a pleasant masque, coherent for its time, but not remarkable except in its tasteful restraint from mentioning Prynne; the celebration was chiefly remembered for the speechmaking, the music, the dancing and feasting which followed. The lavish scale on which all this was conducted is hinted by the fact that each of the Queen's French musicians found £40 wrapped in his napkin when dined at St. Dunstan's. The total expenses may be computed at $1,000,000 in modern money.[51] Somewhat naïvely in view of such outlay by the members of the Inns, Henrietta, who viewed the occasion properly "as a particular respect to herself," wanted it all done over again. And it was—less than a fortnight later at Merchant Tailors' Hall. In consequence, more than one embryo lawyer failed to meet his assessments and found his chambers "seised and forfited and hee put out of Commons."[52] But what of that—the King invited 120 gentlemen of the Inns to attend his own masque, Carew's *Cœlum Britannicum*, given to the Queen on February 18, and ending as the Stuarts wished the Prynne and all other unpleasant episodes would end: *a cloud passeth overthwart the Scene, leaving behind it nothing but a serene Sky.*

Amateur theatricals in polite circles thrived after Henrietta had appeared in *The Shepherd's Paradise;* they form an interesting phase of Cavalier Drama and a separate chapter will be devoted to them. The Queen herself refrained from acting parts in those at the court, but she continued to produce them. On December 21, 1635, the season following the Inns of Court masque, she presented to her husband (eight days before presenting him with another child) *The Pastoral of Florimene*[53] done by her maids in French. This play, only the description and argument of which were published, was of a type, to be described later, indigenous to the court, and in the absence of any known author the Queen herself may be suggested.[54] Popular prejudice failed to prevent Charles and Henrietta from appearing conspicuously in Davenant's masques. These took greater liberties in disposing their royal persons than earlier types would have dared; the Queen as Indamora in *The Temple of Love*, as the Earthly Deity in *Luminalia*, and the King as Britanocles in *Britannia Triumphans*, as Philogenes in *Salmacida Spolia* figure prominently both in the fables and the spectacular background. In the last the Queen, *enceinte* once more, was hoisted in an engine especially devised by Inigo Jones, so that she might make her entry, descending from a cloud.

Henrietta's almost defiant espousal of the drama extended, within limits, even beyond the court. She was, of course, throughout the period, the patron of a professional company of actors, the members of which received biennially from the Lord Chamberlain their four yards of bastard scarlet and three and a half yards of crimson velvet as nominal grooms of her chamber,[55] meager livery, by the way, compared with that issued to adorn the persons of actual chambermen. Christoper Beeston had organized in the very year of the marriage "Queen Henrietta's Men," a second-rate troupe which occupied the Phœnix or Cockpit in Drury Lane until the plague of 1636-37 closed the theatres; at the cessation of the plague Richard Heton, "one of the Sewers of Her Majesty's Chamber Extraordinary" headed a new "Queen's Company" which acted at Salisbury Court until the final prohibition of plays. Sir Henry Herbert and the Earl of Dorset had both a hand in this second organization, and it may be that the Queen expressed the wish that her troupe, which came frequently to court, be a good one.[56]

More interesting, however, is her association with the King's Company at Blackfriars. Henrietta probably set the precedent for English royalty in attending public performances. In the season 1635-36 the visitor Charles Prince Palatine wrote home mentioning Blackfriars, "where the quene saw Lodwick Carlile's second part of *Arviragus and Felicia* acted, w꜀ʰ is hugely liked of everyone."[57] In this same season he himself accompanied her to this theatre to see "Alfonso."[58] Earlier, May 13, 1634, and later, April 23, 1638, two other visits by the Queen are recorded, one to see a play by Massinger, and the other to see Davenant's *Unfortunate Lovers*.[59] It has been assumed that these were not public performances which Henrietta attended, but that the theatre was chartered (as was done on occasion in Elizabeth's reign) especially for the court.[60] But it is doubtful if this assumption will hold. The presence of King Charles is recorded at none of these performances. It is true that the company received for two of them £10 from the crown, the regular fee for court plays; but this proves nothing; the Queen would not have paid her admission in shillings. Let us recall again her background. Her father, Henry IV of France, had watched plays at the public fairs between gambling at the booths, and her brother, Louis XIII, went often to the Hôtel de Bourgogne.[61] Why should not she behave in kind, ignoring as before the English conventions? Afternoons at the Blackfriars were becoming gay and fashionable;[62] the marvel would be if Henrietta had never looked in upon them. A condescension as great is definitely recorded on February 23, 1636, when the Middle Temple gave a masque to the Prince Elector— "the Queene was pleasd to grace the entertaynment by putting of[f] majesty to putt on a citizens habitt, and to sett upon the scaffold on the right hande amongst her subjects . . . Mrs Basse, the law-woman, leade in this royal citizen and her company."[63] One day, years later, Thomas Killigrew was boasting to Pepys of the glories of Restoration playhouses compared with those of the preceding reign; the King came now, he said, "then the Queene seldom and the King never would come."[64] This grudging exception in the case of the Queen need not have been made had Blackfriars been chartered for the court; it is more likely that Henrietta again put off majesty and sat amongst her subjects.

One further instance of the Queen's interest in the professional theatre may be given. In the winter of 1634-35, a French company led by Josias de Soulas, alias "Floridor," visited England. England had

not proved hospitable in the past to French companies and their custom of employing actresses. In 1629 a troupe of strollers had been
"hissed, hooted, and pippin-pelted from the stage,"[65] and in *Histriomastix* Prynne had referred to their performance, with his customary
ardor, as "an impudent, shameful, unwomanish, gracelesse, if not more
then whorish attempt."[66] But this did not prevent the Queen from entertaining Floridor's company at Denmark house, then recommending
it to the King for a visit to Whitehall, and finally exerting her power
that it should be allowed to act on certain days at the Phoenix until
a new play house could be erected. So much was this company in favor
with her majesty that Sir Henry Herbert refrained from making money
by it, a difficult thing for him to do. "The French," he wrote, "offered
mee a present of 10 *l.;* but I refused itt, and did them many other
curtesys, *gratis,* to render the queene my mistris an acceptable service."[67] Some of the courtesies were to the prejudice of the native companies, as we shall see later when observing how the courtly preoccupation with drama was, for the popular stage, no unalloyed blessing.

We must turn from Henrietta to lesser figures of the court. The
Queen provoked the court's invasion of the drama, but naturally she
alone did not accomplish it. She was not compelled to act alone; queens
young and fair have never been. The courtier is the most sensitive of
all creatures in adapting himself to the niceties of his environment; if
they are required by his habitat, he can bud dramatic tendencies with
biological efficiency. Henrietta had not been long in England before
Whitehall became a breeding place for plays.

We may note first an increase in the type of courtiers whom poets of
the day loved to call the "Noble Mæcenas." Persons near to the Queen,
no writers themselves, hastened to patronize the drama. She herself had
protégés among the popular playwrights, and Francis Lenton (trafficker
in jingling conceits), who in 1629 could call himself "The Queen's
Poet," by 1634 had modestly to reduce his title to "One of her Majesties Poets."[68] She smiled upon the efforts of the aging Heywood; James
Shirley called himself "Servant to Her Majesty" on the title page to
The Bird in a Cage; William Davenant signed himself "Her majesty's
servant" from the time he was commissioned to write *The Temple of
Love.* These Queen's poets had no official standing, but Davenant
succeeded to Jonson's rank as court stipendiary; poet laureate in effect
if not formally so designated. Some of the Caroline courtiers needed no
cue from Henrietta to patronize the drama. This is true, I believe, of
the most generous of them, William Cavendish; while Philip Herbert
did so simply in character as a Lord Chamberlain and an Earl of Pem-

broke. On the other hand the Earl of Dorset, in attacking Prynne, in abetting the efforts of Richard Heton's company at Salisbury Court (though here he had some property interest in the venture), and in encouraging the dramatic sallies of Joseph Rutter and Francis Quarles, no doubt was motivated by his associations as head of the Queen's household. It was not until Sir John Winter had become Secretary and Master of Requests to Henrietta that he was dubbed by Tatham "the most worthy Mæcenas."[69] The Digbys, also in the Queen's circle and, like Winter, zealous Catholics, interested themselves in playwrights; Sir Kenelm extended hospitality to Rutter, and earned from Cowley the compliment "Practioner and Patron of the Arts."[70] Endymion Porter, courtier par excellence and amiable gentleman withal, was in the Somerset House clique, and extended really vital kindnesses to Davenant, as well, according to the letter, as to "all poets." Henry Jermyn, too, successor to Montague as Henrietta's favorite in chief, won plaudits for his kindness although there is no evidence how he earned them until he gave refuge to Cowley and Davenant during the Exile. At Oxford the elegant Dr. Brian Duppa encouraged the poetic efforts of young Christ Church men such as Cartwright and Mayne.

But the emergence of the courtier playwright is the more vital element in this movement. Exquisites of the Household, often secure in the reversion of great estates, began to busy themselves with acts and scenes, willing to expose their brain progeny not at court theatricals only, but in the playhouses and on the book stalls of London. To realize what this means in the way of social evolution requires another moment of retrospect.

In the England of Elizabeth and James writing for the public stage was *ipso facto* a stigma of inferior social rank. It is true that early in Elizabeth's reign such pedigreed folk as de Vere, Sackville, and Sidney wrote for the entertainment of the court, and Gascoigne himself rated indubitably as a gentleman. It was not long, however, before even this type of authorship was left mostly to the more menial Lyly, Peele, and Nash, and henceforth when nobles such as Fulke Greville and William Alexander turned dramatists, they wrote closet plays and shunned the thought of actual representation. There is no need to mention school plays, for in such works young gentlemen could claim the student's privilege. From the outset, writing for the public was the function of the gifted plebian: Marlowe, Shakespeare, Jonson, Dekker, Heywood—the men whose names connote most to lovers of the drama—were humbly reared. Dangerous as it may seem to generalize about the station of a group of men numbering several hundred, it is remarkable how small is the need for qualification. Many playwrights, to be sure, were recruited among the sons of small gentry, but for these the theatre was a last resort. Talent and education, unpoised by money to buy a clerical living or influence to attain some genteel form of civil employment, often spelled a career as a playwright. Such was the case of Lodge, who, about 1589, determined "To write no more of that whence shame doth grow,"[71] and subsequently became a physician. Such too no doubt was the case of Marston, who forsook drama for a pulpit in Hampshire. We think of Greene and his exhortation to his fellows to shun the stage; of Henslowe and his string of hacks and servlings. In the reign of James a greater number of the writers seem to have been gentlemen by birth, but there is little change in the status of their occupation. Typical of his group was John Fletcher, well born and well nurtured but declassé; he lacked patrimony, his father had died in debt and royal disfavor. Most dedicatory epistles, be it remembered, were suggestive of mendicancy, and could scarcely be written by the gentle according to the strictures of the day. The one true exception to our rule is Francis Beaumont, his father a judge in a family still prospering. But Francis was a younger son, and susceptible to the good company of Fletcher and Jonson, he felt that he could gypsy for a space in Bohemia; incidentally his marriage seems to have put an end to it. Upon Jonson the gentry showered affection and praise, but this was simon-pure patronage. His social sphere was the city, and those who picture him mingling on equal terms with the masquers at Whitehall fail to comprehend the arrogance of the Stuart court—where the Lord Chamberlain might break his staff over the shoulders of scholarly Thomas May, and seal the affront with a payment of £50.[72] Down to the very end the low standing of the playwright is all too manifest. It seems from his prefaces that Ford would rather have been considered a lawyer's clerk than a dramatist; the prefaces of genuine amateurs are laden with deprecation. Hemming's publishers proclaimed him "above the sphere of common writers";[73] and in dedicating his *Rebellion*, 1640, Thomas Rawlins, medallist at the mint, wrote with insufferable complacence, "I have no desire to be known by a threadbare cloak, having a calling that will maintain it wooly."

Walter Montague, however, was a scion of gentility, and a gentleman of the privy-chamber to the King. His *Shepherd's Paradise*, written for the Queen and so nicely keyed to her tastes that it helps explain his rapid rise in her favor, was, with one exception, I believe, the first full-fledged courtier's play to be acted for forty years.[74] The excep-

tion is *The Deserving Favorite,* acted about 1629, and, as we learn from
its dedication to several grooms of the royal bed-chamber, "at first not
design'd to travell so farre as the Common Stage." The author, Lodowick Carlell, was also under the influence of Henrietta, and though
his offices were master of the bows and privy-chamber man, his real
function was to continue writing courtly plays. The gulf between writers for the "Common Stage" and even so small a courtier as Carlell is
implicit in the dedication to the latter of Dekker's *Match Me in
London,* the humility of which, to us now, is nothing short of poignant.
Soon to enter the lists with these others was Thomas Killigrew, companion to Montague, page to King Charles, and betrothed to Cecilia
Crofts, who had acted Agenor in *The Shepherd's Paradise.* That these
courtiers were encouraged by the crown is no matter of inference.
The prologue to the second part of Carlell's *Passionate Lovers* tells
how,

> . . . most Apollo's beams break from the throne,
> And with a double sweetness doth invite
> All that have gifts, in Verse or Prose to write.

At first some amusement, perhaps a little contempt, was aroused
by these elegant amateurs. "Our French Cavaliers are come home,"
observed a correspondent to Wentworth referring to Montague among
others;[75] and in his "Session of the Poets" Suckling rimed at their
expense:

> In haste from the court two or three came in
> And they brought letters, forsooth, from the Queen;
> 'Twas discreetly done, too, for if th' had come
> Without them, th' had scarce been let into the room.

But the mode thrived, and for all Suckling's facetiousness, we soon come
upon this piece of news: "Two of the King's Servants, Privy-Chamber
men both, have writ each of them a Play, Sir John Sutlin and Will
Barclay, which have been acted in Court, and at the Black Friars, with
much Applause."[76] Among others recruited to the group were Henry
Killigrew, Aston Cokain, William Habington, Richard Lovelace, the
Earl of Newcastle, and the Earl of Westmoreland. No doubt the efforts
of some died in parturition, and those of others never reached the
printer. How epidemic was the fashion is intimated in Cartwright's
The Siege:

> I will turn
> Poet myself; it is in fashion, Lady;
> He's scarce a courtier now, that hath not writ
> His brace of plays.[77]

The most amusing contemporary comment appears in Killigrew's *Parson's Wedding:*

Careless. A knight and write plays? It may be, but 'tis strange to us. So, they say, there are other gentleman poets without land or Latin; this was not ordinary. Prithee, when was he knighted.

Jolly. In the North, the last great knighting, when 'twas God's great mercy we were not all knights.

Wild. I'll swear, they say there are poets that have more men in liveries than books in their studies.

Captain. And what think you, Gentlemen, are not these things to start a man? I believe 'tis the first time you found them lie at the sign of the Page, Footmen, and Gilded Coaches; they were wont to lie at the Thin Cloak. They and their muses made up the family, and thence sent scenes to their patrons like boys in at windows, and one would return with a doublet, another with a pair of breeches, a third with a little ready money, which, together with their credit with a company, in three terms you rarely saw a poet repaired.[78]

It is not needful at this point to indicate how the courtier playwright found imitators in town and university, how he survived during the Interregnum, and became a dominant figure in Restoration drama; this matter will concern us in later chapters.

The court's invasion of the theatre consisted not only in the creation of a special group of writers, with whom professional playwrights soon found themselves in competition, but also in the creation of a special type of play, which some of the professionals soon found it wise to imitate. Such an uncompromising product of the old school as Richard Brome began to feel honestly perturbed. The London companies faced audiences of increasingly fastidious tastes; the habitué of Westminster was now their best customer and he was acquiring a relish for plays composed in his own milieu and often produced at court with scenery and gorgeous costuming such as the public theatres could not afford. Testimony of how a courtly audience could impose its foibles on those who strove to please is offered by several royal visits to the universities. When Peter Hausted published his *Rival Friends,* acted at Newmarket during the progress to Cambridge of 1632, he lamented bitterly the cruelty of his audience. The courtiers had found his satire upon women impolite in the presence of their ladies, and had deplored his rude realism. My village girls, he explains, "spoke no strong lines but plaid at Chackstónes, when it may be some of our butterfly-judgments expected a set at Mav or Primivisti." During the visit to Oxford in 1636, the court was regaled first with an old-fashioned academic allegory, but " it had more of the Moralist than the Poet in it. And though it was well penned, yet it did not take with the courtiers as it did with the togated crew."[79] Later Cartwright's *Royal Slave* was presented, and this received the palm. Here was a play after the court's own heart; its success made the author, and startled the heads of the university.

To define the species of play which the court created will require a separate chapter.

---

[1] *Calendar State Papers, Spanish*, 1558-67, p. 404.—The Queen showed her greatest enthusiasm Sept. 4, 1566, when *II Palamon and Arcyte* was performed at Christ Church, Oxford, and here she seemed moved less by the play than by the antics of the boy actors; see the description quoted in M. S. Steele, *Plays and Masques at Court* (Yale Univ. Press, 1926), pp. 31-32.

[2] J. Nichols, *Progresses James*, II, 162.

[3] Anthony à Wood, *Athenæ Oxonienses* (ed. Bliss), III, 522.

[4] Joseph Q. Adams, *The Dramatic Records of Sir Henry Herbert* (Yale Univ. Press, 1917), p. 55 *et passim.*—Hereafter this work will be cited by title alone.

[5] *Dramatic Records of Sir Henry Herbert*, p. 54.

[6] *Ibid.*, p. 22.

[7] *Ibid.*, p. 54.

[8] Prologue at Blackfriars.

[9] Dedication to the King.

[10] Letter from Prince Charles to King James; cf. A. Strickland, *Lives of the Queens* (ed. 1878), v. 194.

[11] July 21, 1625; cf. *Historical MSS Commission*, LXXX, 68.

[12] See Enid Welsford, *Court Masque* (Cambridge Univ. Press, 1927), p. 190, where Daniel's *Tethy's Festival*, 1610, is instanced as an exceptional case wherein the actors were of good birth.

[13] *Héroard's Journal*, E. Soulié et E. de Barthélmy. (Paris, 1868), II, 118, 121.

[14] G. Lanson, "Etudes sur les origines de la Tragedie classique en France," *Revue d'Hist. Lit. de la France*, X (1903), 418.

[15] H. Prunières, *Le Ballet de Cour en France* (Paris, 1914), pp. 116, 126.

[16] *Ibid.*, *passim*.

[17] *Cal. State Papers, Domestic*, 1625-26, p. 179; *Private Correspondence of Lady Jane Cornwallis* (London, 1842), p. 138.

[18] *Historical MSS Commission*, XVI, 47.

[19] *Cal. State Papers, Venetian*, 1625-26, pp. 345-346.

[20] *Cal. State Papers, Domestic*, 1625-26, p. 273.

[21] *Historical MSS Commission*, XXIV, 478.

[22] A. Strickland, *op. cit.*, p. 227.

[23] *Cal. State Papers, Venetian*, 1625-26, p. 520.

[24] *Strafforde Letters*, I, 262.

[25] *Ibid.*, I, 177.

[26] *Cal. State Papers, Venetian*, 1632-36, p. 445.

[27] H. Ellis, *Original Letters Illustrative of English History*, Series II (1827), III, 260.

[28] *Court and Times of Charles I*, T. Birch, ed., 2 vols. (1849), II, 176.

[29] *Cal. State Papers, Venetian*, 1632-36, p. 28.

[30] *Court and Times of Charles I*, II, 214.

[31] *Ibid.*, II, 216.

[32] *Ibid.,* II, 187.

[33] *Historical MSS Commission,* II, 282.

[34] *Cal. State Papers, Venetian,* 1632-36, p. 86.

[35] G. Smeeton, *Historical Tactics* (1820), p. 13.

[36] Discussed with charity by E. N. S. Thompson, *The Controversy between the Puritans and the Stage, Yale Studies in English,* Vol. xx (1903).

[37] *Prynne Documents,* Camden Society (1877), p. 2.

[38] *Histriomastix* (1633), p. 236.

[39] *Court and Times of Charles I,* II, 222.

[40] *Ibid.,* II, 224.

[41] *Cal. State Papers, Domestic,* 1631-33, p. 524; cf. also *Prynne Documents,* p. 52.

[42] *Prynne Documents,* pp. 10-11, 25.

[43] *Ibid.,* pp. 86-90.

[44] *Black Books of Lincoln's Inn,* II, 317-318.

[45] *Cal. State Papers, Domestic,* 1637, p. 332.

[46] Addresses to Readers of *The English Traveller,* and *A Maidenhead Well Lost;* and "A Prologue to their Sacred Majesties at Hampton Court"; see further A. W. Ward, *Dramatic Literature,* III, 245, n. 1.

[47] *Historical MSS Commission,* XXIII, pp. 2, 34.

[48] *Strafforde Letters,* I, 207.

[49] For a complete description see A. W. Green, *Inns of Court and Early English Drama* (Yale Univ. Press, 1931), pp. 124 *seq.*

[50] *Dramatic Records of Sir Henry Herbert,* p. 54.

[51] A. W. Green, *op. cit.,* p. 126.

[52] *The Pension Book of Gray's Inn,* I, 317.

[53] *Dramatic Records of Sir Henry Herbert,* p. 55; *Cal. State Papers, Venetian,* 1632-36, p. 499.

[54] See above, the allusion to her as author of the pastoral of 1626.

[55] P. R. O., Lord Chamberlaine's Books: L. C. /5/132/pp. 125, 201, 210 *et passim.*

[56] J. Q. Adams, *Shakespearean Playhouses* (1917), pp. 355, 379-380.

[57] *Historical MSS Commission,* II, 118.

[58] *Dramatic Records of Sir Henry Herbert,* p. 75.

[59] *Ibid.,* pp. 65, 76.

[60] J. Q. Adams, *Shakespearean Playhouses,* pp. 232-233; M. S. Steele, *Plays and Masques at Court* (Yale Univ. Press, 1926), p. 248.

[61] *Héroard's Journal,* I, 383, II, 91, *et passim.*

[62] See below, p. 149.

[63] The mask was Davenant's *Triumphs of the Prince D'Amour;* see *Dramatic Records of Sir Henry Herbert,* p. 56.

[64] *Pepys Diary,* Feb. 12, 1667.

[65] Quoted by W. J. Lawrence, *Elizabethan Playhouse,* I (1912), p. 130.

[66] *Histriomastix,* p. 414.

[67] *Dramatic Records of Sir Henry Herbert,* p. 61.

[68] *DNB,* XXXIII. For her patronage of Heywood, see below, p. 155.

[69] Dedication of *Love Crowns the End,* 1640.

[70] Dedication of *Love's Riddle,* 1638.

[71] E. K. Chambers, *Elizabethan Stage,* III, 409.

[72] A. Chester, *Thomas May* (Philadelphia, 1932), p. 49.

[73] Dedication of *The Fatal Contract,* 1653.

[74] During this period Robert Cecil and Henry Lee wrote occasional speeches in entertainments for Elizabeth, and William Percy may have written that series of plays, *Arabia Sitiens*, etc., the auspices of which have not yet been made entirely clear. David Lord Barry, not demonstrably a courtier, but certainly of the courtly class, seems to have felt a momentary impulse to follow the lead of Beaumont, if *Ram Alley* indeed be his. For the date of Carlell's *Osmond*, see below, p. 100.

[75] *Strafforde Letters*, I, 373.

[76] *Ibid.*, II, 150.

[77] Act IV, Scene vii.

[78] Act III, Scene ii.

[79] Anthony à Wood, *History and Antiquities of Oxford*, II, 408.

II

THE CAVALIER MODE

CAVALIER plays are not racy and roistering comedies; they are decorous, indeed very solemn things. The few comedies produced by our courtly school are frail children of Middleton-Jonson grandparentage and might have been begotten by some lesser Richard Brome; for the time being these may be disregarded. The typical Cavalier play is "an ornate, spectacular, rhetorical, sentimental, fortuitous medley."[1] The array of adjectives here appropriated was applied originally to the Greek romances; it is a curiosity of literary history that it fits as exactly the products of Carlell, Cartwright, and Killigrew as those of the semi-mythical Longus, Tatius, and Heliodorus. The plot materials of Cavalier plays derived, in fact, almost exclusively from tales of the Greek decadence. We shall dwell on this point for a space. The story told is important; moreover, while there has been agreement that many Caroline themes came from the "romances," there has been some justifiable indecision—we shall see why—as to what particular themes and what particular romances.

It is natural that the drama of the courtiers should have reflected the tastes of their circle, and at the Caroline court the fashionable ladies (and gentlemen too) from Henrietta down were immersed in a peculiar kind of reading. The Countess of Warwick in her pious memoirs tells what a corrupting influence a maid of honor to the Queen could be upon those untarnished by Whitehall; when Elizabeth Killigrew came to live at the Boyle house, she enticed others to spend time like herself "in seeing and reading plays and romances, and in exquisite and curious dressing."[2] A character in Marmion's *Antiquary* recites the common knowledge of the day: at court "every waiting-woman speaks perfect Arcadia" and gentlemen "lie abed and expound Astræa, and digest him into compliments."[3] In Cokain's *Obstinate Lady*, Vandora "does nothing all day but read little comedies, and every night spends two or three hours on a great tragedy of a merry fellow, Dametas, and a company of strange named learned lovers." She asks a suitor, "You have read many histories?" And anxious to ingratiate himself he replies, "Many, lady! I am a worm in a book: I go through them."[4]

It was too early for the Vandoras of the day to be reading the *romans de longue haleine*,[5] La Calprenède and Scudéry had yet to marshal their phalanxes of squat octavos upon the world. Yet there was no dearth of congenial fiction. From Charles Sorel's *Lysis, ou Le Berger Extravagant,*[6] an "anti-romance" which appeared before the so-called heroic romances had achieved full vogue, we get an excellent knowledge of the best sellers of the early seventeenth century. In Book XIII the character Clarimond arraigns romances, and while he mentions many writers from Homer to Ariosto, he places heaviest obloquy and responsibility upon the latter day Greeks. We know of the recrudescence of interest in the *Daphnis and Chloe* of Longus, the *Erotica* of Achilles Tatius, and the *Æthiopica* of Heliodorus through the number of translations being published. Clarimond passes next to the three famous pastorals, Montemayor's *Diana,* Sidney's *Arcadia,* and D'Urfé's *Astrée.* These, we may note, were indebted as much to the Greek writers as to the Italian Sannazaro, particularly the *Arcadia,* which for all its pastoral embellishments approximates Heliodorus in English.[7] It is not surprising that Sidney figures largely in a French satire; his romance had a continental reputation untouched by the works of Shakespeare or any other Elizabethan. At this point the advantage of surveying literature through the eyes of a contemporary appears. The modern historian of fiction tends to pass from the pastorals to the next peak, the French heroic romances in their full bloom;[8] Dunlop confines his treatment of these to the works of Gomberville, La Calprenède and Scudéry. Sorel, in contrast, lingers over an intermediary group of tales, those at the height of popularity at the time of the inception of Cavalier drama. Clarimond outlines and condemns the romances of Henri Vital d'Audiguier, John Barclay, and François de Molière. These in order were *Histoire tragicomique de nostre temps sous les noms de Lysandre et de Caliste,* 1616, *Argenis,* 1621, and *Les Advantures de Polixene,* 1623. Although d'Audiguier's *Lysandre et Caliste* alters the region of adventure from the lands of the Mediterranean to Burgundy, Holland, and England, and although Barclay's *Argenis* is interlarded with enlightening discourses so that it long passed as political allegory, these tales and others like them are close imitations of the Greek romances. This is true also of Desmarets de Saint-Sorlin's *Ariane* and Gomberville's *Polexandre,* both published by 1632 and therefore available to the Caroline court. There is no need to itemize English imitations of the *Arcadia* or minor French and Spanish romances of the type already indicated. The nature of Vandora's books is apparent. Nearly all were available in English, and all we repeat, especially those freshest when our courtiers began to write, had their basis in Greek fiction.

The extent to which an imitation of a Greek romance could achieve popularity during the third decade of the seventeenth century is shown amply by John Barclay's *Argenis*. This book, shrouded in "fame's twilight," is worth pausing with, not only as a source of Cavalier drama but, together with the *Arcadia,* as England's chief influence on the makers of the heroic romance. The accident of its appearing first in Latin has barred it from mention by most historians of English fiction,[9] and the degree to which it contributed to the genre of *Le Grand Cyrus* has never been fully acknowledged. Of course it may be an error to claim *Argenis* as an English product; one cannot imagine a more international book. Written in the universal language in Rome, by a peripatetic Scotchman[10] born in Lorraine, educated in France, and for some time resident at the English court, it was first published at Paris and within ten years translated into French, Spanish, Italian, English, and Dutch. Editions of French translations by three different authors appeared singly and in pairs every year for a decade after its appearance in 1621.[11] It was dramatized by du Ryer and by Calderón. An English translation was licensed for the press, October 2, 1623, by "Beniamin Iohnson"; a translation by Kingsmill Long actually appeared in 1625, and was re-edited in 1636; another edition by Sir Robert Le Grys and Thomas May appeared in 1628 and 1629, upon His Majesty's Command, together with a *Clavis* "for the satisfaction of the Reader, and helping him to understand what persons were by the Author intended . . ." One reason for this popularity was that the book contained something for everybody: edification for the moralist, instruction in statecraft for the ambitious, alleged allegorical mysteries for the curious. But what interested most both the author and the mass of his readers was the story itself, the star-crossed lovers, the rival friends, their high pitched emotions, their destinies slowly unwinding through exotic adventures. One need only read the *Argenis,* recognize it as a favorite book of the genteel world of 1630, and he is prepared for the nature of Cavalier plots.

The Greek romances and such imitations of them as the *Argenis* must be viewed in composite when one discusses the sources of Cavalier plays. So close is the resemblance among all the romances and all the plays that it is dangerous to assert that any particular romance is the source of any particular play. An exception may be made in the case of such plays as frankly dramatized individual romances—further testifying to their popularity. The *Æthiopica* itself was dramatized in John Gough's *Strange Discovery,* and in an anonymous play, still in manuscript, *The White Ethiopian;* Sidney's romance was dramatized in

Shirley's (?) *Arcadia*, and in another anonymous play, also still in manuscript, *Love's Changelings Change;* D'Urfé's pastoral was dramatized in Leonard Willan's *Astrea;* and Greene's *Menaphon* in Thomas Forde's *Love's Labyrinth.* A few other plays such as Glapthorne's *Argalus and Parthenia,* and the anonymous *Andromana,* both sired by the *Arcadia,* present undisguised episodes from the parent stock. But such plays are the merest handful compared with the many which may claim at least a superficial originality. It is often the practice of the source-hunter in following the spoor of a plot to give tongue as soon as he has found a similarity in an older work; the latter is hailed as The Source, and clairvoyance soon extricates a column of verbal parallels, never very convincing to anyone but the huntsman himself.[12] The practice is especially deceptive when a relationship between specific works is argued on the basis of their common use of widely distributed themes. Cavalier plays make use chiefly of such themes, and it will be safer to compare them with romances of the Greek school not individually but in the mass. It will also be more revealing, because sources are significant in the degree to which they display general tendencies.

The plot of the typical play, like the plot of the *Æthiopica,* the *Arcadia,* or *Argenis,* will present us with a background of political and military strife among two or three neighboring states. In the plays, the states may be those of central Europe or even of the British Isles, but usually the ultimate source of the themes is suggested by the retention of a locale in Sicily or Sardinia or the other isles and coastal lands of the Mediterranean. Whatever the geographical location or era portrayed, a Mediterranean atmosphere lingers in the form of crews of pirates who prey upon and capture the chief characters, or rescue them from watery graves and lend aid to their cause. Pirates and bands of free-booters are everywhere in these plays. Against this backdrop stand out beautiful and virtuous ladies and valiant and magnanimous men—never more than a degree removed from royal station—and the problem is to unite them suitably in wedlock. The task is difficult! Barriers are presented by politics, by apparently unequal rank, by rivalry, by apparent consanguinity (usually because of the mystery surrounding the birth of one or more of the lovers), and by the designs of lustful villains. The lustful villain, to be sure, is a constant factor, not only in romances of the Greek school and in Cavalier drama, but also in Elizabethan drama; wherever unstained virginity is portrayed, lust must appear as a foil and a hazard, even though relegated, as in Italian pastoral drama, to satyrs and centaurs, those not too distant cousins of earthbound Caliban. Finally there intervenes the disappear-

ance and apparent death usually of one lover in each pair; in some
plays characters are slain and restored to life as habitually as in the
Erotica itself. But all barriers melt away, and Cavalier plays, like
Greek romances, end in pacification and wedlock. Like Boccaccio's
novels of the second day, each play tells a tale of evil fortune turning
to good.

Certain episodes are endlessly repeated. Frequently a woman will
follow, serve, and share the vicissitudes of her lover in the disguise
of a boy.[13] In Davenant's *The Distresses,* Basilonte chides Amiana,

> Some tale in Dieava [Diana] de Monte Mayor
> Taught you this trick of wand'ring after your
> lover.

But Montemayor's Felismena had taught this trick to Shakespeare's
Julia in *The Two Gentlemen of Verona* and perhaps to Sidney's Zel-
mane over fifty years before. The trick is common in the subsequent
plays of Shakespeare and his fellows. Montemayor must have borrowed
it from the Italian novellas where it is common and whither Elizabethans sometimes went for it directly. It is possible that the device
entered the novellas through the medium of Greek romances. Although
it occurs explicitly in none of those extant, it is congenial to their type
of episode, with the fortitude and initiative of their heroines and their
universal use of incognitos and disguise.

Another, and more basic, situation in Cavalier plots may also trace
an indirect descent from Greek fiction. We shall call this the Rival
Friend Dilemma. In its perfected form the situation is as follows. A
noble stranger becomes the friend and ally of a princely brother and
sister. The princess falls in love with the noble stranger, but he falls
in love with the prince's sweetheart. The friends become rivals, love
clashes with honor, ethical and emotional stresses assume such a complexity that hearts ache among the characters, heads among the readers.
Then the noble stranger discovers to his dismay that he is the brother of
the prince's sweetheart; thus freed from his ill placed attachment in
this quarter, he suddenly reciprocates the love of the princess and
brother and sister wed sister and brother. This situation occurs in some
variation in Carlell,[14] Suckling,[15] Mayne, in all but two of the eight
plays of Thomas Killigrew,[16] and in a score of others beside.[17] While
it does not occur in Longus, Heliodorus, or Tatius, it does occur in all
its perfection in Barclay's *Argenis.* A shadowing of it in *Euphues* is
more distinct in Lyly's source, the eighth novel of the tenth day, and
in Boccaccio's source, the old French tale of *Athis and Prophilis.* The

latter, with its numerous medieval progeny, is believed to derive from a Greek romance now lost.[18]

Often linked with the situation above, but sometimes occurring independently of it, is the Child Recovered theme. A chief character in the play is discovered to be the son of illustrious parents, lost to them as a babe, whereupon he is saved from impending execution, freed from a love-friendship dilemma, or simply proved eligible to wed his sweetheart of high degree. To justify our treatment of sources so to speak in gross, we may point out that the Child Recovered theme occurs in *The Pastoral of Florimene,* Hausted's *Rival Friends,* Wilson's *Inconstant Lady,* Carlell's *Deserving Favorite,* Killigrew's *The Prisoners, The Princess,* and *Bellamira her Dream,* Suckling's *The Goblins,* Rutter's *Shepherds' Holiday,* Peaps's *Love in its Ecstasy,* Cowley's *Love's Riddle,* Quarles' *Virgin Widow,* Jaques' *Queen of Corsica,* Davenant's *The Distresses,* Shirley's *Coronation* and *Two Gentlemen of Venice,* Brome's *Lovesick Court,* Nabbes' *Tottenham Court,* and Cokain's *Obstinate Lady,* besides in *The White Ethiopian,* Gough's *Strange Discovery,* Willan's *Astrea,* and Forde's *Love's Labyrinth.* In the decade before the closing of the theatres an average of two new plays each year could be counted on for this theme. English playwrights of the period naturally could not countenance infant exposure by parents, so the babies in most of these plays were lost originally through political expedience or the perfidy of a nurse. But in other respects the traditional complexion of the theme is retained. The lost child is recognized at last by some token that he has clung to doggedly through the years. In the *Æthiopica* one of Chariclea's tokens had been a pantarbe; in Wilson's *Inconstant Lady* the token is a scarf (admirably durable) but a minor character in the play is named Pantarbo! Suckling, scorning the commonplace, chose as the token for his lost child a diamond elephant.

To seek a specific source for the Child Recovered theme in these plays may seem supererogatory—some things are simply common property. Lost children, after all, are sometimes recovered in life; this is one of those flowers of human experience such as have been suggested as the basis of all fiction.[19] Babes were exposed, yet reserved for a glorious fate in the *Old Testament,* the *Metamorphoses,* the *Marvels beyond Thule.* The pervasiveness of the theme is illustrated by scholarly attempts to fix the source of Greene's romances. Fawnia's loss and recovery in *Pandosto* has been cited as a direct borrowing from Heliodorus.[20] But it has also been suggested that Fawnia is related to the children taken from the patient Griselda of Chaucer's *Clerk's Tale.*[21]

In this case there is further descent through Petrarch and Boccaccio, with collateral lines in Breton lai and popular ballad,[22] back perhaps to Greek fiction. *Pandosto* itself has been cited as a source of Greene's own Menaphon, but the Child Recovered theme in the latter has been traced back through a tale in William Warner's *Albion's England* (IV, xx) to an Anglo-French version of the *Lay of Havelock the Dane.*[23] Greene's romances remind us of the *Thracian Wonder,* and the *Winter's Tale,* not to mention *Pericles* and other Elizabethan plays where lost children are recovered. John Fletcher was especially fond of the theme. And as we think of plays, we remember how the child recovered figures largely in Guarini's *Il Pastor Fido,* Bonarelli's *Filli di Sciro,* besides other Italian pastorals, and, bridging even the distant era of Greek romance, in the *Menæchmi* and *Captivi* of Plautus. Nevertheless the Child Recovered theme remains the special property of Greek and derivative prose romances. It furnishes the pivotal situation in the *Æthiopica.* It plays an important part in D'Urfé's *Astrée,* Barclay's *Argenis,* and Desmarets' *Ariane.* Clarimond in Sorel's *Lysis,* commenting on its omnipresence in romances, conjectures a starting point in the *Daphnis and Chloe* of Longus. Its constant appearance in their favorite fiction explains why our Cavalier dramatists seem to have been leagued in a society for the perpetuation of cruelty to children.

The fact that certain elements in the stories told by our school of dramatists appear in old English and Continental tales (including the medieval and chivalric romances), in Elizabethan plays, in Italian pastorals, and in such contemporary French drama as formed "Floridor's" repertory at the Phoenix, should not obscure the truth of our generalization that Cavalier plots owe nearly everything to tales of decadent Greece. These tales had fed many streams, and these streams had many branches spreading like rivulets over a delta. The fact that the Cavalier playwright was familiar with these streams as well as with their fountainhead helps to explain why his borrowed themes appear only in generic form. In this respect he contrasts remarkably with the older playwrights. In Boccaccio's ninth novel of the third day Giletta by a sleight upon Bertramo conceives twin sons and secures a ring as proof of their paternity. This story retold by Painter became the source of Shakespeare's *All's Well that Ends Well.* In reading Shakespeare we can perceive at a glance that he had been reading Painter and not Boccaccio. But should this story appear in a Cavalier play, we could not tell whether the author was following Boccaccio, Painter, or Shakespeare, or whether he had simply been reading *Genesis,* where, be it remembered, Tamar disguised as a harlot gets twin sons (and a trinket) from Judah. Our dramatist would have altered all details and chosen his own character names. In contrast with the Elizabethan playwright, who appropriated material boldly, the Cavalier playwright seems furtive. Yet this impression is unfair to him. Following almost subconsciously his composite sources, he felt indeed that he was being highly original. So testifies many a deprecatory, self-conscious, and, at the same time, assertive and even querulous prologue. He was, of course, being only pliant, ingenious—and indescribably repetitive. We must leave this matter of the nature of Cavalier stories. In his preface to his translation of Sorel's *Berger Extravagant,* John Davies wrote that all romances were alike, and his sample plot would serve as a composite synopsis of Cavalier plays:

. . . the Damosel certainly to be relieved upon the point of ravishing, a little child carried away out of his cradle, after some twenty years discovered to be the son of some great Prince, a girl after seven years wandring and cohabiting, and being stole, confirm'd to be a Virgin, either by a Panterb, Fire, or a Fountain: and lastly all ending in marriage, and that all of a day, and in the same place, where to make up the number, somebody must be fresh discovered, some suddenly change their affections, and others rise as it were from the dead.[24]

To a similar slur in the body of the work, a lover of romances opposes this delectable defense:

. . . Clarimond hath said . . . he imagines that all Authors steal one from another, nay he hath been so unjust as to say that there are few adventures in the *Argenis* which are not as common in other Romances; but he does not consider aright. If there be a war in a book, or the ravishing of a maid, or the death of a King, and that in another there be the same accidents, does that make the books alike? It cannot be, for upon that account, the Roman History were no other thing then the Greek, because in both there are wars, ravishings of maids, and deaths of Princes; the circumstances make difference enough between things. Wars are begun upon divers occasions, maids may be ravished divers waies . . .[25]

Here is justice for the Cavalier playwright! He supplied the divers occasions and the divers ways, even though his were the same old wars and the same old ravishings—all so happily ineffectual.

The people who prosecuted these wars and rescued these maids are our next concern. Characterization in any true sense does not appear in these plays. The *dramatis personæ* are restricted to a few undifferentiated types—all silhouettes in black, white, and gilt—animate but unalive. What the Cavalier dramatist actually did was make his characters the exemplars and expositors of a body of faddish notions about etiquette, ethics and the emotions. These notions expounded in monologues or long casuistical debates sometimes occupy entire scenes; they are worth attention for the glimpse they afford into the courtly mind. John Davies' sample plot of a romance mentions "a girl—confirm'd to be a Virgin, either by a Panterb, Fire, or a Fountain." This episode, climactic in the *Æthiopica* and persistent elsewhere, is not utilized in Cavalier plays—gallantry forbade it. The virginity of a heroine is never seriously in question, and in general there is a less physical view of sex and courtship than we find in Greek fiction. These playwrights had as their background not only Greek fiction but also a later product of the ages—Chivalry—though theirs was Chivalry of a recent and somewhat spurious brand. They had been inoculated with the honeyed virus of D'Urfé just as surely as had Mairet, Auvray, Rayssiguier, and other dramatists of contemporary France.[26]

It is unnecessary here to describe the ideals of the *précieuses*[27]—their devotion to D'Urfé, their dilute emotions, their refined sentiments, their nice code of etiquette, their exploitation of platonic love. Suffice to say that with the establishment of Henrietta Maria in England *préciosité* crossed the Channel, and ladies of the court toyed with an attempt to make the *Astrée* canonical at Whitehall as it was at the Hôtel de Rambouillet. Their success was not spectacular, for most Englishmen, even at court, were apt to be unimpressed by involved pretense—especially by the unpointed ardors of platonic courtship, which seemed to them a species of grouse-shooting with the grouse omitted. Henrietta herself, though refined and virtuous, was of a more robust type than the typical *précieuse*. Nevertheless the ideals of D'Urfé occasioned volumes of talk, and even won some lip service—devout murmurings disturbed on occasion by the unharmonious birth of a child by one of the Queen's unwedded maids of honor. In 1634 James Howell wrote, "The Court affords little News at present, but there is a love call'd Platonic Love, which much sways there of late; it is a Love abstracted from all corporeal gross Impressions and sensual Apetite, but consists in Contemplations and Ideas of the Mind, not in any carnal Fruition."[28] William Davenant at the Queen's command glorified ideal devotion in a masque, *The Temple of Love;* then in a play *The Platonic Lovers,* he gently lampooned the fad for the popular stage. The cult lingered to leave a mark on the prose and verse of Waller, Suckling, Habington, and a number more.[29]

With all this in mind let us open at random our first important Cavalier play, Montague's *Shepherd's Paradise,* to observe what the characters are like and what they talk about. It may help animate this scene if we keep in mind the court performance; Queen Henrietta and the Marchioness of Hamilton are on the stage:

Bellesa. You believe, then, Moramente, he will love again, and by a high success shall know he was reserved by heaven for more than he could wish at first? You think that heaven doth allow of love's twice?

Moramente. As it doth intend, Madam, all good should rise to its perfection, our minds are but love's pupils at the first, which fit themselves but to proceed and take degrees; and so our second love is a degree wherein our souls attain to experience that employs itself in love's refinement. So, not by the first step, but by this gradation, love ascends unto its highest.

Bellesa. I will allow you, Moramente, love is no irradiation of a light into our souls whose first instant brightness is in its perfection. But may not the first spark be kept alive and raised unto as high a light as can the second, which is kindled still by putting out the first?

Moramente. 'Tis not an extinction of the flame, 'tis but a change of the material that fomented it; so second loves have this advantage, they being the first instant in that height the first was long a'growing to, and have the first comparison to raise themselves by, which must prove it higher by having got above it.

Bellesa. These degrees of elevation, Moramente, you require in love infer this consequence, that love should be a continual motion, by change aspiring to transcendency. For if comparison doth raise it so, he is to blame that takes but one. For by your inference the number must exalt the last unto the greatest height. Your inconstancy doth not concern us so, as you should strive to prove it a virtue to us.

Moramente. In this degree, Madam, which I have named love comes to touch a point, after which all motion is a declination. I do not allow love's lightness or variety contributors unto its height. I do agree the glory of it is in a consistency in this elevation the second love attains to because the first cannot know how high it is. Had I thought inconstancy a virtue, Madam, I ne're had been blest with this so great a joy of seeing you.[30]

Now this, distressing though it may be, must be recognized as something *new* in English drama. In older plays, even those we term philosophical, such as *Hamlet,* the gnomic speech when it occurs nearly always elucidates character, out of which grows conflict and dramatic crisis. But the Cavalier plays following Montague (who we shall confess offers an extreme instance) are full of oracular utterances included for their own sake. Drama lapses and action comes to full stop while the characters weave their fine spun disquisitions, and split hairs already of gossamer thinness. Sometimes to be sure these discourses are imbued with a tone of hauteur, pathos, or moral urgency, so that a slight effort will remind us that we are reading a play, but just as often we might think we were reading pages from a conduct book in dialogue. The discourses of the characters are not exclusively, or even principally, about platonic love; all phases of love are treated, of courtship, of jealousy, of honor—but all artificially and within a pitifully narrow range. Should the Noble Stranger offer his own life a sacrifice for that of the Prince, the Prince is likely to dilate on lowly-mindedness—such

as would induce anyone to believe that *he* would permit such a sacrifice. This quality in the plays is vital in distinguishing them, their content and general tone. Returning now to the matter of characters, we
shall say this: the people in Cavalier plays are *précieux,* true to life only
in their loquaciousness, and when we have said this we have said
all.

One must be temperate in defining Cavalier drama; and the language of the plays is even more likely than their characters and content
to provoke summary condemnation. Of course there is some diversity
in the style of various authors, but all of them—the fact may as well
be acknowledged at once—substitute a high-pitched rhetoric for the
poetry of the Elizabethans. "I shall never abstain from those fine things,
hyperboles and similitudes," says the romance reading courtier in
Cowley's *The Guardian,*[31] and we know from the correspondence of the
day that there was a grandiloquent argot actually in use at court. The
rhetoric of the plays, while always fluent, is vivacious and colorful in
some writers, languorous and dull in others, and the difference may
spell an entertaining or an intolerable experience for the reader. It is
cheering to realize that the sample quoted from Montague represents
the Cavalier style at its worst.

The form employed is rhythmic prose, usually (though not in Montague) masquerading as blank verse. Blank verse weakened by the
mannerisms of Fletcher had become increasingly emasculate even
among professional and university playwrights, but the final stages
of debility appear in the plays of actual courtiers and their Interregnum imitators. These lacked the stamina or the desire to achieve
any sustained technical proficiency, and while they themselves seemed
confident they were writing verse, their printers were not so certain.
When Cokain issued a second edition of *The Obstinate Lady,* he rebuked the printer of the first—"although that comedy be very much
of it writ in number, he put it forth as if the most part of it were
prose."[32] The same complaint was lodged for Henry Killigrew in the
preface to *Pallantus and Eudora,* 1653, pirated as *The Conspiracy* in
1638. Henry's more productive brother, Thomas Killigrew, was less
particular. His *Princess* and *Claricilla* had originally been printed as
blank verse, but he let them be reprinted as prose in the folio of his
collected works. No one would suspect the transfer. There is a likeli-
hood that an opposite practice also existed among some printers—that
of printing as blank verse what was intended as prose. Blank verse
was traditional in play-books and a better bid for sales; moreover it
was easier for a compositor to set up lines of irregular length, and it
would be tempting for mid-seventeenth century printers to add to

their many malpractices that of making a line of type for each line of
writing on a manuscript page. The following, from *The Loyal Lovers,*
by Cosmo Manuche, may be an example of such compositor's blank
verse:

> Noble friends, I thank you. But that must not be the way.
> for first her Father will not send her with a less guard
> than two, from whom, we cannot take her (with our security)
> without we take their lives (which all the Gods forbid)
> but they'll pursue us strictly.
> No, no, I have contrived a way much safer . . .[33]

This same phenomenon, utterly unmetrical lines lacking capitals except at sentence heads, yet set up in uneven lengths, appears also in
Sir William Lower's *Horatius,* Richard Flecknoe's *Love's Kingdom,*
and elsewhere. But this goes beyond normal practice among our plays;
there is usually at least a dim echo here and there of the old pentam-
eters. There is much inequality even within individual plays, and, in
some, like Lewis Sharpe's *Noble Stranger,* each act will begin with
fairly regular verse, so that the reader may trace a progressive disintegration as the act proceeds.

There remain to be distinguished a few interesting minor qualities
of Cavalier drama. We might have noted in touching on their language
how rhythmic eloquence rises at intervals to crescendos of rant and
bombast, illustrations of which will be quoted later in an analysis of
their increasing grandiosity and their relation to the heroic plays of
the Restoration. Yet despite their heroic tone these plays reveal a
marked feminism. This quality was partly due to the spirit of the
times, reacting against that anti-feminism of Jacobean England which
had broken out in such diatribes as those by Swetnam the Woman-
Hater. However the feminism of Cavalier drama is more directly attributable to *préciosité,* and to the fact that Cavalier plays were
calculated to the meridian of court ladies, principally the Queen.
Women were, after all, the most avid readers of romances. One by
John Kennedy, with a title worth quoting in full, *The Historie of
Calanthrop and Lucilla, conspicuously demonstrat'ng the various
mutabilities of Fortune in their Loves, with every severall circumstance
of joyes and crosses, fortunate exploits and hazardous adventures, which
either of them sustained before they could attaine the prosperous event
of their wished aimes,* 1626, was republished in 1631 with the covering
title *The Ladies Delight.* While Montague writes for "the inspir'd and
more refin'd part of men,"[34] Carlell frankly admits that it is "the gentler Sex that gives life to his muse";[35] Killigrew's dedicatees form a
procession of fashionable ladies. Titles such as *Claricilla* and *Aglaura*

begin to appear, following the precedent of *Argenis* and *Ariane* among
the romances. No play by Shakespeare and few by his fellows had been
so titled (though some of Shakespeare's might well have been) and
Shirley comments on the novelty of the fashion in altering the title of
Love's Victory to *Rosania.*[36] Many plays, like most romances, followed
a fashion not so new by taking the name of their pair of lovers. A
greater number of women characters also appear, one play, *The Female
Rebellion,* offering an amusing instance of complete reversal of earlier
practices; not only are there more women than men, but the men in the
dramatis personæ are relegated to the foot of the column, time-honored
place for women. The women in Cavalier plays, like those in Greek
romances, tend to dominate the scene. Frequently they direct the action, and always the fate of men and nations hangs poised on their
sacrosanct desires.

The feminism of these plays goes far to explain another striking
quality—their almost uniform freedom from ribaldry and coarseness.
These are by far the cleanliest plays in all our older English drama.
This has been scored as a triumph for Prynne and his *Histriomastix,*[37]
but nothing could be further from the truth. At the same period comedies on the popular stage were reacting against unsympathetic Puritanism by going to unparalleled degrees of license. Cavalier plays are clean
because the court was beginning to boast a veneer of refinement, and
court ladies must needs be protected against embarrassment. This influence in operation is displayed in a play written not by a courtier but
by a popular dramatist; the court prologue to Massinger's *Emperor of
the East* reads in part:

> He durst not, Sir, at such a solemn feast,
> Lard his grave matter with one scurrilous jest;
> But labour'd that no passage might appear,
> But what the Queen without a blush might hear.

It was easy for the Cavalier dramatist to observe the proprieties because of his usual, though not invariable, custom of eliminating from
his play the comic underplot with its complement of free-spoken buffoons. Anything comic would appear sacrilege in most of these plays.
The writer's tone is solemn, his rôle almost prophetic. He would have
preferred the elevation of tragedy had not tragedy entailed the harsh
obligation of killing off noble gentlemen and beautiful ladies. The
compromise achieved makes these plays a distinct variety of tragicomedy: though happy in ending there is no relaxation in seriousness
of tone; many plays end in solemn rites—a coronation, a religious procession, or the like. Henry Killigrew shows how a Cavalier playwright
might have his cake and eat it. *Pallantus and Eudora* is introduced as

"Tragedy" and though all the worthy characters are prospering at the end, the play concludes with a blazing funeral pyre and solemn obsequies—conducted for a dead usurper and tyrant!

And now to recapitulate. If we recognize the typical Cavalier play as a schematic dramatization of the action of Greek romance, peopled by Platonics who deliver themselves of undramatic essays, written in florid cadenced prose, feministic in tendency, grave and refined in tone, we begin to discern it as a distinct type in English drama. To apply a hybrid phrase to a hybrid thing, we may call the type an heroical but *précieuse* tragicomedy of *anagnorisis*. It is not hard to distinguish this type from the drama of Shakespeare's ascendency. Its materials alone do that—ancient fantasies of incident, modern artificialities of thought. At its height, Elizabethan drama ranged far for material, but turned oftenest to transcripts of actual human life, in history, biography, and short story, or else pumped life's blood into the veins of romance. The more subtle distinction is between Cavalier and Fletcherian dramatic romance.

One might recall the chivalric setting of *The Knight of Malta*, the romantic plight of Bellario, the girl page in *Philaster*, or, even outside the realm of tragicomedy, the impassioned friendship scenes between Amintor and Melantius in *The Maid's Tragedy*, and draw the conclusion that Cavalier drama is no more than Fletcher poorly imitated. Fletcher heightened the romantic hue of tragicomedy, showed a fondness for glittering artifice, reveled in sentimentality, sacrificed truth to theatrical expediency, and employed type characters, some of which he endowed with "heroic sensibilities."[38] Fletcher showed the way for Cavalier drama, and courtly writers sometimes follow him closely. Yet they resemble him most when at their least characteristic. Shirley is his true son, not Carlell or Killigrew.[39] The departure goes beyond the fact that he was, as they were not, a true poet and artist. There is a difference in kind as well as in quality.

In most respects Fletcher played the game in the old way. He wrote for no courtly coterie absorbed in their genteel fads; he was a practical playwright pleasing a popular audience with popular methods. He wrote romantic dramas, not romances in dramatic form. His plays are so skilfully knit as to produce the maximum in theatrical effect. Cavalier plays are permitted to sprawl, in the fashion of the *Æthiopica,* and to reckon little with dramatic principles: in two part plays there is no *dénouement* at the end of the first part;[40] the action simply breaks off and the audience must return upon a later day to witness the remainder of the "Story." Although the plays could not follow the structure of the romances, where the plot is pieced out like a jig-saw puzzle

by subsidiary histories recited by the characters, they approached the
same effect by withholding information, by resorting to sketchy exposition full of dark hints, by imbuing everything with an air of mystery,
and presenting a tangle of action all but inextricable. Fletcher gives
us the dramatically traditional suspense and climax, Cavalier playwrights give us secrecy and surprise. Fletcher's action is organic; that
is each episode is, to a reasonable degree, the outgrowth of those which
have preceded. In Cavalier plays, in place of a chain of events welded
by forces we can observe, we find pure fortuitousness. Rather than have
his character make up his mind to go any place, the playwright prefers
to have him captured and dragged to his destination by irrelevant
robbers. There is an illogicality of action, a perverseness of behavior
foreign to Fletcher but quite native to the prose romances. We are
reminded of the ending of the *Æthiopica,* where disaster almost results from Chariclea's stubborn, and pointless, refusal to talk. Almost
any Cavalier play would end within two speeches, its misunderstandings and crossed purposes dissolved, if the characters would do and say
what was natural and obvious at the moment. The popular failure of
The Faithful Shepherdess left Fletcher disgruntled and disinclined to
experiment, but it is doubtful, after all, if there was much disparity
between what his audiences expected of him and what he wanted to
give. Fletcher was coarse and full of animal spirits. Rarely does he
omit the comic underplot, or at least a few scenes of earthy humor. No
better illustration of the existence of a new school of drama can be
given than the nice sobriety of Thomas Killigrew's *The Prisoners* and
Claricilla. Killigrew too, as his later comedies reveal, was coarse and
boisterous, but in writing serious plays he had to observe the proprieties of his school.

As a playwright of the old school, Fletcher was mindful of the worth
of his action. He and his audiences valued this action for itself, and not
solely for its atmosphere or for the posturing it might provoke. It is
true that the plot materials described earlier in this chapter are all
utilized by Fletcher as well as by the Cavalier writers; in fact few situations possible to romantic fiction are absent from the half-hundred
plays associated with Fletcher's name. He loves to disguise fair ladies
as boys and to buffet them and their lovers dangerously in strange lands
and on the high seas. He lets love unite enemies and love-rivalry divide
friends. He restores lost children to their right, and brings to heel
piratical kidnappers and wicked usurpers. Frequently the Cavalier
writers must have found in Fletcher materials ready to their hand. Yet
Fletcher's stories are different from those of his courtly successors. In
adapting his materials he was independent and resourceful, and al-

though he laid under contribution so much of the exotic fiction of his day, he intertwined with what he borrowed so much that was his own, so much that was native and real, that his plots, unlike those of the Cavalier playwrights, are not repetitious, do not form predictable patterns.

Reality raises its head in Fletcher even when he is at his most exotic. His characters are usually creatures of flesh and blood; they are not, like Cavalier characters, personified theories. In especial instances, it is true, Fletcher shows a tendency to produce the latter, and that recurring type now stamped by the critical commonplace, "the bluff old soldier," sometimes resigns complex humanity to become, like Æcius in *Valentinian*, only an emblem—an emblem of Fletcher's conception of liegeman's fealty. But characters of this kind are exceptional in Fletcher. In *Valentinian* we also meet Lucina, who is no mere emblem of chaste womanhood; she is a woman first, a chaste woman afterwards, and is never inflated to superhuman proportions. The degree to which Fletcher's characters are physical and psychological realities is illustrated by Arbaces in *King and No King*. With Tigranes, Spaconia, and Panthea, Arbaces is involved in a variation of what has been described above as the "rival friend dilemma" where love-rivalry is complicated by consanguinity. In a Cavalier play the love of Arbaces for his sister Panthea would show as the merest "straw man" of an emotion, foreordained to yield, after a forensic display, to the prior claims of magnanimity and ethical rectitude. Not so in Fletcher. The infatuation of Arbaces is all too convincing; the reader is protected by no sheen of unreality, no metaphysical elevation.

In *préciosité* Fletcher displays scarcely a trace of interest. His characters do not halt in mid-career to expound doctrine, platonic or otherwise. The dialogue remains always dramatic. The serious plot of *The Humorous Lieutenant* is of a type almost to have compelled Fletcher to write drama of ethical debate, yet he did not do so. Two plays, *Valentinian* and *Monsieur Thomas*, actually drew their plot materials from Part II of the *Astrée*,[41] yet they show an utter imperviousness to the characterization, diction, and philosophical mood of D'Urfé. It is worth observing that both of these plays were written, as the critics agree, by Fletcher alone.[42] *The Lovers' Progress*, founded on d'Audiguier's *Lysandre et Caliste* seems to have been revised by Massinger at a time when the Cavalier mode had begun to establish itself; and here we find such a speech as the following:

> How is my soul divided! Oh Cleander,
> My best-deserving husband! Oh Lisander,
> The truest lover that e'er sacrificed

To Cupid against Hymen! Oh, mine honour,
A tyrant, yet to be obey'd! and 'tis
But justice we should thy strict laws endure,
Since our obedience to thee keeps us pure.[43]

For a character thus to present us with a thesis is not typical of Fletcher's method.[44] To put to a practical test the question of whether a true distinction between Fletcherian and Cavalier tragicomedy exists, one need only read the dialogue quoted from Montague's *Shepherd's Paradise* and then ask himself if he has ever read anything like it in Fletcher —in *The Faithful Shepherdess* or elsewhere. Or one may read in succession Fletcher's *Love's Pilgrimage* and Carlell's *Passionate Lovers*. Both are tragicomedies of persecuted sweethearts, exotic in atmosphere and peregrinating in design, but there the resemblance ends: Fletcher's is a drama of love and high adventure, Carlell's a dramatic exposition of ardors and elegant behavior.

Richard Flecknoe was justified when, in 1664,[45] he spoke of Fletcher's manner being "turned a new way" by the Caroline courtier. In some aspects of its artificiality the "new way" was, to be sure, quite old— older indeed than the time of Fletcher. Plays had been "courtly toys"[46] in earlier stages of dramatic history; the gallantries of Richard Edwardes and the affectations of John Lyly had been calculated to please gentility.[47] Some of the old dramatic romances whose titles alone survive, *Chariclea, Cloridon and Radiamanta, Phigon and Lucia, Philemon and Philecia*,[48] and others must have displayed kindred features with Sidney's *Arcadia*, as do Cavalier dramas themselves. We must bear in mind that the plays under discussion are the expression of a class, and that the contrast they present with popular drama is explainable only upon that basis. In analyzing the reasons why, in Italy, Il Lasca warred in vain against *anagnorisis*, why the plots of the *Commedia erudita* never rose above "Mistakes between two brothers, confusions of sex, discoveries that poor girls are the lost daughters of princely parents,"[49] John Addington Symonds has the following to say: "None of these five species [of Italian drama; i.e. comedy, tragedy, masque, pastoral, Florentine religious *Feste*] can be called in a true sense popular; nor were they addressed by their authors to the masses of the people. Performed in private by pious confraternities or erudite academies, or exhibited on state occasions in the halls of princely palaces, they were not an expression of the national genius but a highly cultivated form of aristocratic luxury."[50] Had it not been for the upsurge of English popular drama, and what has been called "the triumph of realism,"[51] most Elizabethan and seventeenth century plays would have conformed to a mode not unlike that described in the present chapter.

Sooner or later in discussing Caroline drama, we must consider the question of decadence. Are the Cavalier playwrights decadent authors? It may seem to contradict much that has already been said, especially about the reliance of these authors upon Greek romance, if one ventures to deny it. Fletcher, Ford, and Brome are more decadent than Montague, Carlell, and Killigrew. Decadent authors are over-ripe, Cavalier playwrights had scarcely arrived at green. Of course, if false taste and poor technique are evidence of the blight, Cavalier plays are decadent—but so also are those rococo whatnots, once displayed in Victorian parlors, now secreted in dim lumber-rooms. It is certainly a sign of decline in the vitality of popular drama that Cavalier plays were given a hearing in the public theatres and were permitted to deflect the development of later professional playwrights. A taste less staled would never have tolerated these plays, but we should not display moral indignation if a Caroline famine has followed an Elizabethan feast. This is in the nature of things. The term decadence usually carries with it a sense of moral obliquity, and from such a charge Cavalier plays can be triumphantly acquitted. They are astonishingly innocent productions. The fact that a character, unaware of the relationship, will often fall in love with and woo his own sister does not mean that there is dalliance, as in Fletcher and Ford, with the theme of incest; in fact there never is—there is simply a love of coincidence, and a grasping at every opportunity to add to the perplexity of lovers. The Cavalier hero never has a wayward impulse; torrents of precept rain upon him if he so much as wavers into jealousy or fickleness. These plays were one of the most wholesome interests at the court of King Charles, and like *préciosité* itself, they helped to civilize our ancestors.

---

[1] S. L. Wolff, *The Greek Romances in Elizabethan Prose Fiction* (New York, 1912), p. 235.—For influence of the Greek romance, see also, M. Oeftering, *Heliodor und seine Bedeutung, Literarhistorische Forschungen,* XVIII (1901).

[2] *Autobiography of Mary Countess of Warwick,* T. C. Croker, Ed., *Percy Soc. Pub.* (1848), p. 4.

[3] Act II, Scene i.

[4] Act I, Scene i; Act II, Scene i.

[5] But they were imported promptly, see T. Haviland, *The Roman de longue haleine on English Soil,* Philadelphia, 1929.

[6] Translated as *The Extravagant Shepherd. The Anti-Romance: or the History of the Shepherd Lysis,* London, 1653. Preface signed John Davies.

[7] S. L. Wolff, *op. cit.,* pp. 262-366.

[8] Some of the intermediate romances are treated by W. Von Wurzbaci, *Geschichte des Französischen Romans* (Heidelberg, 1912); and by H. Kœrting, *Geschichte des Französischen Romans im XVII Jahrhundert* (Oppeln and Leipsig, 1891).

[9] It is not discussed by S. L. Wolff, *op. cit.*, or J. Jusserand, *English Novel in the Time of Shakespeare* (1890); Dunlop places it among political allegories.

[10] For an excellent account of Barclay, see K. N. Colvile, *Fame's Twilight* (London, 1923).

[11] For a bibliography and source study, see K. F. Schmid, *John Barclay's Argenis, Literarhistorische Forschungen*, XXXI (1904).

[12] I have made this error in *Thomas Killigrew* (Philadelphia, 1930), pp. 150-159, where I insist upon Desmarets de Saint-Sorlin's *Ariane* as the particular source of Killigrew's early plays.

[13] Typical variations of the device appear in Carlell's *Passionate Lovers,* and *Arviragus and Philicia,* Suckling's *Brennoralt, or The Discontented Colonel,* Cokain's *Obstinate Lady,* T. Killigrew's *Cicilia and Clorinda,* Manuche's *Loyal Lovers,* and Wm. Killigrew's *Siege of Urbin.* Concealed identity of some form occurs in nearly every Cavalier play.

[14] *The Deserving Favorite.*

[15] *The Goblins.*

[16] *The Princess, Claricilla, The Prisoners, The Pilgrim, Cicilia and Clorinda* (2 parts), *Bellamira her Dream* (2 parts).

[17] Montague's *Shepherd's Paradise,* Mead's *Combat of Love and Friendship,* Wm. Killigrew's *Siege of Urbin* and *Selindra,* etc.

[18] S. L. Wolff, *op. cit.*, pp. 248-261.

[19] See J. C. Dunlop's Introduction to his *History of Prose Fiction,* revised ed., 2 vols. (London, 1896).

[20] S. L. Wolff, *op. cit.*, p. 425.

[21] T. H. McNeal, "The Clerk's Tale as a Possible Source for Pandosto," *PMLA*, XLVII (1932), 453-460.

[22] *Chaucer Society Publications,* Series II, v, 176.

[23] Joseph Q. Adams, "Thomas Forde's Love's Labyrinth," *Studies in Language and Literature in Celebration of the Seventieth Birthday of James Morgan Hart* (New York, 1910).

[24] *The Extravagant Shepherd* (1653), sig. A2.

[25] *Ibid.*, Book XIII, p. 77.

[26] D'Urfé's influence on the French drama is discussed by O.-C. Reure, *La Vie et les Œuvres de Honoré D'Urfé* (Paris, 1910), Chapter XV.

[27] The ideals are now familiar; cf. J. B. Fletcher, *The Religion of Beauty in Woman and Other Essays on Platonic Love in Poetry and Society* (New York, 1911).—D'Urfé's code had, of course, medieval and early Renaissance foreshadowings; for the sources of *Astrée,* cf. B. Germa, *L'Astrée d'Honoré D'Urfé* (Toulouse et Paris, 1904), Part II, Chapter II. A good analysis of D'Urfé's love code appears in K. M. Lynch, *The Social Mode of Restoration Comedy* (New York, 1926) pp. 46-51. (The code was never effectively interpreted in seventeenth-century England.) For D'Urfé's influence on the literature of the time, cf. J. B. Fletcher, *op. cit.*, pp. 166-205, and A. H. Upham, *The French Influence in English Literature* (New York, 1911), pp. 321-344.

[28] *Familiar Letters,* J. Jacobs, Ed., 2 vols. (London, 1892), I, 317.

[29] J. B. Fletcher, *op. cit.*, pp. 166-205.

[30] *Shepherd's Paradise* (1659), pp. 62-63.

[31] Act III, Scene iv.

[32] See author's address, *A Chain of Poems*, 1658.

[33] *Loyal Lovers* (1652), p. 37.

[34] Preface to *Shepherd's Paradise*, 1659.

[35] Epilogue to Part I, *Arviragus and Philicia*.

[36] See the Dublin prologue.

[37] A. W. Ward, *English Dramatic Literature*, III, 245.

[38] For Fletcher's innovations, see J. W. Tupper's introduction to his edition of Davenant's *Love and Honour* and *The Siege of Rhodes*, Belles-Lettres Series, 1909.

[39] F. E. Schelling, *Elizabethan Drama* (1908), II, 426-427, makes such a distinction between Davenant on the one hand and Carlell and Killigrew on the other, and, in general, suggests the point of view developed in the present chapter.

[40] See Carlell's *Arviragus* and *Philicia* and *Passionate Lovers*, and T. Killigrew's *Cicilia and Clorinda* and *Bellamira her Dream*. The latter two must have been designed as "closet dramas."

[41] *Variorum edition Beaumont and Fletcher*, A. H. Bullen, gen. ed., IV, 210, 326.

[42] See E. H. C. Oliphant, *The Plays of Beaumont and Fletcher* (Yale Univ. Press, 1927), pp. 142-145, 146-148.

[43] Act I, Scene i.

[44] Judging chiefly by the plays published in his life time; however, speeches like the above are rare anywhere in the Beaumont and Fletcher folio, although a number of the plays, while still part of an unpublished theatrical repertory, must have undergone Caroline revision.

[45] In the preface to *Love's Kingdom*, where we find the first truly historical view of English drama. Flecknoe erred in naming Suckling as leader of the new school.

[46] See the Prologue to Richard Edwardes' *Damon and Pythias*, 1565.

[47] Lyly followed so closely his private pattern of play-making, and time has preserved so little of the courtly drama before Lyly, that it is impractical, unfortunately, to pursue the comparison.

[48] *Documents Relating to the Office of the Revels in the Time of Queen Elizabeth*, Albert Feuillerat, Ed., *Bang's Materialien* (Louvain, 1908), pp. 145, 175, 213, 238.

[49] John Addington Symonds, *Renaissance in Italy*, 2 vols. (New York, 1935), II, 237-238.

[50] *Ibid.*, II, 231.

[51] W. Thorp, *The Triumph of Realism in Elizabethan Drama* (Princeton dissertation, 1928). Dr. Thorp, however, considers realism only as opposed to didacticism.

III

CAVALIER DRAMA AND THE RESTORATION HEROIC PLAY

A DETAILED account of plays in the Cavalier mode from the time of Montague to the time of Dryden will appear in later chapters. The mode survived during the Commonwealth and the earlier years of the Restoration. In 1663 or 1664, when the Duke of Buckingham first drafted his *Rehearsal,* Henry Howard, Robert Stapylton, and William Killigrew were sharers in his ridicule; and as he or his clique revised the burlesque from time to time, Davenant, Robert Howard, and Dryden were permitted to succeed each other as its prime dramataster.[1] Dryden was viewed, neither as the inventor of a new kind of play, nor as a disciple of Corneille, for whom Buckingham had doubtless the correct courtly respect, but simply as the legatee of those whom we shall list as the last of the Cavaliers.[2] That the view was substantially correct, and that the heroic plays of the Restoration represent a culmination of the Cavalier mode, is the opinion to be advanced in the present chapter. It is not the opinion that has generally prevailed.

The belief that the heroic play is isolated from earlier types of English drama, that it came into being partly as an imitation of French classical drama, partly as a Restoration invention, has enjoyed wide currency in the past and enjoys considerable currency still. The basis of the belief is clear. First, there is the testimony of the heroic dramatists themselves. In his *Essay of Heroic Plays,* Dryden asserted that the "first light we had of them" was *The Siege of Rhodes,* and conjectured that Davenant had "heightened his characters . . . from the example of Corneille." Such refinements upon Davenant's manner as appear in his own plays, Dryden implied were the result of his own inspiration (experienced while reading Ariosto) to make drama comply with "the greatness and majesty of an heroic poem."[3] Then the Earl of Orrery, in a letter quoted in Dodsley's preface to his collected plays,[4] stated explicitly that he composed in rime because Charles II preferred the French to the English fashions in drama. The rime of the heroic plays weighed heavily in Dodsley's day and throughout the eighteenth century[5] in suggesting their origin; however sketchy may have been acquaintance with pre-Restoration drama, it was common knowledge that the English playwrights, in contrast with the French, had used unrimed verse. In the early nineteenth century, the theory of French dominance was amplified when Scott edited Dryden and added to French classical drama the *romans de longue haleine* as the inspiration of the heroic plays.[6] That the plays and the romances contained material in common was easily capable of demonstration. Finally, the fact that the heroic plays rose into prominence shortly after the Restoration has contributed greatly to the belief in their foreign inspiration. Conscious of the fact that the Stuart court had been living in exile, critics have naturally inferred that a taste for French literature was cultivated abroad, and that the acquired taste induced imitation upon the return to England.

With the extension of knowledge of the entire range of English drama, it has become apparent that the traditional view of the origin of the heroic plays would have to be modified. In 1874, Symonds made out a case for the plays as a native English growth.[7] Ward in his *English Dramatic Literature,* although taking much the position of Scott in respect to the genesis of the type itself,[8] created a greater sense of the continuity of English dramatic tradition than had previously existed; and in 1903 Saintsbury, fortified by Ward's history and his own familiarity with the byways of English literature, stated that the theory of imitation of the French as the sole basis of the heroic plays was now "almost impossible to sustain except by mere ignorance."[9] But it is difficult to stem the momentum of long established belief, and in 1912 Edmund Gosse confidently asserted that "there was no continuity between the plays written under Charles I and those written under Charles II, and the first thing to be done, in appreciating the latter, is to dismiss all consideration of the former. . . ."[10]

Few in recent years have gone so far as Gosse, but there has been a tendency in a number of monographs[11] to revert to the approximate position of Scott; to minimize the importance of native tradition, and to divide between Continental critical theory and French drama and prose romance the honor of begetting the heroic plays. Some of the comment has been made in connection with the effort to pick the "pioneer" heroic play. Dryden's assertion that the "first light" of such plays was *The Siege of Rhodes* is itself inaccurate, yet it is more accurate than more recent assertions; for in Davenant's play, actually on the stage before the Restoration, appear most of the details of the final pattern. But this fact has not prevented *The Indian Queen* of 1664, or *The General* of 1662, from being nominated as the first heroic play. None of these plays contains all the characteristics of *The Conquest of Granada,* yet all contain some of them; and we should view them equally as stages in a process of evolution; or, better, we should admit some latitude in our conception of the type itself. There is danger in identifying the type with a limited number of its qualities, and in fixing the attention upon too narrow a field of literary history.

The most recent definition of the heroic play characterizes it as "a wholly serious play, composed in rimed verse, with a tone befitting heroic poetry, and concerned with the lofty sentiments of persons in high station."[12] The phrase "a tone befitting heroic poetry" as applied to the rhetorical bombast of the plays expresses the evaluation of their authors rather than our own, but otherwise this definition may be accepted as just. The rime of the plays, it is now generally agreed, is not their most essential quality, for, as Mr. Nicoll has observed, the rime was "a passing external fashion"[13] which died out relatively early while other of their features lived on well into the eighteenth century. However, since rime was truly a conspicuous feature of the plays in their years of greatest vogue, and since so much is made of it by those arguing French origins, it is equitable to admit it into a definition.

Our object now is to trace the various ingredients of the heroic plays as they made their appearance in earlier English drama—more specifically in drama of the Cavalier mode. The believers in an English tradition behind the heroic plays have often failed to carry conviction because they urged a comparison of the plays with the drama of Marlowe and Fletcher, ignoring that body of drama, now fallen into obscurity, but produced by and for the same social order as were the heroic plays themselves.

Let us look first at the fables of the heroic plays. In story material, except for an increased use of the supernatural, there is little to distinguish those written before and those written after Dryden's *Tyrannic Love,* so we shall restrict our purview to the former. Limits of space will allow only brief synopses.

In *The Siege of Rhodes,* Part I, 1656, Alphonso's jealousy of his wife Ianthe, provoked by the courtesies she has received from Solyman the Magnificent, is dissolved when Ianthe rivals his own valor in repulsing the Turkish Emperor's assault upon Rhodes. In *The Siege of Rhodes,* Part II, 1659?, Ianthe is sent from Rhodes to make terms of peace with Solyman. In the Turkish camp her charms inflame the jealousy of Roxolana, the Emperor's wife, but these same charms at last win Roxolana's friendship, and magnanimous terms of peace for Rhodes—in spite of the fact that Alphonso, in a jealous relapse, has led out the Rhodians in a futile assault upon the Turks.

In Orrery's *The General,* 1662, the brave steadfastness of Altemera in love and virtue sets at naught the lustful designs of a kingly usurper and his insidious son, so that she is at last united with her brave though impetuous lover, Lucidor. The latter she will consent to marry only with the permission of Cloriman, his worthy rival, to whom she owes much, and whose valor has overthrown the lustful tyrant and restored the true king.

In Howard and Dryden's *Indian Queen,* 1664, Montezuma asks for the hand of Princess Orazia as his guerdon for defeating the Mexican enemies of the Incas, but he is repulsed by her royal father because of his obscure birth. He revolts to the Mexican side, defeats the Incas, and captures Orazia and her father. Then both he and his captives are imprisoned as a result of Mexican treachery. Zempoalla, the usurping Mexican Queen, falls in love with Montezuma, and her paramour General Traxalla with Orazia, but neither Montezuma nor Orazia will shun death by yielding to these loves or by letting the other yield. They are about to be sacrificed to the gods when the true queen, Amexia, arrives with her forces: Traxalla is slain, Zempoalla takes her own life, Montezuma is discovered to be Amexia's princely son, and is united to Orazia. Diversity of incident is furnished throughout the play by Zempoalla's honorable son Acacis, who is Montezuma's friend in arms and hapless rival in love.

In Orrery's *Henry V,* 1664, the English king displays an honorable anxiety to win the hand of the French Princess Catherine, not by right of his recent glorious victories, nor yet by prohibiting the rivalry of his faithful subject, Owen Tudor, who also loves Catherine, but rather by the force of true love and by a willingness to hazard all personal dangers. The path to the realization of his desires is paved by political dissensions among the French themselves, and by the noble readiness of Owen Tudor to place friendship above love.

Orrery's *Mustapha,* 1665, begins with Roxolana interceding with Solyman on behalf of Queen Isabella as the all-conquering Turks lie before the Hungarian city of Buda. The two sons of Solyman, Mustapha and Zanger, become rivals in love for Isabella, but remain fast friends withal. Fearing that her own son, Zanger, will be slain after the Turkish custom when his elder stepbrother, Mustapha, succeeds to the Emperor's sceptor (and not knowing that these two have mutually sworn to share the throne and not to outlive each other), Roxolana makes the fatal error of joining with the Vizier Rustan in a plot to inflame Solyman's anger against his elder son. In consequence, both Mustapha and Zanger perish, while Roxolana is banished from her husband's life. Only the Hungarian Queen, who has been ever constant to her deceased spouse, profits by these lethal jars of Islam.

In Dryden's Indian Emperor, 1665, Montezuma of *The Indian Queen* is portrayed in his advanced years, as the widowed father of two sons and a daughter, and the ward of two daughters and a son of his erstwhile persecutor Zempoalla. Montezuma's sons are rivals for the love of one of Zempoalla's daughters, while he himself has a weakness for the other. Zempoalla's son is in love with Montezuma's daughter. Complicated enough already, this amatory web becomes more so when Cortez leads a force of Spaniards against the Mexicans; and, amidst the alarms of war, falls in love with Montezuma's daughter while one of Zempoalla's daughters falls in love with him. Love collisions whip in a mælstrom of military encounters, but Cortez emerges victorious alike in love and arms. Only he and his Mexican princess, and one pair of native lovers, survive; Montezuma and the other principals, some of whom have blackened themselves with treachery, having perished on the weapons of their enemies, or heroically by their own hands.

Orrery's *Black Prince*, 1667, save that it substitutes an intrigue-ridden court for the more usual beleaguered city and armed camp as the scene of action, and the same author's *Tryphon*, 1668, add no new essential to the type of story material already indicated, and need not be described. *The Conquest of Granada* itself tells a tale much of the same pattern as that of *The Indian Queen*.

What we have then in the heroic play is a story of vexed love affairs against a background of war, international and civil. The forces separating the lovers are, in the first place, physical, created by the hazards of war and the plots of the lustful, and overcome at last by the valiant prowess of the hero and the constancy of the heroine; and, in the second place, emotional, created by jealousy, the claims of honor, rivalry between friends, etc., and overcome at last by compromise, fortuitousness, and simple evaporation. In a word, we have the same story formula in the heroic plays that we have in the dramatic romances of the Cavalier mode, as the reader will recognize by the description in the preceding chapter, or, more clearly, if he will persevere through the numerous synopses to appear in later chapters. There is not a theme, in fact scarcely an incident, in the heroic plays which had not been utilized in the drama of the three preceding decades, not once but many times. The new playwrights retained more interest in such devices as the rival friends and the hero of unknown birth, than in others, such as pseudo-fatalities and the piratical kidnapper, but whereas some of the old freight was pitched overboard, little new freight was taken on. The passionate, scheming woman, such as Zempoalla of *The Indian Queen* and Lyndaraxa of *The Conquest of Granada*, is seldom encountered in Cavalier drama, but she is no foreign importation; she probably evolved as the result of Elizabeth Davenport's phenomenal success in the rôle of Davenant's Roxolana, and of the delight of Restoration audiences (witness the comedy of the day) in the spectacle of skilful deceit. Such characters as Solyman, not portrayed as heroes perhaps, but as admirable despite their bloody despotism, had long been growing in favor; so testify Melcoshus in Carlell's *Osmond*, and Misander before his conversion in Cartwright's *Siege*. Dryden put himself to some pains to justify his use of the supernatural, but he did so because of the strictures against it in Davenant's *Preface to Gondibert*,[14] not because there lacked precedent in earlier heroic drama. The Cavalier plays had made constant use of oracles, visions, magic balms, and such miraculous machinery as the prophetic witch in Carlell's *Arviragus and Philicia*, the salvation of Cratander at the sacrificial altar in Cartwright's *Royal Slave*, and the direct intervention of the gods to establish the true royal succession in Quarles's *Virgin Widow*. The exotic locale of the action is least of all an innovation of the time of the Restoration; Sicily holds the palm as the favored land of the Cavalier plays, but Lower's *Phoenix in her Flames* had gone to Arabia Deserta, Cartwright's *Royal Slave* to Persia, Carlell's *Osmond* to the camps of the raging Turk, while others had sought out Alexandria, Bithynia, Ethiopia, and other outlandish lands. The realm of the Incas was first brought on the English stage in Davenant's Commonwealth show, *The Cruelty of the Spaniards in Peru,* the source of which was not a French romance but *The Tears of the Indians,* an English translation of a Spanish descriptive pamphlet.[15] It was inevitable that Restoration playwrights should finally invade China, and thus complete the circumnavigation of the globe. The apparition of English historical figures in Orrery's *Henry V* and *The Black Prince* seems at first glance to distinguish his material, in these two instances at least, from that of the Cavaliers, but the distinction is more apparent than real. In these two plays the characters are unimportant, in fact almost unrecognizable, in their historical aspect; King Henry and Prince Edmund are the usual heroes of exotic romance, and the English and French setting is little more convincing than the British setting of Stapylton's *The Stepmother,* or Carlell's *Arviragus and Philicia.*

The similarity of the materials of the Cavalier and the Restoration dramatist raises the question whether the latter borrowed directly from the former. To the present writer it seems likely that he sometimes did. The quartos and de luxe folios of the Cavalier plays had been available for years, and because of the courtly status of the authors must always have attracted the attention of the fashionable. Then, in addition to new plays written by survivors of the Cavalier generation and acted

early in the Restoration period, a number of old ones were revived:
Pepys saw *The Lost Lady*, *Argalus and Parthenia*, *Love and Honor*,
Brennoralt, *Aglaura*, *Claricilla*, and *The Princess* during his first year
of play-going, and others later on.[16] The plot of Orrery's *Mustapha*
certainly profited from suggestions in Denham's *Sophy* as well as in
Davenant's *Siege of Rhodes*, and the plot of the same author's *The
General* from suggestion in Suckling's *Brennoralt*. Orrery, considering
that his drama has been called so French, was remarkably familiar with
the native English plays of Sir John Suckling, who, by the way, had
already become an aureate tradition. The lover's question in Suckling's
Brennoralt

> . . . shall this fresh ornament
> Of the world, this precious loveliness
> Pass, with other common things, amongst
> The wastes of time?[17]

is echoed in Orrery's *The General*

> Shall all these charms of body and of mind
> Which late so bright in Altemera shined,
> Like other common things of Nature's birth,
> Be now reduced perpetually to earth?[18]

Brennoralt's resolution, "I will raise honour to a point it never was
. . ."[19] may well have inspired Owen Tudor in Orrery's *Henry V*, "Why
should not I, ev'n I alone, raise Love and Honour to a height unknown?"[20] Owen Tudor's set exposition of his love and friendship
dilemma,

> His favor wounds much deeper than his hate.
> I must unworthy, or else wretched prove,
> Be false to Honour or else false to Love.
> To which of both shall I precedence give?
> I'm kill'd by this, by that unfit to live . . .[21]

is justly considered one of the targets of the famous one-shoe-off-and-
one-shoe-on parody in *The Rehearsal*, but it is noteworthy that Buckingham's editors have been reminded of similar speeches in Davenant's
Love and Honor and in Quarles's *Virgin Widow*. It was common
among the Cavalier plays for vexed heroes to be very explicit in re-
hearsing their problems—like Charistus in Cartwright's *Lady Errant*,

> O my Lucasia!
> O my Olyndus! divers ways I bend,
> Divided 'twixt the Lover and the Friend.[22]

It is needless to labor the point that the heroic playwright of the Restoration sometimes borrowed directly from his Cavalier predecessor. It

is undeniably true that he went often for his material to La Calprenède and Scudéry.[23] But a false emphasis has been placed upon this fact. He went to La Calprenède and Scudéry just as the Cavalier dramatist had gone to the Greek, English, Spanish, Italian, and French predecessors of La Calprenède and Scudéry, and would have gone to these also had they been available when he wrote. The crucial consideration is the type of material the dramatist seeks after, not the place where he finds it. The Cavalier and the Restoration writer sought after the same material, and found it at different points along the same stream: the sensational romance of decadent Greece and of Europe in the latter sixteenth and in the seventeenth century—not a "French," but a distinctly international product.

It is, of course, not enough to argue the generic identity of the story ingredients in Cavalier drama and in the heroic plays. These ingredients might have been employed with entirely different emphasis in the two bodies of drama. The fact is, however, that they were not. Dryden's assumption that *he* decided that a play, like an epic poem, should express the heroic ideal and elevate love and valor to majestic heights is amusing in view of the thoroughness with which Cavalier playwrights, without prefatory theorizing, had committed themselves to the heroic ideal a generation before. The heroic ideal itself, as distinct from the fables furnishing the vehicle for this ideal, was a renaissance growth so widely diffused that it is impossible to say that it passed directly to Dryden from Tasso, or to Dryden from Davenant's *Preface to Gondibert*, whither it had passed from French critical theory, notably Scudéry's *Preface to Ibrahim*.[24] The heroic ideal in literature may be briefly described as a late renaissance coding of classical criticism, affirming allegiance to the dogma that the purpose of literature is instruction, that instruction is best conveyed through pleasing example, that the epic is the most elevated form of literature and the richest in pleasing example, and that anything aspiring to epic rank must include illustrations of virtue and exclude illustrations of the meaner vices. The conception of virtue was purely aristocratic, limiting the quality to the traits of epic heroes: physical courage, prowess in arms, magnanimity, and fidelity to a code of personal honor. This was *heroic virtue*, and that patterns of perfection in heroic virtue far transcending nature must appear in literature worthiest of the name is implicit in the criticism of Sidney, Puttenham, Jonson, Alexander, and Hobbes before *The Preface to Ibrahim* was written. *The Preface to Gondibert*, with its elucidation of the heroic ideal (and its modification of it, which gave Dryden a chance to dispute), is as easily traceable to native English theory as to that of the continent.[25]

The application of the heroic ideal was elastic in practice. Philip Sidney could couple the names of Homer and Heliodorus as a matter of course, and could fancy his own *Arcadia* as descending from the *Iliad* as well as from the *Æthiopica*. The Greek and derivative prose romances were admired and used for illustration by adherents of the heroic ideal from Sidney onwards; and the Cavaliers, in dramatizing the substance of these romances, dramatized their spirit as well, and anticipated Dryden's avowed purpose of bringing the heroic ideal to the stage. The Cavalier dramatist concentrated upon patterns of perfection in heroic virtue just as surely as did his Restoration successor, and the latter must be considered as continuing, not as importing or inventing a tradition.

The heroic ideal, with its theoretical basis, produced, both in Cavalier and Restoration drama, characters who are heroical in speech and action because of their obligations under a code of gallantry, characters belonging to a class of *professed* heroes who must preserve an *esprit de corps*, characters who are prompted to valorous deeds and large accent not so much from inner urge as from external compulsion. Carlell's Aviragus and Dryden's Almanzor express the same class heroicism—a type which must be distinguished from the individualized heroicism of Shakespeare's Henry V, or even Marlowe's Tamburlaine. The heroic ideal, as defined in preceding paragraphs, did not appear in English drama as early as in English prose romance. It is for this reason that those who have remarked only the "King Cambyses' vein" and the artificiality of the heroic plays, and have cited only the conqueror plays of Marlowe and the romances of Fletcher as their English antecedents, have failed to convince disbelievers in their basis in English tradition. A reader of *The Conquest of Granada* and of *Tamburlaine* receives utterly contrasted impressions, despite the fact that these plays contain heroic bombast in common. The strenuousness, the superhuman conceit, the egotistical rant of a Maximin or an Almanzor, as it appears not so much in the early rimed plays of Davenant and Orrery as in the matured productions of Dryden and his imitators, must be weighted only as a detail of behavior. Tamburlaine and Almanzor behave alike in this detail—both speak the language of Jove's thunder—, but the two are vastly different in essence. Tamburlaine's high-astounding terms are uttered un-selfconsciously, as a fitting orchestration to his conquest of the world. His is an authentic rant; his boasts must match his deeds: Almanzor's deeds must live up to his boasts. Fletcher's exalted strain, though more like the forced growth of the Restoration, rarely relates to physical prowess and military conquest, as the epithet "lily-livered"[26] applied to his heroes tends to suggest. When he pulls out the heroic stop to the full, there is likely to be a suggestion of satire in his tone—as in the familiar portrait of Arbaces in *King and No King;* Arbaces is a ranter but is "no king." Fletcher and his fellows usually employ heroic rant for adverse characterization, or even caricature, and the villains, not the heroes, as in the heroic plays, are most addicted to it. When Davenant in his earliest and most Fletcherian phase permits a character to cry,

> I am the broom of heaven; when the world grows foul,
> I'll sweep the nations into th' sea like dust.—[27]

he is portraying an Albovine, a bloodthirsty barbarian who drinks from the skulls of conquered enemies and is capable of such improprieties as

> Fill me a bowl, where I may swim
> And bathe my head, then rise like Phœbus from
> The ocean, shaking my dewy locks.[28]

In the heroic plays, a character may proclaim his single-handed ability to sweep nations into the sea, and yet remain a pattern of propriety. But this is true also in romances of the Cavalier mode. In both bodies of drama, we find conventionalized valor generated in the heroic ideal, together with a heroic verbal extravagance once considered worthy only of Bobadils or barbarian conquerors; in both "all things drawn as far above ordinary proportion of the stage, as that is beyond the common words and actions of human life."[29] A few brief quotations from our Cavalier plays may be helpful. When Suckling's Brennoralt cries,

> I will raise honour to a point
> It never was—do things of such
> A virtuous greatness she shall love me;
> She shall; I will deserve her though
> I have her not . . .,[30]

he stands far from Tamburlaine but very close to Almanzor; here is valor as virtuous perfection, from ethical necessity. The Cavalier hero habitually conquers by generic right; and, able to perform impossibilities, readily admits his ability. When Pausanes and Hipparchus in Killigrew's *Prisoners* lend their arms to the King of Sicily, towns fall before their might:

This way, this way . . . the gallant reapers went; sure by this their sickles are dull'd, and their hands weary with grasping such full victory; when the word was given, they charg'd through their fellows, and like lightning scal'd and leap'd the wall, where once entered, cowards lose not faster than they gain'd ground . . . 'twas as if they had flown, not fought, for conquest.[31]

Pausanes' mistress is sought "through the straits of a thousand wounds," and, mark you, his heroism is always self-conscious:

'Tis honest, nay 'tis honorable; and when can a young man die better . . . Thou see'st I have hunted from danger to danger all my life but to find a name, or one to own me, and cannot compass it; therefore to choose I'll leap into this danger, for from this glorious end I may in story force one.[32]

"Ye Gods!" cries the King of Sicily, "What strange kind of men are these?" The hero in *Pallantus and Eudora,* the single play of Thomas's younger brother is epitomized as

> . . . th' inimitable
> Matchless, not to be counterfeited, or
> Resembled, Great Pallantus! Whom as none
> Can reach in a noble action, so none
> Can equal in a gallant presence![33]

Cartwright's King in *The Lady Errant* is of even grander proportions:

> With his uncover'd head he dares the thunder,
> Slights hail and snow, and wearies out a tempest;
> Then after all, he shakes himself, and gives
> Rain, as the heavens did before, but with
> A more serene aspect . . . other wars
> Are not so manly as his exercises,
> And pitched fields often are more easy service
> Than his mere preparations.[34]

Misander in the same author's *Siege* is at once so martial and so sensitive of his honor that when his counsellors venture a word of advice, he must exercise heroic restraint to refrain from slaying them.

Many Cavalier heroes can match Dryden's, rant for rant. Falorus in Cokain's *Obstinate Lady* cries,

> Not Mercury pleading in her defence
> With oratory able to stint Jove's wrath
> When he has bespoke the thunderbolts of the Cyclops
> To wreak some injury, should ever win me
> To her bed![35]

In Jaques's *Queen of Corsica* Florimond proves his quality with,

> . . . sooner may you make the flowing sea
> Fast to the shore, and never more return
> Into the hidden bowells of herself
> Than me swear this . . . You command a thing
> Wild horses and enraged elephants
> Can never draw me to.[36]

And Calidor is not behindhand,

> Flatter the bear
> With honey when th' hast robb'd her of her whelps,
> Or take the angry lion by the paw
> When thou hast prick't him, but my noble
> Rage is not to be deluded . . . Draw! that I
> May send thee straight to Hell![37]

There is something especially Almanzor-like in the rant of Pæologus in Swinhoe's *Unhappy Fair Irene:*

> Villain, but that my spirits all
> Are charm'd with noble pity to this maid;
> And passion, stifl'd in remorse,
> Lies swounding for a while,
> I'd hack an epitaph upon thy flesh
> That all might shun thee.[38]

If Almahide must be chaste simply because Almanzor thinks her so, what of the fair Irene who cannot die because Pæologus still lives!

> My love, do'st think she lives?
> Fond, she cannot die:
> Her soul's in me, and mine in her reciprocal,
> So while I live, she cannot die;
> But I may die in her; but I'm alive;
> Therefore she is not dead.
> Then I'll go seek her here;
> The contaminous bed of this grim tyrant
> Shall not detain her from me;
> And e're I'll go without her,
> I'll leap destruction in the face,
> And kiss the instrument of my decease.[39]

There is no need to multiply examples of Cavalier rant. The *Siege of Rhodes,* said Dryden, although the first light of the heroic plays, did not comply enough with "the majesty of an heroic poem,[40] and it is true that Davenant's play is fairly restrained; but Dryden was guilty, unconsciously perhaps, of suppressing evidence; "the greatness and majesty" of the type he exploited was old when *The Siege of Rhodes* was written. Heroicism in action and speech, inferior to Dryden's in quality, but no different in kind, saturates plays of the Caroline and Commonwealth period. He may have believed that in the heroic play he was creating "an imitation (in little) of an heroic poem," but we are privileged to doubt that he worked upon a self-conceived artistic principle suggested by a few lines in Ariosto. It is even less possible to believe that his heroics were an immediate importation from abroad, and were inspired by the classical drama or heroic poems and romances of the French. About the French hero, elevated model of the chivalric virtues though he may be, and a conqueror of thousands, there is an aloofness and frigidity on the one hand, and a faintness and languor on the other, that distinguishes him from Dryden's. The impulse which created Cavalier heroics is the impulse which created Dryden's. The stream of specious romance watering and watered by the literature of Italy, Spain, France, and England during the gloaming of the Renaissance instigated a universal cult of heroic virtue, and its exemplars in each nation were given a national twist. In England this twist was British arrogance, expansiveness, and verbal muscularity. Tamburlaine and Almanzor are indeed compatriots, although between the two flows the stream of Greek romance and attendant critical theory, such as had laved the shores of Fletcherian drama, and had inundated that of the Cavaliers.

The heroic plays are notable not only for a peculiar brand of valor but for a peculiar brand of love, and that their love like their valor is a continuation rather than an innovation in English drama is the next point to be illustrated. In epic literature proper, love had been adjudged too soft an emotion, and its appropriate setting too pacific, for it to be allowed a prominent place; but in decadent romance, which as we have noted was admitted to the rank of epic literature by Sidney, love occupied not only a prominent but a preëminent position. A reconciliation was needed if the passion of love was to be elevated to the rank of the other virtues in harmony with the heroic ideal, and this reconciliation was effected by making love itself heroic. Love becomes heroic if it strikes with sufficient suddenness and intensity one previously immune to it, or if it subjects the lover to sufficient trials of endurance. Kisses are not themselves heroic, but one may exercise his prowess in perfectly tremendous deeds in order to win the right to kiss; or, conversely, he may exercise his magnanimity in heroic proportions by relinquishing his right to another, let us say a friend, a brother, a royal master, or one for whom the beloved has conceived a prior passion. Love becomes heroic when the romancer or playwright deals with its hardships rather than with its amenities.

The wide interest in the love doctrines of D'Urfé may be partially attributable to the craving for the heroic. At first glance, nothing seems more unlikely than that these doctrines could be forced into the framework of epic or dramatic literature, and it is true that, even in France, the most successful interpreters of D'Urfé's subtleties were the authors of letters and lyrical poems. However, to seekers after the heroic, there was one inviting quality in the doctrines of D'Urfé: they seemed, at least to the blunt-minded, to add a perfect host of hardships to the

condition of being in love. Not only was the emphasis largely upon
sacrifice and restraint, but the typical conversation between lovers was
a contest, an intellectual battle, in which the participants marshalled
all the forces of casuistry and similitude to determine how, when, and
whether they should love. We can sympathize with Zanger in Orrery's
Mustapha when he sighs:

> Among the priests of love there casuists be,
> Who Love's religion vex with sophistry.[41]

Sometimes the dialectical encounters between lovers, or rivals in love,
prove more exhausting than armed combat. One may conjecture that
many readers of the *Astrée* perceived, not that the code of love expounded by Sylvandre was gracious and refined, but simply that it
was *difficult*.

In the heroic drama of Cavalier and Restoration authors alike there
are few scenes of love-*making*, few addresses to tender sentiment; and
wooing, if wooing it may be called, progresses amidst the blare of
martial trumpets and the sighs of ethical perplexity. In winning love
the hero must conquer armies, in relinquishing love he must conquer
himself. Dryden emphasized the physical barriers to love, Orrery, who
was more decidedly a Platonic, the spiritual; but both were following
a tradition already established in English drama. Thomas Killigrew
had emphasized, in the same manner, the physical barriers, Walter
Montague the spiritual, thirty years before. There is no need to quote
parallel scenes in Cavalier and Restoration plays in view of the descriptions of the former that will appear later on. It will grow wearisome
then to repeat of play after play that the hero gains his love after
settling with his might the wars of Sicily and Sardinia, or is separated
from her, sometimes for ten long acts, by the fanciful claims of honor,
or relinquishes her to his friend at last as testimony of his magnanimity.
The similarity between the old and the new lies not only in outline
but in detail. Tag with rime the love encounters of Carlell, Cartwright,
and Killigrew, and you have the love encounters of Orrery and
Dryden.[42]

With mention of the word "rime" we arrive at an interesting crux.
The rime of the heroic plays is a technical feature, an externality; and
in such features, sudden changes and departures from native tradition
are more easily credible. Yet even in technique, the heroic plays reveal
less sudden change and departure from native tradition than is frequently imagined. In tracing the origin of rime in the heroic plays
we need not begin, *ab ovo*, with miracle drama, although Dryden himself would be our justification, with his comment that rimed plays in

England were "not so much a new way amongst us as an old way new reviv'd."[43] Despite the survival of rime for a few special uses in regular types of drama, and more generally in masques, blank verse and prose—and after Fletcher an unhappy cross between the two—had formed the medium of English drama for nearly a century before the Restoration, distinguishing it from the coeval of other nations and giving the rime of the heroic plays, when it appeared, the status of an innovation. One impulse behind the adoption of rime must have been the dissatisfaction with the laxity into which the writing of blank verse had fallen; in the words of Saintsbury "the set of English taste toward the rhymed decasyllable had been more and more marked for some forty years before [the Restoration]."[44] Couplets appear at intervals in the drama chronicled in the present history, and though not until after *The Siege of Rhodes* are they prevalent enough to suggest an accepted vogue, their presence indicates that the return to rime was a natural if not inevitable phenomenon. That form of the rimed decasyllable, known as the closed couplet, and imitated from the Latin elegiac distich, was not new in the Restoration or even in the earlier seventeenth century,[45] but skill in its use among English writers had spread slowly. The couplets written by Denham in his contribution to Catherine Phillips' *Horace* are readily distinguishable from those he had written in his youth.[46] It is to be expected that those which appear in Cavalier plays will not be finished examples of the type.

We shall avoid quoting the familiar scene in couplets in Denham's Caroline tragedy, *The Sophy*.[47] We shall avoid also lingering with instances where couplets are employed for traditional purposes: when Roscius speaks in rimed decasyllables in Randolph's *Muses' Looking Glass*,[48] he is discussing drama, and seems naturally to fall into the conventional verse of prologues and epilogues; when Caronil in Cokain's *Obstinate Lady*[49] does so, he is indulging in sententious utterance. However, in Quarles's *Virgin Widow*, printed in 1649 and written seven years earlier, couplets appear in passages which simply advance the plot:

Museus

.................Weigh Heaven with Hell,
Compare harsh owls to warbling Philomel,
Weigh froth with honor, or dejected shame
With the down-weight of an illustrious name.
Pulchrella woos thee with a siren's song,
But brave Panthea's more Heroick tongue
Chaunts strains of honor: false Pulchrella sheds
The tears of crocodiles; Panthea treads
High steps to triumph, where thy growing name

Shall stand recorded in the hall of fame.
But take thy course. Th' advice is only mine,
Thine is the interest, as the chance is thine:
This only know, Ballarino's tongue proclaims,
Palladius dares not fight, but with his dames.

Palladius

The scales are turned. Panthea, lodge thou here
Next to my heart. Pulchrella, lie thou there.
[Puts that in his bosom, tears the other]
Farewell, my soft embraces; sports, stand by:
Ballarino, if Palladius lives, shall die.

Museus

So now it works. If either hap to fall,
I, the sole-second to both parties, shall
With my breath'd sword do justice to the other
Crowns weigh no friends: ambition knows no brother.[50]

If such riming with Quarles may have been only a whim, it was other-wise with Mildmay Fane, who rimed inveterately, not only in his masque *Raguaillo D'Oceano,* but in the whole series of plays he produced between 1641 and 1650, alternating between blank verse and couplets and obeying a strong impulse to pass from the former to the latter even within the same speech:

If to be nobleness of our extractions
Such moderation had been shown was fitting,
Rather like friends we might have been admitted
Into your highness' presence than thus captives;
Nor should you have disdained a league of peace
To those so much concern'd your fame's increase:
Our present state, as it falls out, proves thus
Triumph to you, but ignominious
Unto ourselves. We had the world at will
(The lesser one at least), but when to ill
We did employ our powers, no wonder then
At once we lost our castles, towns, and men—
Nay, and ourselves, that's worse; you govern all;
No marvel then that all at your feet fall . . .[51]

Enjambment and end-stopping side by side characterize Fane's couplets. The same mingling appears in the undated manuscript play, *The White Æthiopian,* and argues for a date of composition during the Commonwealth, that is, before the Restoration crystallization of the "heroic couplet." The play is interesting because heroic in theme, and rimed throughout:

Chariclea

My fortune which you seem willing to know
My brother to you might more proper show,
For bashful silence might more proper fit
To questions made by man, a maiden wit;
Yet seeing you are so civil as to crave
That which you might compel, I have
A willingness, and think a captive may
Unto a victor, being bid, to say;
And that without exceeding the just bound
Which modesty in virgins might confound:
Know then that Ionia was my place of birth,
The city Ephesus the place on earth
Where first I breath'd . . .[52]

Sherburne's *Medea* of 1648 is written in octosyllabic and old-fashioned decasyllabic couplets; and *The Famous Tragedy of King Charles I*, 1649, is sprinkled with the latter, somewhat less old-fashioned. A banner year for rimed plays was 1651, with the appearance of Denny's *Shepherd's Holiday*, Prestwich's *Hippolytus*, Willan's *Astrea*, and the anonymous *Marcus Tullius Cicero*. Of these the most interesting to a student of the heroic plays is *Astrea:*

The chiefest point wherein ye agitate
Is if love's essence subject be to fate,
Perishable or not; love hath two objects
The body and the soul; since both effects
This shepherd feels, the gods in me pronounce
The body perishable, such love he renounce:
But since the soul's love, as herself, cannot die,
He that continue to eternity.
. . . .

Now, Mistress, leave that shepherd, I suspect
That with his venom he will thee infect
His false axioms have buried one alive
So will they thee, if thou with him survive.[53]

Thus Willan tagged the Platonic doctrine of Sylvandre and the anti-Platonic doctrine of Hylas. Good or bad in its prosody, and it is certainly not good, the fact remains that in *Astrea* we have a play wholly in couplets, and with at least its "amatory battledore and shuttlecock" in common with the heroic plays of the Restoration. Flecknoe's *Love's Dominion*, 1654, and Baron's *Mirza*, 1655, are occasionally heroic in tone and occasionally fall into heroic couplets. G. Cartwright's *Heroic Lover* is in couplets throughout, and although not published until 1661, was, or so the author tells us, "penn'd many years ago."

In 1656 the rimed play actually made its appearance on the stage,

in Sir William Davenant's *Siege of Rhodes,* Part I, and that this play
and its sequel, also probably staged before the Restoration, profoundly
influenced the verse form of subsequent dramatists would seem beyond
dispute: Dryden gave full credit for the use of the heroic couplet in
Restoration drama to Davenant, "who at once brought it upon the
stage and made it perfect . . ."[54] Although other measures appear in
both parts of *The Siege of Rhodes,* closed couplets predominate. A
number of influences must have acted upon Davenant to impel him to
compose in rime. One, habitually ignored, is that he had served Fulke
Greville in the latter's last years, and may have acted as amanuensis
while his master was revising his earlier poetic work and, in Davenant's
own words, "with too much judgement and refining spoyled it."[55]
Greville's philosophical dramas *Alaham* and *Mustapha,* published in
1633, are both rimed, and in the latter such verses as

> Unhappy state of ours! wherein we live,
> Where doubts give laws, which never can forgive;
> Where rage of kings not only ruins be,
> But where their very love works misery,[56]

are not untypical, and are not distant relatives, when all is said, of
"heroic couplets." Davenant also must have shared that dissatisfaction
with formless blank verse, and that "set" of taste toward a more disciplined medium which we have been tracing. Then he needed novelty
of form for his presentations. Drama as such was prohibited by Puritan
law, and blank verse had been a badge of drama before the closing
of the theatres. Rime was part of Davenant's disguise, as was his
christening his works "operas" and having them chanted in *stilo recitativo* in imitation of the Italian opera of the period—itself, be it
remembered, in rime. Finally there was the example of French drama.
Weakening the claim of the last as a prime influence upon Davenant
is the fact that French dramatic rime had not induced imitation before, even when French influence in other directions was strong at the
court of Charles and Henrietta, and when "Floridor's" repertory was
creating a stir in London; or even when Englishmen such as Rutter
and Lower translated actual French plays.

In *The Siege of Rhodes* appear passages in the heroic quatrains of
Davenant's *Gondibert,* a measure which Dryden acknowledged borrowing from Davenant in writing *Annus Mirabilis.* It is significant of
Davenant's influence that heroic quatrains replace in several instances
the heroic couplets of both *The Indian Queen* and *The Indian Emperor.* Such quatrains appear also in *The Female Rebellion,* probably
written in 1658. This play contains passages heroic in tone written in
heroic couplets, several instances of rimed stichamythia, and an actual

reference to the distich in the text.[57] Rimed stichamythia also appears in Meriton's *Love and War*, printed in 1658:

Aberden

For too rash counsel often breeds within
A subject height, which may be call'd a sin;
And that in prodigality, then done
Beside its shifts, it can no other shun,
But come to ruin.

Yernomy

Ay, it is so, but this is not so bent
Because, great King, we have your counsel in't.

Aberden

But for I know rash counsel doth maintain.

Fafrisius

Fear not that thought, for it will prove most vain

Aberden

If it be so, yet danger may be worth.

Buzarian

It cannot be, it is a thing of mirth.[58]

Rime seems not to have encouraged Meriton to lucidity; but the very title *Love and War* is engaging to students of the origins of heroic plays, and one might, if robust enough to associate himself with such a clownish client, claim this play as a "pioneer."

We are in a position now to read with a sense of proportion a statement made by Orrery in a letter of January 23, 1662: "I presumed to lay at his majesty's feet a tragi-comedy, all in ten-feet verse and rhyme . . . because I found his majesty relished rather the French fashion of writing plays than the English."[59] Since 1661, Orrery had written two plays, *The General*,[60] and another now non-extant, using rime, as we see by his remarks, in conscious imitation of the French. Shortly afterwards, English writers, in close contact with Orrery in Dublin or the court of Charles in London, began using heroic couplets in translating Corneille: Mrs. Phillips in her *Pompey*, acted in Dublin in 1663; Carlell in his *Heraclius*, printed in 1664; and Waller, Sedley *et al.* in their *Pompey the Great*, acted at the Duke's House in 1663 or 1664. By 1664 heroic couplets in plays were no longer a novelty; they had penetrated into parts of such plays as Howard's *Blind Lady* and *The Vestal Virgin*, Flecknoe's *Erminia*, Stapylton's *Slighted Maid*, Tuke's *Adventures of Five Hours*, Sir William Killigrew's *Ormasdes*,

Etherege's *Comical Revenge*, and Dryden's *Rival Ladies*; and in this year appeared upon the London stage the first full crop of rimed heroic plays, Howard and Dryden's *Indian Queen* in January, and Orrery's *Henry V* and *The General* respectively in August and September. By 1668 couplets were recognized as the standard medium for heroic plays and continued to be so recognized until about 1676. In some quarters they have always been regarded as the distinguishing feature of such plays.

If we pause now to sum up whence came this convention, we shall see that there were two sets of impulses: one, a simple desire for change, represented by the tentative experiments with rime during the Caroline and Commonwealth period, culminating in that play of highly composite inspiration, *The Siege of Rhodes;* and the other, emulation of the French, as represented in the work of Orrery and the English translators of Corneille. The first of these sets of impulses, abetted by the growing popularity of the heroic couplet in non-dramatic verse and by the remarkable senility into which dramatic blank verse had fallen, must be granted priority in point of time. In the opinion of the present writer, it must also be granted priority in point of force. *The Siege of Rhodes* was a tremendously popular play on the stage from 1661 onward, whereas London audiences had been given no opportunity to applaud Orrery until after *The Indian Queen* had made its appearance. Orrery employed the distich with greater facility than any dramatist had done before, and through his personal prestige he gave an impetus to the new mode, but in no sense is his *General* the first heroic play, or the first transitional play in rime. *The Conquest of Granada* would probably have appeared in its present form had Orrery not written at all, and the riming convention of the heroic plays at their height is not exclusively, or even primarily, a debt to French classical drama.

We have dwelt thus extensively on the origin of the rime in the heroic plays because rime is not only their most spectacular formal characteristic but also their most uniform. In other matters, details of construction, observance of the unities, and the like, there is so much diversity among the plays themselves that it is difficult to discuss them as a unit. Davenant reduced the number of characters and simplified the story of *The Siege of Rhodes*, but probably less in imitation of the French, or even in compliance with those pervasive impulses we term "neo-classical," than as result of the physical limitations upon his Commonwealth theatre. Orrery's plots are fairly simple, but his stories are fairly complex; that is, he uses (and without marked success) the medium of a letter, a confession, or the like, to convey knowledge of a series of intrigues which a Cavalier dramatist would have displayed in action. Dryden's *Indian Emperor* is as complex and episodic as the average Cavalier play, and *The Conquest of Granada* itself, with its three distinct narrative interests, is by no means simple. In general however, there is a greater observance of the unities, eclectic though it may be, and an infinitely greater sense of craftsmanship in the heroic plays than in Cavalier drama, and the change is owing, at least in part, to influences from abroad.[61] The criticism of the day is eloquent of the compromise being effected between English tradition and foreign example in matters of technique.

We must remember, however, that Jonson had made the English very conscious of the claims of classical dramatic theory, and not only he, but such of his disciples as Brome and Nabbes had been remarkably faithful in observing the minor unities before 1642. In plays of the Cavalier mode, formless though they usually are, there is one significant step toward the technique of the heroic plays. By eliminating the comic as they normally do, they achieve, if not unity of time, place, or action, at least unity of tone. One feels in reading such plays as Killigrew's *Prisoners,* Cartwright's *Royal Slave,* and Carlell's *Osmond* that they are at least "all of one piece." That Caroline playwrights and audiences were conscious of this as a change is attested by Brome's complaint,

> And such are only good those leaders cry;
> And unto that belief draw in a faction,
> That must despise all sportive merry wit
> Because some such great play had none in it.[62]

To compensate for the deletion of the comic, the Cavalier dramatists had offered an increase in theatrical display, and thus in an additional respect paved the way for Restoration theatrical usage. The Cavalier dramatists loved scenic effects as much as their successors, and often disposed their characters about the stage in operatic groupings; there is the elaborate ceremonial of dancing slaves at the end of *The Royal Slave,* the symbolic dance of statues come to life at the end of *The Siege,* and the blazing funeral pyre exhaling perfume at the end of *Pallantus and Eudora,* the last scene of which "consisted onely of musick and shew." Flecknoe's *Love's Dominion* and Willan's *Astrea* are among plays continuing to display a love of music and show during the Commonwealth period. While on matters of detail, we may note that the double-barreled heroic plays, with their stories continued for ten acts, are foreshadowed in Carlell's *Arviragus and Philicia* and *The Passionate Lovers,* and in Thomas Killigrew's *Cicilia and Clorinda* and *Bellamira her Dream.*[63]

Although the emphasis of the present discussion of the origin of the Restoration heroic plays has been placed on their relation to the drama of the Cavaliers, it is not the intention of the author to suggest that the Cavalier and Restoration plays form a unit totally segregated by their mutual characteristics from all earlier English drama, or to suggest that because they both reflect the tastes of a courtly class, they have nothing in common with popular drama. To do so would be to substitute one error for another. Cavalier drama had roots in Fletcher, just as Fletcher had roots in the Elizabethans, including Shakespeare. Literature is just as continuous as the succession of generations that produce it; and wars, exiles, and ordinances against stage plays can no more break its continuity than they can annihilate a race. It is sufficient if, in proof of continuity, our discussion has related the heroic plays to the body of romantic drama that immediately preceded them, and has demonstrated that they represent a culmination of native English tendencies clearly in evidence before the closing of the theatres. Totalling the argument bluntly, they are more *like* the Cavalier plays than they are like those of any period in any other nation; they are essentially a home-grown product. Were Cavalier plays more widely read, and had there been no court exile in France to distract the attention of students, it would never have been suggested otherwise. To appreciate the meaning of the heroic plays in the history of English literature—in the history of the English people— we must view them in relation to the social background and artistic fashions of a generation before.

---

[1] For the original of Bayes (formerly "Bilboa"), see Allardyce Nicoll, *Restoration Drama* (1928), p. 236; and the introduction to M. Summers' edition of the *Rehearsal* (1914).

[2] Discussed below, Part II, Chapter VII.

[3] *Essay of Heroic Plays*, prefixed to *The Conquest of Granada*, 1672.

[4] See below, p. 66.

[5] A representative view appears in Samuel Johnson's *Life of Dryden*.

[6] Scott's introduction to *The Conquest of Granada*, in his edition of Dryden.

[7] *Academy*, March 21, 1874.

[8] III, 309-317.

[9] Introduction to the *Mermaid* edition of Dryden. Asserting the native origins are F. E. Schelling, *Elizabethan Drama*, II, 307-370; J. W. Tupper, Introduction to *Belles-Lettres Series* edition of Davenant (1909); A. Nicoll, "Origin and Types of the Heroic Tragedy," *Anglia*, XLIV (1920), 325-336, and *Restoration Drama*, pp. 82-90; see also Cornell Dowlin and K. Lynch, noted below.

[10] Introduction to the *Everyman* collection of Restoration plays (1912).

[11] L. N. Chase, *English Heroic Play*, Columbia diss. (1903); M. L. Poston, "Origin of the English Heroic Play," *MLR*, XVI (1921), 18-22; P. J. Pendlebury, *Dryden's*

Heroic Plays: A Study of Origins (London, 1923); F. W. Payne, "The Question of Precedence between Dryden and Orrery with regard to the English Heroic Play," *RES*, I (1925), 173-181; W. S. Clark, "Roger Boyle, Earl of Orrery, and his successors in the English Heroic Play," *Harvard University summaries of theses*, II (1930), 168-170; Articles on the subject by Professor Clark, relating chiefly to Orrery, appear in *RES*, II (1926), 206-211, 280-283; 459-460; *MLN*, XLII (1927), 16-20, 381-383; *MLN*, XLIV (1929), 1-6; *RES*, VI (1930), 191-193; *RES*, VIII (1932), 437-444.

[12] W. S. Clark, "Definition of the Heroic Play," *RES*, VIII (1932), 437-444.

[13] *Restoration Drama*, p. 91.

[14] Published separately from *Gondibert*, Paris, 1650, and with *Gondibert*, London, 1651; a modern edition of this landmark in criticism is contained in *Critical Essays of the Seventeenth Century*, J. E. Spingarn, Ed. (Oxford, 1908), Vol. II. Dryden's views of heroic literature are frequently offered in polite difference with Davenant's.

[15] L. Hotson, *Commonwealth and Restoration Stage* (Harvard Univ. Press, 1928), p. 166.

[16] No early Restoration performances of the plays of Cartwright and Carlell are recorded, but performances may have occurred; their titles appear in a list of plays reserved to the use of the King's Men; see A. Nicoll, *Restoration Drama*, p. 316 *Arviragus and Philicia* was revived in 1672.

[17] *Act* III.

[18] Act V.

[19] Act III.

[20] Act II.

[21] Act II.

[22] Act II, Scene vi.

[23] The fact is emphasized in a number of the essays listed above in Note 11. See also A. W. Ward, *op. cit.*, III, 309; and H. W. Hill, "La Calprenède's Romances and the Restoration Drama," *University of Nevada Studies*, II, No. 3 (1910); III, No. 2 (1911).

[24] But see the ground-breaking article on this subject by C. G. Child, "The Rise of the Heroic Play," *MLN*, XIX (1904), 166-173.

[25] The case is thoroughly put by Cornell Dowlin, *Davenant's Preface to Gondibert* (Philadelphia, 1934), Chapter V.

[26] F. E. Schelling, *Elizabethan Drama*, II, 195, quoting Oliphant.

[27] Act II, Scene i.

[28] Act II, Scene i.

[29] Dryden's *Essay of Heroic Plays*.

[30] Act III.

[31] Act III, Scene v.

[32] Act V, Scene II.

[33] Act V.

[34] Act IV, Scene v.

[35] Act II, Scene ii.

[36] Act II, Scene iii.

[37] Act III, Scene ix.

[38] Page 2 of the quarto, 1658 (not divided into acts and scenes).

[39] *Ibid.*, p. 4.

[40] *Essay of Heroic Plays*.

[41] Act III.

[42] Excellent illustrations appear in the only article on the subject, K. Lynch," Con-

ventions of the Platonic Drama in the Heroic Plays of Orrery and Dryden," *PMLA*, XLIV (1929), 456-471. W. S. Clark disputes the force of this article, and Dr. Lynch replies, *PMLA*, XLV (1930), 623-626.

⁴³ *Epistle Dedicatory to The Rival Ladies*, 1664.

⁴⁴ Introduction to the *Mermaid* edition of Dryden.

⁴⁵ Once propounded as the invention of Waller and his circle by Edmund Gosse in *From Shakespeare to Pope* (1885), the closed couplet in earlier writers, especially Jonson, has been discussed in Professor Schelling's corrective essay "Ben Jonson and the Classical School," *PMLA*, XIII (1898), 221-249; and in Elizabethan poets, especially Grimald, by G. P. Shannon, *PMLA*, XLV (1930), 532-542; and in Chaucer by M. A. Hill, *PMLA*, XLII (1927), 845-861. R. C. Wallerstein, *PMLA*, L (1935), 166-209, traces the process of development between the years 1625 and 1645.

⁴⁶ See the introductory essay by T. Banks, *The Poetical Works of Sir John Denham* (Yale Univ. Press, 1928).

⁴⁷ Act IV, Scene i.

⁴⁸ Act I, Scenes ii & iii.

⁴⁹ Act II, Scene ii.

⁵⁰ Act III.

⁵¹ *De Pugna Animi*, Act V, Scene v; see below, p. 201.

⁵² Harleian MS 7313, fol. 9.

⁵³ Act II, Scene iii.

⁵⁴ *Epistle Dedicatory to The Rival Ladies*. The epistle is addressed to Orrery, who is complimented upon his own use of rime.

⁵⁵ John Aubrey, *Brief Lives*, A. Clark, Ed., 2 vols. (Oxford, 1898), I, 205.

⁵⁶ Act II, Scene i.

⁵⁷ Edited from Hunterian Museum MS by Alexander Smith, 1872; see pp. 59, 70.

⁵⁸ Act I, Scene i.

⁵⁹ Quoted by F. W. Payne, *RES*, I (1925), 173-181.

⁶⁰ W. S. Clark, "Further Light upon the Heroic Plays of Roger Boyle, Earl of Orrery," *RES*, II (1926), 209; "Early Stage History of the First Heroic Play," *MLN*, XLII (1927), 381-383.

⁶¹ A survey of such influence appears in C. V. Deane, *Dramatic Theory and the Rhymed Heroic Play* (Oxford, 1931).

⁶² *Prologue to The Antipodes*.

⁶³ The distinction between these and Elizabethan serial drama has been noted above, p. 41.

IV

THE TREND IN COMEDY

THE Cavalier generation is associated in our minds with gayety, charm, and even with the more engaging sort of moral delinquency. We see it in terms of the better known songs of Sir John Suckling, a dramatic counterpart of which would make the ideal social comedy. It seems inevitable that the plays of the Cavaliers should have prepared the way for that critical comedy of fashionable posturing and amorous siege, perverse but perfect in its kind, that reached its highest expression in the plays of Etherege, Wycherley, Congreve, and Vanbrugh. Yet such proves not the case. Cavalier drama was prevailingly serious, sentimental, romantic.[1] Of the scores of plays written by genteel amateurs between 1633 and 1664, only a scant dozen have laughter as their principal object, and few of these are impressive either artistically or historically. The Cavaliers had their lighter side, and this side influenced the ways and works of the generation that followed, but the influence was not exercised through the drama. Cavalier comedies are thoroughly imitative, and anticipate the Etheregean mode only in the degree that professional comedies had done so.

Of the playwrights upon whose work the present history is centered, the first to write comedies were the young gentlemen of the universities. In their serious plays, these modish scholars had forsaken academic tragedy and allegory to imitate courtly romance,[2] but since the courtiers had established no vogue and provided no model in comedy, there was nothing our scholars could do but imitate the professional humorists; they did not wish to jeopardize their standing as men of the world by writing old-fashioned Plautine farces and collegiate satires. Cartwright's *The Ordinary, c.* 1635.[3] Mayne's *City Match,* 1636, and Cowley's *The Guardian,* 1642, resemble each other so much in material and manner as to illustrate, in themselves alone, the Caroline stereotype in comedy.

In *The Ordinary,* a certain young Londoner named Meanwell woos and weds the heiress Jane, at the same time revenging himself upon old Simon Credulous, who has defrauded his father, by marrying off young Credulous to Jane's serving-maid. In *The City Match,* young Plotwell, also the son of a bankrupt, wins Susan Seathrift for himself and Timothy Seathrift for his sister, imposing in the process upon old Seathrift and upon his own usurious uncle, Warehouse. In *The*

Guardian, young Truman wins his beloved Lucia, after pitting his wits against his own crochety father and against Lucia's designing guardian, Blade. The three plays, of which Cowley's is best, Cartwright's by far the poorest, all are remarkably similar: all are coarse and bourgeois in tone, all have to do with marriage and marriage portions, all contain a pair of romantic lovers, all are full of complex trickery involving among much else the humiliation of at least one character by a deceptive wedding ceremony, all feature a group of tavern-roarers or "blades."[4] The dialogue is characteristic of contemporary comedy. It strives for those effects of high-spirited jollity which professional writers like Brome and Davenant were able to achieve through a spontaneous redundancy of speech then passing current as wit. The word *wit* itself, like its synonym *fancy,* still implied no more than intellectual resourcefulness, which might express itself in literary composition either as a poetic image or as a comic similitude. "Wit," said Davenant, "is . . . the dexterity of thought";[5] and, years later, Dryden, paying homage to Davenant's own wit, said, "Nothing was proposed to him upon which he could not suddenly produce a thought extremely pleasant and surprising."[6] It was only gradually that the comic issue of wit was expected to have not only ingenuity but also a satirical thrust. There is little such thrust in the wit of Cartwright and Mayne. In his attempts to display an entertaining fertility of intellect by paralleling ideas and piling up similitudes, Cartwright achieves only pedantry and dullness. Mayne does somewhat better, but such speeches as

> He has a cough that nightly drowns the bellman;
> Calls up his family; all his neighbours rise
> And go by it, as by the chimes and clock . . .[7]

are perhaps too typical. Cowley's wit is more edged than that of the other two, and one of his gallants, the similitude-loving Puny, has been considered prophetic of the foppish false-wits of Restoration comedy.[8] In most of his scenes, however, Cowley, like the rest, was simply manufacturing, with obvious strain, bumptious speeches for conventionally conceived Citizens, borrowing the rude realism of the popular stage. None of these scholars felt a kinship with his material; Cartwright italicized his virtuosity by disclaiming, in his prologue, a knowledge of the life he portrayed. A university wit may have been able to fancy himself in the rôle of a Meanwell or a Truman, for a plump marriage portion, then as always, was a notable equalizer; but, for the rest, Bread Street and its burghers were things to be despised.

We have then, in the plays just reviewed, the current modification

of the London of Middleton and the Londoners of Jonson (sadly de-
vitalized)—in a word, just an echo of the popular comedy of the day
as it was being produced by Marmion, Davenant, Nabbes, Glapthorne,
and Brome. True it is that the comedy of Brome and his fellows reveals much of the ground-plan of Restoration comedy of manners. The
Restoration playwrights themselves produced a comedy of situation
exploiting the relationship of type characters to their milieu, with
stories consisting of a web of petty intrigues or plot "interests,"[9] rather
than a comedy of universal human traits elucidated in the stress of
a major action. The Restoration playwrights, too, portrayed a conflict
between an older generation, mercenary and depraved, and a younger
generation, unscrupulous but idealistically intent upon living its own
life. Dragon-guarded marriage portions, stolen matches, and gulling
wedding ceremonies remained staple plot materials. Blades were re-
christened Rakes, and were endowed with new manners, but were not
discarded. But interesting as may be, in its social and literary implications, the bourgeois warp of the "high" comedy of the Restoration, it
does not elevate the historical importance of the comedies of Cartwright, Mayne, and Cowley; of these, all that can be said is that they
bear the same relationship to Restoration comedy of manners as do
the more capable plays of Brome.

Toward the very end of the pre-war period three realistic comedies
issued from actual courtiers, as distinct from courtly residents at the
universities: the Earl of Newcastle's *The Variety* and *The Country
Captain,* and Thomas Killigrew's *The Parson's Wedding*—all evidently
written, and acted at Blackfriars, about 1639 and 1640.[10] Two of these
plays anticipate the actual atmosphere of Restoration comedy of manners, in a way that the university plays do not; yet one may say of
their authors, as of the university wits themselves, that they merely
followed a professional lead—the lead, however, of James Shirley rather
than of Richard Brome.

Thomas Killigrew's career will be described in a later chapter.[11]
That of Newcastle (1593-1676) is too well known, through history and
the congenial "Life"[12] by Lady Newcastle (her single work not wholly
sub-literary), to necessitate much review. Newcastle is unique among
Cavalier dramatists—as a prime courtier who never wrote a courtly
play. From the beginning, he set himself apart from the amateur pur-
veyors of dramatic romance and aligned himself with the popular
school. For the romantic vein even of the professional writers he cared
little—for the "Spanish perfume" of Beaumont and Fletcher, the
"liquorish and sugar candy" of the pastoralists, and, when they had

appeared upon the scene, "the foolish, phantastical, heroick fustian"
of the Restoration tragedians. But Jonson! Ah "he was the honour of
his nation and the poet of poets."[13] The first of Newcastle's plays is
eloquent of his devotion to Jonson: *The Variety, c.* 1639, is little
more than a scrapbook, wherein the story of several courtships laden
with the usual bustling intrigue forms merely a frame for the
"humours" portraits of a news-monger, a worshipper of the past, a
country simpleton and his mother, a French dancing master, a band
of professional "jeerers," and the members of a female academy of
fashion—all, or nearly all, of whom had appeared in the Jonsonian
gallery itself.

Newcastle was, in Langbaine's phrase, "our English Mæcenas"[14] to
a succession of poets from Jonson and Ford to Dryden and Shadwell,
and deserves our gratitude accordingly; but his habit of enlisting the
literary assistance of his protégés renders it difficult for us to extricate
and appraise his personal contributions to dramatic literature. It is
probably Newcastle who is shadowed forth in Sharpe's *Noble Stranger,*
1640, in the person of the martial nobleman, Philomuses, who writes
plays and keeps "stipendiary poets."[15] Lady Newcastle, when she herself turned playwright, unconsciously reflected upon the methods of
her husband when she expressed the regret that she had had on the
Continent no professional playwright to "tie together" her scenes.[16]
There has recently come to light a dramatic manuscript written in
Newcastle's own hand, *A Pleasant & Merrye Humor off a Roge,*[17] and
its eleven episodic and farcical scenes illustrate the quality of Newcastle's
unaided efforts. Shadwell wove a revised version of most of the scenes
into *The Triumphant Widow* (a comedy reminiscent of Jonson's *Magnetic Lady*), and this was acted as Newcastle's at Dorset Garden in
1674. After reading Newcastle's draft, one is inclined to give whatever
credit is due for *The Triumphant Widow,* and indeed for Newcastle's
other late comedy, *The Humorous Lovers,* 1667, to Thomas Shadwell.[18] Oddly enough, the ducal collaborator seems to have confined
his efforts to scenes below stairs. When Ben Jonson had died, Newcastle had transferred his patronage to James Shirley, whereupon the
latter "did much assist the Duke in the composure of certain plays."[19]
Amusing testimony to the probable extent of this "assistance" was
offered in modern times by A. H. Bullen, who, coming upon a manuscript copy of *The Country Captain,* printed it confidently as by James
Shirley, unaware that the play was known and had been printed in
1649 as the Earl of Newcastle's.[20]

Even if Shirley had had no immediate hand in *The Country Cap-*

tain, the precedent furnished by his own earlier comedies would deny that play much claim to originality in type. *The Parson's Wedding* also had the advantage of Shirley's example, but it was probably written wholly by Killigrew, who must be given credit for his adaptability. The two plays will best be discussed together. In *The Country Captain,* Sir Francis Courtwell, a polite roué, pursues the all too-willing Lady Huntlove, wife of an unsuspecting country gentleman. Needing a stalking-horse, he persuades his cousin, Master Courtwell, to pay suit to Lady Huntlove's sister. Having by this means gained admission to the Huntlove manor house, Sir Francis secures the consent of his quarry, but the efforts of the pair to cuckold the Squire all fail by ludicrously narrow margins. Master Courtwell falls honestly in love with the sister, and wins this sparkling beauty in rivalry with "Cavalier" Device, a Frenchified gallant. In *The Parson's Wedding,* two fashionable rakes, Tom Careless and Ned Wild, contend with two country gentlemen, Constant and Sadd, in courtship of a young widow and her companion, Pleasant, both of whom are handsome, wealthy, and witty. The suit of the countrymen is hopeless from the start so that they can scarcely be considered seriously as rivals, but a feud springs up between the ladies and their city gallants which threatens to render the latter's suit hopeless also. The feud is only terminated when the gentlemen force the ladies to marry by compromising their reputations. Both plays have low-comedy sub-plots which provide the titles, and, in the case of *The Parson's Wedding,* most of the scenes. In Newcastle's play, Captain Underwit, a ridiculous neophyte soldier, is tricked into marrying a lady's maid by the device of an intercepted letter describing her as an heiress. In Killigrew's play, a venal dissenting clergyman is forced to wed a sprightly demimonde; and an amorous "platonick," Lady Love-all, is imposed upon by a series of practical jokes. We have already noticed punitive misalliances forced upon gulls in the university plays; indeed they are inescapable throughout the realistic comedy of the day.

   The Country Captain and *The Parson's Wedding* are not without intrinsic interest. They would be improved by pruning, especially in the scenes of low comedy, and *The Parson's Wedding* is awkwardly constructed, but both plays contain scenes of true comic vitality and a few characters who are both individualized and true to life. The dialogue has not that stylistic distinction which makes certain comedies of the Restoration remarkable simply as illustrations of superb English prose, but it is well written, and wittier, in the modern sense of the term, than that of the university comedies or that of many contemporary professional ones. The badinage smacks of the drawing-room at least as frequently as of the tap-room. In their upper spheres of action, the two plays, mutually or individually, display many of the features of the social comedy of the Restoration. We find pitched battles in repartee, an atmosphere of contemporary English high life, an avowed antagonism between the sexes, amatory intrigue among the fashionable and well-born, the rake as hero and the witty and sophisticated lady as heroine, and a satirical attack upon rusticity, on one hand, and, on the other, upon fashionable affectation, especially as it appears in foppish pretenders to wit. Had not Shirley's comedies already appeared upon the stage, these plays would have to be accredited with taking a decisive step toward the type of comedy written by Etherege. However, if we are to retain the proper sense of proportion, we must keep Shirley constantly in mind, even though we may disregard for the moment his actual hand in *The Country Captain.*

A reader fresh from the romantic plays of the Cavaliers, with their superlative elevation, will be struck most forcibly by the equivocal moral tone of the two plays. In 1664 Samuel Pepys called *The Parson's Wedding* "bawdy,"[21] and the word was not ill-chosen. Newcastle's language is less licentious than Killigrew's, but his is the guiltier theme; Lady Huntlove commits adultery in intention if not in fact, and her fifth-act reformation is not impressive. Killigrew's Widow and Pleasant do not share the vices of their gallants; they are chaste, and admirable. The "platonick" Lady Love-all is unchaste, but she is not admirable. Mistress Wanton, the demimonde, is unchaste and admirable, but she is not a lady. These distinctions are significant. But while Killigrew basically may have been on the side of the angels, his language is so wantonly coarse as to obliterate any such impression. That a Cavalier who had written intensely ethical plays could become ribald with gusto is a reminder that he lived in two worlds of morality, the theoretical and the actual. At the very time when the refined sentiment of D'Urfé was being injected into courtly drama, a dissolute life was considered fashionable among courtly writers. Thomas Randolph did much to create a pattern of conduct later followed by Suckling and Killigrew. A curious link between these three is a passage describing the sensual charms of a ripe girl of fifteen, which appears first in *The Muses' Looking Glass,* is imitated and enlarged upon in *Brennoralt,* and again *ad nauseum* in *The Parson's Wedding.* Newcastle, of course, had never succumbed to the platonic cult, and Killigrew must have written his play as a public exhibition of his change of heart. Neither writer can be accused of beginning the moral decline of English comedy. Marital infidelity as a comic theme had appeared in such plays as Middleton's *Chaste Maid in Cheapside,* with its outrageously funny Touchwood Sr. and Lady Kix, in Fletcher's *Wild Goose Chase* and *Rule a Wife and*

Have a Wife, and, more recently, in Shirley's *The Gamester* and Brome's *Mad Couple.* The courtly writers before 1642 carried the decline no further than the professional writers, and the point they reached was still considerably short of the Restoration nadir; immorality was not yet on the intellectual plane, and characters did not rationalize their behavior; rakes still enjoyed their sins rather than the commission of their sins.

The Country Captain and *The Parson's Wedding* are most interesting, after all, not for their dubious morality, but for their atmosphere of social high life and their satirical portraiture. Unlike the university wits, Newcastle and Killigrew drew their material from their own world of fashion. There is an intimacy about *The Parson's Wedding* and a particularity about its characterization which suggest that its Parson, its Captain, its Courtier, its Platonic Lady, and so on, were portraits of actual people. The impression becomes a certainty when we reach the interesting tag-epilogue; the Captain addresses Lady Love-all:

They say you have a great power over the Parson. If you can prevail with him to express his anger in some satiric comedy (for the knave has wit, and they say his genius lies that way), tell him 'tis expected he should be revenged upon the illiterate Courtier that made this play.

Shirley's association with *The Country Captain* is enough to suggest that in this play also some of the characters may have been drawn from life. It is Shirley to whom we must look as the chief harbinger of the Restoration tendency to seek the material of comedy among posturing members of polite society. In November, 1632, Shirley narrowly escaped punishment and was forced to revise *The Ball*—not because it trespassed politically, but because, as Sir Henry Herbert said, "ther were divers personated so naturally, both of lords and others of the court . . ."[22] In the first scene of *The Lady of Pleasure,* itself a highly sophisticated play, Shirley threatened to satirize in earnest some day the "antic gambols" of the fashionable world. His *Hyde Park* and especially his *Gamester* exploit the foibles of the élite, and come very close indeed to the type of comedy sometimes considered indigenous to the Restoration.

The note struck so clearly by Shirley is not, to be sure, wholly silent in Cavalier plays other than the two comedies by Newcastle and Killigrew. In a few of the romances such as Suckling's *Goblins,* Cokain's *Obstinate Lady,* Cartwright's *Lady Errant* and *The Siege,* Mayne's *Amorous War,* and Berkeley's *Lost Lady,* the Cavalier dramatists interrupted their high heroic seriousness long enough to let their ladies and gentlemen indulge in a little gay social banter. The "anti-platonic" appears—a character who, like D'Urfé's Hylas, is humorously skeptical about that ideal love which consists in "ideas of the mind, not in any carnal fruition."[23] Sex innuendo appears, and the repartee, among minor characters at least, is apt to become slightly salty. Usually, however, there is simply a gracious interchange of mildly sophisticated shafts concerning love and marriage—for instance in Cartwright's *Lady Errant:*

> Tis not in fashion, Sir, to love your lady—
> At least you ought not to profess it:

or,

> . . . Husbands are at best
> But a sad kind of pleasure; one good look
> And a salute's enough at any time.[24]

If the Cavaliers had developed an individual type of comedy, as they did of dramatic romance, it would have been a comedy of love and marriage debate, resembling the light scenes in the works just mentioned, and capitalizing the conflict between *précieuse* theory and actual human practice. Davenant's *Platonic Lovers,* a professional play, provided a hint of the direction such comedy might take, but the nearest approach to the type by an actual courtier came after the Restoration, in Sir William Killigrew's *Pandora.*[25]

The fact that the courtly writers did not create an individual type of comedy, and that *The Country Captain* and *The Parson's Wedding* can be considered as little more than sports, and Shirleyan echoes, is significant in itself. Certainly the material for high comedy was at hand. The correctly provocative type of social intercourse was as old as the Renaissance, as the charmingly affected dialogues of Castiglione are sufficient to prove. Shakespeare had not been at a loss for material in writing *Love's Labour Lost,* and Lyly, Day, and other Elizabethans were able to strike from genteel mannerisms momentary flashes of high comedy. In the early seventeenth century the intense individualism of the Elizabethan age subsided, and an increased conformity, gregariousness, and delight in social intercourse were the result. We need only glance at the statutes designed to make the gentry reside on their country estates instead of yielding to the lure of London in order to recognize the growth and magnetism of Polite Society. Gentlemen had long since discovered that the pulse of life could be quickened by a conversation with a wit, a flirtation with a beauty, or a game of primero, more conveniently than by an expedition to the Indies. Ladies were seeking destinies less exclusively domestic than had formerly been considered sufficient for all but the most grand. Such "normalizing" works of literature as *The Courtier* and *Euphues* were succeeded by

D'Urfé's *Astrée;*[26] and Henrietta Maria and such able lieutenants as
the Countess of Carlisle followed the example of the Marquise de
Rambouillet by becoming missionaries of etiquette to a social coterie
of which they formed the rallying points. The rise of Puritan and democratic opposition to those in high places helped to crystallize the social
coterie, for in their increasing isolation the fashionable idlers were
forced to turn in upon and discover themselves. Fashion is the result
of abrasive contact; wherever there is extensive social intercourse, an
artificial code of conduct is sure to evolve, and this code is sure to work
its comic restraints upon individuals within its pale. Dorothy Osborne[27]
was fifteen years of age before Charles and Henrietta were forced to
vacate Westminster. That the period in which she had grown up was
lacking neither in a cultivated society nor in the insight to perceive
with amusement at times its own artificialities is illustrated by her
letters to Temple, written a decade later.

There was certainly, in Caroline days, manners of a kind to supply
fair game for satirical treatment. There was also a group of young
men, with a first-hand knowledge of these manners, who had recently
turned to play-writing. In fine, the same conditions prevailed which
prevailed during the Restoration, with such fruitful results. That the
Cavaliers made so little use of their opportunities is a commentary
upon the spirit of their age, and, by implication, upon the spirit of
the age of the Restoration. The Cavaliers wrote to please their Queen,
whose tastes they shared. They were romantic in their outlook upon
life. They were not yet cloyed with gallantry, nor prepared to write
upon social attitudes in a spirit of disillusion. They were inhibited,
besides, by the critical dogma that tragedy had to do with the misfortunes of the mighty, comedy with the absurdities of the mean. It
would not have been in the *esprit de corps* to display the absurdities
of the mighty in public places. Restoration writers were not so restricted, both because *esprit de corps,* like other forms of idealism, was
at low ebb and because the drama had become a less public institution.
In the theatres, once they had been deserted by the masses, the classes
could enjoy the parade of their follies with a degree of privacy. It is
notable that Shirley, like Fletcher, his chief predecessor in satirizing
high life, was *declassé;* he had the necessary personal experience to
write of Society, while his descent to the rank of a common playwright
permitted him to write of Society objectively. And the age was not
yet ready for what he had to offer. *The Lady of Pleasure,* although
the best comedy of its generation, was not the most popular, and
Shirley deserted the type with this play, seven years before the theatres
were banned. The attitude of Sir Henry Herbert is very revealing.

Herbert had a strict sense of propriety and an acute consciousness of the class to which he belonged; he smiled approvingly at *The Young Admiral* but frowned at *The Ball*. If audiences wished to laugh, they could laugh at citizens, not at "lords and others of the court."[28] What were citizens for? When social comedy came into its own during the Restoration, it had been forced to wait, not for a native precedent, and certainly not for the example of Molière, but for a generation relaxed from those restrictions which chivalry imposes upon itself. *The Country Captain* and *The Parson's Wedding* may be given credit for helping to convey Shirley's type of comedy over into the new period and giving it fashionable authority. They seem to have been revived on the Restoration stage earlier than Shirley's own comedies. Pepys saw *The Country Captain* on October 26, 1661, and pronounced it "silly," as he was apt to do anything connected with the name New-castle. His reference to that "bawdy, loose play" *The Parson's Wedding* has already been mentioned.

As we leave the Caroline period, it is to be expected that a survey of the comedy of manners will provide us with few examples of plays by professional playwrights. While the theatres were closed, condi-tions were adverse to the development of professionals, and when the theatres were reopened it took several years for writers to achieve pro-fessional status. But whereas the writing of social comedy was left almost entirely to authors with courtly connections, such as Margaret Cavendish, James Howard, and Thomas Southland, or to bookish amateurs such as John Wilson, and Richard Head, the mark of the popular comedy before 1642 remains indelible in their work. Oc-casionally, however, there appears a suggestion, in certain details, of the character that social comedy would assume after 1664.

The period of the Commonwealth produced only one comedy of any significance, but this one, usually ignored,[29] has features of considerable interest. An advertisement of a play "written by a person of learning and eminency" was appended to Montague's *Accomplished Woman*, published by Bedel and Collins in 1656, and in the same year the play appeared: *The Hectors, or The False Challenge*, "a comedy writ-ten in the year MDCLV." Phillips and Winstanley attributed it twenty-five years later to Edmund Prestwich, but the attribution is without value.[30] The prologue promises "a strain in a new way":

> Here is no dabbling poet, nor no bare
> Poor Belgick Captain, but what's most a wonder,
> You shall but once read here of blood and thunder;
> No academic wit, the senses five,
> Or liberal sciences not here contrive

Into a play he doth, or wedding make
Upon Parnassus, or a story take
From Lucian. I shall puzzle you, you'll cry,
What a device then can this play e're be?

Little of this promised originality appears in that portion of the play providing the title. For the hackneyed themes of academic drama, to which the prologue chiefly refers, the author substituted, like Cartwright and Mayne before him, the hackneyed themes of popular comedy. Hadland,[31] who has lost his fortune in the late wars, consorts with Castor and Slur, the usual tavern blades, called in this instance "Hectors." The three impose on silly La-gull by tricking him into expensive duels, and upon Justice Quorum by involving him in the usual mock marriage. This is the Bromean material of farcial intrigue among the London citizenry used by so many writers of Caroline comedy. What gives the play its claim to attention is a second plot, which sets the comic scene among a higher and more subtle social group. In this portion of the play occurs a battle of wits between the gallant Mr. Wellbred and the sprightly Miss Love-wit, who resemble in everything save emancipation from morals the witty beaux and beauties of Restoration comedy of manners. There are also the capricious Miss Crisis, who must be converted to Mr. Knowwell as a sensible and discreet if not scintillating husband, and, finally, little Miss Bud, who is just home from boarding school and who follows about in mute admiration a coxcombical pretender to fine manners and brilliant speech.

The plot is too rambling and the characters too discursive for *The Hectors* to be fit for the stage, but its dialogue is often written with distinction and reveals an author turning critical attention upon his own polite social stratum to exploit its comic possibilities. The atmosphere of the drawing room and the manners of those who frequent it are carefully conveyed. Conflict between the sexes with the weapon of wit is here, although battle is joined within the field of moral propriety; and the characters have discovered that the most absorbing thing in life is their own foibles and ideas. In easy and familiar prose, they display their conversational prowess upon such subjects as city compared to country life, intellectuality in women, the proper etiquette of husband and wife, duelling, painting and patching, the conceit of the town beau. Remarks are often shrewd, as well as wittily phrased, and the general tone of enlightenment is such that one is constantly tempted to patronize the play as "modern." As in Restoration comedy of manners itself, the impression upon the reader made by certain scenes is that of satirical essay rather than of drama.

The Hectors is remarkable also for another characteristic of Restoration comedy of manners. This is a detail of technique, evasive and rather difficult to define. It consists of a careful attention to, and reproduction of, the minutiae of the progressing scene. The term *realism* scarcely conveys the idea, for *realism* has an overlay of larger meaning, and suggests attention to basic rather than to external realities. Elizabethan drama, as illustrated by plays as old as *Arden of Feversham,* is full of realism as we use the term, but Elizabethan drama is also full of conventional ellipses, is never shackled by fidelity to undramatic detail. In Restoration comedy, dramatic movement sometimes defers to plausibility in small externals (as when a character explains his entrance with the comment that his coach has broken down outside the house); and, in the dialogue, the hesitancies and inconsequentials of actual conversation are in some measure preserved. Something was woven into the texts of plays that harmonized with the increasingly illustrative fashion of mounting performances, and although the two tendencies may have been mutually accelerating, at first they were the twin effects of a common cause. When Saintsbury discusses the relations of Restoration and Caroline comedy, he mentions the "modernity"[32] of such plays as Shirley's *Hyde Park,* and it is this reportorial quality, this extra-dramatic verisimilitude, to which he evidently has reference. The quality is one of those which the term "naturalness" is sometimes made to apply. Although less discussed than other qualities of Restoration comedy, it is of historical importance, related as it is to the growth of the scientific mood and to the advent of such novelists as Defoe and Richardson.

The impulse to reproduce rather than to represent synoptically was a constantly growing one during the seventeenth century, and only incidentally reflected in the art of the drama, as we may judge by the fact that a play as isolated as *The Hectors* reveals it even more clearly than *Hyde Park.* A few lines from the first scene of *The Hectors* may be quoted:

Bud. Really, Cousin, there was a rare gentleman in the slash'd doublet and button'd cap; me thought he talk'd incomparably.
Love-Wit. Whom doth she mean?
Pate. Mr. La-gull certainly.
Crisis. Alas, poor soul!
Pate. Well, I must be going.
Crisis. Nay, prithee stay a little longer.
Pate. No, I have appointed to meet one.
Crisis. Who? Mr. Hadland, I'll warrant you.
Pate. 'Tis no matter for that.

Crisis. Well, I hope when you come to lie at this end of town again, we shall more enjoy your company.

This dialogue, although admirable in its way, reveals something that is not all pure gain; what is gained in naturalness is lost is a sort of dramatic lassitude, and such is true in a measure of much modern drama. The same type of phonographic recording of actual conversation occurs in some of the dialogues of Lady Newcastle,[33] also written during the latter years of the Interregnum, and gives her otherwise anomalous drama some slight historical interest.

Verisimilitude through extraneous detail appears in some of the earliest plays written after 1660. Witness the interpolations concerning the coaching arrangements in the opening speeches of Howard's *Committee,* 1662:

Mrs. Day. Now out upon't how dustry 'tis! All things considered 'tis better travelling in the winter; especially for us of the better sort, that ride in coaches. And yet, to say truth, warm weather is both pleasant and comfortable; 'tis a thousand pities that fair weather should do any hurt.—Well said, honest coachman, thou hast done thy part. My son Abel paid for my place at Reading, did he not?
Coachman. Yes, an't please you.
Mrs. Day. Well there's something extraordinary, to make you drink.
Coachman. (Aside) By my whip, 'tis a groat of more than ordinary thinness—Plague on this new gentry, how liberal they are.—Farewell, gentlemen. Pray when you come by Reading, let Toby carry you.

Thomas Porter's *The Villain,* 1662, provides an instance of the quality we have been discussing penetrating even into a serious and romantic play:

Clairmont

Are the players good that are in town?
Monsieur d'Elpeche, you know, you are a virtuoso.

D'Elpeche

They say themselves they will do wonders for us;
I never saw 'em act.

Brisac

I think the self same band was once at Orlean.

Bontefeu

The same, Sir, had the great mischance.

Clairmont

What was it, prithee?

Bontefeu
Acting Orpheus' descent into Hell,
Their fire-works set fire on the stage,
Which burnt some part o' th' town.[34]

Here is plausible small talk utterly unrelated to the action of the play or the individual traits of the speakers, inserted simply as part of the background.

In casting about for comic subjects, several early Restoration writers resorted simply to reporting current incidents and scenes; the little group of obscure comedies which resulted have no merit as drama but are interesting as straws in the wind. *The Presbyterian Lash*, 1661, which reported scandal about the Puritan clergyman, Zachary Crofton, is described elsewhere.[35] Resembling it somewhat is *A Witty Combat*, 1663, by "T. P.," which reports, with Jonsonian embellishments in the portrayal of character, the career of Mary Carleton, here called Madam Moders, an adventuress of the day who was brought to trial for snaring a husband by posing as a German princess. Richard Head's *Hic et Ubique, or The Humors of Dublin*, 1663,[36] fulfills the promise of its prologue:

Here's no Utopian stories, nor such things
As some men fain, that fly upon the wings
Of fancy only.................
Experience teaches what we have to say.

With little attention to plot, the play mirrors a phase of the life of the times; its account of a company of English bankrupts seeking to recoup their fortunes in Dublin is written in a key resembling that of the "novels" of Aphra Behn. The anonymous *Knavery in All Trades*, 1664, discards plot almost entirely, and reveals in its gossipy, intimate dialogue only the author's interest in the London about him—in the activities of those new-fangled places of entertainment called coffee-houses, and in the troubles of merchants with their wives and their pilfering apprentices. The coffee-house patrons converse in this vein:

Has any of you seen the play of Harry the Eight?
Many years ago I did.
So did I.
'Tis rarely set forth, they say.[37]

They proceed to discuss Fowler and other actors of the good old days of the Fortune, with their only reason for so doing the fact that people do talk about such things in actual life.

The comedies written between 1660 and 1664 other than those already mentioned invite little attention.[38] John Wilson's *The Cheats*, Thomas Southland's *Love a la Mode*, James Howard's *English Mon-*

sieur,[39] Richard Rhode's *Flora's Vagaries,* and Dryden's *Wild Gallant* were all acted in 1663, and Alexander Greene's *The Politician Cheated* was printed in the same year. All these plays are marked by denatured Jonsonism and much hectic intrigue, usually farcial and dealing with courtship, of precisely the same nature as that which had appeared in the comedies of Brome and his professional and amateur contemporaries before 1642. The method of multiplying and interweaving this intrigue was typically English, although the intrigue itself sometimes resembled that of Spanish drama of cloak and sword, itself frequently adapted during these first years of the Restoration.[40] None of these comedies is notable for its naturalness of manner or its atmosphere of high life to the degree of *The Hectors* of 1655 or of Shirley's comedies before 1642. There are a few scenes of effective satire in *The Cheats;* an arresting company of hard, technically chaste but essentially impure, females in *Love a la Mode;* a fairly amusing fop in *The English Monsieur;* and a rather pleasant hoyden admirably suited to the talents of Nell Gwyn in *Flora's Vagaries;* but otherwise little that compels interest.

The Wild Gallant, owing perhaps to the subsequent prominence of its author, is sometimes singled out as having made unique contributions to the type of comedy perfected during the Restoration, but the truth is that Dryden's play is neither very good nor very original. In fact it is a Bromean comedy, with a plot and dramatis personæ compounded of the tag ends of numerous older plays. The original relationship between roistering Mr. Loveby and sprightly Lady Constance is about the same as that between Young Pallatine and Lucy in Davenant's *The Wits,* and the lady's method of paving the way to a marriage with her gallant (through a pretended pregnancy) is anticipated in May's *Old Couple* and Brome's *Sparagus Garden.* No issue can be made of the pair of witty, bantering lovers: these indeed became a standard feature of later comedy of manners, but they had already appeared in a score of plays older than Dryden's—some, in fact, older than Shakespeare's own *Much Ado About Nothing.* Beatrice and Benedick themselves, by the way, had reappeared upon the stage in Davenant's *Law Against Lovers* just before *The Wild Gallant* was written. The ingredients that were to go into social comedy after 1664 had all been gathered before 1660, and by a very gradual accumulation.

It is with justice that Etherege's *The Comical Revenge, or Love in a Tub,* 1664, has frequently been selected as marking a divisional point in the evolution of comedy of manners. Although four-fifths of the play is a commingling of old-fashioned farce and old-fashioned tragicomedy, the few scenes involving Sir Frederick Frollick and his courtship of the widow Rich are of a piece with the later comedy of Etherege himself and of his most gifted successors. The new element in these scenes is not of a kind that need be traced to literary precedent either at home or abroad; it is an attribute rather of the author's own style and personality. Sir Frederick Frollick himself is only a more cultivated Wilding of *The Gamester*, Young Pallatine of *The Wits*, Tom Careless of *The Parson's Wedding*, Sir Francis Courtwell of *The Country Captain*, or Mr. Loveby of *The Wild Gallant*. Considered generically the materials and methods of the Sir Frederick scenes are all present in English comedy of the preceding thirty or thirty-five years. What makes the difference is that these materials and methods had never been used before by Sir George Etherege, and Sir George Etherege was the first author with superior comic talents to appear in his generation. New personalities in literature create new, or apparently new, departures. When Sir Frederick Frollick discharges the opening salvo of Restoration wit, "Men are now and then subject to those infirmities in drink which women have when they're sober," Etherege is simply creating a similitude, the device upon which playwrights had long exercised their ingenuity, and its satiric thrust of sex antagonism represents impulses that had long been gathering force. What distinguished Etherege's similitude from those, let us say, of Cartwright, is its superb success. The newest element in it, as in the scene where it appears, is the individual skill of the writer.

The element of novelty in the Sir Fredrick Frollick scenes derives not only from individual literary skill but also, in large measure, from the spirit that informs them—that is, from the philosophical temper of their creator. Sir Frederick himself, polished, gallant, sophisticated, owing nothing to seriousness or to tyrannical imperatives, bathed in the aura of his whimsical debaucheries, is symbolic of an ideal. The admirable rakes of Elizabethan drama, from Prince Hal in *Henry IV* to Wellborn in *A New Way to Pay Old Debts* had been at bottom sound and substantial citizens; Sir Frederick is *not* at bottom a sound and substantial citizen, and for this reason he is not besmirched by his indiscretions and is in no need of rehabilitation. To reform him were to ruin him; he is the new pattern of perfection. The Ned Wilds and Sir Francis Courtwells of the plays which intervened between Elizabethan and Restoration comedy illustrate that the ideal represented by Sir Frederick was not entirely new, but in Etherege this ideal was for the first time wholly codified and accepted. The ideal was certainly not borrowed from Molière! As the Restoration period continued Molière furnished plot materials to writers, and furnished a standard of technique—in exploiting the ludicrous in character and situation with a refinement that had evaded the boisterous Elizabethans—, but in every fundamental aspect Molière's comedy is different from that of contemporary England and cannot be considered as its sire.

The character of Sir Frederick exemplifies only a detail of the temper of Restoration social comedy, but it is representative. The temper as a whole has been admirably analyzed by Mr. Palmer, Mr. Dobrée, and others.[41] Of whatever evolutionary processes it may have been the outgrowth, the peculiar accentuation of this temper, its radical sharpness of outline, can be explained only as reaction. Restoration social comedy was an expression of that same social coterie which had previously expressed itself in a type of drama utterly antithetical—romance of the Cavalier mode. This is in the nature of things. The coat had been worn one way, and now it was turned inside out. The chief contribution of the Cavalier generation to the social comedy of the Restoration was in organizing the coterie which this comedy was to interpret, and in providing the precedent for gentlemen of the necessary social experience to write plays.

---

[1] Even among the professional writers, realistic comedy was in the descendent. Between 1630 and 1642, the professionals wrote about four serious and romantic plays to three comic and realistic ones; the amateurs about five to one.

[2] See below, Part II, Chapter II.—In one respect the departure was less radical than might be supposed; some of the Latin academic tragicomedies had utilized the same exotic materials and from the same ultimate sources as the plays of the Cavalier mode.

[3] No record of the original performance of *The Ordinary* is known; for the stage history of *The City Match*, see p. 144. *The Guardian* was presented during a passing visit of Prince Charles to Cambridge, March 12, 1642; for its altered form, *Cutter of Coleman Street*, see below, pp. 183-185. Cowley had written, besides a pastoral play (see below, pp. 119-120) a Latin comedy, *Naufragium Joculare*, acted at Cambridge in 1639. A fourth English university comedy of popular inspiration is George Wilde's *Love's Hospital*, 1636, discussed below, p. 140.

[4] It was his tavern-roarers whom Cowley converted into the cashiered Cavaliers of *Cutter of Coleman Street*.

[5] *Preface to Gondibert*, 1650.

[6] *Preface to The Tempest*, 1670.

[7] Act IV, Scene vii.

[8] K. M. Lynch, *Social Mode of Restoration Comedy, University of Michigan Publ.*, III (1926), 100-101.

[9] For a discussion of the structural resemblances between Bromean and Restoration comedy, see C. E. Andrews, *Richard Brome, Yale Studies in English*, XLVI (1913), 54 seq.

[10] It is possible that *The Parson's Wedding* was not acted until after the Restoration; see my *Thomas Killigrew* (Philadelphia, 1930), p. 190n.—For the dates of Newcastle's plays, see P. T. E. Perry, *The First Duchess of Newcastle and her Husband as Figures in English Literary History* (Cambridge, 1921).

[11] See below, pp. 104-109.

[12] *The Life of William Cavendish Duke of Newcastle*, C. H. Firth, Ed. (London, 1886).

[13] *The Triumphant Widow*, Act IV, Scene i; although the writing of this scene is probably Shadwell's, the sentiments were Newcastle's as well as Shadwell's; similar sentiments are expressed in *The Humorous Lovers*, Act I, Scene ii.

[14] G. Langbaine, *English Dramatick Poets*, p. 317.

[15] Act II.

[16] "Epistle to the Readers," *Plays written by the Thrice Noble, Illustrious Princess, The Lady Marchioness of Newcastle*, 1662.

[17] Edited from a holograph manuscript at Welbeck Abbey, by Francis Needham, *Welbeck Miscellany No. 1* (1933).

[18] In addition to the plays written with Shadwell, Newcastle furnished Dryden with the "bare translations" (John Downes, *Roscius Anglicanus*, p. 28) out of which *Sir Martin Mar-all* (1667), was fashioned. A. Nicoll, *Restoration Drama*, pp. 172-173, gives Molière's *L'Etourdi* and Quinault's *L'Amant Indiscret* as the plays translated, but *Sir Martin Mar-all* is enough unlike these to be to Dryden's credit as an original play.

[19] Anthony à Wood, *Athenæ Oxonienses* (ed. Bliss), III, 739.

[20] Harleian MS 7650, see *Old English Plays*, Vol. II (1883).—Bullen called the play *Captain Underwit*. For the speculation on the Cavendish-Shirley collaboration, see P. T. E. Perry, *op. cit.*, pp. 100-112.

[21] *Pepys Diary*, October 6 & 11, 1664.

[22] *Dramatic records of Sir Henry Herbert*, p. 19.

[23] See above, p. 36.

[24] Act IV, Scene ii; Act V, Scene iv.

[25] Discussed below, pp. 242-243.

[26] Professor Lynch (*Social Mode of Restoration Comedy*) lays great stress on the influence of D'Urfé upon English comedy. According to Professor Lynch, D'Urfé's influence produced, beginning in Caroline days, a social milieu regulated by a code charmingly gracious but artificial, and drama began to reflect an interest in characters less as individuals than as members of this milieu, obligated to submerge their natural selves in conformity with rigid rules of wit and fashion. The intelligent and admirable people (and characters) deferred to the code gracefully and with success, the stupid and pretentious awkwardly and with ludicrous strain. The ultimate result was a Millament and a Sir Fopling Flutter, both poseurs and therefore comic, but comic on entirely different planes. Professor Lynch maintains also that the bantering lovers of Restoration comedy, and the "proviso" betrothal scenes, owe their literary ancestry, chiefly via Dryden, to D'Urfé's *Astrée*.

[27] See below, pp. 202-203, 229.

[28] See above, p. 78.

[29] The play recently has been discussed as a source of Wilson's *The Cheats*; see M. Nahm's edition of the latter (Oxford, 1935). A number of drolls and comic interludes were written during the Commonwealth (See Part II, Chapters V & VI), but these have little bearing on the development of social comedy.

[30] Phillips and Winstanley depended upon Langbaine and sometimes misunderstood his arrangement of plays under various authors. For how *The Hectors* may have been given to Prestwich in error, see the suggestive comments by Langbaine, *English Dramatick Poets* (1691), pp. 13-14, 533. Nothing is definitely known of Prestwich; but a clue to his identity is provided by the admission of Thomas, grand-

son of Edmund, Prestwich to Gray's Inn in 1649. Our author may have been Thomas's younger brother or cousin. If so, he came from Hulme Co., Lancaster. See *Register of Admissions to Gray's Inn*, J. Foster, ed. (London, 1889), pp. 173, 252. For Prestwich's *Hippolytus*, see below, p. 216.

[31] Possibly this name, and some of the action, were imitated from Day and Chettle's *Blind-Beggar of Bednal-Green*.

[32] Introduction to the *Mermaid* Dryden.

[33] Discussed below, pp. 229-233.

[34] Act II.

[35] See p. 186.

[36] It appears from their title pages that *A Witty Combat, Hic et Ubique*, and *Knavery in All Trades* were all acted at private entertainments. The title *Knavery in All Trades* is applied to a play performed by citizens in 1655, but the play on that occasion seems to have been *The Knave in Graine* of 1640; cf. H. Rollins, *SP*, XVIII (1921), 318.

[37] Act III.

[38] That is, in the search for a "new note" in social comedy. Adaptations of older comedies, by Davenant and others, and original romantic comedies are not relevant to the present discussion. Thomas Thomson's *English Rogue* (1660?), and *Life of Mother Shipton* (1661) belong in neither of these categories, but they are eccentric productions of small significance. Early Restoration comedies relating to the English political conflicts, Tatham's *The Rump*, Howard's *The Committee*, Cowley's *Cutter of Coleman Street*, and Lacy's *Old Troop* are noticed below, Part II, Chapter IV.

[39] For the date of this play, see Ethel Seaton, *LTS*, Oct. 18, 1934, corr. For the dates of the others, see A. Nicoll, *Restoration Drama*, pp. 348-376 *passim*.

[40] See below, p. 239.

[41] John Palmer, *Comedy of Manners* (1912); Bonamy Dobrée, *Restoration Comedy* (Oxford Press, 1924); H. T. E. Perry, *The Comic Spirit in Restoration Drama* (Yale Univ. Press, 1925); K. M. Lynch, *op. cit.* (notes 8 and 26 above).

PART TWO
SURVEY

THE COURTIER PLAYWRIGHTS

CAVALIER drama is not uniformly fantastical and inartistic—there are gleams in the darkness; yet it is safer for the reader's peace of mind if he views it outside the realms of art or concedes it a place of privilege there, if he withdraws his thoughts from the poetic drama of Fletcher and his elders, and thinks in terms of literary and social history. Most literary histories are chronicles of victories. Behold here some major defeats. There is enlightenment in them. And for the unhistorically minded there may be charm in the quaint, the characteristic, the utterly absurd.

Walter Montague's *The Shepherd's Paradise,* already mentioned a number of times, is a perfect Waterloo of literature, but it precipitated the Prynne episode, introduced *préciosité* to the English stage, and gave countenance to courtier playwrights; therefore, though given only passing mention in most histories of the drama, it and its author may claim fuller treatment here. Montague (1603-77) wrote no more plays, and his career on the whole is that of a political intriguer and Catholic prelate.[1] Son of the first earl of Manchester, he cut short a career at Cambridge to travel abroad, and had scarce reached his majority when he was employed by Buckingham in the elaborate diplomacy attending the betrothal of the young King Charles and Princess Henrietta. Later he was sent on a number of missions, often semi-official and veiled in secrecy, and at the time of the break between King and Parliament he was in bad odor as agent of the Queen. He had been converted to Catholicism by legerdemain miracles wrought by Ursaline nuns at Loudun, and had journeyed to Rome to become a father of the oratory, so that when his reputation with Pym's cohorts drove him to France, one of the first of the exiles, he was ready for a career in the church. He became Abbot of St. Martin's, near Pantoise, but he was never far removed from the sphere of small intrigues in great circles. There may seem little in his career to indicate the fashionable playwright, but Montague's play was really quite in character. As a young man he was known as a Frenchified gallant, and was entirely at home amid courtly artificialities. Sworn as Gentleman of the Privy-chamber Extraordinary in 1631,[2] Montague wrote his play soon after; his readiness to furnish amusement, as well as his newly professed Catholicism, cemented with the Queen a friendship which may have begun at the time of her marriage negotiations. He was a lady's man—in a demure clerical way—and his piety and *politesse* won the friendship also of the Queen and Queen Mother of France; his other venture into secular literature was a translation of a French book of harmless homily published as *The Accomplished Woman* in 1656.

The acting of *The Shepherd's Paradise* has already been described. Apparently it was not revived after the winter of 1632-33, and although it circulated in manuscript, it was not published until 1659. The paradise of the play is a retreat for the lovelorn, where the shepherds—masquerading gentry quite untrammeled by sheep—find "a peaceful receptacle of distressed minds, and a sanctuary against fortune's severest executions." To this sanctuary, which proves in fact a very stiffly organized little commune, retreats Prince Basilino alias Moramente who loves but must conquer his love for the subject Fidamira. He does so by the arduous method of falling in love with Saphira alias Bellesa, the intensely chaste and theoretical Queen-elect of the shepherd's paradise. Fidamira herself retreats hither, as does her secret suitor Agenor. Everyone takes an assumed name, Fidamira becoming Gamella, Agenor becoming Genorio; and the habit is troublesome, especially since the former proves to be neither Gamella nor Fidamira but Miranda, sister of her erstwhile lover Basilino, and her secret suitor proves to be neither Genorio nor Agenor, but Bellesa's brother Palante. These relationships when finally revealed bring blessed surcease to a tangle of crossed purposes, for the various lovers find they may pair off without violating so much as a by-law in that vast unwritten charter which governs right sentiment and honorable behavior.

The plot is of little importance in this endless, amorphous play. Its hundred and seventy closely printed pages are devoted to elaborate exchanges of civilities, comments on actions and impulses, ethical casuistry, analyses of the love code. The characters all speak in paragraphs, and everywhere is ingenuity, abstraction, meaningless nuance. To this the occasional songs offer little lyrical refreshment—as witness this sample couplet:

> I find a glowing heat that turns red hot
> My heart, but yet it doth not flame a jot . . .[3]

The prose is like parody of the language of thought, and lacks the color achieved by later Cavalier rhetoricians. It is dull, pedantic, clotted with syllogistic patterns and labored conceits:

Basilino. Mistake not, Madam; the only thing in this world impossible to you is the guiltiness of my mind. Tis not in my power to be so complacent unto you as to afford it you. Your ill opinion of it may be so heavy on its innocence as to bow it out of its own frame; but even then it will become an arch triumphant whose very incurvation will become a beauty, as it was made so by the weight you laid upon it . . .[4]

Need we continue? A sample of Montague's dialogue has already been quoted.

It is little wonder that Patrick Carey wrote,

> But tell me pray, if ever you
> Read th' English of Watt Montague,
> Isn't it more hard than French?[5]

and Suckling,

> Watt Montague now stood forth to his trial,
> And did not so much as suspect a denial;
> But witty Apollo asked him first of all,
> If he understood his own pastoral.[6]

Thus *The Shepherd's Paradise* struck some of the cleverer of Montague's fellows. It falls below the plane even of its own class. Nevertheless Montague attained the prestige of the pioneer; it is an irony of human conduct that some especially ludicrous fad which everyone is laughing at one moment everyone is imitating the next. *The Shepherd's Paradise* stamped an imprint on subsequent Cavalier drama.

Lodowick Carlell (1602-75), the next of our courtly dramatists, had a greater flair for literature than Montague, and honored the theatre not with one dully resonant salute but with a fairly continuous volley. Lodowick[7] was the son of one of King James's huntsmen, of a family swept to Westminster from the border regions of Brydekirk in the wake of the Stuart accession. He was a nimble and versatile courtier. By 1629 he was established as gentleman of the bows to the Queen and groom of the privy-chamber to both their majesties. From 1629 on, he was receiving from the Queen £60 as a groom, £61, 10s. as master of the bows and stringhounds.[8] In September, 1635, he became gentleman of the bows in ordinary to the King,[9] and was granted £85, 5s. yearly for "good and faithful service heretofore done unto us and here after to be done."[10] Besides his annuities, he drew from the Lord Chamberlain his costly raiment as groom of the chamber, his satin gown, his velvet doublet and coats, of green cloth and marble cloth, lined with silk and trimmed with fur;[11] and as master of the bows and stringhounds, his standard and "barehide," and gold-thread and silk and leather leashes.[12] How cosily he warmed his niche amidst the silken splendors of Whitehall, and how strangely he contrasts with Thomas Carlyle, later product of the family of Brydekirk! He governed hounds and wrote plays for his Queen. His prologues and epilogues are eloquent of his kingly and queenly inspiration, and at the Restoration, in returning to drama with a translation from Corneille, he tells how the work had taken birth at Denmark house because her Majesty "loves plays of that kind . . . my most gracious Mistress whom I have so long serv'd, and in former Plays not displeas'd."[13] Drama was his pastime, the hunt his honorable vocation:

> This Author hunts, and hawks, and feeds his deer,
> Not some, but most fair days throughout the year.
> Such rude, dull, heavy scenes expect you then,
> As after suppers vapours from his pen . . .[14]

Rude scenes! What kind of huntsman was this? one puzzles in wandering through these plays—dim, faintly scented corridors hung with faded tapestry that might have been designed by some fanciful child. He was a small Caroline courtier, docile and romantic, dedicated to "good and faithful service," as unreal to us now in his marble coat checking the string hounds on their silken leashes as one of the characters in his own plays. He was not soft—lest we mistake the nature of these courtiers; appointed one of the keepers of Richmond Park he was shrewd enough and capable enough to retain the position in the Interregnum, and at the Restoration he regained court subsidies and wrested from life a comfortable old age.

In 1629 was published, hesitantly and with assurances from both author and printer that it had been tossed off as a gentleman's whim, *The Deserving Favorite* "as it was lately acted before the King's Majestie, and since publikely at the Black-friers . . ." The story tells of the maiden Clarinda and her rival lovers: Lysander, son of an exile; and the "deserving favorite," who is a Duke and kinsman of the King. Lysander tries to blacken his own character so that Clarinda may choose the more fortunate suitor, but her constancy equals his magnanimity. Soon Lysander's own constancy is tested, for the King's lovely sister falls in love with him while secretly tending the wounds which he has received in a duel with the Duke. When his whereabouts is betrayed by Jacomo, lustful villain of the tale, and he is about to be executed, for slaying the Duke, that gallant rival reappears alive, saves him, and dissolves their rivalry by revealing him to be Clarinda's brother. Now though Lysander and Clarinda may not wed each other, they are both provided with mates of the royal blood; and their exiled father, who proves to be no other than the mysterious hermit who has coöperated with the Duke in unraveling their twisted fates, is restored to the King's good grace.

This play is at once one of Carlell's better efforts and his nearest approach to Fletcherian tragicomedy. It is diffuse and complex, but less so than his later plays, and the language is adequate in its ornate and mellifluous fashion despite the laxity of the blank verse. Since it preceded *The Shepherd's Paradise,* it is practically free from "Platonic" philosophizing; yet its story materials,[15] the chivalrous rivals, the exile returned in disguise, the adversary restored to life, the lover proved his sweetheart's brother with happy consequences, form the pattern of later Cavalier drama; and Carlell shares with Montague what honor there is in establishing the new mode.

This courtier's essays in drama were casual and sporadic. We hear of no successor to *The Deserving Favorite* until 1634, when Mildmay records in his diary having seen *The Spartan Ladies* performed.[16] This title appears in the *Stationers' Register,* September 4, 1646, in an advertisement published with Middleton's *More Dissemblers besides Women,* 1657, and in a list of plays belonging to the King's Men in 1669,[17] but no copy survives and there is nothing to indicate the nature of the play except its feministic title.

Carlell's next play that can be dated, *Arviragus and Philicia,* displays Cavalier drama in its accomplished form, including the impregnation of Montaguean *préciosité.* It is almost wholly in undisguised prose, and its length alone is reminiscent of the romances. The work is divided into two parts, each of five acts, and with no suggestion as in older serial drama of mutual independence of parts. It was acted at the Cockpit in Whitehall, April 18 and 19, and at Hampton Court, December 26 and 27, 1636.[18] Other performances at court and at the Blackfriars are recorded in this year,[19] and in 1672 the play was revived at Lincoln's Inn Fields with a new prologue by Dryden—alone, perhaps, of Carlell's plays to appear on a Restoration stage.

The plot is too ramified to be told in detail. The time is some ancient age, heroic but sophisticated, and the place is Geoffrey of Monmouth's British Isles with an atmosphere suspiciously akin to that of the helter-skelter lands of Greek romance. The King of Britain has slain the King of "Pictland," and has reared the Pictish Prince Arviragus with his own children, Guimantes and Philicia. Arviragus has become a conqueror for Britain and has fallen in love with Philicia, but he insists at last upon his natal right to rule over Pictland. The British King and Prince are as bad and fraudulent as the British Princess and Arviragus are good and highminded, and hatred leads to intrigues, intrigues to open conflicts, until there is a series of military operations so complicated by baseness on one side and chivalry on the other that it is impossible to distinguish victories from defeats. The actions of Arviragus are always restrained by his refusal to follow one step with its logical successor,

and Philicia is fettered by the conflict of duty to her father with love
for his opponent. Little is accomplished at the end of Part One except
the assassination of the King of Britain by one of his own villains. In
Part Two a new force enters the play. The Danes invade the island,
led by Queen Cartander, who captures Arviragus, plans to sacrifice
him to the gods, but falls in love with him instead and makes him her
general. Philicia joins Arviragus, disguised as the inevitable page, and
jealousy is added to the complex passions of Cartander, so that her
impulses and actions become utterly vertiginous. Throughout the story
Arviragus has been squired by a faithful friend, Guiderius, who has a
lovely sister Artemia. A lucky circumstance! for Cartander finally con-
tents herself with Guiderius, her captive's "other half," and Guimantes,
who has become a reformed character upon succeeding to the British
throne, makes honorable proposals to Artemia. Thus the way is cleared
for Arviragus to wed Philicia, and three weddings unite Britain, Denmark, and Pictland in a beautiful amity.

If this synopsis seems complex, the reader may be thankful that he
has been spared the involved military tactics, the trafficking with witch-
craft and murderous enterprise on the part of the villain Adrastus, the
divided loyalty of Guiderius's father Eugenius, the tests of love and
fidelity practiced by Guiderius and others upon Philicia, the claims of
Cartander's former lover Oswald, and a host of minor episodes and
complications. The play is a congeries of romantic accidents, all suf-
fused with heroic gallantry and diaphanous sentiment. Both Arviragus
and Philicia are so sensitive that they are difficult of approach. They
meet friend and enemy alike with injured sensibilities, insulted honor,
self-righteous loquacity—torrents of chop-logic. Arviragus especially,
for all his indubitable (though strangely inoperative) military prowess,
is a sensitive plant. Note in the following scenes from Part II, Act I,
which will furnish a sample of Carlell's dialogue, how this hero detects
a taint in each succeeding speech of Guiderius, whose only offence has
been to offer his life for his friend by pretending to be the first captive
of the Danes.

Arviragus. But if it shall appear you have done this slily, usurp
upon my right as being first if not as soon a prisoner, the breach upon
your part will show like arrogance, I having more years practic'd the
ways of death with greater frequency to arm me for the encounter.
Had you (as I did once suspect) attempted to supplant me in Philicia's
love, from her perfection I would sooner find excuses than for this
intrusion; her falsehood could not taint my honor, but here in this
rivalry for death, if it be due, to magnify a seeming friendship you
struck in me the brand of coward, so yielding up to chance or policy
that little fame that I have purchast by my loss of blood.

Guiderius. O speak not this, Sir! Your pure fame is mounted to a height that slander cannot reach.

Arviragus. 'Tis just I now suspect your friendship, that dare injure truth. Fame that depends upon the breath of man can ne'er be freed from its Creator; all that we can do to keep it pure is that the ingredients be made up of truth, and then the Gods approve of our ambition. That sacred friendship be not injured, I am resolved if you were taken prisoner first to glory in that confidence which you shall show in death, and after, if it grows within my power, revenge it to the full.

Guiderius. Not on the Queen?

Arviragus. That as you please. If I be found the proper sacrifice—.

Guiderius. You! O, Sir, remember Philicia. You must not think of dying.

Arviragus. No?—Yes, young man, and when I think upon Philicia, I am more engaged the gods destroy not their own ordinances, nor bring us unto glory or to joy but by the ways of virtue. Honor they have appointed for the soul of all men's actions, and when I fail in that, can they in justice grant me the continuance of so great a blessing as Philicia's love? . . .

Not all of *Arviragus and Philicia* is so densely ethical. This style is more characteristic of the second part with its difficult reconciliations. Part One is not lacking in action ingeniously developed, lively dialogue, variety, suspense, and scenes of theatrical effectiveness. But throughout the material is bizarre, and the place might as well be the Bithynia, Sicily, or Sardinia more usual in Cavalier plays. The author hints at a source in his epilogue to Part One, and the *Historia Regum Britanniæ* was evidently in his mind. But the relation of the play to the *Historia* is superficial. It would be to lose the advantage of our preliminary treatment of sources if we paused to note here the points of contact between *Arviragus and Philicia* and the *Æthiopica.* Suffice it to say that for everything not a stock device of tragicomedy, we need look no further than to Heliodorous and D'Urfé, or other breeders in their line, as sire and dame. The play is such a composite, such an elegant medley of gallantry, passion, and politeness that it is no wonder that at court it was "hugely liked of everyone."[20]

Since Carlell's plays, like those of other courtiers, seem to have required no licensing, it is difficult to date them when no specific performances are recorded. In 1657 "Two New Plays," *The Fool Would be a Favorite* and *Osmond the Great Turk,* were published "as they have often been acted by the Queen's Majesty's Servants with great applause." Since the company of this name came into existence in October, 1637, and since in 1638 the prologue to Part Two of *The Passionate Lovers* proclaims that Carlell will write plays no more, one might by a literal interpretation of the evidence place these plays in the season of 1637-38. However, the company of the title page might possibly be a misnomer for Queen Henrietta's Men, established in 1625, or Carlell might have changed his mind about writing no more, so it is unwise to be dogmatic in dating these plays. It seems unlikely that the play "Osmond the Great Turk," recently discovered to have been licensed September 6, 1622, by Sir John Astley after he had "refused to allow it at first"[21] was identical with Carlell's play despite its identical title. The prefatory material to *The Deserving Favorite* seems to stamp that as a first play, and in Carlell's *Osmond* there seems to be nothing that would evoke the prohibition of the censor. Carlell may have re-worked the *Osmond* of 1622, in the writing of which, though he was then a youth of twenty, it must be conceded as possible that he had a hand.

Of the two plays in question *The Fool Would be a Favorite* has the lesser interest. Alone of Carlell's plays it descends to a comic underplot, which concerns the tricks played upon the yeoman Gudgeon by the courtiers with whom he is ambitious to mingle, and which gives the play its title. The main plot is a romance of love. Philanthus is such an embodiment of the grand passion that he dare defy the edict "They do not love at all, that can love twice," and woos successively Miranthe, Aurelia, and Lucinda; after many travails and considerable bloodshed, he sacrifices Lucinda to the embraces of his friend Agenor, and con-tents himself with the highly temperamental Aurelia—a consummation staged, not inappropriately, at the tomb where this hero is supposed to be dead and buried. The play is full of the themes and sentiments common to Cavalier drama, and is really such a loosely articulated organism as will permit the maximum of scenes in which lovers sep-arated by honor, etiquette, and misunderstanding, may voice passionate love plaints, analyze themselves and others, and threaten self-slaughter at the least excuse.

Osmond the Great Turk has more individuality than most of Car-lell's plays. It is a tragic tale of Osmond's fidelity to Melcoshus, grim Emperor of Tartary. He sacrifices his fair Christian captive, Despina, whom he loves and who loves him, to the bed of his emperor. When the latter finally slays Despina, as he has already slain his own son, because he must remain the ruthless and inviolable leader of warriors, Osmond checks a momentary impulse to vengeance and dies at the side of his leader in repulsing the swords of traitors. This story, the back-ground for which may have been furnished by Knolles's popular *His-tory of the Turks,* is not the usual one of Cavalier drama: as a rule love and duty are reconciled; here love is lost and duty wins a voluble Pyrrhic victory. On the other hand the play is as full of minor romantic intrigue, and, despite its high heroic tone, almost as full of sentimentality and ethical cant as the other plays of Carlell and his group. When Osmond surrenders Despina to the Emperor, he indulges in the following speech:

Pardon, dread Sir, that man who shall affirm he hath an humbler soul towards great Melcoshus than Osmond, I dare defy him to the trial with his sword or faithfullness, which makes me, Sir, assure you you are in danger of your liberty. See not her face, for 'tis a woman, so far I'll warn you, a weeping one, until you do withal consider— She's your slave's slave (I mean my prisoner); were she less worthy she had been my mistress, but being thus excellent who can deserve to look on her but you? Let her be covered still, for if I draw this veil, you then must yield, the thought of all your glories laid aside, and in her heavenly eyes read your captivity.[22]

Osmond remains firm in the face of Despina's lingering tenderness for him:

Despina. Osmond, how e're the Emperor in my command o're him makes all the empire subject to my will; yet if you kneel I must not be exempt, for well you know I love you.
Osmond. I fear—.
Despina. Yet not as heretofore; 'tis now a sisterly affection.
Osmond. Thanks heaven![23]

In his impassioned swan song, Osmond affirms that his fidelity to the Emperor will extend into the next world,

. . . So, methinks, I see Despina stand ready to embrace me, but for Melcoshus' sake, even there again I will refuse her.

Those who have accused Fletcher of subservience to the theory of divine right of kings should read this play. Melcoshus is sacrosanct in all his bloody tyranny, fit idol for the worship of heroes, converting Osmond to belief in the justice of his actions by the most amazing dialectal perversions of logic and ethics. His barbaric splendor reminds us of Davenant's gentler Solyman the Magnificent, and in general this play and its characters take a long stride towards the heroic dramas of a later day.

In the play which he resolved would be his last, *The Passionate Lovers,* Carlell produced another ten-act romance like *Arviragus and Philicia.* Since the first part was acted alone at Somerset House, July 10, 1638,[24] it seems likely that the second part was not then completed, for the two are continuous. On the eighteenth and twentieth of December of this year the two parts were acted successively at Whitehall, with the second part repeated on the twenty-seventh.[25] The title-page informs us also of performances at Blackfriars. King Charles must be held responsible along with Carlell for the story which follows.[26]

Agenor, son of the King of Burgony, decides for state reasons to conceal his love for his cousin Clorinda, and to have his younger brother, Clarimant, pretend to woo her. But Clarimant begins to love in earnest, and Agenor's troubles are increased by the plotter, Cleon, who also loves Clorinda and is ambitious to wrest the succession from the true heir to the throne. Driven by conspiracies to escape from his own realm, Agenor takes refuge in neighboring Neustrea, where he weds under peculiar circumstances the Princess Austella. Clorinda follows him hither in the ill-chosen company of Cleon, and a rape is narrowly averted when Agenor comes upon them during a hunt. Learning that her savior and erstwhile lover is married, Clorinda asks to meet his wife, preserving meanwhile her present male disguise. This is no unreasonable request in a romance, nor one which could readily be refused. Clarimant now reappears on the scene as acting ruler of Burgony in the decease of the father and absence of the elder brother. He relieves himself of some obscure grievance against Neustrea by enforcing subjection, proclaims his brother King of Burgony, then offers to fight him for deserting Clorinda, all in rapid succession. Clorinda, still in disguise, averts the duel, and Agenor and Austella are happily reunited. In Part Two, Cleon, who had apparently been slain in Part One, reappears as lively and villainous as ever. The business of this second part is obviously to unite Clarimant and Clorinda in marriage; but this joyous consummation is delayed not only by Cleon's renewed villainies, but by Clorinda's vows of love to Agenor (whose marriage would render them no longer binding to any but a *précieuse* princess), by her designs to wed Clarimant to Austella's younger sister Olinda, by the jealousy which her male disguise occasions Olinda's suitor, the Prince of Aquitain, and by the latter's becoming enamored of her when she proves no man but a beautiful woman. The various villains of the piece unite forces and enlist the aid of a "Druid" or shyster hermit; Clarimant and Clorinda are captured and taken to sea where the latter is given her choice of death or marriage to Aquitain— a choice complicated by her new vow to wed no other if she weds not Clarimant; the ship burns, Agenor comes to the rescue and slays Aquitain; Cleon and his fellow villains perish in the flames, and Clorinda consents to marry Clarimant—as she might as well have done many long acts before.

This play, more than *Arviragus and Philicia*, is not drama but a romance acted out. We are informed casually during its peripatetic course that the King of Burgony has died, that the identity of Clorinda is now known, and so on. There is no perceptible structure, and no climax, unless we admit each new scene to be a climax. Running parallel with the physical action, the disguisings, the wars, duels, fire, etc., and largely unrelated to this action, is another stream of interest: the ethical and sentimental emotions of the characters. With these inner conflicts we never really come to grips, for although there is a great deal of talk about them, they are dissolved, whenever a decision is threatened, by some spectacular new physical development—an invasion, kidnapping, or the like. While there is plenty of action and the characters are often battered and bleeding, the basic situation, if such it can be called, is curiously static throughout—the delayed decision of certain obviously eligible couples to make a match of it. The artificiality of this delay, the general unreality of the conflict, results from the standardized nature of the protagonists. They are all so uniformly noble that they duplicate each other, and distinctions among them and conflicts between them can only result from accidents superimposed by the author—imbecile villainies by outsiders, misunderstandings, the binding nature of unreasonable vows. Here is negation of all reality, a dream world in the Antipodes; in moments of impatience one wonders what mind bemused could have felt at home in this phantasmagoria.

In the year 1664 Carlell, an elderly man now, responded to the impulse of an awakening dramatic era and to the return of Henrietta to England by translating Corneille's *Heraclius* into respectable though somewhat wooden heroic couplets. The work is to his credit (though, as he tells us with some pique, it was refused by the players), for some of the other Cavaliers, such as Montague and Killigrew, could not achieve meter of any kind. This is Carlell's only Restoration play, *Two Fools Well Met* having been assigned to him by Downes[27] in confusion of this writer with James Carlisle. His contribution to drama consists of those courtly plays which have been described. Much that has been said of them might apply as well to plays by other authors of the courtier group. It is difficult to epitomize Carlell otherwise than negatively, to point in him to any distinctive qualities or "notes." If he can be said to have any favorite theme among the common romantic stock, it is that of fidelity of noble man to royal master; if his language, alternating between verbose prose and prose-like verse, can be said to have any outstanding quality besides a chaotic syntax, it is an indescribable langour which his own epithet "vapours" does not ill describe. Except for Montague, he is the most fibreless of the Cavalier writers.

His interest now is purely historical; his plays call for silence, or for compassion.

Despite his traffic with drama, Carlell was an old-fashioned courtier governing his life with a decorum befitting his elegant calling. Other courtly dramatists were younger men, modelled upon a newer ideal of gallantry, matching more nearly the popular conception of the Cavalier. In this younger set moved Thomas Killigrew (1612-83)[28] who has become, not with entire justice, traditional as a roisterer and roué. Killigrew belonged to a somewhat improvident younger branch of an old Cornish family, which ever since the accession of Elizabeth had been filling minor places in the court. His father was vice-chamberlain to Queen Henrietta Maria, and as a young boy Thomas became a court page, to the detriment of his formal education as well, perhaps, as to a saner modelling of his character. He was handsome, witty, volatile; and after travels abroad, he returned to the court, wedded a maid of honor, and proceeded to immerse himself in debts by his extravagance as a man of fashion. Almost as prompt an exile as Montague, he served severally the Stuarts on the continent, as fiscal agent, amateur diplomatist, and groom of the chamber, until he managed to repair his fortunes in the Low Countries by a fairly remunerative second marriage. At the Restoration he returned to England, where he secured a patent as manager of the King's Players and many royal favors besides, until age and infirmities debarred him from his beloved rôle of man of affairs and merry wag. In old age he was estranged from all his family save the ne'er-do-well son of his first wife, his necessities relieved only fitfully by his royal master Charles II. Killigrew was a coarse and theatrical swaggerer, none too trustworthy either in his conversation or his claims upon the treasury, but he had his romantic ideals and personal loyalties, and lived an active enterprising life in no wise degraded for all his inveterate yearning to cut a dashing figure. Like other gallants of his generation, he was a more wholesome personality than the wits and beaux of the Restoration, who were softer and more cynical if no more debauched than their Cavalier elders.

One of Killigrew's sisters, as well as his fiancée, acted a part in *The Shepherd's Paradise,* and he himself was an actor in court theatricals; this hobby, together with a craving to be in the mode, and a friendship with Walter Montague, no doubt led him to authorship. The plays with which we are concerned chiefly here, *The Prisoners, Claricilla* and *The Princess,* were written just before and during a journey with Montague into France and Italy during the winter of 1635-36, and were acted by the Queen's Company at the Phœnix before plague closed the theatres in May, 1636.[29] *Claricilla* was revived in a clandestine performance of 1653, and several times during the Restoration (as was *The Princess* also on one lamentable occasion) by a playhouse manager not averse from passing his own wares on somewhat reluctant audiences.

Killigrew's plays are entertaining for their sheer bravura and unabashed excess. Here we have Cavalier drama with its heroic tones unmuted by restraint. The first of them, *The Prisoners*, tells of two noble youths, Hipparchus and Pausanes, who rebel against their pirate chieftain, Gallippus, to prevent the ravishing of Lysimella, sister of the King of Sicily, to whom they surrender themselves as prisoners. Pausanes falls in love with Lysimella, and she is not unaffected, despite her chagrin at weakness for a nameless wanderer. When the two prisoners participate in a Sicilian attack upon Sardinia, the enemy proves to be ruled by two lovely maidens, Eucratia and Leucanthe. Hipparchus falls in love with one of these, the King of Sicily with the other. Lysimella, following Pausanes to the front, is kidnapped by Gallippus, who thus climaxes a series of spectacular villainies. (We learn, by the way, that he has been persecuting her ever since Pausanes was a child, so she must be a woman of fairly advanced years.) There follow pursuit, storm, shipwreck, the death of Gallippus, and the discovery that the two prisoners are Sardinian princes stolen by the pirate as babes. They are, of course, the brothers respectively of Eucratia and Leucanthe, so that in the usual fashion a triple marriage is arranged among the three sets of brothers and sisters, linking Sicily and Sardinia in a marital alliance well-nigh indissoluble.

The scene of *Claricilla* is again an indeterminate Sicily. Claricilla, daughter of the true King, is rescued from a usurper largely through the prowess of her cousin Melintus, who for some obscure reason is serving her father in disguise. The love of this pair is opposed by the restored King, who has his own choice for her hand, and by the King's lustful favorite Seleucus. Melintus is considerably battered in body, reputation, and, as he tremulously conceives, in *honor*, by the forces pitted against him, but he finds unexpected allies in a friendly band of pirates with whom his brother Philemon is attached as a slave incognito. Seleucus is revealed to the King of Sicily in his true colors and the obstacles are removed to the marriage of Melintus and Claricilla— but not before Philemon has been revealed also as a lover of Claricilla but heroically willing to relinquish her to his friend and brother.

In *The Princess* there are more crossed loves, more wars, more pirates, more Sicilians. Rome has conquered Sicily, but since there is a Roman Prince and Princess, Virgilius and Sophia, and a Sicilian Prince and Princess, Facertes and Cicilia, the experienced reader draws immediate comfort from the prospect of another politico-matrimonial amnesty.

Before such an amnesty may occur, however, both princesses are captured by pirates, Cicilia must be rescued from a Neapolitan slave-mart by Virgilius and Facertes (fast friends despite their national enmity), and Sophia must withstand the ardent wooing of the pirate leader Cilius. After all have been properly jostled through many militant encounters up and down many storm-racked coasts, they are brought miraculously together for a climactic conflict followed by a climactic reconciliation. Cilius proves to be no true pirate at all, but another Sicilian Prince, long lost brother of Facertes and Cicilia. He relinquishes Sophia in deference to his brother's claims, and while sacrifices are in order, ethical Cicilia forgives her country's wounds and consents to wed Virgilius. Even the pirates seem ready to become good citizens.

Reviewed thus briefly these plays seem pretty much alike—as indeed they are in their main ingredients—, yet each has its own chaotic diversity of incidents and intrigues. All are involved, mysterious, full of surprises—perfect examples of the dramatic type defined in a preceding chapter. The characters are loquacious and sensitive, with minds thoroughly addled by the doctrines of the salons, yet Killigrew was most interested after all in plot, action, adventure, and high heroism. Utterly unselfconscious, he disguises his handsome personages by clapping black patches over their eyes, and displays their valour by puncturing them with wounds and sustaining their heroism during vast drainage of blood. Oddly enough we can perceive through the ludicrousness of all this his genuine ability. He is *naïf* and fantastic, but not dull. His scenes at times have verve, and his gusty rhetoric vivacity and color. Inexperienced as a writer and unschooled save by romance-reading and the social intercourse of the court, he relied on a native fluency which never failed.

Like other cavalier plays Killigrew's are inaccessible, and despite the limitations of space a brief sample must be quoted. There follows a fragment of one of the numerous discovery scenes, that in *Claricilla* where Melintus finds his brother Philemon a slave in the pirate band of Manlius. The reader may wish to exercise himself by trying to restore these speeches to the blank verse of the first edition:

Melintus. To what strange fate am I reserv'd, or by what sin have I pull'd down this curse of a general hate upon me that all paths I tread are arm'd against me? Ha! more enemies? Nay then, Melintus, yield, for 'tis visible thou war'st with heaven. (He spies 'em.)

Manlius. What art thou that with such pains hast to this place hunted thy ruin, and thus with injurious wounds in the dead of night awak'd our anger?

Melintus. Prithee go forward with thy injury; such another charm will call back my anger and then I shall be safe, for it hath ever yet been prosperous though that success made me unfortunate.

Manlius. Leave thus vaingloriously to urge your former success, for 'twill be no ground now to build a future conquest on. And therefore yield thy sword, and quickly, before I command it and thy head. Know my power here rules even thy fate.

Melintus. Yield my Sword? By what other privileges do I hold my life among my enemies? Prithee look upon me, and if thou canst read these characters, they'll tell thee I was not born to yield, and though thou art the glorious master of the sport, and I, unfortunate by a cross fate, am hunted into the toil where danger on all sides begirt my innocence, yet with the lion I dare be angry with my bonds, and although I may become thy prey, yet I will not be thy scorn.

[At this point Manlius orders the slave Philemon to seize Melintus, but the slave recognizes Melintus as his brother, joins forces with him, and the two vanquish the pirates.]

Manlius. My wonder waits upon this fellow's acts.

Melintus. What art thou that thus in less than a man hides more than a god?

Philemon. What am I? A soul with her old clothes on, a slave with wounds and crosses torn; and yet in better fortunes I have known your face.

Melintus. If thou hast mercy in thee, tell me who thou art.

Philemon. Mark me well, dost thou not see thyself here? Not yet? (He weeps.) Now I am sure thou do'st in these crystal drops; friendship will guide Melintus to know Philemon.

Melintus. Philemon! Oh ye gods! New weights to sink me!

Philemon. Oh! 'tis a powerful rod that Melintus' friendship strikes with. A thousand miseries have smote upon this rock, but never any that made water issue through till now.

Melintus. Oh Philemon, Philemon, what cannot friendship do? 'Tis from her living springs this dew falls.

Manlius. Melintus and Philemon! What change hath begot this misery? (He kneels to Melintus and Philemon.) Oh noble Princes, upon my knees I beg, when your surprised joys are over, you'll shower a pardon upon unfortunate Manlius.[30]

It may be remarked by the way that Killigrew's romances, providing his rakish tendencies had early buds, are a tribute to the platonic fashion at court—they are tremendously elevated. This is not true of his comedies, written under other than courtly influences; in fact these, *The Parson's Wedding, c.* 1641, and *Thomaso, or The Wanderer,* 1654, present a truly startling contrast. His additional romantic plays, loyally produced as closet drama during the Commonwealth period, may be disposed of briefly.

The Pilgrim, possibly written for the strolling players serving Prince Charles in Paris in 1646, is a tragedy, and more nearly approaches the Fletcherian type of drama than Killigrew's other works. In fact its theme is much like that of Shirley's *The Politician*. It turns upon the discovery by Prince Cosmo that his mother, Julia, is an adultress and a traitor to her magnanimous second husband, the Duke of Milan; and the play ends with the son unknowingly slaying his own father, and the mother unknowingly slaying her own son. Corrupt elders are contrasted with their virtuous children, the story developing love affairs between the son and daughter of Julia, and the son and daughter of Milan, noble passions harrowed by fate from the beginning and predestined to end in sorrow. From the absolute standard, if one should venture to apply such to Killigrew's work, *The Pilgrim* is his best play with the possible exception of *The Parson's Wedding*. Though it is needlessly complicated, often ill-adapted for acting, and too extravagantly emotional, it contains scenes effectively developed and passages of sincere feeling.

When our dramatist was sent as Royalist ambassador to the states of northern Italy, he occupied his unlimited leisure by composing two huge dramatic romances, *Cicilia and Clorinda* and *Bellamira her Dream*, each in ten acts after the manner of Carlell, and each a perfect depository for all the plot materials, heroics, and sentiments of the Cavalier mode. These surpass in their extravagance anything else in the tradition. In *Cicilia and Clorinda*, 1649-50, the background is the conquest of Savoy by the Romans. Two noble Savoyards, Amadeo and his sister Clorinda, provoke a series of passionate love rivalries when they go to conclude a peace with their enemies. It appears that they shall be matched with Otho and Cicilia, the children of the Roman governor; but Manlius, a Roman general, Lucius, his feverishly temperamental brother, and Orante, a degenerate Lombard lord, have each looked upon Cicilia and Clorinda with the eye of desire, honorable and otherwise; and the resulting tangle of conflicts, the alarms and excursions, are a miracle to contemplate. Pages would be necessary if one were to retell this story in detail; suffice it to say that lustful Orante is slain at last; a third heroine is developed as a mate for Manlius; and the rest are paired off, only Amadeo being left unmated—his matchless excellences of character being left him as consolation for his lonely state.

If such is possible, *Bellamira her Dream*, 1650-52, is even more involved and more fantastic than its companion. An old fratricidal war has placed on the throne of Sicily the brother of the true king. This usurper has two noble children, Leopoldo and Bellamira; while in the neighboring wood there dwell as foresters (unaware of their true identity) the two children of the former king, under the names Pollidor and Phillora. The object of the story, of course, is to unite in marriage these pairs of royal cousins. A civil war, the intrusion into the realm of Spanish Prince Almanzor, and the passion of the noble Sicilian Palantus for Bellamira are merely the beginning of the sequence of aids and obstacles to this consummation. Bellamira falls in love with Pollidor by seeing his image in a dream, and Pollidor with Bellamira by looking upon her picture,—circumstances giving the play its subsidiary title, *The Love of Shadows*. Hurdling a universal history of romantic adventures, let us be content to add that the appropriate matches are made at last, and peace is restored to Sicily. Thomas Killigrew wrote these two plays *for his own amusement!* No better illustration could be offered of a Cavalier's predilections when in serious or sentimental mood.

More famous than Killigrew among Cavalier writers are Carew, Denham, Lovelace, and Suckling, all of whom had some contact with drama. Carew's masque, *Cœlum Britannicum*, has already been mentioned; and Denham's *The Sophy*, written when he was not yet of the courtly circle and remained uninfluenced by courtly tastes, belongs to the next chapter. The plays of Richard Lovelace (1618-58) have not survived. It is enlightening to note how this handsome and congenial, however futile, youth was garnered in by the feminine circle at court. He was at Oxford during the progress thither of Charles and Henrietta in 1636, and a great lady in the Queen's retinue, susceptible to his charm, secured for him from Laud an expeditious M.A.[31] Whereupon he left the university to shine with mild luminosity at court. He served in the two expeditions against Scotland, the so-called Bishops Wars, out of which experience issued a tragedy, *The Soldier*, just as out of his student career had issued a comedy, *The Scholar*, acted at Gloucester Hall in 1634 and afterward at the Salisbury Court theatre.[32] The later of these plays must have been of the type we are reviewing, perhaps resembling Suckling's *Brennoralt, or The Discontented Colonel*, also an outgrowth of experience in the Bishops Wars. Probably little has been lost by the extinction of Lovelace's plays, their quality doubtless conforming with that of the body of his works rather than of "Althea" and "Lucasta," but they would have been interesting for an amplification of his plaintive, autobiographical vein.

Usually bracketed with Lovelace, though his superior in literary gift, is Sir John Suckling (1609-42)—almost a symbol of the Cavalier legend. Modern research has been remiss in attention to Suckling's life, but its main outline is well known and need only be suggested here.[33] Son of an able official who had risen from master of requests and comptroller in the royal household to become secretary of state and privy-councillor, feathering his nest in the process, young Suckling concluded an easy sojourn at Cambridge and Gray's Inn to find himself heir to a rich estate. After travels abroad, diversified by volunteer service in the army of Gustavus Adolphus, he returned to London to plunge into the festivities of town and court. He strove for distinction as a wit, a town rake, a reckless gambler. His wealth like his energies was expended lavishly. Garrard, in reporting how he and his fellow privy-chamber-man, William Berkeley, had each written a play, tells how Suckling's "cost three or four hundred pounds setting out, eight or ten suits of new cloaths he gave the Players; an unheard of prodigality."[34] To the King's cause in the Bishops Wars he donated a troop of one hundred tall men mounted on superb steeds and wearing uniforms of white and carnation silk—a company beautiful to look upon, but justifying, when in action with Suckling at its head, contemporary opinion that it was more fitted for pageantry than warfare. The concluding extravagance in Sir John's life was his *opera-bouffe* part in the royalist plot of 1641 to bring armed force to bear on Parliament—a fiasco followed by his flight to the continent, rapid dissolution of an overtaxed constitution, and death reputedly by his own hand. Suckling, for all the scintillant dash of his verse and the glamour of his myth, was a pathetic figure. His reputation for gallantry was largely posthumous, contemporaries estimating him as a coxcomb. Although he prided himself on his adventurousness and athleticism, his frail physique made him submit on one occasion to a public beating by Sir John Digby. One so percep-tive might have found a higher rôle than that of the *enfant terrible;* it is a misfortune for literature that he chose to shine as a gallant and lived in a period of turmoil. We glimpse the obscured side of his char-acter in his fondness for the company not of sparks alone but also of poets and philosophers, and of his tendency to vary the merriment of a summer excursion by taking along a cartload of books. Drawn into a different circle, he might have denied us the colorful story of his career but left more such sensitive poetry as "A Ballad of a Wedding"—perhaps, also, some better plays.

Suckling's first play, *Aglaura,* was written as a tragedy in the winter of 1637 and transformed to tragicomedy by carpentry upon the ending in the spring of 1638,[35] so that a reversible fifth act would admit of productions in either the revised or "the tragicall way." It was produced with a sumptuousness unjustified by its quality, and was then printed in folio—a format which in the opinion of honest Brome was entirely too commodious for it.[36] The scene is a corrupt court where the King lusts after his son's sweetheart and the Queen lusts after her husband's brother. A purer love affair is that between Prince Thersames and Aglaura, chorused by the pallid enamourment of the maiden Orithie for Thersames, and of Semanthe for Aglaura's brother Zorames. Zorames, serving incognito in the King's guard, has been a lover of the Queen. The whole is a nebula of love-affairs, noble and debased, swirling in a vortex of personal and political intrigues. The King is slain at last by assassins in mistake for his son and rival, Thersames, while Thersames is slain by Aglaura in mistake for the King. Aglaura dies of grief, Zorames is poisoned by the Queen, and the Queen is dispatched by Zorames's faithful servitor. "What have we here? a churchyard?" sapiently observes a minor character in contemplating the death of seven major personages among incidental casualties. The few survivors go off to drown themselves in tears.

A catastrophe so far-reaching might at least have had the virtue of finality, but such was not to be. Suckling, as dauntless resurrectionist, proceeded to make all the encounters of the fifth act result not in deaths, but in curable wounds. With a cool,

'Tis strange, perchance you'll think, that she that died
At Christmas should at Easter be a bride . . . ,

he displayed how the King and Queen became reformed characters, and how the pairs of young lovers were happily united in marriage. Suckling's dramatic fragment of doubtful date, *The Sad One*, first printed in the third edition of *Fragmenta Aurea*, contains plot materials identical with those of *Aglaura*, but its several excellent scenes and its interesting dialogue suggests that it might have proved a better play.

Aglaura resembles typical Cavalier drama less than Fletcherian tragedy of court intrigue, with greater excesses and complications and a more fetid and unwholesome atmosphere. Some of D'Urfé's influence is apparent in the platonic affections of the women of the play, and in the "anti-platonic" scoffings of one Orsames, who considers the new love "a mere trick to enhance the price of kisses," but this element is subsidiary and affects the major characters not at all. The play is amateurish and ill-conceived; its personages are so busy gaining material ends in love and politics; in planning murders, rebellions, rapes, or their circumvention, in dark tunnels under involved circumstances, that characters fail to emerge and emotional subtlety is brushed aside. The mother, father, and son whose desires conflict are mutually cold, indifferent to their relationship, and since there is no apparent compunction or sense of guilt, the consanquinity motif, through sheer carelessness of the author, is pointless and lacking in force. The speeches are strident, the scenes hysterically vigorous and often repulsive. The concluding carnage is less objectionable than the distorted sensuality of the characters, their sordid passions and insane words. Such a brutalized production makes one recognize the disinfectant function of true Cavalier drama; the courtiers were better off telling their elegant tales of discovered princelings than in working such unsavory variations on Jacobean tragedy.

In his subsequent plays Suckling wrote more in the manner of his fellow courtiers. *The Goblins,* which may be placed conjecturally between his two plays of known date, eschews lust and villainy in major characters. Orsabrin, storm-tossed to the shores of Francelia after captivity among pirates, lends aid to Samorat, whose suit to Sabrina is opposed by her brother's desire that she wed the ruling Prince. The two allies, after worsting Sabrina's brothers, are captured, rescued, re-captured, successively by authorities of the state and a kind of Robinhood fellowship of freebooters or "Goblins" who live underground and humorously mete out preëmptory justice by posing as "hell's wards." Orsabrin falls in love with Reginella, ward of the leading Goblin, and after narrow escape from a state execution, his and Samorat's guerilla courtship is rewarded when he proves to be the lost brother of the ruler, and the Goblins a band of political refugees from some old Francelian dissension.

The materials are those of the Greek school of romance, crossed, as we are reminded by mention in the text of Mendoza's *Querer por solo Querer,*[37] by Spanish drama of cloak and sword. The play is riotously full of action, its episodes following in mystifying succession through countless fragmentary scenes. Excess of ingenuity makes the story all but unintelligible despite the intended clarification of the conclusion. Yet there are some witty, some poetic lines. A gay atmosphere, notably where confessions are wrung from a poet and others by the ghostly impositions of the Goblins, reminds us less of tragicomedy than of a type of romantic comedy at that time all but extinct. No better in craftsmanship than *Aglaura,* it is a more enjoyable play.

Suckling's best play, *Brennoralt, or the Discontented Colonel,* can be dated with fair accuracy by an allusion to the treaty of Berwick and political sentiments inspired by its author's experience in the Bishops Wars. Like most Caroline courtiers, Suckling was impatient of the civil disturbances of the times; wise policy by Charles, he believed, would banish strife and leave the realm to peace and pleasure. The discontent of Brennoralt, though he is portrayed as a queller of Palatine rather than Scottish rebels, is Suckling's own. Brennoralt's belief that he could negotiate more shrewdly than his king does not impeach his infinite loyalty; in Act III he cries,

> Dost think, 'cause I am angry with
> The King and state sometimes, I am
> Fallen out with virtue and myself? Draw!

Brennoralt will be quoted in a later discussion of war plays, but its political allusions are purely incidental; its heroic-romantic unreality makes it kin with typical Cavalier drama as will appear with a brief résumé of the plot. Brennoralt, a large-souled warrior, loves Francelia, daughter of a rebel governor. Francelia is also loved by the gallant rebel Almerin, who in turn is loved by Iphigene, a woman serving as a man in the royal forces. Almerin slays Francelia in a fit of jealous rage provoked by Iphigene's politic attentions to her while still in male disguise, and Brennoralt slays Iphigene whom he mistakes as the assassin. All this takes place in the rebel fort at Menseck, which Brennoralt has stormed almost single-handed as proof positive of his heroic worthiness of Francelia. Having dispatched the women, the two men proceed to avenge their errors on each other. Almerin falls and Brennoralt, inappropriately, lives on—more tragically discontented than ever.

The play has the weaknesses inherent in a puerile plot and stereotyped characters, but it is redeemed in measure by felicity of language and a number of compelling scenes. It is more graceful than *Aglaura,* less disjointed than *The Goblins,* and is developed with exhilarating gusto. One of its curiosities is that Almerin reciprocates posthumously the passion of Iphigene, thus lending a sublime pathos to the concluding duel of the two heroes, for it appears now that each has slain the other's true love. A few speeches from this scene will illustrate Suckling's facile intensity:

Almerin

> The title of a kingdom is a trifle
> To our quarrel, sir. Know, by sad mistake
> I kill'd thy mistress, Brennoralt,
> And thou killd'st mine.

Brennoralt

> Thine?

Almerin

> Yes, that Iphigene,
> Though shown as man unto the world,
> Was woman, excellent woman!

Brennoralt

> I understand no riddles; guard thee. (Fight and pause.)

Almerin

O, could they now look down, and see
How we two strive, which first should give revenge,
They would forgive us something of the crime.
Hold! pr'ythee, give me leave
To satisfy a curiosity—
I never kissed my Iphigene as woman.

Brennoralt

Thou motion'st well, nor have I taken leave.
          [Each kisses his dead love.]
It keeps a sweetness yet, as 'stils from roses,
When the flowers are gone. (Rises.)

Almerin

Even so have two faint pilgrims, scorch'd with heat,
Unto some neighbour fountain stepp'd aside,
Kneel'd first, then laid their warm lips to the nymph,
And from her coldness took fresh life again,
As we do now.

Brennoralt

Let's on our journey if thou art refresh'd.

Almerin

Come, and if there be a place reserved
For height'ned spirits better than other,
May that which wearies first of ours have it.
          (Fight a good while; Almerin falls.)

Brennoralt

If I grow weary, laugh at me, that's all.

Almerin

Brave souls above, which will be, sure,
Inquisitive for news from earth,
Shall get no other but that thou art brave.[38]

Suckling was less the *précieux* than other courtly dramatists, and
was more willing to be bound by the exigencies of dramatic effectiveness. It was his consciousness of the splendor of earlier drama, and his
fear of serving up "cold meats,"[39] that made him rival his contemporaries in exoticism of story and treatment. What distinguishes his plays
from those of the other Cavalier dramatists is their occasional evidence
of his authentic gift of poetry. His blank verse is as lax as that of his
fellows, and he is normally as shrilly rhetorical as they, but now and
then he writes lines of the purest beauty—slipping a few fresh buds

into his garlands of artificial roses. The descriptions of his heroines will often have a detailed loveliness:

> Sweet as double violets, and wholesome
> As dying leaves of strawberries . . .
> Hair curling, and cover'd like buds of marjarom,
> Part tied in negligence, part loosely flowing—[40]

As we should expect, it is the physical beauty of woman that has most power to wrest from him true feeling in place of hollow eloquence, and sensuality mingles with his finest poetry. But he can also separate the two; in one scene of *Brennoralt* a roistering Cavalier frenzies his companions with a libidinous description; in another a lover looks upon his mistress and cries:

> Heavens! shall this fresh ornament
> Of the world, this precious loveliness
> Pass, with other common things, amongst
> The wastes of time? What pity 'twere!

Most amateurs of literature will prefer Suckling as he was, for he has woven a glittering thread into the pattern of English art, but we cannot evade the truth that he developed imperfectly, that he was spoiled by his times.

Suckling's plays, of all those of the Cavalier school, had the most successful stage career. All three were produced at Blackfriars before the closing of the theatres, and *Aglaura,* probably the others as well, was presented at court.[41] At the Restoration all three were successfully revived by the King's Men from 1661 at least until 1668, Pepys seeing each of them at least once, and *Brennoralt* four times.[42] *Aglaura* was acted in both versions, and the pathetic rôle of the heroine helped to win Kynaston his early reputation.[43]

Sir William Berkeley's *The Lost Lady* has a career parallel with that of *Aglaura.* Berkeley (1609-77) and Suckling made their dramatic debut at the same time in 1637,[44] and *The Lost Lady* was performed at Whitehall, March 26, 1638, one week before Suckling's play.[45] It, too, was published in folio, and was revived in the Restoration.[46] *Cornelia,* another play probably by Berkeley, has not survived. It failed on the Restoration stage, proving "to witty for the vulgar sort."[47] Although called a "New Play" at that time, June 1, 1662,[48] it was probably an unacted product of earlier days, unless we are to believe that its author returned to dramatic composition after an interval of twenty-five years and varied his routine as Governor of Virginia by shipping off a play for production in London. To biographical data already available about Berkeley—courtier, Cavalier, and after 1641 stubborn royalist colonial—may be added here that he was born at Hanworth in 1609,[49] was the first cousin of our dramatist, Thomas Killigrew,[50] and was appointed a gentleman of the privy-chamber extraordinary in 1632.[51]

To any who picture all our early American settlers as unswervingly rugged, *The Lost Lady* will occasion some bewilderment. Prince Lysicles of Thessaly interrupts his elaborate mourning for his murdered loved one, Milesia, in order to court Hermione, the mistress of his friend Eugenio. His apparent infidelity is merely a ruse to save Hermione from the mercenary matchmaking of her father, but no one knows this until his behavior provokes a series of almost fatal accidents. The most critical of these is his poisoning of a Moorish soothsayer, Acanthe, whom he is led to believe, after a conversation with what appears to be Milesia's ghost, has been an instrument in his bereavement. But Acanthe, after the author solemnly lets the blacking be washed from her agonized face, proves to be Milesia herself—not murdered, but willing to appear so in order to spy upon the endurance of her suitor's love. Happily she recovers from her richly deserved poisoning, Eugenio is reassured of the honorable motives of Lysicles, and the friends are reconciled and united to their several loves. *The Lost Lady,* so appealing as to have occasioned an amateur performance during the Interregnum with sprightly Dorothy Osborne as the heroine,[52] is concerned even more than the average Cavalier play with the tenets of the love code and expounds, possibly at second hand the doctrines of D'Urfé. There is detailed analysis of that constancy which must extend beyond separation, as in the case of Hermione and Eugenio, or even beyond the grave, as in the case of Milesia and Lysicles. Hermione "loves" Eugenio whereas she only "adores" Lysicles—familiar cant among "Platonics." One character, Ergasto, like Hylas in the *Astrée,* is an infidel in ideal love. He and the coquettes, Irene and Phillida, supply a number of wit combats at times gently ribald, and there is much of the sensual and cynical peeping from behind the author's polite pretence. The play is static and talkative, and falls flat at moments of crisis, but it is worth reading. There is intellectuality in the dialogue, the moderate tone of which sometimes contrasts oddly with the extravagant situations. Although nothing of a poet, Berkeley commanded a fluent literary English, some of his polished scenes suggesting high comedy in an unexpected way.

Berkeley and the others who have been discussed thus far were courtiers in the most literal sense; that is, they were appointees, usually privy-chambermen, in the King or Queen's personal suite. Another member of the household, the Earl of Newcastle, greater in name and function than any of the other writers, should be mentioned again at this point. Although Newcastle refused to write like a courtier,[53] he may not have written for the stage at all except under cover of the unconventional new fashion. Sir Kenelm Digby, groom of the King's chamber, and author of a romance based on his courtship of Venetia Stanley (a courtship strangely compounded of platonic and unplatonic impulses),[54] followed the lead of fellow courtiers at least to the extent of translating Italian pastoral plays. Digby's *Amyntas* and *Il Pastor Fido* have not survived.[55] No doubt many other plays emanating from the court failed to reach the printer. A tragicomedy with the suggestive title *Nothing Impossible to Love* was written by Sir Robert Le Grys, royally commissioned translator of Barclay's *Argenis,* but nothing is heard of this play after the appearance of the title in the *Stationers' Register* and Warburton's list.[56] *The Governor,* acted at St. James February 17, 1637,[57] was evidently written by one Sir Cornelius Formido, but this play also was never printed.[58] A number of titles of lost anonymous plays gleaned from the *Stationers' Register* of the Commonwealth period suggest in themselves alone the courtly type of play under discussion: for instance, *The Noble Ravishers, Castara, or Cruelty without Lust, Pity the Maid, The Supposed Inconstancy, The Woman's Law, The Woman's Masterpiece,* etc.[59] Probably the supply was greater than the demand. Richard Brome, archenemy[60] of the Westminster playwright, that "dandling on a Courtly lap," informs us that subsidized performances were not uncommon. Says he, ". . . the great and curious Poets" supply not only plays but "money, too, to have 'em acted." And he warns the popular audience, "You pay as much for your seats at them as at these, though you sit ne'er the merrier, nor rise the wiser, they are so above common understanding."[61]

There remain to be treated in the present chapter certain writers who, though not post-holders in the royal household, revolved in the circle of Whitehall and were susceptible to its influence because of their attendance upon some great lord. One such dramatist was Joseph Rutter, about whom we know little except that he was an intimate of Sir Kenelm Digby[62] and the tutor of the two sons of Henrietta's lord chamberlain, the Earl of Dorset. At Dorset's suggestion Rutter translated Corneille's *Cid,* the first part of which was published in 1637, and the second part, at the King's command, in 1640. In his dedication Rutter not only compares Dorset with Don Roderigo of the play but politely alleges that Dorset's two noble sons have participated in the translation. In his "Session of the Poets" Suckling with the propensity of the pot to call the kettle black dubbed the translation bombastic, but its blank verse is actually quite restrained, the work competent and deserving of its success when acted at Whitehall and the Phoenix theatre.

The translation of Corneille was preceded by an original play, *The Shepherds' Holiday,* also acted at Whitehall and the Phoenix, probably shortly before 1635, when it was published with commendations by Ben Jonson and Thomas May. For his epilogue Rutter penned a dedication to Charles and Henrietta—

> whose lives have brought
> Virtue in fashion, and the world have taught
> That chaste innocuous sports become the stage
> No less than civil manners do the age,

and his work is such as would have delighted this amorous and romantic pair. Appropriately dubbed "pastoral tragicomœdie" the play subordinates the intricate love affairs of several pairs of true pastoral characters to the sojourn among the Arcadian shepherds of the Princess Sylvia, sweetheart of lowly Thyrsis, until conveyed away by her importunate suitor Cleander. In time fortunately to avert disaster, Sylvia is discovered to be not the King of Arcadia's daughter but Cleander's own sister. Thus one barrier to her union with Thyrsis is removed, and this union proves a glorious one when Thyrsis is discovered to be no humble shepherd but the King of Arcadia's son, the circumstances of whose loss and recovery elucidate the terms of the usual brain-fatiguing oracle.

This play, quite above the Cavalier average, is well-planned and clear, its blank verse light in touch, at times almost poetic. From D'Urfé's *Astrée* Rutter has borrowed the name of Hylas, scoffer at platonic love, for one of his personages, and Hylas's character for another; and in general his work shows as much the influence of French as of Italian pastoral. This is characteristic of courtier plays in the Arcadian mode, notably, as we have seen, of Montague's *Shepherd's Paradise.*

Cavalier pastorals and heroic tragicomedies converge in type. In so far as Cavalier pastorals may be compared with the Italian, they resemble the work of Guarini and Bonarelli much more than that of Tasso; but they far surpass even the later Italian pastorals in romantic intricacy and adventurousness; and court intrigues as well as interloping gentlefolk tend to obscure the Arcadian background. Tasso, though the epitome of the courtly writer, at least preserves the illusion of rustic simplicity; his Cupid complains that mother Venus, "vain and ambitious, thrust me upon mere courts, crowns, and sceptres . . . I will inspire humble hearts with noble sentiments . . . I am Love among shepherds as among heroes." Guarini's shepherds, though kin of the gods, are shepherds still; and Fletcher and Randolph, most successful among English imitators of Tasso and Guarini, admit no characters of greater station than high priests of sylvan shrines. In contrast, courtly pastoralists, such as Rutter, are so anxious about nothing as to get the shepherds away from their sheep, to establish them at court as the lost children of noble parents. They have an ancient precedent for this in the *Daphnis and Chloe* of Longus.

The few years following the Queen's acting in *The Shepherd's Paradise* not only produced Rutter's play but witnessed quite a vogue for pastorals at court, Fletcher's *Faithful Shepherdess* being revived the very next season with the common actors wearing the costumes dignified by the queen and her ladies in their histrionic adventure.[63] On December 21, 1635, *The Pastoral of Florimene* was acted in French by the Queen's maids of honor.[64] Only the argument of this play survives, but this is enough to suggest that the country setting was purely incidental. Again we find multiple courtships complicated by disguise, interrelationship, and a permanent *brouillerie d'amour*, the whole no doubt retarded originally by *précieuse* sentiment in the fashion of Montague. The production was enlivened by intermedii of masque and anti-masque effect, songs in praise of the King, and an elaborate setting, "no Scœne but that of the pastoral [being] twice seene."[65]

It was about 1633 that Abraham Cowley, himself ultimately drawn into the royal circle although at this time still a King's scholar at Westminster, originally wrote his pastoral *Love's Riddle*. No doubt it was revised, however, before its publication in 1638 and dedication to Sir Kenelm Digby. Pastoral drama seems to have formed a bond between Digby, Rutter, and Cowley. In *Love's Riddle*, as in Rutter's *Shepherds' Holiday*, a heroine of high degree has flown to the shepherds to escape the importunities of an unwanted lover. The maiden, one Callidora, in this case dons man's attire, and is almost slain by her brother Florellus because her assumed masculinity quickens the pulse of Bellula, his shepherdess sweetheart. A revelation of identities, discovery that Bellula is not a shepherdess born but the lost sister of Callidora's rejected suitor, and a convenient if somewhat abrupt readjustment of affections paves the way for a triple wedding among three sets of brothers and sisters—all of whom may now cease masquerading in their homely weeds and return to the elegancies of the city. The use as in *The Shepherds' Holiday* of an underplot involving the loves of authentic shepherds combines with the three crossed courtships of the main plot to make Cowley's pastoral extremely intricate, but it is deftly plotted, is at times even dramatic, and thoroughly successful in its own ornate and conventional realm. Cowley might have become an excellent playwright, as we shall see in reviewing his later work. In this his initial essay, the hackneyed pattern of the story and certain scenes of ungracious mirth are counterpoised by language often delicately embroidered, tender, and poetic. *Love's Riddle* is far superior to Rutter's play despite its similarity in many minor details as well as in type and story design.

The variety of pastoral produced by Rutter and Cowley is carried still closer to ordinary Cavalier dramatic romance in W. Peaps's *Love in its Ecstasy*. About Peaps's life, investigation has yielded nothing save what he himself has chosen to tell in the edition of his solitary play. In 1649 he shared the common royalist discontent at the prohibition of drama and saw fit to venture into public with a work written long since when he was a gentleman student at Eton. Presumably this places his pastoral not far in date of composition from those of Montague, Rutter, and Cowley, although, as we shall see, gallant Arcadianism persisted in plays actually written during the Interregnum. *Love in its Ecstasy* Peaps calls "a kind of Royall Pastorall"—and with reason, for there are no less than four kings among the characters! The plot turns on the "superplatonick" love of King Charastus for a subject, his temporary resignation of his crown so that he may equalize his station with hers until their marriage, and the tyranny of Bermudo, who tries to perpetuate his vice-regency by banning love and marriage in all Lilybeus. This situation winds into a maze of inter-family courtships, miraculous reappearances of the supposedly slain, lost princes recovered, and the like, both the story and the high-astounding language suggesting Thomas Killigrew more than any known pastoralist. The habit of the characters of disguising themselves as shepherds is the sole claim of this unhappy work to classification as pastoral.

There is no evidence that *Love in its Ecstasy* or Cowley's *Love's Riddle* was ever acted, or that *Florimene* or Rutter's *Shepherds' Holiday* was revived after 1635. Other pastorals produced in the decade before the closing of the theatres and affected in some degree by court tastes will be mentioned hereafter. Those described above sufficiently illustrate the power of the Cavalier drama to divert into its own mode a type of play hedged in originally by the most restrictive conventions, many of them quite opposed to the grandiose.

We may return now to our roll of playwrights in touch with the court through their standing with its noble officials. Francis Quarles (1592-1644) is not usually considered a courtier, and his sphere in fact was chiefly elsewhere, but like Joseph Rutter he was connected with the Earl of Dorset, whose influence secured him his place as chronologer of

London.[66] Quarles's single dramatic effort, *The Virgin Widow, c.* 1641, strives to conform with the Cavalier mode, and does so in materials if not in general tone. Nothing could be more fantastic than the fate of Katreena, transferred into a humble family in infancy but restored to her queenly state by direct intercession of the gods, who waft the royal crown to her head in the same stroke with which they exterminate most of the members of the usurping family. Since Katreena has retained virginity during her marriage to an old usurer (poisoned in the course of the play), her accession fulfills an oracle that the next king shall be the son of a maid, wife and widow. Although distinctly not *précieuse*, the play has all the plot involutions of typical Cavalier romance, including a love affair between the heroine and a mysterious stranger— proved oddly at the end to be the husband of the usurping queen, destined to retain his post as King consort during the reign of Katreena. Elements of comedy and tragedy amateurishly interwoven make *The Virgin Widow* an indescribable mixture, not uninteresting despite its eccentricity. When published in 1649 after private performance by young Royalists at Chelsey, the printer asserted it would not only sweeten the brackish tempers of a deluded age but would prove that Quarles could be "delightfully facetious as divinely serious," and indeed the play does indulge in certain jollities scarcely predictable of the pious author of *Emblems*. Less in discord with his usual religious vein was the single dramatic effort of George Sandys (another privy-chamberman by the way), who rendered into English couplets the *Christ's Passion* of Hugo Grotius. This work, done during the absence of the court on the Scottish expeditions, is just one more illustration of the playwriting tendencies of the time and place: "Thus in the shadow of your absence," says the author to his liege, "dismissed from arms by act of time, have I, in what I was able, continued to serve you. . . ."[67] We can only conjecture which Charles would prefer, the consistent gravity of Sandys or the romantic escapade of Francis Quarles.

If Dorset, the Queen's Chamberlain, may be held partially responsible for the dramatic efforts of Rutter and Quarles, Pembroke, the King's Chamberlain, may be held wholly responsible for those of two additional sub-courtiers. The plays of Henry Killigrew and William Habington were evidently written upon Pembroke's commissions, once on the occasion of the marriage of his son, and again when he wished to entertain the royal family. The career of Henry Killigrew (1613-1700), Doctor of Divinity, Councillor of the Duke of York, royal chaplain, and Master of the Savoy,[68] contrasts in every respect except in lifelong devotion to the Stuart cause with that of his elder brother Thomas. Yet his single play, *Pallantus and Eudora*, "Design'd for an entertain-

ment of the King and Queen at Yorke House at the Nuptials of Ladie
Mary Villiers, and the Lord Charles Herbert,"[69] is identical in kind
with *The Prisoners, Claricilla,* and *The Princess,* for the two brothers,
so different in maturity, were in youth affected alike by their associations at court. *Pallantus and Eudora* tells the story of a prince incognito shipwrecked on the shores of Crete in time to join forces with
another stranger prince in aiding the rightful king overcome a usurper.
One of these allies falls in love with the true king's sister, the other
with the usurper's daughter, so that in the usual way ethical and sentimental develop side by side with political and military complexities.
It is little wonder that when the play was performed at Blackfriars,
Lord Falkland had to defend it against the charge that its youthful
characters were impossibly profound by revealing that he who "writ
the whole play was himself no older."[70] Perhaps only one so young as
Henry Killigrew could have been so owlish. An induction, designed
for the production of the play at the court marriage and printed when
it was pirated in 1638 as *The Conspiracy,* condemns rude comedy and
maintains, quite without cynicism, that tragedy more befits the solemnity of a great marriage. The young King of the play never smiles
except in approbation of good deeds, and at the end even the court
buffoon resolves to repent of his merriment and grow serious. The
long oratorical preachments of the characters, albeit they check the
heroic action to a somewhat shambling pace, are not lacking in eloquence. Perhaps this younger Killigrew's work rises slightly above the
plane of his brother's, but we may honestly doubt the publisher's assertion that *Pallantus and Eudora* enlisted Ben Jonson among its host
of admirers.

Superior in every way to the above, and indeed to most Cavalier
plays, is *The Queen of Aragon* by William Habington (1605-54),
author of *Castara.* Though a devoted Catholic, Habington was related
by marriage to a branch of the Herbert family, the fact perhaps ex-
plaining his association with the Earl of Pembroke. Sir Henry Herbert recorded that on April 9, 1640, "my Lord Chamberlen bestow'd a
play on the Kinge and Queene, call'd *Cleodora, Queene of Arragon,*
made by my cozen Abington. It was performed by my lords servants
out of his own family, and his charge in the cloathes and sceanes which
were very rich and curious. In the hall at Whitehall."[71] The royal
couple was so well pleased that the entertainment was repeated. Then
there was a performance at Blackfriars, and in the custom of fashionable plays, a publication in folio. Revived in the Restoration, the play
delighted Samuel Pepys: "To the Duke of York's playhouse, and there
saw, the first time acted, *The Queene of Arragon,* an old Blackfriars

play, but an admirable one, so good that I am astonished at it, and wonder where it hath lain asleep all this while that I have never heard of it before."[72] Others since Pepys have been pleasantly surprised by this play. Into the story of a queen fought over by three intrepid warriors—her own rebellious general, a Castilian general, and the latter's king—is injected a novel undercurrent of democratic spirit. Allowed to choose freely among her suitors by the magnanimous renunciation by each of his military or other advantages, the Queen refuses the monarch and takes the man—resolved not to be such a one as,

> . . . reserves her love
> To serve her profit, and exposeth it
> To the merchant that bids highest.[73]

Elsewhere the author brands titular greatness "the envy but of fools," maintains that "no distinction is 'tween man and man," and at one point puts into the mouth of a common soldier a stirring vindication of the dignity of the lowly born.[74] Such sentiments are a startling apparition in Habington's circle. Surprising too is his evaluation of one of the types which comprised this circle:

> Though he talk positive, and bustle 'mong
> The soldier lords, pretend to embassies
> And state-designs all day, he'll drink,—you guess the rest.
> He'll quarrel too, then underhand compound.
> Why, for a need he'll jeer and speak profane;
> Court, and then laugh at her he courted. Madam,
> Forgive him his pretence to gravity,
> And he's an absolute Cavalier.[75]

One begins to realize that this author's espousal of chastity in *Castara* and elsewhere, for which he has become almost notorious, may have owed less to the platonic fad at court than to a brave personal conviction. Independence of spirit is not the sole merit of *The Queen of Aragon*. It is dramatic only at intervals, and there is an air of unreality about it, notably in the unperturbed decorum of the ladies amidst the alarms of war, but its design is simpler, its verse less fibreless, its elevation less specious than is the case with most Cavalier plays; and the language is that of a man who may claim honestly the quality of a poet.

The Queen of Aragon is about the last of the plays by courtiers acted before the closing of the theatres. After 1640 these courtiers had something else to think of, for the troubles in the North over King Charles's bishops, and the increasing turmoils at home, were beginning to engross all attention. The writers discussed were in close contact with Whitehall and Denmark House. Their number has not been swelled by inclusion in the present chapter of such gentlemen-about-town as John Denham, Sir Aston Cokain, and Sir William Lower, and of such fashionable residents at the universities as Jasper Mayne and William Cartwright (both smiled upon by majesty itself). The multiplication of amateur playwrights in town and university during the 'thirties merits a chapter in itself; it was mainly by recruits to the latter group, emulating courtly writers, that the Cavalier mode was continued during the Interregnum.

Before describing the spread of courtly influence, we must indulge in a word of deprecation concerning the plays of the courtiers themselves. As critics we are much too hard on these men. It is true that their drama often approaches the ridiculous. It is also true that the plays most worth reading prove to be by courtiers who achieved greater distinction in another form of literature. On the other hand, there is latent talent discoverable in some of the worst of these plays by some of the obscurest of these playwrights. What, we should ask, could normally be expected of a group such as this, considering their training and opportunities. For one thing, the courtiers were neophyte authors, denied by circumstances the time to work out their apprenticeship. Greater writers than they would rank humbly in our esteem if judged solely on the basis of their early efforts. It does not follow that the courtiers would have produced fine work in a more mature stage of development, that their aims would not have continued misdirected, their talents largely wasted. But it does appear that they might have achieved that circumscribed excellence displayed by the heroic plays of the Restoration, the dramatic type towards which their experiments were tending. We leave the plays of the Caroline courtiers mournfully aware that we have not ascended so much as a hillock in Darien, yet more inclined to blame the *zeitgeist* than the authors themselves.

---

[1] A biographical notice appears in *DNB*, xxxviii, 270.
[2] P. R. O., Lord Chamberlain's Books, 5/132/p. 281.
[3] *Shepherd's Paradise* (1659), p. 112.
[4] *Ibid.*, p. 119.
[5] *Trivial Poems* (1651), p. 7.
[6] "Session of the Poets."
[7] A biographical sketch appears in C. H. Gray, *Lodowick Carliell . . . and "The Deserving Favorite"* (Chicago, 1905). The name is spelled "Carlile" in official documents, "Carlell" on title pages, "Carliell" in signatures traced by C. H. Gray.
[8] P. R. O., Accounts Various ("Establishment of Henrietta Maria"), 438/7², 438/11, 438/13, 438/15, 439/3.
[9] P. R. O., Lord Chamberlain, 5/134/p. 32.
[10] P. R. O., E 403/2459/20 (Auditor's Patent Books).
[11] P. R. O., Lord Chamberlain, 5/51/p. 154.

[12] *Ibid.*, 5/134/p. 388.

[13] *Heraclius* (1664), "Author's Advertisement."

[14] Prologue to Part Two, *Passionate Lovers.*

[15] C. H. Gray, *op. cit.*, pp. 57 ff. urges Solorzano's *La duquesa de Mantua* (1629), as the source, but see above p. 31.

[16] F. G. Fleay, *Biographical Chronicle*, I, 46.

[17] A. Nicoll, *Restoration Drama*, p. 316.

[18] *Dramatic Records of Sir Henry Herbert*, pp. 56, 57.

[19] *Ibid.*, p. 55, and title-page; also see above p. 19.

[20] *Historical MSS Commission*, II, 118: a letter from Charles Prince Palatine during his residence in England, 1635-36.

[21] W. J. Lawrence, "New Facts from Sir Henry Herbert's Office Book," *LTLS*, Nov. 1923, p. 820.

[22] Act I. For the theme of *Osmond* elsewhere in English drama, see below, p. 219.

[23] Act IV.

[24] *Dramatic Records of Sir Henry Herbert*, p. 76.

[25] *Ibid.*, p. 77.

[26] See above, p. 10.

[27] *Roscius Anglicanus*, p. 31.

[28] For a life and critical study, see the present author's *Thomas Killigrew Cavalier Dramatist* (Univ. of Pennsylvania Press, 1930).

[29] *Ibid.*, pp. 145, 172.—The author has erred in stating that these plays were acted at the Phoenix *after* the plague.

[30] Act IV, Scene i. Quoted from folio *Works*, 1664.

[31] Anthony à Wood *Athenæ Oxonienses* (ed. Bliss), III, 460.

[32] The prologue and epilogue appear in *Lucasta*, 1649.

[33] The present notice is based on *DNB*, LV, 140; Aubrey's *Brief Lives, passim*; the memoir in Hazlitt's edition of Suckling's Works, 2 vols. (1892), and contemporary allusions.

[34] *Strafforde Letters*, W. Knowles, Ed., 2 vols. (London, 1739), II, 150.

[35] Dated by Garrard's letter, Feb. 7, 1638, in conjunction with the two lines from the prologue to the altered version quoted below.

[36] Brome compared the play to a babe in the great bed at Ware; cf. "Upon Aglaura printed in Folio," *Five New Plays*, 1656.

[37] Act IV.

[38] Act IV.

[39] See the historically interesting epilogue to the altered version of *Aglaura*.

[40] From *Brennoralt*. In *Aglaura*, Act IV, first appeared the lyric, "Why so pale and wan, fond lover?"

[41] See the title-pages, and *Dramatic Records of Sir Henry Herbert*, p. 76.

[42] H. McAfee, *Pepys on the Restoration Stage* (New Haven, 1916), pp. 126-128; *Dramatic Records of Sir Henry Herbert*, p. 118.

[43] Downes, *Roscius Anglicanus*, p. 19.

[44] See Garrard's letter cited in notes 34 and 35.

[45] *Dramatic Records of Sir Henry Herbert*, p. 76.

[46] *Ibid.*, p. 117; *Pepys Diary*, Jan. 19 and 28, 1661; A. Nicoll, *Restoration Stage*, p. 315.

[47] L. Hotson, *Commonwealth and Restoration Stage*, p. 246.

[48] *Dramatic Records of Sir Henry Herbert*, p. 118.

[49] D. Lysons, *Environs of London*, 6 vols. (London, 1796-1811), V, 99.

[50] Margerie Killigrew's will, P. C. C., 71 Clarke; this establishes the fact that his mother was the sister not of Sir Henry (as in *DNB*, IV, 368) but of Sir Robert Killigrew.

[51] P. R. O., Lord Chamberlain, 5/132/p. 305.

[52] See below, pp. 202-203.

[53] See above, pp. 74-75.

[54] *Private Memoirs of Sir Kenelm Digby* (London, 1827).—The "unplatonic" portions, separately printed as "Castrations from the Memoirs," are usually found bound into the volume.

[55] *Poems from Sir Kenelm Digby's Papers*, G. F. Warner (Roxb. Club, 1877). *"Dedication of Amyntas,"* p. 1; fragment of *Il Pastor Fido* (Act II, Scene v), pp. 4-6.

[56] W. W. Greg, "The Bakings of Betsy," *The Library*, Series III, II (1911) p. 247. It is possible that the author of the play was Robert Le Grys the younger.

[57] *Dramatic Records of Sir Henry Herbert*, p. 58.

[58] A play called *The Governor* was entered in the *Stationers' Register*, Sept. 9, 1653, with Formido named as the author. I have been unable to identify him. F. G. Fleay, *Biographical Chronicle*, I, 235, speaks of his play as extant in MS., but this is an error; see below, p. 225.

[59] See below, p. 285.

[60] See below, pp. 152, 154.

[61] Epilogue to *The Court Beggar*, printed 1653. This epilogue evidently post-dates the composition of the play.

[62] *DNB*, L, 31.

[63] *Dramatic Records of Sir Henry Herbert*, p. 53.

[64] *Ibid.*, p. 55.

[65] *The Argument of the Pastorall of Florimene*, 1635.

[66] *DNB*, XLVII, 94.—A reference to Richelieu as still living (Act IV, Scene i) dates his play before 1642.

[67] Dedication to the King.

[68] A. Harbage, *Thomas Killigrew*, pp. 34-37.

[69] Postscript to the edition of 1653.

[70] Publisher to the Reader (ed. 1653).

[71] *Dramatic Records of Sir Henry Herbert*, p. 58.

[72] *Pepys Diary*, Oct. 19, 1668.

[73] Act V.

[74] Act III, Scene i; Act II, Scene i.

[75] Act III, Scene i.

II

AMATEURS OF TOWN AND UNIVERSITY

THE sporadic efforts of a host of "miscellaneous" playwrights complicate the pattern of Elizabethan and seventeenth century drama from the very beginning. Authors of one or two plays, occasionally of considerable merit, form a continuous procession to confuse the student and exercise the historian. Not often can these visitors to the theatrical world be grouped, as in the case of the courtier playwrights, because of a common background and a common inspiration. Sometimes they are authors in other fields experimenting with drama, sometimes actors trying to double their capacity in the theatre, sometimes complete unknowns who must have been discouraged early in their dramatic aspirations; frequently they are undergraduates and fellows of the universities following a time-honored precedent in providing local instruction and entertainment. In the past, such playwrights had tended to imitate the type of play and the mannerisms popularized by the leading professionals of their day; or, at the universities, to produce allegorical and satirical types indigenous to the place and, it seems, perennially satisfying. But after 1633 the fad for dramatic authorship at court made amateurs of town and university look less exclusively to professional or traditional sources for their inspiration. In London, even those amateurs who displayed little aptitude for innovation were recruited among gentlemen who would not have written at all had it not been for the fashion set by the *haute monde* of Westminster, At one of the universities, the Cavalier mode was adopted so cordially that old academic types of drama were almost wholly abandoned.

The influence of courtly drama upon the academic amateur is brought into sharp relief by a comparison of the plays of Thomas Randolph, whose period of authorship falls just before *The Shepherd's Paradise* was produced at court, with those of William Cartwright, whose period falls just after. William Cartwright (as we shall see) rivalled the courtiers in their own peculiar vein. Thomas Randolph, though sprightly and popular, was an academic of the old school. As a "son of Ben," he injected Jonsonian humours into most of his plays, but he retained touch with Aristophanes and Plautus as well as with university satirists and allegorists before him. Such "shows" as *Aristippus* and *The Conceited Peddlar* might have been written at the

time of the *Parnassus* plays. The persistence of the devices of the morality in academic backwaters is illustrated in *Plutophthalmia Plutogamia*
and even in *The Muses' Looking Glass*. *Amyntas* has no academic
flavor, but is traditional in another way. Patterned evidently upon
Guarini, it reveals no interest in the pastoralism of contemporary
France; and resembles Fletcher's *Faithful Shepherdess,* written over
twenty years before, more nearly than it does Rutter's *Shepherds' Holiday,* written only five years after. *The Jealous Lovers,* in telling its tale
of brothers wooing their own sisters through ignorance of identity, has
only its plot materials in common with those courtly dramas in which
lost babes and entangled courtships were about to figure in sentimen-
tally heroic situations. It is Plautine comedy pure and simple, reminding us of *The Comedy of Errors* more than of *Love's Riddle, The Deserving Favorite* and other all but contemporary works. *The Jealous
Lovers* was presented to the court during the royal progress to Cambridge in 1632. During this same progress, though at Newmarket rather
than at Cambridge itself,[1] was presented Peter Hausted's *Rival Friends*
in which again we have cradle exchanges and entangled courtships as
the basis of the plot. Here the treatment is romantic enough, but in an
old-fashioned way, with disturbing intrusions of satire and realism.
Crude in conception and robustious in spirit, it seems refreshingly
vigorous and youthful to the modern reader; but, as we have seen,[2]
it displeased the court, which was already craving that elegance and
refinement about to be supplied in superlative measure by the courtiers
themselves.

Once we have recognized Cavalier romance as a fairly distinct type,
isolated by its heroical and *précieuse* features, and once we have
perceived that it emerged and exerted its influence after 1633, the year
of Queen Henrietta's appearance in *The Shepherd's Paradise,* we have
a new instrument which, used with sufficient caution, will help fix the
period of activity of certain dramatists. The plays of William Hemming, Randolph's schoolmate while at Westminster and friend thereafter, have been placed conjecturally in 1637 and 1638.[3] Of these plays,
one, *The Jew's Tragedy,* is a bookish chronicle based on Josephus's
tragic account of Vespatian and Titus, and the other, *The Fatal Contract,* is of the lust-and-bloodshed variety, featuring a sinful queen
against the background of a semi-historical French court. Neither shows
the slightest evidence of the courtly influence so permeant in 1637 and
1638. Inconclusive in itself, this quality is suggestive in the light of
other facts. Tragical foreign histories, like *The Bloody Brother* and
Thierry and Theodoret by Fletcher and his collaborators, were being
imitated in the twenties. Davenant's *Albovine* of 1628 illustrates the

type, and it seems probable that Hemming's *Fatal Contract* was contemporary with this. *The Jew's Tragedy* offers more decisive evidence of an early date. In his epilogue Hemming writes,

> The lofty Buskin, and the learned Bay
> Are not expected to adorn our Play;
> Our Author deemeth these fair trophies fit
> To grace the raptures of a riper wit.

Evidently the play is a closet drama written by a young man. Since this author's non-extant *Coursing of a Hare* was acted at the Fortune in 1633,[4] he would scarcely have considered any later play either unripe or unworthy of the "lofty Buskin." It seems likely that Hemming and Randolph were writing at the same time, thus escaping equally the influence of courtly romance.

Both Randolph and Hemming were university men whose dramatic activity seems to have ceased just as they were about to embark upon a career of writing for the popular stage. Another university man flirting with the same plan and at about the same time was Arthur Wilson, whose *Swisser* was acted at Blackfriars in 1631[5] during the author's belated career at Oxford. In view of its date it is not surprising that this play should exploit the blustery passions of the lords of ancient Lombardy, historical at least in their names, and should resemble in type, despite its happy ending, Davenant's *Albovine* and Hemming's *Fatal Contract*. Wilson was still interested in the drama as late as January 14, 1633,[6] when his last play, *The Corporal,* was licensed for acting at Blackfrairs, and it is possible that a third play, of doubtful date, *The Inconstant Lady,* was written after the courtiers had created the Cavalier mode. This readable though sometimes ridiculous tragicomedy, in depicting the passion of a Duke for the fair maiden Cloris until she is proved his own daughter stolen as a babe, suggests in several ways the fantasia of the new romances, but it also contains elements wholly foreign to the type (for instance a central character by no means exemplary of ideal womanhood), and at no point offers proof positive of the influence of Montague and Carlell.

Randolph, Hemming and Wilson, moving in an urban-academic borderland as they wrote their plays, were none of them especially well born or especially opulent, and might have drifted like scholars before them and like their contemporary, James Shirley, into the ranks of the professional playwrights. Together their work offers a fair idea of the nature of dramatic dabbling (though Randolph's plays were considerably more than that) just before 1633. After 1633 a surprising number of amateurs other than the courtiers were men of independent means or lucrative occupation. Not all of their plays, to be sure, are in the Cavalier mode. *The Ward,* by Thomas Neale,[7] Middle Templar and heir to the estate of Sir Thomas Neale of Hampshire, is self-designated a tragicomedy, but it eschews the romantic materials at this time implicit in the type. Actually this play, both odd and interesting, is a tract inspired by the author's indignation at the vagaries of the law, and presents as its central character a pathetic little orphan who has been victimized by a bad will. *The Swaggering Damsel,* by Robert Chamberlain, clerk to Queen Henrietta's solicitor-general, is a belated (and quite charming) romantic comedy; *The Valiant Scot,* by "J. W. Gent.," a belated (and well written) chronicle drama. Other isolated plays of these latter years are Alexander Brome's *The Cunning Lovers,* one of the pleasantest comedies of the decade; and Henry Burnell's *Landgartha,* an Irish play founded on Swedish history. Thomas May's *Old Couple* seems to have been first acted in 1636,[8] though first written some years before; revision, perhaps, may account for the fact that, here, exotic romance is superimposed on Jonsonian comedy of manners.[9] *Imperiale* by Sir Ralph Freeman, *The Rebellion* by Thomas Rawlins, and *The Tragedy of Messalina* by N. Richards are all tragedies, interesting in their testimony of the latterday proneness to seek originality in mere excess, but fairly conventional in their several types. Freeman was a wealthy entrepreneur and government official, Rawlins a prospering engraver at the mint (where Freeman was titular Master Worker), and Richards, although now disproved the Cambridge scholar and school-master of St. Albans,[10] seems also to have been a man of substance, one of the landed Richards of Rowling, Kent.

Another author of a solitary tragedy was Francis Jaques, whose *Queen of Corsica,* 1642, remains in manuscript.[11] Nothing is known of this proselyte to drama, but his name suggests that he was one of the numerous younger sons of Sir Roger Jaques, Mayor of York and father of several Inns of Court students. His tragedy is interesting only for its manner of grafting new courtly ornaments upon old dramatic stock. Queen Achæa, infatuated with Calidor, a nameless wanderer to the shores of Corsica, woos him through the unwilling agency of Florimond, her erstwhile suitor and his sponsor at court. The wedding ceremony of this disparate pair has scarcely ended when Achæa amazes herself by giving birth to a child. "Are these your marriage nights in Corsica!" exclaimed Calidor with pardonable annoyance. But it develops that Achæa is really the innocent victim of Florimond, who has violated her during an opium-induced sleep; this crime is greater than he himself contemplated, for he proves to be his victim's half-brother. The *dénouement* consists of wholesale slaughter in which innocent and guilty alike are huddled to atonement. The design of the play is old; incest has cast its pestilential shade athwart other court intrigues since Fletcher's *King and No King*. But Jaques has supplied a faddish complement of rival friends, nameless wanderers, *précieuse* sensibilities, and verbal heroics. Calidor is lifted bodily from contemporary court romance.

> Men call me Calidor:
> But you have made choice of a friend in me
> That knows nor kin or parentage; acquainted
> With nothing in myself but my misfortunes;
> And if you ask my country, I know none
> But the wide world, nor anything in it
> But rapines, murthers, incest, pride, and scorns;
> Who by the tempest of my passions hurl'd
> To surly seas, by them betray'd to pirates,
> And by those pirates cast upon this shore
> 'Mongst land-wolves; and from them into your mercy
> Comes your poor broken friend . . .[12]

One is amazed to come upon several genuinely interesting scenes amidst the miserable execution and atrocious taste prevailing in this play.

Judging by the interchange of commendatory verse, most of the gentlemen writers of the day knew each other, and judging by the content of this verse, were unwilling to be confused with common playwrights. Rawlins's *Rebellion* was

> . . . not for the span
> Or greasy thumbs of every common man.

None the less it was acted on the public stage, a distinction denied the average amateur play. Attempts by newcomers most likely to be tested in the theatres approached the type of the new courtly romances. Lewis Sharpe's *Noble Stranger, c.* 1639, tells the tragicomic tale of Prince Honoria, who in the guise of a nameless warrior wins the heart of the princess whom international diplomacy has predetermined as his bride. It lacks the "Platonic" embellishments of full-blown Cavalier romance, and the same degree of heroic inflation, but its material and general tone suggest the type. Commendatory verses testify to "oft cramm'd Theatres," and one wonders why Sharpe failed to fulfill his promise to write a "higher strain" thereafter.

Less fleeting than the above in their sojourn with the dramatic muse were three more gentlemen of the town who felt the dramatic urge in the latter half of the Caroline reign—Aston Cokain, William Lower, and the more notable John Denham (1615-69). None of these seems to have been a courtier in any sense prior to 1642, yet each subsequently attained to the free masonry of the "Cavaliers"; each became a conspicuous Royalist and was awarded the dignity of knighthood. In fact there is similarity in several phases of their careers. All three were county heirs, who, following university days, gravitated to London and moved in the environs of the Inns of Court. Denham had already come into his estate and been called to the bar by 1641 when, in the words of Edmund Waller, "he broke out like the Irish rebellion"[13] with his tragedy *The Sophy*. One is inclined to question Waller's testimony to the popularity of this play, not that it lacks desert, but that it stands so aloof from the fashions of the day. It is one of the most original plays of the Caroline era. Simply and skilfully Denham adapts an episode in contemporary history: portraying the fear-engendered cruelty of the Persian King Abbas to Mirza, his glorious son; Mirza's vengeful impulse to slay his own child Fatyma because she is the delight of the King's old age; and finally, after the villains who fomented these ills have joined their victims in tragic deaths, the succession to the throne of Mirza's young son, the Sophy. The play is simple, dignified, clear, and if notable neither for prosody nor poetic delicacy, yet full of fine thoughts and eloquent lines. Mirza is a nobly melancholy rather than tragic figure, but there is a moving pathos in his portrayal, notably in that scene where he weakens in his resolve to slay Fatyma; the latter's childish prattle recalls Hubert's in *King John*. Assailing our emotions delicately rather than through mass attack, Denham departs from the usages of his day, his play portending, in its restraint and reality, a type of classic tragedy which in England never materialized. Talent was not lacking; conditions in the reign of Charles were simply adverse to its development. The air was vitiated. Denham was a dilettante, slighting his own work with the boast, "He did it when he had nothing else to do."[14] Like Cowley, he might have made a first rate dramatist. It is unfortunate that his one further contribution to drama was no more than the fifth act of Catherine Phillips' translation of Corneille's *Horace*.

Aston Cokain (1608-84) was another literary dilettante, less talented than Denham but also less flippant; he pretended no disdain for authorship and was naïvely proud of his acquaintance with the literati. As member of a wealthy and well-connected Derbyshire family[15] and as kinsman of Philip Stanhope, first Earl of Chesterfield, it seems probable that he could have won some minor appointment about the court, but he apparently preferred a career of self-cultivation and companionship with poetic wits and worthies of his day. After sojourns at Trinity College, Cambridge, and at one of the Inns of Court (in neither of which institutions does he seem formally to have matriculated), he made several extended visits to Italy, returned to England to wed, and by 1639 had become master of an estate. On February 21, 1643, Oxford, which by this time was distributing degrees in reward for loyalty, conferred an M.A. upon him, and he remained a staunch Royalist throughout the troubles. It is fair to remember this, as well as his tendency to dabble in unprofitable letters and be a boon tavern companion of the wits, when seeking reasons for the evaporation of his family fortunes and the impoverished last years of his long life.

Cokain's first experiments in authorship came during his travels in Italy. In 1635, while residing in Venice, he translated *Dianea,* the Italian romance of Loredano;[16] and at this time, or during an earlier visit in 1632-33, he wrote his play of *Trappolin, creduto Principe, or Trappolin Supposed a Prince.* His remark in the Prologue,

> . . . it is no translation; for he ne're
> But twice in Venice did it ever hear . . .

proves more ingenuous than most protestations of the kind, for the Italian original was *commedia dell' arte* and hence available to Cokain only in *scenari* or in actual representation; there was no text to translate.[17] The plot centers about one of those folk heroes—witty and spirited underlings—of which Figaro is a sophisticated descendant. Lowly Trappolin, transformed by magic into the likeness of Duke Lavino, revenges himself upon former oppressors and sets state business merrily awry, the while various love intrigues develop spasmodically in a topsy-turvy court. One would expect an Englishman of Cokain's time to convert such material into a mere Bromean comedy of courtship, but such proves not the case. Something of what must have been the spirit of *commedia dell' arte* is preserved—crispness, spontaneity, a certain naïveté, and, amidst farcical action and impudent dialogue, an inkling of democratic philosophy.

Cokain's next play, *The Obstinate Lady,* is of native inspiration. No mention of this work antedates its publication in 1657, but its allusions to the Cockpit and Blackfriars and other features of pre-war London suggest a date of composition prior to 1642. The play, sad to say, is a piebald cross between comedy of manners and Cavalier romance. Lucora obstinately disdains her suitor Carionil until he disguises himself as a blackamoor, whereupon she exclaims, "He is the brav'st proportion'd African I ever saw," and consents to an elopement. Disgusted by this, Carionil spurns her for her sister Cleanthe, who has been kidnapped as a babe and has entered his service disguised as a boy. A faithful friend, Falorus, who has been wont to feel sympathetic agonies when Lucora proved cold to Carionil, now woos her himself, and successfully, but not until he has suffered further agonies lest courting his friend's mistress, even though now discarded, may smack of treachery. There are several additional courtships—one of which is interrupted when the wife of the suitor returns from the dead—but the circumstances of these need not be detailed. The play is bad; such a mixture could scarce be otherwise. Borrowed situations, badly assorted themes, and language alternating between smart repartee and strained rhetoric reduce it far below the level of *Trappolin*. Yet there are several good passages, in which these oddly named Londoners shadow forth an actual social milieu. But the witty and realistic dialogue of one moment will change in the next to love-and-friendship casuistry or heroic bombast. When Lucora is about to sing, Carionil exclaims,

> Forbear awhile to play upon the spheres
> Ye servants to the deities! The gods
> Will blame you, if your music keeps the air
> Of her all-ravishing harmony from their ears.[18]

Essentially imitative at best, in this play Cokain swings like a weathervane among the variable winds of traditional fashions and the new Cavalier mode.

Also heterogeneous, yet not uninteresting, is Cokain's last play, *The Tragedy of Ovid*. This was probably a new composition in 1662 when it was first published, for the author had been reissuing his older plays for the preceding six years and would scarcely have withheld this. The scene is the city of Ovid's exile, Tomos in Pontus, and the play takes its titles from the fact that the poet intrudes from time to time reciting autobiographical—and quite irrelevant—passages, including one during his death throes. The main plot concerns the mad cruelty of jealous Bassanes towards his wife Clorina and his erstwhile friend Pyrontus. The innocent wife dies of grief with the heart of murdered Pyrontus bound in her hands. The crime is avenged and Bassanes slain, but tragic consistency is marred by a compensatory ending, in which the brother (and avenger) of Pyrontus weds the sister of Clorina. Ethical without conviction, and passionate in pedestrian verse, this play can be exactly described by the adjective *hollow*. Its interest derives from its many literary echoes (including a musical divertisement, of operatic type but imitative, nevertheless, of Peele's *Arraignment of Paris*), and from a few scenes of Roman low life in which Cokain exercised his latent talent for comedy of manners. A quaint underplot in which a debased Captain Hannibal pits his bravado against an animated corpse evokes at moments an effective atmosphere of horror; clearly the episode derives from some variant of the Don Juan story, probably Italian in view of Cokain's professed interests.

Of Cokain's three plays only *Trappolin* appears to have been acted.

No claims are made on the title pages of *The Obstinate Lady;* and the legend "Intended to be Acted shortly" on that of *Ovid* bespeaks only a touching optimism. *Trappolin,* however, displayed considerable vitality. Acted during the Restoration with a new prologue by Duffet, it was altered by Tate as *Duke and no Duke* in 1684, and by Drury as *The Devil of a Duke,* a ballad opera, in 1732, until, after many revivals, it reached the last stage of its metamorphosis when, in 1818, it appeared at Covent Garden as a "comic melodramatic burletta."[19]

One can only say of Cokain, that, without being wholly contemptible, he is one of the most distraught and tasteless writers of his time. He was curiously susceptible to influences, foreign and native, old and new. His *Masque at Bretby,* a little entertainment which will be described hereafter, shows unmistakable reminiscences of both Spenser and Milton. Since he was naturally vacillating, was undisciplined by practical contact with the theatre, and lived in a period of disintegration, experiment, transition, it is not remarkable that his plays are inchoate, and, except for *Trappolin,* worth while only for details.

More homogeneous than Cokain's (though superior in nothing else) are the plays of William Lower (1600?-1662), who confined his efforts to the Cavalier mode. Like Thomas Killigrew, Lower was of Cornish stock.[20] After a youth of fashionable aimlessness, he entered the army and captained a troop in the Bishops Wars. This troop seems to have deserted *en masse.* In fact our shreds of information about Lower never present him in a distinguished light. The only records of his service during the Civil Wars, when he became Lieutenant Colonel and royal governor of Wallingford, concerns his failure to collect a levy from the town of Reading and his imprisonment by Parliament. Living at the Hague during the last years of the Interregnum, he sought a place in some royal household, placing himself before the eyes of prospective patrons by the exercise of his pen. At this time, and again shortly before his death, he succeeded in making good his claim to family inheritances. The assertion by his kinsman, Dr. Richard Lower, that he was "an ill poet and a worse man" seems to have been evoked by a jealousy over money; certainly we have record of no serious sins perpetrated by Sir William other than his lyrical poems.

In 1639 was printed—there is no evidence that it had been acted—Lower's first play, *The Phoenix in her Flames,* a prime illustration, save that it ends unhappily, of dramatized romance of the Greek school. Damascus having been laid waste by barbarians, Prince Amandus wanders into Arabia where he is captured by desert bandits. He averts the rape of Princess Lucinda, a fair Egyptian captive, and becomes first the leader and then the reformer of the bandits. Later, as general of the Arabian army, he repulses the invasion of the Prince of Persia, betrothed of Lucinda. Lucinda herself has fallen in love with her rescuer, but Amandus fails to respond, for his heart is engaged to the Arabian Princess Phoenicia. The latter now replaces Lucinda as the heroine, and after Amandus, whose love she reciprocates, is slain by the treachery of rivals, she commits suicide by inhaling spiced smoke such as that in which the Phoenix is reputed to expire. Considering its complexity, the play is clearly developed, its plotting and its novel conclusion being its chief distinctions. Amandus, superlative both in military prowess and emotional sensitiveness, is another prototype of the conquerors in the heroic plays of the Restoration. The play is not unlike Carlell's *Arviragus and Philicia* and *The Passionate Lovers,* except that Lower shows less aptitude for the dialectal subtleties of *précieuse* dialogue. The verse is stronger and the phrasing less drab than in any later composition by the author.

After the long interruption of the wars Lower returned to dramatic authorship—via translation. While dwelling at the Hague during the last years of the exile, he published Englishings of two plays by Corneille, *Polyeuctes,* 1655, and *Horatius,* 1656; and of two by Quinault, *The Noble Ingratitude,* 1659, and *The Amorous Fantasme,* 1660. Two more, of plays by Scarron, *Don Japhet of Armenia* and *The Three Dorothies, or Jodolet Boxed,* were not printed, but the former survives in manuscript while the latter was formerly part of the collection of Skeffington Hall. *Scævoli,* a tragedy, mentioned as "now in press" and attributed to Lower in the advertisement in Montague's *Accomplished Woman,* 1656, was probably also a translation. Lower's translations have little to recommend them, in fact not so much as evidence of an exact knowledge of French. And although the author's linguistic ability increased somewhat as he progressed through the series, his literary ability did not; his are the baldest and most literal versions imaginable, and couched in the most decrepit blank verse. Usually too there is nothing to indicate to the unwary that Lower was not the original author of these plays; in this matter, however, the guilt may be the printer's.

Of the plays he translated, Lower paid special tribute to Quinault's *Noble Ingratitude,* in assuring the Queen of Bohemia in his dedication that it was "one of the best that hath been presented upon the French stage." The noble ingratitude in question is the obligation of one Almanzor to avenge his sister's wrong even against his rescuer and friend. After endless complications in which women display their emotional tremors, and men roar like sucking doves, all is reconciled by marriages among sets of brothers and sisters. We touch familiar ground

here; Quinault's play belongs to much the same tradition as the dramatic romances of the English courtiers.

In the midst of his activity as a translator, Lower published *The
Enchanted Lovers*, 1658, which, though someday it may be proved
otherwise, must still be considered an original play. In type it is one of
those gallant pastorals spun out of the terrific love entanglements of
genteel disguiselings, such as have already been discussed as a typical
contribution of Cavalier drama. The pastoral retreat in this case is
Erithrea, which is ruled over by the enchantress Melissa; and the principal refugees are Thersander, "a Cavalier disguised in the habit of a
Shepheard," and his loved one, Diana. Persecuted by Melissa and her
magic, these two live and die in alternation, and mourn for each other
in regular shifts, thus carrying tragicomic technique in this matter to
its logical conclusion. Finally they (and the reader) are released by the
intervention of the goddess of the hunt. The studious plotting of this
play fails to redeem the indescribable flatness of the language—

> If the nymph knew the love I have for you,
> I would expect no other usage from her;
> She would without doubt cause me to be carried
> Into some fearful island where I should
> Be rendered miserable all my days:[21]

Such are its prosey rhythms and prosey phrases. In a later chapter
the reader will be reminded of Lower as a writer of plays at a time
when the stage in England was interdict, but there will be no further
need to discuss the plays themselves. The author is a lesser man even
than Cokain, interesting only as a sign of his times, praiseworthy only
for his industry.

Thus far little has been said of plays written by actual residents at
the universities subsequent to 1633, yet here the infiltration of courtly
romance is especially interesting. University playwrights had been
showing increasing susceptibility to outside influences for some time,
and latterly had not been adverse from offering their efforts to the
world. Says Freed in Shirley's *Witty Fair One*, 1628,

What makes so many scholars, then, come from Oxford and Cambridge,
like market-women, with dossers full of lamentable tragedies and
ridiculous comedy, which they might here vent to the players, but
they will take no money for them.[22]

The gibe is repeated wittily in Newcastle's *Country Captain*,

. . . There will be a new play shortly, a pretty play, some say, that
never heard it; a comedy written by a professed scholar: he scorns to
take money for his wit as poets do.

Lady. He is charitable to the actors.
Sister. It may be repentence enough in them to play.[23]

Plays in the English vernacular had gradually won their way. As late as 1615 Tomkis felt called upon to apologize because *Albumazar,* acted at Trinity College, Cambridge, was in English,

> If't be a fault to speak this foreign language,
> (For Latin is our mother tongue) I must entreat you
> To frame excuses for us, for whose sake
> We now speak English.[24]

Yet little more than a decade later Trinity auditors could appreciate the jest in Randolph's *Aristippus,*

> . . . his [Ennius's] verses are in Latin, but because the audience are scholars, I have translated them into English that they may be understood.

Needless to say, only a fraction of Randolph's dramatic work is Latin. But while the university writers had not waited upon the court fad for authorship, to produce an increasing number of English plays, these plays had tended to retain an academic flavor—that is, a dwelling in serious drama with moral allegory, and in lighter drama with topical satire and Plautine farce. This element in Randolph, most recent and popular of the university writers in 1633, has already been noted.

The appearance of the courtier playwrights and the creation of the Cavalier mode had an effect on university drama almost political in its significance. At Cambridge where the atmosphere was increasingly Presbyterian and anti-royalist, courtly romances found not a single imitator. In fact, whereas Latin plays persisted,[25] the only play in English certainly acted at Cambridge between Randolph's time and the closing of the theatres was Cowley's comedy of manners, *The Guardian,*[26] presented on March 12, 1642, while Trinity was receiving a passing visit from Prince Charles. An attack in the Prologue upon such Puritan zealots as Prynne expresses the attitude of the author rather than of the university, which was soon to expel Cowley for his Royalism. Another play, discordantly titled *Adrasta, or The Woman's Spleen and Love's Conquest,* 1635, while never acted, may have been written by a Cambridge student while still in residence. The author, who protests that his play has pleased the "prime wits of both the Universities," signs himself John Jones, Eugenius; and a John Jones took his B.A. in Queen's College in 1636,[27] remained at the university and, about 1638, played the part of Archiater in Johnson's *Valetudinarium.*[28] This may be our author, but of course one cannot be certain of anything respecting a person named John Jones. The play, a tragicomedy, concerns the persecution of the lovers Lucilio and Althea by the splenetic Duchess Adrasta. After both seem to have been hounded to death (in the most complex manner conceivable), and to have been buried in state by grieving parents, they reappear alive, but delay a while their happy union by posing as spirits. The speeches, written in fairly regular blank verse (as those of even the later academic plays are apt to be) are much too long for the stage; and pedantry intrudes from time to time, once in the form of that old donnish device of the ambiguously punctuated letter. Perhaps the most interesting feature of the play is the dedication, wherein the author voices a touching plaint against the Players, who returned his manuscript after "a slight and halfe viewe of it." He comforts himself at last—

. . . What tho it was never acted? I hold the deepe and solid eare a more faithful messenger to the understanding than light spectators: such I mean as applaud only of toyes and bables . . . are like Americans meerely taken with bels, rattles and Hobby-horses, not relishing the perfection of Nature nor solid Art . . .

The dedication, like several other things about *Adrasta,* including a satirical underplot, reminds one of Peter Hausted's *Rival Friends.* It is not certain that Jones was a Cambridge author; and be that as it may, the fact remains that at Cambridge plays in the vernacular decreased in number during the last decade before the wars and no author showed any community of taste with the playwrights of the court.

In contrast, at Oxford there were more English plays produced in the half dozen years before 1642 than in all the preceding years combined, and their type reveals the affinity of the university. Oxford was Royalist in sympathy, and its tastes and interests were converging with those of the court. Since 1630 Laud's chancellorship had helped link the university with the Stuart cause; before long Oxford was to provide the King with a refuge and capital. Dr. Brian Duppa, Dean of Christ Church and vice chancellor of the university, typified the Oxford spirit. Handsome and courtly, he gained the favor of Laud and Dorset and became tutor to the King's sons, yet condescended to sponsor *Jonsonus Virbius,* a book of homage to a professional playwright.

In August, 1636, Archbishop Laud was the host at Oxford of Charles and Henrietta, the Princes, and the nobles and ladies of the court. Since the Prynne episode, which was not yet closed, there had been no better way to display loyalty and a contempt for Puritanism than by entertaining their Majesties with plays, and on this occasion no less than three were offered by the authors and actors of the university.

Studious planning had aimed at variety, and the three plays were
utterly divergent in type. The first, presented by the students of
Christ Church on August 29, was *The Floating Island*, by William
Strode, self-important Orator of the university. The play is a moral
allegory, the Floating Island symbolizing Man or the Human Heart,
and the action depicting the chaotic rule of Queen Phancy when she
is rebelliously substituted for King Prudentius and his counsellor In-
tellectus Agens. Despite the masque-like effects of an elaborate setting,[29]
the play could not have been made lively, such a character as Liveby-
hope displaying few human qualities even though chummily called
"Liveby" by the other personages. Although the court openly displayed
its boredom,[30] in its type the play was less completely moribund than
we might at first suppose.[31] Moral allegory is the Phoenix of dramatic
types: *Microcosmus*, written by Thomas Nabbes only a few years before, received a warm popular reception and created an interest in
"moral masques" which, as we shall see, persisted during the Interregnum. Strode was simply a dull writer, and no one need feel obliged
to follow the advice of his recent editor to read his play three times,
even though one is thus assured of discovering many occult qualities,
including a forecast of the discovery of radium.[32]

The next play presented to the noble and royal visitors, this time
by the students of St. John's, was George Wilde's *Love's Hospital*. An
examination of this play, which is still in manuscript,[33] reveals something better calculated to the holiday mood of the courtly auditory.
Wilde's play is comedy of manners of Jonson-Middleton stock, less
pungent than those of Brome but similar in type. Such comedies reigned
on the contemporary popular stage and were invariably imitated by
the Cavalier writers on the few occasions when they worked the lighter
vein. In *Love's Hospital* most of the humor is supplied by the beautiful Facetia's four suitors, who are respectively deaf, dumb, halt, and
blind; while romantic action is injected into the plot by a fifth suitor,
the comely Comastes, who triumphs alike over the infirm quartette and
over philandering Lysander, the choice of Facetia's eccentric father.
The play is full of boisterous intrigue, and is at times honestly amusing.
Wilde,[34] who deserves an editor, had already written two Latin plays,
Hermorphus and *Euphormus sive Cupido Adultus*, and was to write
another English piece in the year following the royal visit. This play,
also acted by the students of St. John's and thereafter left in manuscript,[35] is a rimed rudimentary pastoral, *The Converted Robber*, interesting less for its romantic fable than for its setting on Salisbury
Plain and the Spenserian brogue of its shepherd folk. *Love's Hospital*
is the more considerable of Wilde's English plays, and seems to have

enjoyed a fair success with the court. "It was merry and without offense," said Anthony Wood, "and so gave a great deal of content."[36]

Wilde's star was dimmed, however, by the astonishing success of the last of the trio of plays offered to the court. In the evening of the same day, August 30, the students of Christ Church redeemed the failure of Strode's allegory by presenting, again with fine scenic effects, William Cartwright's *Royal Slave*. This was Cavalier romance—directly aligned with the courtly plays of Montague, Carlell, and the rest. We are not surprised then that it "much delighted his Majesty and all the nobles," who commended it as "the best that ever was acted."[37] The Lord Chamberlain was "so transported with it that he swore mainly he never saw such a play before."[38] It was not forgotten when the Oxford progress was past. In the November following, Henrietta requested of Laud that the scenery and Persian costumes be sent from Christ Church to the royal seat at Hampton Court, where the professional actors might be compared with the students in enacting the play.[39] On January 12, 1637,[40] the performance was given, again at great expense and with acclaim. The author wrote a new prologue and epilogue and received an honorarium of £40; his play was twice issued in print by 1640.

Why greatness was thrust upon William Cartwright (1611-43)[41] as either man or poet no modern student will understand; his contemporaries seem to have selected him arbitrarily as a paragon. Externally his career was ordinary. His father, of middle class Gloucestershire stock, kept a tavern for a time (as did the elder Davenant), but was himself an Oxford graduate. Young William was diligent and "bright" at Cirencester School, Westminster, and Christ Church, always careful to cultivate the right people and the right opinions. Christ Church, like Westminster School, was a breeding place for poets, and Cartwright gained the friendly interest of Dr. Duppa. After mounting, through his Bachelor's and Master's degrees in 1632 and 1635, he took orders and became finally junior proctor of the university. When rebellion threatened in 1642, Christ Church, foremost of the colleges in loyalty as in poetry, went through the motions of arming, and Cartwright's selection as one of the "Council of War" for Oxford earned him considerable uneasiness when Lord Say led a Parliamentary force into the town and stirred up the academic rookery. A year later he died, just when Oxford had become the royalist capital and the Stuart cause was at its zenith. In spite of this premature death (perhaps partially because of it), William Cartwright became a cherished memory. King Charles is said to have worn mourning for his loss. "The most noted poet, orator, and philosopher of his times" and "the most florid

and seraphical preacher of the university . . . the utmost man could
come to . . . in whom hallowed fancies and reason grew visions and
holy passions, raptures and extasies, and all this at thirty years of age"
—such are the encomiums of Wood, Fell, and Lloyd.[42] "In thee Ben
Johnson held Shakespeare's quill," said Jasper Mayne in commending
the 1651 collection of Cartwright's works, thus reminding us that
Cartwright himself had said "Shakespeare to thee was dull . . ."[43] in
commending the works of Fletcher. Some of the most talented poets
of their time joined Mayne in hymning praises, the number of commendatory verses prefixed to the collected works occupying a quarter of
the volume.[44] The object of this adulation was an affable young man of
quick but common intelligence, sinuous in exploiting his mediocre
talents; and, beneath his poetic, philosophic, religious skin, a con-
formist to the bone. But let us be tolerant still.

Cartwright had already written a comedy, *The Ordinary*,[45] when
The Royal Slave was produced. It had paid Jonson the compliment of
imitation and must explain the old dramatist's plaudit, "My son Cartwright writes all like a man,"[46] for, superior though they are in other
respects to this bit of coarse and unclerical buffoonery, his subsequent
plays are anything but masculine. *The Royal Slave* drips with *préciosité*. Cratander, captive of the Persian King Arsamnes, is appointed
mock ruler for three days, after which he is to be sacrificed to the sun
god. He proves a miracle of justice, valor, and stoic wisdom, winning
at last the platonic love of Queen Atossa. Triumphant alike over
treachery and scorn, he gains the reverence of his enemies, but at the
expiration of his reign insists heroically that the gods shall have their
sacrifice. However, when he is led to the altar, the sun is eclipsed, and
in deference to the omen this royal slave is spared and made ruler
of his native Ephesus. Elevation of tone and grandiloquence of style
give the play an almost religious atmosphere. A sample of the style is
furnished by some of the expositions on platonic love. Cratander can

> . . . distinguish betwixt love and love,
> 'Tween flames and good intents, nay between flames
> And flames themselves.[47]

To her husband Queen Atossa pleads the cause of her love for this
slave,

> Doth not the sun (the sun which yet you worship)
> Send beams to others than yourself? Yet those
> Which dwell on you lose neither light nor heat,
> Coming not thence less vigorous, or less chaste.
> Would you seal up a fountain? or confine
> The air unto your walk? Would you enjoin

The flow'r to cast no smell but as you pass?
Love is as free as fountain, air, or flower,
For't stands not in a point; 'tis large and may,
Like streams, give verdure to this plant, that tree
Nay that whole field of flowers, and yet still run
In a most faithful course toward the bosom
Of the lov'd ocean.

Arsamnes succumbs to this remarkable exegesis, albeit none too heartily

. . . the vine that climbs
By conjugal embracements 'bout the elm
May with a ring or two perhaps encircle
Some neighboring bough, and yet this twining prove
Not the offence, but charity of love.[48]

For all its arboreal trimmings this smacks somewhat of scholasticism, and Cartwright can be the absolute pedant. On the other hand, his style is eloquent, and about Cratander, however spurious he may be in substance, is thrown an aura of dignity.

Two additional romances by Cartwright are of uncertain date. The dedication to one, *The Siege, or Love's Convert,* claims that King Charles saved the manuscript from destruction by its contemptuous author; and the prologue and epilogue of the other, *The Lady Errant,* suggests performance before some polite private audience. The few years following the success of *The Royal Slave* seem the most likely period for their production, especially since Humphrey Moseley in printing these works asserts that all were written before the poet was twenty-five.

The Royal Slave with its sacrificial motif betrays an obvious affinity with Greek romance. So also does *The Siege,* even though the author notes that its plot grew from a suggestion (evidently a very slender one) in Plutarch's *Life of Cimon.* The tyrant Misander besieges Byzantium and demands as tribute Leucasia, fairest virgin of the land. He stabs her in a fit of barbaric distrust; then remorse turns his lust to love, and him from a ferocious conqueror into a perfect professor of amatory-philosophic casuistry. Leucasia drinks a love potion, believing it the poison sent by her father to dispatch Misander, and through this agency comes to reciprocate the latter's love. The initial atmosphere of violence and rapine alters completely to one of peace and amorousness. Elsewhere the play deals with a hunt after the wealthy old widow Pyle by several Byzantian nobles, and is thus rendered less homogeneous than *The Royal Slave* although in the main it has the same tone. The change wrought in Misander by the power of love is wholly miraculous; in gazing at Leucasia.

> . . . his nimble soul
> Did visibly climb up into her eyes
> By their own beams.[49]

In his blank verse as in his lyrics Cartwright revels in conceits. A dominant note in the play is feminism, yet it appears that love alone saves women from complete irrationality:

> Love then doth work in you, what reason
> Doth perform in us, here only lies the difference:
> Ours wait the lingering steps of age and years,
> But th' woman's soul is ripe when it is young.[50]

For the rest, there is the baroque background and all the heroic yet delicate passions of the Cavalier mode.

In *The Lady Errant* the Prince of Crete, after an ornamentally bloody encounter with Olyndus, his dearest friend, wins the hand of the Princess of Cyprus, although their parents are at war. Not the enmity of their nations, but the Prince's noble distemper of jealousy is the chief obstacle to the match, while oracles, disappearances, ethical hazards, and a female rebellion in Cyprus (thwarted at last by one "lady errant" who is pledged to succor men in distress) offers additional complications. In this play as in the others, Cartwright displays his skill as a rhetorician, in which department he was inferior to none of the court playwrights. He was not lacking either in the instincts of the showman: his plays are remarkable for their conscious spectacularity, each one containing ceremonials or pageantry of an almost operatic quality, with the grouping of characters carefully indicated in the text.

Among Oxford playwrights is also numbered Jasper Mayne (1604-72), another "quaint preacher and noted poet" and Cartwright's friend and fellow scholar at Christ Church. Mayne's life,[51] until the Wars, parallels that of his more famous, though actually less capable, companion; but he lived to suffer the hardships of Royalists during the Interregnum and to enjoy the triumph and material rewards of the Restoration. His comedy of manners, *The City Match,* was intended for the royal visit of 1636, but evidently two Christ Church plays were deemed sufficient and the St. John's comedy by Wilde was given precedence; however Mayne's play was "sent for to Hampton court"[52] and was afterwards acted at Whitehall and, with a display of reluctance by the author, at Blackfriars "at the King's price."[53]

Another play, *The Amorous War,* was probably written a year or so later when romantic drama had established its absolute supremacy.[54] The "war" is a holiday sort of engagement in which King Eurymedon of Thrace attacks King Archidamus of Bithynia, ostensibly because the latter has eloped with his sister Roxane, but actually to woo his enemy's sister Barsene. The court ladies involve themselves in the conflict by tanning their faces and posing as amazons. For the alarms of war soon are substituted a series of amorous intrigues, engaging though indelicate, and all ends with marriages and the union of Thrace and Bithynia. The materials, which include sea captures and the like, are those of the Cavalier mode, but the tone is more humorous than heroic, and the type of amorousness revealed is not platonic. Sometimes the speeches suffer from length, but the language is good and the resourceful plot well worked out. The play makes interesting reading for the very reason that its author succumbed only partially to prevailing fashion.

The roster of Christ Church plays is not yet complete. Robert Mead, who took his B.A. in 1638, his M.A. in 1641, and later served valiantly as a captain for King Charles,[55] had the pleasure of seeing the gentlemen of Christ Church enact his *Combat of Love and Friendship*— "a stoop, when his youth was willing to descend from his then higher contemplations."[56] The title is descriptive: three pairs of lovers, interlinked as usual by family ties and friendships, enmesh themselves in a web of unnecessary difficulties, to succumb at last to their obvious destiny of matrimony. Jealousy, honor, friendship, love—these are the themes, developed of course dialectically rather than dramatically. There is some moderately successful comedy in the love rivalry between a soldier and a poet who are forced by their mistress to assume each other's mannerisms, but in the upper realm of action all is the passionate plaints of faddish romance.

Oxford colleges other than Christ Church may claim our two concluding plays, *The Strange Discovery* and *Sicily and Naples*, both printed in 1640. The identification of John Gough, author of the first, with the Merton doctor of divinity of that name must remain purely conjectural, but it is certain that the latter's activities as a preacher about the university and a "jealous son of the Church of England"[57] is no argument against it. *The Strange Discovery* takes us to one of the wellsprings of Cavalier drama, for it is a dramatization of the *Æthiopica* of Heliodorus. However, it lacks all the refinements of the new mode, and is developed simply as a play of adventure and sex intrigue. Written in regular though uninspired blank verse, it serves as a passing abbreviation of the famous Greek novel. It is not adapted to the stage: at that point where Theagenes and Chariclea meet at their devotions, we come upon the following insertion,

Theagines takes the taper with a great deal of reverence from the hand of Cariclea, and sets fire to the altar, but first he was in a maze

at the exceeding beauty of Cariclea, and she as much with his; they
both smiled a little and blush'd, and then became pale again: in
conclusion he falls in love with her, and she with him.[58]

These, somewhat difficult, stage directions indicate the narrative nature of the play.

Samuel Harding, author of *Sicily and Naples,* was a student of
Exeter, who took his bachelor's degree in 1638.[59] From the address
to the reader, it appears that the play was left unacted, and that the
author was anxious to have it appear that "his toy" was forced into
print by his friends. These friends, one of whom was Robert Stapylton, contributed a quantity of commendatory verse to the volume,
wherein the author was compared with Shakespeare, Jonson, Randolph,
and Suckling to their common disadvantage. In the play itself court
treacheries, seductions, accidental incest, and tripartite war among
Naples, France, and Sicily lead up to the "fatal union" in death of
King Ferrando and Calantha, his bethrothed bride. This action, of
course, is not typical of the Cavalier mode, suggesting rather the late
Fletcherian tragedies of the popular stage, but the play is of very mixed
type, and the author's method of disguising his characters, withholding
their identities, etc., shows the influence of the latest romantic school.
The play is obscurely plotted, ugly in atmosphere, and indubitably
hard reading.

Although *Sicily and Naples* is no strong argument in point, the
bulk of late university drama illustrates with clarity, as in a lesser
degree does amateur drama elsewhere, the carrying power of the new
dramatic fashion initiated by the Caroline courtiers. Whether university drama in English as a whole gained or lost in quality and ap-
propriateness need not be debated. Milton no doubt would have
objected to young divines "writhing and unboning their clergy limbs"
in the amorous wars of romance, no less than as the "buffoons and
bawds"[60] of satirical comedy. Certain it is that the dramatic ambitions
of the young divines were stimulated. A stately nod, or the responsive
glance of a bright eye, was worth striving for; a success like Cartwright's
might spell the beginning of a career; it would be pleasant to get one's
degree as Richard Lovelace had got his.[61] The years 1635 to 1642 are
unrivalled in the production of university plays in English, concentrated though they were at Oxford and, indeed, at Christ Church College—that academic outpost of Westminster.

---

[1] G. C. Moore Smith, *College Plays* (Cambridge, 1923), p. 291.
[2] See above, p. 24.
[3] F. G. Fleay, *Biographical Chronicle,* I, 276.

[4] *Dramatic Records of Sir Henry Herbert*, p. 34.

[5] Cf. MS edited by A. Feuillerat, 1904.

[6] F. G. Fleay, *op. cit.*, II, 278. This licensing is not listed in *Dramatic Records of Sir Henry Herbert*. A fragment of *The Corporal* is extant in manuscript: Bodleian, MS Douce C. 2.

[7] For the MS of this play, dated Sept. 16, 1637, and other works of Neale see MSS. Rawl., poet. 79. For Neale's entrance in the Middle Temple see *M. T. Records, Minutes of Parliament*, II, 769.

[8] W. J. Lawrence, "New Facts from Sir Henry Herbert's Office Book," *LTLS*, Nov. 29, 1923.

[9] A. Chester, *Thomas May* (1930), pp. 80 *seq.*

[10] G. C. Moore Smith, *N. & Q.*, Tenth Series, XI, 461-462.

[11] British Museum, Lansdowne MSS, 307.

[12] Act I, Scene i.

[13] T. H. Banks, *Poetical Works of Sir John Denham* (Yale Univ. Press, 1928), Introduction.

[14] Prologue to *The Sophy*.

[15] *DNB*, XI, 224-225; *Alumni Cantabrigienses*, I, 1, 362.

[16] Not published until 1654, but dated Venice, 25. Oct., 1635, in the author's epistle.

[17] H. Spaemann, *Aston Cokains Werke* . . . Munchen diss., summary (1923); K. M. Lea, "Sir Aston Cockayne and the 'Commedia dell'Arte'," *MLR*, XXIII (1928), 47.

[18] Act I, Scene i.

[19] *Works of Cokain*, J. Maidment & W. H. Logan, eds., p. 118.

[20] A life appears in W. B. Gates, *The Dramatic Works and Translations of Sir William Lower with a Reprint of "The Enchanted Lovers,"* Univ. of Penna. thesis (1932).

[21] Act V, Scene i.

[22] Act IV, Scene ii.

[23] Act I.

[24] The Prologue.

[25] J. Rickets' *Byrsa Basilica, c.* 1633; T. Sparrowe's *Confessor, c.* 1634; P. Hausted's *Senilis Amor*, 1636; W. Johnson's *Valetudinarium*, 1638; A. Cowley's *Naufragium Joculare*, 1639 (cf. G. C. Moore Smith, *College Plays*, p. 70).

[26] The play is discussed above, pp. 72-74.

[27] *Alumni Cantabrigienses*, I, II, 486.

[28] G. C. Moore Smith, *op. cit.*, p. 88.

[29] For an extended account of the circumstances of these royal entertainments see Anthony à Wood, *History and Antiquities of Oxford*, II, 408-413.

[30] See above, p. 24.

[31] Another Oxford moral allegory, Richard Zouche's *The Sophister*, usually dated *c.* 1638, is an earlier play; *Fallacy or the Troubles of the Great Hermenia*, Harleian MSS, 6869, No. 2, is a version of it, and is dated August 13, 1631.

[32] Other remarkable claims are made for Strode in the introduction to his poetical works by B. Dobell, London, 1907. Dobell, and E. G. Hoffsten (*The Floating Island*, Univ. of Pa. thesis, 1908) both misconstrue the play as a political allegory.

[33] British Museum Additional MSS, 14047.—The title page bears the date August 29, 1636, but Wood's account indicates that it was given on the afternoon of the thirtieth.

[34] No life appears in *DNB*, but facts are available in *Alumni Oxonienses*, and

Anthony à Wood, *Athenæ Oxonienses*, III, 720. An edition has long been promised in W. Bang's *Materialien*.

[35] B. M. Add. MSS., 14047.

[36] Anthony à Wood, *Hist. and Antiquities of Oxford*, II, 411.

[37] *Evelyn's Diary* (ed. Bray), I, 421.

[38] *Cal. S. P. Domestic*, 1636-37, p. 114.

[39] Anthony à Wood, *Hist. and Antiquities of Oxford*, II, 413.

[40] *Dramatic Records of Sir Henry Herbert*, p. 57.

[41] The most complete life appears in the excellent edition of Cartwright's verse; R. C. Goffin (Cambridge, 1918), pp. xl-xli.

[42] Quoted in the above, *passim*.

[43] Beaumont and Fletcher folio, 1647.

[44] At this even certain contemporaries were amused.

[45] See above, pp. 72-74.

[46] R. C. Goffin, *op. cit.*, Introduction.

[47] Act III, Scene iv.

[48] Act III, Scene v.

[49] Act I, Scene v.

[50] Act V, Scene viii.

[51] *DNB*, XXXVII, 162-163.

[52] Anthony à Wood, *Hist. and Antiquities of Oxford*, II, 413.

[53] Cf. Prologue. The play is discussed above, pp. 72-74.

[54] But see Act V, Scene iii, in which certain allusions suggest an Interregnum revision.

[55] *Athenæ Oxonienses* (ed. Bliss), III, 342; *Alumni Oxonienses*, 997.

[56] Stationer to the Reader.

[57] A. à Wood, *Athenæ Oxonienses*, III, 524.

[58] Act II, Scene viii.

[59] *Alumni Oxonienses*, 648.

[60] *Apology for Smectymnuus*.

[61] See above, p. 109.—Lovelace's *The Scholar* was acted at Gloucester Hall, Oxford, 1634.

III

THE PROFESSIONAL PLAYWRIGHTS

AT the time of Queen Henrietta's appearance in *The Shepherd's Paradise,* the popular stage was very sensitive to influences from Westminster. Because of the growth of Puritanism and the gradual loss of the city audience, the theatres were depending more and more upon attendance by the gentry of Whitehall, the inns of court, and the environs of Holborn, Drury Lane, Fleet Street, and the Strand. The geography of the theatrical district illustrates the fact: in the reigns of James and Charles the active companies migrated steadily away from Shoreditch and the Bankside toward the western suburbs. "Private" theatres were provided, where spectators could sit in enclosed comfort. In the final years of the pre-war period, it is the King's Men at Blackfriars, the Queen's Men at Salisbury Court, and the King and Queen's Boys at the Phoenix about whom we hear most, and whose names appear almost invariably on the title pages of new quartos. The Globe is now no more than a summer theatre used occasionally by the King's Men, and the other Bankside theatres have fallen to base uses. The Fortune and the Red Bull, with the combined disadvantages of being open-air houses and off Society's beaten track, witness the precarious fortunes of second rate troupes. About 1632 or '33 King Charles renovated the Cockpit in Whitehall as a regular "theatre royal" for the performance of plays at court.[1] It is apparent that the two Restoration playhouses governed by royal patentees were not a peculiar product of a new era, but were the culmination of a trend already distinct in 1633.

Blackfriars itself, unmistakably foremost of the theatres, was within the old city walls but at their western extreme. The atmosphere here during the 'thirties was not unlike that of the early Restoration houses. The congestion of sedan chairs and coaches at play-time offered a serious traffic problem.[2] We hear of a dispute between the Lord Chamberlain and the Duke of Lennox over a key to one of the playhouse boxes.[3] The gallants were in full strut then as later, and a combat between Will Crofts and the pugnacious Lord Digby[4] reminds us of a similar one between Henry Killigrew and Buckingham at the Duke's House in 1667.[5] Even the performance of Davenant's *Love and Honor* in the coronation robes of Charles II and his peers[6] is less exclusively typical of Restoration times than it might seem.[7]

While there is sometimes a note of regret in prologues and epilogues for the loss of the old City audience, with its enthusiasm and uncritical tastes, the actors were grateful for, even flattered by, the growth of their fashionable clientele. But as the court began to take up drama in earnest, certain disadvantages began to appear. Between the gorgeous setting of court theatricals and the barren stage of the playhouses the contrast was becoming painful. Caroline audiences were quite familiar with scenery, not in masques alone but in plays. Flecknoe so informs us explicitly in his preface to *Love's Kingdom,* 1664, and there is ample evidence of his accuracy. At those gala times when the courtiers wrote or acted in plays, scenery was the normal thing. Henrietta and her ladies, of course, were granted the finest of scenic backgrounds when they acted Montague's pastoral; among the sketches of Inigo Jones preserved in the Duke of Devonshire collection are those of several sets for this play as well as of the costumes for the queen and the modestly skirted male impersonators. When the curtain rose upon *The Pastoral of Florimene,* acted by Henrietta's maids, the proscenium arch appeared to frame the stately temples of Delos, and in the subsequent scenes only one setting was twice repeated.[8] Several sketches by Inigo Jones of the setting of Carlell's *Passionate Lovers* still survive.[9] Aubrey tells us that Suckling's lavishness in setting out *Aglaura* was expressed not only in the costumes but also in scenes.[10] Henry Killigrew's *Pallantus and Eudora* "had scenes fitted to every passage of it."[11] Herbert's report of the performance of Habington's *Queen of Aragon* mentions "the cloathes and sceanes, which were very riche and curious."[12] Amateur theatricals even outside the court sometimes were elaborately set. Milton's *Comus* was provided with scenes at Ludlow Castle, as were Jonson's entertainments at Welbeck and Bolsover when Newcastle was host to the King. When the Earl of Westmoreland's *Candy Restored* was performed by his children and guests at Apthorpe in 1641, there was a pastoral landscape, and on either side of the stage "a treble entry over which Heroes, men of Armes, and Battles painted . . . which . . . turn silently about at the change in states fortune, and are backt with nothing but fresh greenes & faire garden landskipps which consent in uniformity with the scene itself—the traverse being drawne."[13]

On special occasions at court, the professional players acting in plays from their own repertory were aided by the decorative handicraft of the royal architect. When *The Faithful Shepherdess* was acted at Denmark House by the King's Men in 1634, Inigo Jones fitted it with scenes.[14] Heywood's *Love's Mistress,* also acted at Denmark House, was similarly accoutred; and the enthusiasm of the ingenuous old poet as he writes his dedication to Dorset, the Queen's chamberlain, contrasts with the assumed contempt of other professionals:

I cannot pretermit to give a due charracter to that admirable Artist, Mr. Inigo Iones, Master surveyor of the Kings worke, Ec. who to everry Act, nay almost to every Sceane, by his excellent Inventions, gave such and extraordinary Luster; upon every occasion changing the stage, to the admiration of all the Spectators; that, as I must Ingeniously confesse, It was above my Apprehension to conceive . . .

Caroline attacks on scenery have about them the savor of sour grapes. Peter Hausted must have felt that his *Rival Friends* displeased the court visitors to Cambridge in 1632 partially because of the bare stage:

I doe confesse we did not goe such quaint wayes as we might have done; we had none of those Sea artes, knew not how, or else scorn'd to plant our Canvas so advantageously to catch the wayward breath of the Spectatours, but freely & ingenuously labour'd rather to merit than ravish an Applause from the Theatre.[15]

But in 1636, Laud and the scholars of Christ's Church, Oxford, made certain that their plays in entertainment of the King and Queen should not suffer by comparison with productions at court. Strode's *Floating Island,* whatever its other shortcomings, was equipped with all the fittings of movable wings, landscapes, churches, dwelling-houses, practicable ocean billows, and a populous island visibly floating. Cartwright's *Royal Slave* also was staged with "shuts," sun-lit temples and forests, and "as much variety of scenes and motions as the great wit of Inigo Jones . . . could extend unto."[16]

To what extent the managers of the professional stage tried to meet this kind of competition must remain a field of conjecture. It seems likely that the tendency to introduce into plays imitations in little of court masques brought with it rudimentary imitations of Jonesean settings for particular scenes ever since the accession of James,[17] but there is a singular lack of evidence to support the probability until we come to 1635, when Nabbes' *Microcosmus,* masque-like in its entirety, was presented in jubilee-wise at Salisbury Court.[18] As a *tour de force* the players equipped this play with scenes throughout, and won popular acclaim whatever the financial outcome of their venture may have been. It seems likely that when plays by courtiers became the property of the professional companies, Carlell's *Passionate Lovers* for instance,[19] the scenery adorning their original production at court was transported to the public theatres along with the author's text. It is true that the court and playhouse stages were different in size, but scenery can be cut down. On one occasion certainly there was *fear* that such a transference would take place; when the authorities

of Oxford University lent the scenes and costumes of *The Royal*
Slave to the professionals for their performance at Hampton Court,
they took fitting precautions:

These players had procured from the university all their apparel and
the scenes, which the university did not altogether approve of; yet they
lent them, but with a letter to my lord chamberlain, that because they
had provided that entertainment only for their majesties against their
coming to Oxford, they humbly besought, that what they had done for
the entertainment of their majesties might not be made common upon
a stage.[20]

Another report of the affair is even more definite,

At the same time the Chancellor desired of the King and Queen that
neither the Play, or Cloaths, nor Stage, might come into the hands
and use of the common Players abroad, which was graciously granted.[21]

The courtiers, less reticent about letting their plays fall to the use of
the "common players abroad," would scarcely have withheld their
scenery.

But, at best, scenery on the public stages must have been makeshift
and sporadic, not because of ignorance of it or indifference among the
sharers, but because they could not afford it. Normally, plays continued to be declaimed upon a platform in the old way, with, as we
have remarked, a growing consciousness of a disadvantage. The Prologue to Brome's *Court Beggar,* acted at the Cockpit about 1638, protests,

                    . . . no gaudy scene
          Shall give instructions what his plot doth mean:

In similar vein is the Prologue to Newcastle's *County Captain,* acted
at Blackfriars about 1640:

          Gallants, I'll tell you what we do not mean
          To show you here a glorious painted scene,
          With various doors to stand instead of wit,
          Or richer clothes with lace, for lines well writ;
          Tailors and painters thus, your dear delights,
          May prove your poets only for your sight,
          Not understanding . . .

This affectation of contempt should not deceive us. Ben Jonson, in
his famous quarrel with Inigo Jones, was honestly offended in his
artistic sensibilities that the scene-painter should take the wall of the
poet, but for the lesser lights, they merely deprecated what was beyond
their practical means. Old methods were being placed on the de-
fensive, and the sharers must often have wished that their audiences
were less ravishingly entertained elsewhere.

Sooner or later they must have revised their methods of giving plays, and devised a new playhouse economy. The movement was in the wind, for in 1639 William Davenant, the professional nearest the court and most amenable to its tastes, secured a royal patent for the erection of a huge playhouse in Fleet Street, where "plays, musical entertainments, scenes, or other like presentments" might be displayed.[22] Here was innovation rearing its dangerous head, and that hostility arose among proprietors of established companies we know from the attitude of Richard Heton, manager at Salisbury Court. In this new theatre in Fleet Street, says he, "no man can judge that a fellow of our Company, and a wellwisher to those that own the house, would ever be an actor . . ."[23] This attitude, as well no doubt as that of property owners in the vicinity of the projected theatre, and the patentee's lack of financial resources, caused the abandoning of the design, but we may note that Davenant was the progressive entrepreneur who experimented with a scenic stage during the Interregnum. On an earlier occasion the professional companies had had to suffer in silence when a court whim caused an obvious infringement on their rights. In 1635 the French players under Josias de Soulas, "Floridor," who had won the interest of Queen Henrietta, were permitted by royal command to fit up a playhouse in a Drury Lane riding-school, having been specially privileged before to act plays at the Phoenix on Wednesdays and Fridays during lent—"sermon days" when the English companies were prohibited from acting.[24] These Frenchmen, besides, employed women actors, also prohibited (by custom at least) to the natives, although, according to a passage in Shirley's *The Ball*, it was "a thing much desired in England by some ladies, inns o'court gentlemen, and others."[25]

But when all is said, about the educated tastes of polite audiences, it was the professional playwrights more than the managers and actor-sharers who felt a pressure from the court. At least the professional troupes were little affected by the competition of amateur actors, such performances as those of *The Shepherd's Paradise, Florimene,* and *The Queen of Aragon* being relatively few, while professional appearances at court were still numerous and profitable. Amateur authors, on the other hand, threatened dangerous competition. It seems that plays by courtiers did not even require licensing,[26] and since such plays were likely to become town talk, the professional companies were willing enough to present them. We have seen that *Arviragus and Philicia* was "hugely liked of everyone" and *The Royal Slave* was proclaimed "the best that ever was writ." We can imagine the effect of such judgments on the tempers of steady practitioners. Ben Jonson's friendliness toward his university "sons" rarely extended to the courtiers; in complimenting Brome's *Northern Lass*,[27] he comments on the playwright's craft:

> You learn'd it well, and for it serv'd your time,
> A 'prenticeship; which few do nowadays:
> Now each court hobby-horse will wince in rime,
> Both learned and unlearned all write plays.
> It was not so of old: men took up trades
> That knew the crafts they had been bred in right . . .

Commendations by John Ford express more mildly the same sentiment.

Richard Brome became the chief spokesman of professional antagonism toward the gallant interlopers who, with the Cavalier mode, were making his kind of drama old-fashioned overnight. He scoffed cleverly at Suckling's *Aglaura*,[28] at the importation of plays from Oxford,[29] and at the laureateship[30] when it had been won by Davenant, who in a sense had sold out to the court. In his Prologue to *The Court Beggar*, he condemns "handsome love-toys":

> . . . of late (he knows not how) y'are grown
> Deeply in love with a new strain of wit
> Which he condemns, at least disliketh it.

In the Prologue to *The Antipodes, c.* 1638, he continues the attack:

> Opinion, which our author cannot court,
> (For the dear daintiness of it) has of late
> From the old way of plays possesst a suite,
> Only to run to those that carry state
> In scene magnificent, and language high,
> And clothes worth all the rest, except the action,
> And such are only good those leaders cry;
> And into that belief draw in a faction,
> That must despise all sportive merry wit
> Because some such great play had none of it.

And in the Prologue to *A Jovial Crew,* 1641:

> (Our comic writer, finding that romances
> Of lovers, through much travail and distress,
> 'Till it be thought no power can redress
> Th' afflicted wanderers, though stout chivalry
> Lend all his aid for their delivery;
> 'Till lastly some impossibility
> Concludes all strife, and makes a comedy) . . .

There are hints of antagonism in the prologues, epilogues, and commendatory verses of other professional playwrights. In their actual plays most of them resisted, consciously or unconsciously, the Cavalier mode. Yet its influence is sometimes apparent, and it is interesting to trace the effects upon professional work, especially that of the newer arrivals.[31]

In 1633 the professional playwrights still surviving from Shakespeare's day were fairly numerous. Not all of these were active. Chapman, Dekker, and Rowley, though still living, seem to have ended their traffic with the stage, while Ben Jonson was just bringing his career unhappily to a close. But the veteran of them all had not yet retired from the lists. Thomas Heywood (1573?-1641), who had been writing plays in those distant years when the Admiral's Men were giving keen competition to the company of Shakespeare, still exercised his quality, and was adapting himself with engaging humility and good humor to conditions of the new day. From 1631 to 1639 he was poet of the City Pageants. In 1633 and '34 he retorted to Prynne and Prynne's aspersions upon the stage.[32] Between 1630 and '36 he wrote a number of prologues and presentations for plays given at court;[33] perhaps he spoke these lines himself—an aged priest of Thalia. He accepted Queen Henrietta as "the very soul of Amabilitee,"[34] the great patroness of his art, and in 1634 cheerfully brought himself to her notice by dedicating to her his ambitious compilation, *The Hierarchy of the blessed Angels, their Names, Orders, and Offices. The Fall of Lucifer with his Angels.*

Heywood was rewarded for his uncritical readiness when *Love's Mistress, or The Queen's Masque, c.* 1634, was selected, as its title page says, to be "three times presented before their two Excellent Maisties, within the space of eight dayes. In the presence of Sundry Forraigne Ambassadors." The play retells the tale of Cupid and Psyche, but is interspersed with pastoral scenes featuring Pan, singing nymphs and swains, dancing bumpkins, and the like. One character, Midas, mean-spirited and carping, has been interpreted as a caricature of Prynne,[35] but of this attack upon a fallen enemy Heywood must be declared guiltless; Midas despises poetry, but as a materialist not as a Puritan, and he takes a most un-prynnish delight in low comedy. Despite its masque-like ornaments, *Love's Mistress* is dramatic, at least in its earlier acts, and is full of that sweetness distilled from old myths and natural beauty so typically Elizabethan. Gracing this Caroline feast, Heywood has conjured up a spring breeze to replace the scents of perfumery, fresh flower-garlands to replace the gilt and tinsel. *Love's Mistress* contains the strongest blank verse and the truest poetry heard at so late a date in any new play performed at court. One hopes it was appreciated, that it was not alone the scenery by Inigo Jones which, in the words of the delighted and self-effacing author, sent away the noble spectators so "plenally satisfied."[36]

Love's Mistress was successful, but was not *à la mode*. Its type returns us to the time of Lyly and Peele. However, Heywood was willing to learn new tricks. In *A Challenge for Beauty*, acted by the King's Men about 1635, he produced what has been called "the most polite and fashionable of his dramas,"[37] obviously in an attempt to write in the Cavalier fashion. Courtly apparel sits oddly upon a play resembling at the core the author's own *Fair Maid of the West;* and the chronicle structure, the rugged language, the bourgeois tone, and the patriotic note assort quaintly with modish themes of love, honor, and friendship:

> Honour should still precede love; Sir, I will,
> Though I, to cure another, myself kill . . .

The opposed ethical niceties in points of honor expounded in the plays of Montague and his followers must have struck the honest intelligence of Heywood as a kind of game among the characters: the attempts of his Bonavida to match the beauty and virtue of the English maiden, Hellena, against the vaunted excellences of Spanish Isabella, and the "passages of honor" between the English slave Ferrers and his friend and rival, the Spanish Captain Valladaura, are developed naïvely as "contests." The long, stiff strides of Heywood could not be disciplined to the mincing gait and ballet leaps of the courtiers, but that he essayed imitation at all is testimony alike of their prestige and his complaisance.

The attitude of Ben Jonson (1572-1637), proud, opinionated, inflexible, is directly at variance with that of Heywood. Jonson, of course, had his private reasons for resenting the courtly invasion of drama. When he had quarreled with Inigo Jones about whose name should have precedence on the title page of *Chloridia* in 1631, the court had decided, since this testy pair could not work in harmony together, it could spare the poet more readily than the scene-craftsman. Jonson then, despite his skill and long service in writing masques, and his quasi-official standing as laureate poet, had to retire and watch his inferiors such as Townshend, Carew and Davenant take his place. The Lord Chamberlain even stepped in to silence his satirical reprisals upon Jones.[38] Finally his last play when acted at court was "not likte."[39] Jonson was a particular sufferer from the growing sophistication and taste for novelty. His former prestige and the esteem in which he was still held by the literati prevented not at all popular audiences from damning his later works. These, *The New Inn*, 1629, *The Magnetic Lady*, 1632, and *The Tale of a Tub*, 1633, show, we must confess, an attempt to capitalize former success and a tiresome inversion upon old methods. *The Magnetic Lady* begins with labored dogmas, in defense of itself and its author's art, which are singularly unattractive.

It seems likely that Jonson's obscuration as a public figure was pretty complete after 1633. His health was poor. In 1631 he had lost his post as city chronologer through failure to function. It is unlikely that in his last years he was recognized as a critical dictator. His ability to charm a tavern circle must have passed with his ability to write successful plays. There is no evidence that the "sons of Ben" ever composed a literary circle of any compactness, with Jonson as the presiding genius—however proud young men may have been at winning the old master's approbation. Thanks to his pension and the good offices of Newcastle, who sometimes employed him,[40] Jonson was never in the shadow of want, but he was fading none-the-less from popular consciousness. The unusual tribute paid him in *Jonsonus Virbius*, the book of homage which followed his death in 1637, must have been occasioned partially, like so many funeral wreaths in general, by a guilty regret his passing caused his neglectful times.

But while Jonson personally had ceased to be a commanding figure in the period we are studying, the methods he had originated in comedy remained in use. Others more adaptable than he were able to make these methods still palatable. They were utilized, as we have seen, in the comedies of every courtier and gownsman who donned the sock. Their persistence is tiresome in individual minor plays, which are often interesting in the degree that they have escaped "humours." Yet it must be confessed that many comedies, both amateur and professional, are passable, which would be nothing at all had their authors lacked so sound a mentor in comic technique.

Among the professionals who followed the footsteps of Jonson may be numbered Shackerley Marmion (1603-39), who, though derived of landed gentry and educated at Oxford, was forced by indigence to seek a livelihood with his pen, becoming the associate of Heywood, Brome, and Nabbes rather than of the literary dabblers in and about the court. His brief and hectic career,[41] terminated by a fatal illness while he was serving in Suckling's troop during the Bishops Wars, reminds us of those of the early "university wits." *Holland's Leaguer*, 1631, and *A Fine Companion*, 1633, are the usual combination of Middleton's comedy of intrigue in low-life and Jonson's "humours," repulsive in some respects, but the work of a man of talent, with a much better command of blank verse (when he chose to use it) than was common

among new writers of the 'thirties. The only extant play produced by
Marmion after the fashion of courtly drama had set in is *The Antiquary, c.* 1635; this contains more polished dialogue in the manner of
Shirley's social comedy than does the author's former plays, but its
type is true to the tradition in which he had elected to begin his work.

Jonson's chief follower among the professional dramatists was, of
course, Richard Brome (d. 1652?), who, with occasional trading in more
serious wares, industriously supplied his comic staples to the playhouses
for the dozen years preceding their close. While the stamp of Jonson
is always upon his plays, so also is that of Middleton, and his methods
reveal how he could please the taste of popular audiences, how his
reputation could wax while Jonson's waned. For emphasis on character is substituted emphasis on intrigue; the satirist and moralist gives
way to the farceur and ribald jester. But these things everyone knows,
and Brome should be given his due. He has suffered too much from a
kind of critical snobbery, which has stigmatized him as the base imitator
of a greater man whose groom he had formerly been. Brome, after all,
produced such original plays and such first-class entertainment as *The
Antipodes* and *A Jovial Crew.*

We have noticed how Brome, who was working on contract to supply
three plays a year to the Salisbury Court Theatre and who naturally
looked askance at amateur competitors,[42] became the chief spokesman
of professional antagonism toward the courtly invasion and the Cavalier mode. Once, however, he weakened and paid the new fashion
the tribute of imitation. *The Love-sick Court* has been dated *c.* 1629
upon very slender circumstantial evidence,[43] but both its story and
treatment suggest influences not in effect until after the courtier playwrights had appeared upon the scene. Against a background of civil
unrest, capitalized by the machinations of a court villain, the supposed
brothers, Philocles and Philargus, contend for the hand of the responsive but oscillating Princess Eudina. Though the successful suitor
will wear the crown of Thessaly, the rivals are such souls of honor, so
devoted to each other, and so befuddled by the customary obscurities
uttered by a Delphic oracle, that their route to the coveted goal is
most circuitous. Tricked into a duel, each tries to die at the other's
hand, and Philargus apparently succeeds. Then Philocles is revealed
to be Eudina's brother—translated, of course, as a babe. Philargus reappears alive, and he takes Eudina while Philocles takes the crown—
thus satisfying the spectators with an equitable division of the prizes.
In the heroic vein of the rival friends and the ethical confusion of the
Princess, all of whom the author has tried valiantly to endow with
new-fangled sensibility, we discern the leaning toward courtly romance,

even though Brome moves with ludicrous awkwardness amidst the emotional subtleties of his theme. He proved more at ease in tragicomedy on the several occasions when he followed the spoor of Fletcher and Massinger; the Cavalier mode was the peculiar forte of the gallant amateurs.

The last notable disciple of Jonson produced by the professional stage was the earnest, respectable, and uninspired Thomas Nabbes (1605-41). In *Covent Gardens, c.* 1632, *Tottenham Court, c.* 1633, and *The Bride,* 1638, we find reincarnate "humours," accessory, to be sure, to the current preoccupation of popular comedy—the thorny path of a pair of pure and sentimental bourgeois lovers through the thickets of a London Town which seems to have been peopled entirely by mercenary oldsters and rowdy tavern wits. In some respects Nabbes was a more faithful child of Jonson than was Brome. His plays by precept, if not always by example, are strictly moral, even sermonesque, and reveal the author's sense of professional vocation. He was doctrinaire, more so than any dramatist other than Jonson himself, and strove consciously to observe the classical principles of unity. Even *The Unfortunate Mother,* his unacted Fletcherian tragedy, he guarantees will have,

> A constant scene, the business it intends.
> The two hours time of action comprehends.

His *Hannibal and Scipio,* 1635, like Jonson's Roman tragedies, which it imitates, seems to have been undertaken as its author's masterpiece. He studiously explained the structure of the play in his prologue, denoted a new scene with the appearance of each new speaker, carefully read the printer's proofs, and gave all signs that he believed himself here to be contributing to Literature. The tragedy actually is both dignified and interesting.

Nabbes remained severely aloof from Cavalier fashions. His romantic *Unfortunate Mother,* as he assures the reader, contains no mysterious disguises, no "bumbast raptures," no "glorious scene of state." His interest to the student of new or, as in this case, revived currents in mid-seventeenth century drama derives chiefly from *Microcosmus, A Moral Mask,* which as has already been mentioned was produced on the professional stage of Salisbury Court in the full panoply of painted scenes. *Microcosmus* is really a morality play,[44] resembling, in theme, Strode's *Floating Island,* and, in its conventions, dramatic allegories of much greater antiquity. The characters are such abstractions as Temperance, Sensuality, Love, Hope, and Despair, Nature and the five senses, the bodily humours (such as Phlegm and

Choler), together with the functionaries Bonus Genius, Malus Genius, Philosopher, and the like. Pivotal in the action are Physander—the body—and Bellanima—the soul—, the conflict and final reconciliation of these reminding us of the old body-and-soul debates, and much besides. Physander *in extremis* is deserted like Everyman by his fleshly companions. Cumbered though it is with mediæval trappings, the effect of the piece is dramatic; and with its masque-like complement of song, dance, and scenic decoration, it could bid well for success. Nabbes is often alluded to with respect during Interregnum times, and when we observe the popularity of moralities in the private theatricals of that time, we must remember *Microcosmus.*

The remaining professional playwrights active in the 'thirties, Massinger, Ford, Shirley, Davenant, and Glapthorne, occupied themselves chiefly with romantic tragedy and tragicomedy, and may be classified roughly as of the school of Fletcher. Most of their serious plays are in the main stream of Fletcherian tradition and are distinct from those of that Fletcherian tributary—the Cavalier mode. Yet here once more the influence of the latter is perceptible.

Philip Massinger (1583-1640) had actually worked at the same table with Fletcher in collaboration, and might have been expected to succeed him as reigning dramatist after 1625. That honour was reserved for James Shirley, but Massinger remained active, though a little disgruntled it appears, until 1639. His relations with the court were not close, probably through no choice of his own. In January, 1631, Herbert refused to license one of his plays because its reflections of international politics were adjudged to contain "dangerous matter."[45] Just two months later, however, his *Emperor of the East* was performed before their Majesties with the author protesting in his prologue that the play, even in conception, was sacred to the King's pleasure, and was free from all unseemliness. Parts of it might well have been designed to instruct Charles in kingly ethics. In June, 1638, Massinger again provoked censorship, this time by the King himself. Herbert copied down a speech uttered by Don Pedro of Spain in the play, now non-extant, *King and Subject,* beginning

We'll raise supplies what ways we please,

and voicing with peculiar arrogance the speaker's subscription to the doctrine of the divine right of kings. Herbert also copied down Charles's censure, "This is too insolent, and to bee changed," evidently pleased that those who afterwards might cast eyes upon it would have "proof" that his master was no tyrant.[46] Our first impression is that Massinger had been leaning over backward in a display of loyalty and had intended the speech as admirable, but the possibility that the *King and Subject* was identical with the play significantly titled *The Tyrant*[47] casts a different light on the playwright's motives. Like many loyal subjects, Massinger may have deplored absolutism, and may have risen covertly to object. If so, his good intentions would not have been appreciated. In his prologues and epilogues, and even in the body of his plays, there is a note of repining which suggests a sense of neglect. At court,

> There is a drink of forgetfullness, which once tasted
> Few masters think of their servants, who, grown old,
> Are turn'd off, like lame hounds and hunting horses,
> To starve in the commons.[48]

But he admits that he is "a strange old fellow" whose "sullen mood would quickly leave him" would his audiences consent to be pleased.[49]

The exact extent to which Massinger attempted to please by taking a leaf from the book of the courtly playwrights is hard to discover because only one of his later plays survives besides *The Guardian,* a comedy of 1633, and *A Very Woman,* fashioned in 1634 out of an older play. However this single work, *The Bashful Lover,* 1636, is revealing. It is different from Massinger's older plays, and the new notes are in the scale of courtly romance. The bashful lover of the play is Hortensio, a Milanese, whose only plea to Matilda, the Princess of Mantua whom he humbly adores, is—

> That I may not offend you, that is all,
> When I presume to look on you . . .

When Mantua is attacked by the Duke of Tuscany, Hortensio's devotion sublimates into prodigies of valor; he rescues his great rival, Prince Uberti, from death, and Matilda herself from rapine. He is one of those heroes who feels disgraced by defeat no matter what the odds. In all ways the play is a compendium of ultra-romantic themes. Prince Uberti himself and his friend Farneze make heroic sacrifices for each other, and the former grieves jealously when the latter appears to have won death and honor; a hermit Octavio succors the battle-torn warriors and proves a great general in disgrace; the savage leader of the Tuscans is tamed by the beauty and goodness of Matilda, and makes peace with the defeated Mantuans. Finally Hortensio is proved no humble unknown but heir to the dukedom of Milan, whereupon Uberti is persuaded that his path of duty precludes marriage, and Matilda is freed to grant her bashful champion his guerdon.

Not only in its type of story but in its general atmosphere, its exalted tone and heroic intensity, *The Bashful Lover* recalls Carlell and Killigrew. Hortensio's exploits are accompanied with appropriate eloquence, and although Massinger was too good a dramatist to imitate the extra-dramatic discursiveness of the courtier playwrights, and their utter disregard of human realities, it is obvious that he was tending to play their game. His rhetorical art lent itself well to the type, and *The Bashful Lover* may be considered one of the best of the "paleo-heroic" plays. The titles of other later plays by Massinger—the titles are all we have to judge by—: *Cleander*, 1634, *The Orator or the Noble Choice*, 1635, *Alexius or the Chaste Lover*, 1639, and *The Fair Anchoress of Pausilippo*, 1640, suggest, together with the play just reviewed, that the Cavalier mode may have diverted his concluding work into a new phase.

In John Ford (1586- a. 1639), on the other hand, it is unlikely that we should find the slightest trace of influence by the new fashion even if all his plays had survived. Though less the disinterested, occasional playwright than he wished to be thought, Ford's contact with the theatre was less close than Massinger's and from the beginning he had been less susceptible to the stress of popular taste. There is something isolated about his work which the word "bookish" scarcely describes, although it may suggest the tendency he displays, in contradistinction to our other older dramatists, to create plays as literature, to concentrate on his own predilections and develop his own artistic ideals. Unless it is postdated by *The Queen, or the Excellency of her Sex*, which has virtually been proved his,[50] *The Lady's Trial*, 1638, is Ford's last extant play; in fact these, and the effluvious comedy, *Fancies Chaste and Noble*, c. 1635, are the only ones falling within the period of our purview. Neither *The Queen*, despite its congenial basis in the loves and wars of Aragon, nor *The Lady's Trial*, despite its late date, has followed the fashion of courtly romance. Free from the forbidding themes of *'Tis Pity She's a Whore* and *Love's Sacrifice*, they exemplify otherwise Ford's unique and subtle strain.

The playwright who might naturally have been expected to become the chief purveyor of professional entertainment for the court was James Shirley (1596-1666). Although derived of common stock, he was a man of culture who had distinguished himself at Cambridge and become master of St. Alban's, which he had been voted to represent as proctor in 1624.[51] The radical change in his life involving his removal to Gray's Inn and turning dramatist in 1625 increased rather than decreased his wide circle of friends. May, Randolph, Habington, and Stapylton commended his early plays, besides gentlemen of the inns of court and fellow professionals like Massinger and Ford. The dedicatees of his published plays comprise a roll call of the gentry. Newcastle enlisted his services as a collaborator.[52] Yet the fact remains that Shirley, whether through disregard of faddish tastes in drama or through ineptitude as a courtier, missed his preferment; and although it was he who succeeded Fletcher as most popular playwright, it was another, William Davenant, who succeeded Jonson as court stipendiary. And such would probably have been the case even though Shirley had not been disqualified by his Catholicism.

Shirley's plays from 1625 to 1632 were chiefly comedies and tragedies in the school of Fletcher. Between 1632 and 1635, appeared *Hyde Park, The Lady of Pleasure,* and other comedies of manners, more fashionable and sophisticated than anything Fletcher had written, and destined to place Shirley first among those who heralded comedy of the Etheregean type. Although Herbert took exception to *The Ball,* 1632, because of the exactitude of its portraiture,[53] the play had tended to defend the amusements of those in high life from carping outsiders, and seems to have proved quite acceptable to polite audiences. In 1633 King Charles himself provided Shirley with the plot of another comedy of manners, *The Gamester,*[54] which from any reasonable point of view is more objectionable than *The Ball.* In 1633 and 1634, when the court was beginning to take its more active interest in drama, Shirley was in favor. In 1633 appeared *Bird in a Cage,* satirically dedicated to Prynne, the caged enemy, by James Shirley "Servant to her Majesty." In the same year Herbert licensed *The Young Admiral,* and went out of his way to praise it:

The comedy called *The Yonge Admirall,* being free from oaths, prophaness, or obsceaness, hath given mee much delight and satisfaction in the readinge, and may serve for a patterne to other poetts, not only for the bettering of manners and language, but for the improvement of the quality, which hath received some brushings of late. When Mr. Sherley hath read this approbation, I know it will encourage him to pursue this beneficial and cleanly way of poetry, and when other poetts heare and see his good success, I am confident they will imitate the original for their own credit . . .[55]

Performed at court, the play was "likte by the K. and Queen." In 1634 Shirley was selected to be the author of the great entertainment for their Majesties whereby the inns of court repudiated the doctrines of *Histriomastix.*

Bird in a Cage, and *The Young Admiral* are dramatized romance,[56] and therein depart from Shirley's work up to this point. The concession to court taste, however, involved little except selection of material. *Bird in a Cage* treats whimsically rather than in deadly earnest its extravagant theme. *The Young Admiral* is a somewhat nearer approach to the type of play we have been studying, and should be examined with the similar contributions of Heywood, Brome, and Massinger. Vittori, admiral of the Neapolitan fleet, returns glorious from victory over the Sicilians, but is banished by Prince Cesario, who is jealous alike of his conquests and his favor with the beauteous Cassandra. Captured with his beloved one by a second fleet from Sicily, Vittori is given the choice of witnessing Cassandra's immediate execution or of leading the enemy against his native, though ungrateful, land. He chooses the second alternative, only to be further tortured by the knowledge that his own father, held hostage in Naples, is in jeopardy despite his patriotic offer to resist the attack of his offended son. Finally, Cassandra joins forces with Rosinda, a Sicilian Princess whose jilting by Cesario has provoked the war in the first place; and these two bestir their women's wits to effect reconciliations and an end of the combat of love and arms. The young admiral of this play, wandering in disguise, buffeted by fate, torn between love and honor, distempered by jealousy, ready to hold Cassandra in his arms and hurl defiances at overwhelming odds, is almost the heroic figure of the courtly school.

The Young Admiral was written only half a year after *The Shepherd's Paradise* created its sensation at court, whereas *Bird in a Cage* was almost coincident with, Montague's play.[57] In other words the schematized romance of the courtiers, with its platonic affinities, was still in inception, and Shirley could scarcely have imitated it in the plays just reviewed even had he so desired. We examine with particular interest then his plays of the next few years, written when Carlell, Killigrew, and the rest were industriously following Montague's lead. We find that Shirley, although he tended to occupy himself more with romantic and serious themes[58] than he had formerly done, did not substitute gilded manikins for characters, sensibilities for emotions, heroic posturing for dramatic action. In a word he ignored the Cavalier mode. Platonic love and *précieuse* debate interested him not at all—and this remained true throughout his extremely fecund subsequent career. Let us note also that he did not continue to grow in favor expressly as an entertainer of the court. He was so dependent upon his market with the popular stage that in 1636, when plague closed the London theatres, he migrated to Dublin where he could continue to exercise his craft. In 1639, in dedicating his *Maid's Revenge* to Henry Osborne, he said, "I never affected flattery: some say I have lost my preferment by not practising that court sin." His affecting no more the literary artifices of the court may have contributed to this loss of preferment.

A dramatist with Shirley's skill might have written interesting plays in the Cavalier mode. Had he turned to this dramatic type and wrought certain changes in it, in the direction let us say of technical discipline, his serious plays might be more prominent historically than they are now. He is destined to be known more and more by his comedy; his tragedy and tragicomedy, competent and estimable though it may be, suffering from the abundance of earlier work of the same kind, and the inescapable impression of dilution which it conveys to the modern reader. We shall concede, of course, that an impetus from him to the formation of that dubious artistic type, the heroic play, would offer us a poor exchange for his authentic even though attenuated strain of dramatic poesy.

It is to be hoped that Shirley has not been pictured as a sort of martyr to his artistic integrity. He was a practical and successful playwright. Caroline audiences for all their increasingly effeminate tastes must have enjoyed the Cavalier mode largely for its novelty, and even *Arviragus and Philicia* and *The Royal Slave* would have produced a surfeit if presented in endless repetition. Shirley's plays were still the better steady diet. His only error, from the practical viewpoint, was in not deviating at intervals to the new fashion, thus fortifying at court his reputation as a modish writer. The dramatist who showed the most skill in keeping one foot in the public theatre and the other in the royal banqueting halls was William Davenant (1606-68), the venturesome son of an Oxford taverner. Though usually thought of as a figure in the theatrical world of the Restoration, Davenant was a noted playwright and produced the bulk of his original drama before the closing of the theatres. His was no small achievement—succeeding to Jonson's place as writer and pensioner of the court a dozen years after starting from scratch. How he was sent to London at sixteen with two suits of clothes and £40 to serve an apprenticeship to "some good merchant or other tradesman," how he escaped by becoming a page in the town houses of prominent nobility, and then through the good offices of Endymion Porter secured his entrance at court is an interesting story though it cannot be detailed here.[59] During his career as a popular playwright, Davenant was also a soldier, an author of court masques, an indefatigable writer of complimentary epistles to the nobility, and an intimate companion of courtiers such as Porter and Suckling. His later career presents us with the original and—to the student of Caroline trends—the revealing spectacle of a professional playwright who became a royal general and envoy, and was raised to knighthood.

Davenant began his career as a playwright not long after Shirley, but met at first with scant success. *The Cruel Brother*, 1627, *Albovine*, c. 1628, and *The Just Italian*, 1629, are all reminiscent—mostly of

Fletcher. The last is a serious comedy of manners, the others romantic tragedies of lust and bloodshed, eloquent of their author's youthful gusto, but not pleasing enough to the times to save one from failing on the stage and the other from being refused by the actors. A long illness interrupted Davenant's career, but in the season 1633-34 he produced his sprightly comedy, *The Wits,* which like its companion study of manners, *News from Plymouth,* is distinguished by a certain breezy freshness from plays of the same type produced by other imitators of Jonson. *The Wits* suffered at Blackfriars from the persecutions of an inimical clique, but succeeded at court, where it was presented probably through the intervention of the author's friend Endymion Porter, who had previously moved King Charles to restore the text censored by Herbert for alleged profanity.[60]

From 1634 on Davenant's plays alternated between types standard on the popular stage and romances which approximated as closely as any professional work the drama of the Cavalier mode. *News from Plymouth,* 1635, *The Unfortunate Lovers,* a Fletcherian court tragedy, 1638, and *The Spanish Lovers,* a cloak and sword play of Spanish inspiration, 1639, reveal clearly enough the author's continued affiliation with the professional group. On the other hand, *Love and Honor,* 1634, *The Platonic Lovers,* 1635, and *The Fair Favorite,* 1638, were obviously affected by court interests, and must have looked for their appeal chiefly to the most gallant sector of the Caroline audience. Another play, *The Siege,* which first appeared in Davenant's folio of 1673, has been identified, no doubt correctly, with a play licensed in 1629 as *The Colonel;*[61] but since this play also resembles courtly romance, there is weight in the suggestion that it underwent revision after its early appearance.[62] The high-minded reproof given by Bertolina to Florello, whose love for her has made him desert the Florentine army besieging her native Pisa, and Florello's frenzy at the loss of both love and honor together with his subsequent redemption through valor, are all bathed in the refulgent glow of hyper-romantic idealism. The plot reminds us of Shirley's *Young Admiral,* the two plays containing, by the way, one almost identical speech.[63]

When Davenant hit upon the title *Love and Honor* for a play already twice named, he revealed his sensitiveness to currents from the court. Practically any play in the courtly fashion might be fitted with this title. The gentlemen of Whitehall did actually fancy themselves as potential military heroes, while the vocation of the ladies was to master the technique of love, both sexes naturally craving the amenities rather than the fatigues of their several preoccupations. They expected writers to provide patterns of behavior and discourse in a dramatic apotheosis of their own dream-world. In *Love and Honor*, Evandra, doomed captive in Savoy, has three glorious lovers, each of whom asks nothing better than that his life be sacrificed for hers. Evandra herself, and her fellow paragon Melora, are severally determined that only they shall pay the extreme penalty. Displays of tempestuous love and disinterested valor alternate in ingenious succession, until the author springs his surprise and, by wrenching every probability, bathes all alike in a perfumed felicity.

Love and Honor was exactly contemporary with Shirley's *The Opportunity*, a drama of light hearted intrigue. The modish appeal of *Love and Honor*, as well as the friendship of Porter, may explain why Davenant and not Shirley was selected several months later to receive the Queen's commission to write a masque glorifying platonic love. On February 10, 1635, *The Temple of Love* was presented at court, a pleasantly buoyant succession of songs and eccentric dances, amidst which a group of "Persian" youths (including the not overly platonic Lord Goring) avoid the wiles of magicians and find the Temple of Chaste Love, recently established upon the Isle of Natsinga by Queen Indamora—that is, of course, Henrietta Maria. Davenant's conception of chaste love seems to have derived from the connubial compatibility of Charles and Henrietta rather than from the doctrines of D'Urfé, but his efforts were appreciated, as two additional court performances of *The Temple of Love* go to testify. Several months later, he made dramatic capital of the court fad for platonic love by writing a "drama of love debate . . . for and against fruition of love in marriage."[64] In *The Platonic Lovers*, 1635, Duke Theander and Duke Phylomont are each in love with the other's sister; but whereas Phylomont woos with the traditional objectives, Theander's warmth is all of the spirit; he is content to beget reflections in his mistress's eyes, leaving the "coarse and homely drudgeries" of creating children to more common clay. Although Davenant's convictions are on the side of the natural lover, he puts into the mouth of Theander and his soul affinity, Eurithea, words of sweet and tender delicacy.

In *The Fair Favorite* we again have a romance of courtly sentiment and gallantry. Eumena, the platonic mistress and state favorite of a King, is rumored unchaste, and becomes the provocation of an odd combat between two devoted friends, her own brother, who believes the rumor, and her new-kindled lover, who does not. As usual the duel proves fatal only by report, the brother is saved from the scaffold, Eumena weds her champion, and the King forswears platonic dalliance to reciprocate the long-suffering devotion of his faithful Queen. In this play more than in the others the author inclines to sacrifice comic underplot in deference to Cavalier practice.

Although this is not the place to enter into an extended discussion of the poetic and dramatic endowment of Davenant, whom we shall meet again in later chapters, the point may be made that his plays have been unjustly disparaged. Even in these polite romances just reviewed, although he gives us more rhetoric of artificial sentiment and inflated heroics than does Shirley, he never descends to the prolix bathos of the genuine *précieux,* and his plays rise considerably above those of the amateurs at court.

The last professional playwright to appear upon the scene in time to produce any considerable body of work was Henry Glapthorne (1610- a. 1643), whose half dozen extant plays were produced between 1635 and 1640. Too little is known of Glapthorne for us to determine exactly his social and professional affiliations, but it appears certain that he came to London from Cambridgeshire via Cambridge University;[65] and that he moved on the fringe of smart society, aspiring like Davenant, though less successfully, to favor with the great. Lines such as,

Sconce. . . . my ancestors kept the inquisition out of Amsterdam.
Urinal. And brought all sects in thither.[66]

suggest, if not Catholic leanings, at least a strong aversion to the evangelicals. Glapthorne was acquainted with Lovelace, and dedicated plays to Thomas Wentworth, Earl of Strafford, and to Will Murray, groom of the King's bed-chamber.

During his few years of dramatic activity Glapthorne was feeling his way, uncertain whether to join Brome in the school of Jonson, Shirley in the school of Fletcher, or to imitate the Cavalier mode. *The Tragedy of Albertus Wallenstein,* possibly an early play written close upon Wallenstein's death in 1634, is a readable though amateurish tragedy of the not unfamiliar obituary-chronicle type. *The Hollander,* 1636, and *Wit in a Constable,* 1639, are comedies of intrigue and humours, while *The Lady Mother,* 1635, brings domestic strife and romantic passions together to form a remarkably hybrid tragicomedy. The new fashion in playwrighting had certainly gone to Glapthorne's head; he did not hesitate to interrupt realistic intrigue or low farce by sudden explosions of heroic rant, or flowery passages of artificial sentiment. In *The Lady Mother,* for instance, a character—upon very little provocation—will astonish us by blurting out,

For heaven's sake, speak: were he defens'd with clouds,

> Or circled with unsteadfast bogs, my rage
> Should cut a passage to him . . .

Equally surprising in such a play are passages in this vein,

> How prettily these trees
> Bow, as each meant to consecrate a branch
> To the drowned lovers! And, methinks, the stream
> Pitying their hearse should want all funeral rights,
> Snatches the virgin lilies from his banks
> To show their wat'ry sepulchre.[67]

Pathetic fallacy was Glapthorne's forte. Even the farcical *Hollander* contains passages fantastically embroidered with the imagery of flowers, birds, and streams. Conceited nature imagery—unless we except the unique imbecility of nearly all his female characters—is the author's distinguishing badge.

Glapthorne's most interesting plays are *The Ladies' Privilege, c.* 1637, and *Argalus and Parthenia, c.* 1638, Fletcherian romances strongly crossed by the Cavalier mode. The latter, derived from Sidney's *Arcadia,* has given the author scope for exercising his talent for epithalamic and elegiac verse, as he tells his pseudo-pastoral tale of love's tragic hazards. The play is full of the casuistical discussions of the ethics of love and friendship so familiar among the disciples of D'Urfé, while at least one character, Demagorus, speaks—in his own phrase—"the Heroick dialect."

The Ladies' Privilege, dedicated to the "true Example of Heroicke Vertue," Sir Frederick Cornwallis, reveals how the lady Chrisea engages the honor of her true lover, Doria, to renounce his suit, and force his friend, Vitelli, to woo in his stead. Vitelli, after the proper display of soul-strife, forsakes his own beloved one in order to obey the mystifying injunction of his friend. When Doria comes within the shadow of the scaffold by the usual route, as principal in a supposedly fatal duel, his page disguised as a woman pleads the virgin's privilege of rescuing the condemned felon by accepting him in marriage. Finally Chrisea reveals that Doria's supposed victim still lives, that she still loves him, and that her actions throughout have been only a character-test of him and his friend. There is little action or dramatic feeling in this inconsequential play, but its artificialities are not unpleasant, and like Davenant's gallant tragicomedies it offers, with its love-honor-friendship theme, its ethical entanglements, and "strong lines," a measure of the professional concession to the Cavalier mode.

Of three remaining professional playwrights, each of whom has left one extant play produced before 1642, little need be said. John Kirke[68]

and Thomas Jordan were actors; and the old-fashioned bourgeois romance, *Seven Champions of Christendom,* published by the former in
1638, and the riotously indelicate comedy, *Walks of Islington and
Hogsdon,* licensed for the latter in 1641, give a fair notion of the type
of plays relished by the less genteel audiences of the Red Bull. *The
Distracted State* by Jordan's friend, John Tatham, will be mentioned
in a later discussion.[69] The times were unpropitious for writers such
as these. Kirke has the distinction of being the last author mentioned
in the surviving list of plays licensed before the closing of the theatres;
on June 8, 1642,[70] Herbert burned one play received from him "for
the ribaldry and offense that was in it" but authorized a second, with
the timely title, *The Irish Rebellion.* Of neither of these was Kirke
necessarily the author. Jordan and Tatham both lived to see fine
gentlemen monopolize dramatic authorship while they were relegated
to composing the lord mayor's pageants. In the early Restoration was
consummated that courtly usurpation of the stage, the beginnings of
which we have now completely traced.

---

[1] J. Q. Adams, *Shakespearean Playhouses* (1917), p. 304.

[2] *Strafforde Letters,* I, 175; II, 118.

[3] *Ibid.,* I, 511.

[4] *Ibid.,* I, 426.

[5] *Pepys Diary,* July 22, 1667.

[6] John Downes, *Roscius Anglicanus,* p. 21.

[7] See above, p. 119.

[8] See the "Description of the Scœnes and Intermedii" in the synopsis of the play
printed in 1635.

[9] In the Duke of Devonshire's collection; see note 12.

[10] *Brief Lives* (ed. Clark), II, 245.

[11] Postscript to the edition of 1653.

[12] *Dramatic Records of Sir Henry Herbert,* p. 58.—Jones's sketches for this play
and for Carlell's *Passionate Lovers* survive in the Duke of Devonshire Collection, cf.
Designs by Inigo Jones for Masques and Plays at Court (1924), pp. 118, 131-132.

[13] B. M. Add. MS 34, 221, fols. 2-19. For Fane's plays, see below, pp. 198-202.

[14] *Dramatic Records of Sir Henry Herbert,* p. 53.

[15] Address to the Reader.

[16] Anthony à Wood, *Hist. and Antiquities of Oxford,* II, 408-413.

[17] Cf. F. E. Schelling, *Elizabethan Drama* (1908), II, 411.

[18] The scenes are described in the text. That the production was purely a professional venture is assumed by W. J. Lawrence, *Elizabethan Playhouse,* II (1913), 121.

[19] Listed as exclusive property of the King's Men in 1641; cf. *Malone Society Collections,* II, part III (1931), 399.

[20] From a letter dated Jan. 11, 1637, cf. *Court and Times of Charles I,* II, 263.

[21] A. à Wood, *History and Antiquities of Oxford,* II, 413.

[22] J. Q. Adams, *Shakespearean Playhouses,* pp. 424 *seq.*

[23] *Ibid.,* p. 427.

[24] *Ibid.*, pp. 420 *seq.*

[25] Act v, Scene 1.

[26] Note that the licensing of no such play appears in Herbert's records, significant even though these records are incomplete.

[27] "To my old faithful servant . . ."

[28] See above, p. 125.

[29] Epilogue to *The Court Beggar.*—For a similar thrust, see Shirley's verses commending *A Jovial Crew.*

[30] Prologue to *The Damoiselle, c.* 1638.

[31] Not all professional plays are here mentioned. For a standard general classification and evaluation, see F. E. Schelling, *Elizabethan Drama,* Chaps. xvii to xix.

[32] See above, p. 16.

[33] *Pleasant Dialogues and Dramas,* 1637. See M. S. Steele, *Plays and Masques at Court,* pp. 281-283.

[34] Prologue to King and Queen at Denmark House in *Love's Mistress.*

[35] A. M. Clark, *Thomas Heywood* (Oxford, 1931), pp. 138-142.

[36] Dedication to Dorset.

[37] A. M. Clark, *op. cit.,* p. 164.—F. E. Schelling, *op. cit.,* ii, 309-310, describes the play as a "caricature" of courtly drama.

[38] *Dramatic Records of Sir Henry Herbert,* p 34.

[39] *Ibid.,* p. 54. The play was *The New Inn,* probably an old comedy in altered form.

[40] See below, pp. 193-194.

[41] *DNB,* xxxvi, 191.

[42] C. E. Andrews, "Richard Brome," *Yale Studies in English* (1913), p. 13.

[43] F. G. Fleay, *Biographical Chronicle,* i, 36.

[44] Not an isolated phenomenon; note Fletcher's "Triumph of Time" in *Four Plays in One,* Shirley's *Honor and Riches* (1631), and the late moralities written by Dekker in collaboration.

[45] *Dramatic Records of Sir Henry Herbert,* p. 19. *Believe as you List* is adjudged to be this same play "reformed."

[46] *Dramatic Records of Sir Henry Herbert,* p. 23.

[47] *Ibid.,* p. 38, n. 2.

[48] *The Bashful Lover,* Act v, Scene i.

[49] Epilogue to *The Bashful Lover.*

[50] See introduction to the edition by W. Bang, *Materialien zur Kunde,* xiii (1906); see also M. Joan Sargeaunt, *John Ford* (Oxford, 1935), pp. 188-193.

[51] A. C. Baugh, "Some New Facts About Shirley," *MLR,* xvii (1922), 228-235.

[52] See above, p. 75.

[53] See above, p. 78.

[54] See above, p. 10.

[55] *Dramatic Records of Sir Henry Herbert,* p. 19.

[56] *The Arcadia,* also dramatized romance (and based upon Sidney) was published under Shirley's name in 1640, and has been dated 1632; cf. F. G. Fleay, *Biographical Chronicle,* ii, 239. I believe this an earlier play, and not by Shirley, for reasons I have stated in an article scheduled to appear in *Modern Philology.* I am also publishing separately other notes on the Shirley canon not germane to the present discussion. Another and undated dramatization of Sidney's *Arcadia* survives in a scarcely legible manuscript, *Love's Changelings Change,* B. M., Add. MS. Egerton 1994, fols. 293-316. It contains, besides the main plot utilized by the author of the play

published in 1640, the episodes of the capture of the princesses by Cecropia and Amphialus.

[57] *Dramatic Records of Sir Henry Herbert*, p. 34.

[58] *The Coronation*, 1635, approaches in type *The Young Admiral*. For Shirley's departure from comic drama, see A. H. Nason, *James Shirley, Dramatist* (New York, 1915).

[59] I have written a life and critical evaluation, *Sir William Davenant, Poet Venturer*, Univ. of Penna. Press, 1935.

[60] See the prologue; and *Dramatic Records of Sir Henry Herbert*, pp. 22, 54.

[61] F. G. Fleay, *op. cit.*, I, 101.

[62] F. E. Schelling, *op. cit.*, II, 342.

[63] Beginning, "Let mothers still enjoy their sleep." *Young Admiral*, Act III, Scene ii; *Siege*, Act I, Scene i.

[64] J. B. Fletcher, "Précieuses at the Court of Charles I," *Journal of Comparative Literature*, I (1903), 145.

[65] His dates and place of birth have been added to the text while in proof. They are supplied, with other information, by J. H. Walter, *LTLS*, Sept. 19, 1936, p. 748.

[66] *The Hollander*, Act. I. Another unfavorable reference to the Reformation appears in *Wit in a Constable*, Act v.

[67] Act v, Scene i.

[68] W. J. Lawrence, "John Kirke, Caroline Actor-Dramatist," *SP*, XXI (1924), 586 ff.

[69] See below, p. 185.

[70] *Dramatic Records of Sir Henry Herbert*, p. 39.

IV

PLAYS ON THE CIVIL WARS

THE reader has met many sad and sentimental foreign princes in this book, but no English horsemen, winning rebel garrisons in the King's cause and feminine hearts in their own. Where, he may ask, are the plumed and laughing Cavaliers? Although this enchanting fellowship must continue to prove evasive, there is in fact a group of plays which bring us nearer the Cavalier himself and his Roundhead antagonist than those we have been treating. These political plays are scattered through our entire period, but since few of them have either merit as drama or significance in dramatic history, it will work little injury to our general plan to treat all of them here.

Before 1642 allusions to the troubles brewing between King and Parliament are more likely to appear in the court masques than in regular plays. Censorship was clamped down so tightly against political comment on the popular stage that dramatists, no matter how sympathetic with the Royal side, were wary of conveying anything but the most generalized satire. Caroline court masques, on the other hand, were more noteworthy for their politics than for anything else.[1] This dubious dramatic type had long been saved from insignificance only by the genius of Ben Jonson, and with his dismissal as writer for the court, the texts became the merest complement to spectacular displays of scenery and costuming; Inigo Jones governed the sport and reaped the praise of the spectators. Disintegration appeared in the incoherent and fragmentary nature of the fables, and in the pedestrian verse; the antimasques degenerated into series of farcical pantomimes and eccentric dances, in which the influence of the French *ballet de cour* is clearly manifest. William Davenant wrote oftenest and best, but only once or twice was he able to stem the tide toward mere scenic display, and write songs and dialogue that were more than adequate. Masques fitted the temper of the Caroline court, where their brittle splendor was a symbol of Stuart pretensions. Had it not been for their terrific expense in the face of dwindling royal revenues, there would have been more of them. Grumblings were often audible from officials near the exchequer, and even the noble ladies and gentlemen chosen to dance the grand figures with their Majesties were known to demur in view of the outlay for costumes and jewels. In some years masques were intermitted altogether, on the pretext that there were no adequate facilities of space or that the brilliant lights would injure the King's paintings. But when the money was found to produce them, they were produced lavishly—usually in pairs during the pre-Lenten festivals, one by Charles in honor of Henrietta, and another by Henrietta in honor of Charles.

The marriage of Charles and Henrietta did not at first prove the bond of amity between England and France that was intended; and on May 15, 1627, Buckingham presented a masque which, as the Venetian ambassador reported, represented the putting forth of a fleet against the French "to inflame the King's ardour."[2] The Duke himself appeared, and "after him Envy, with divers open-mouthed dogs' heads representing the people's barking."[3] Only a few of the extant masques are as explicit as this in their partisanship.[4] Usually they deprecate strife and emit the warm rays of political optimism. There appear personified abstractions such as Justice, Religion, Affection-to-the-Country, and, above all, Concord. Storm clouds appear in the scene, as a reminder of the storm clouds on the actual English horizon, but at the end these clouds always break away as in Carew's *Cœlum Britannicum*, "leaving behind nothing but a serene sky." Concord and serene skies—a sort of wish-fulfillment—are the standardized form of climax. It was difficult for the courtiers to understand how opposition could exist to the Crown in view of the majestic presence and personal graciousness of Charles and his lovely spouse. The marital felicity and fecundity of the ruling pair were exploited in the masques as if they were a triumph of state business upon which every Royalist could be personally congratulated.

Two of William Davenant's last masques are especially rich in political allegory. *Britannia Triumphans,* 1638, takes for its subject the magnificance of Britanocles (Charles), "the glory of the western world" who "hath by his wisdom, valour, and piety not only vindicated his own but far distant seas . . ." The scenic ornamentation draws its motif from the English fleet, and the masque is actually devoted to the cause of Charles's claim to sovereignty of the seas, and consequent subterfuge in levying ship-money.[5] His enemy is Imposture, who with the aid of Merlin raises the spirits of the "mean and low" including such historic rebels as Cade, Kett, and Jack Straw. His friends, on the other hand, are Heroic Virtue, Action, and Fame. That Imposture represented Puritanism and democratic opposition to the King, was remembered as a grievance as late as 1698, by the anonymous author of *The Stage Condemned,* who devoted fifteen pages of his tract to the evils of *Britannia Triumphans.*[6] *Salmacida Spolia,* an entertainment of especial splendor presented by the King and Queen in unison to illuminate the darkening days of 1640, also takes its entire theme from the relations of Charles to his realm. Charles, that "secret Wisdom" who will banish discord, is represented as "Philogenes or Lover of his People." The classical basis of the piece is borrowed from the legend of the fountain of Salmacis in Caria, where barbarians who drink are "reduced of their own accord to the sweetness of the Grecian customs." The pacific ruler approves this gentle method of conversion. Symbolism occurs throughout: Discord appears in a scene of tempest and darkness, but is banished by Concord and Good Genius of Great Britain, who bring calm and clear skies. The good King invites his people to honest pleasure—an introduction to the series of antimasques. The scene changes to craggy mountains representing "the difficult way which heroes are to pass ere they come to the throne of Honour." A chorus of "beloved people" led by Concord and Good Genius sing praises to the Queen, who descends with her ladies through the clouds to join the King with his gentlemen in the grand dances. The final scene is a glorious city filled with triumphal music; the harmonious spheres float by, and the refulgent skies open to reveal a heavenful of deities. This is all more conciliatory than *Britannia Triumphans*, but the assumption of righteousness there is less offensive than the sweet palliation here—the self-blinding in the presence of facts. That the King and his court should have tolerated such sentimental camouflage is scarcely credible.

No regular plays written before 1642 relate in their entirety to the trouble brewing between King and Parliament in the fashion of Davenant's late masques. Of course many plays, nearly every comedy in fact, persist in the time-honored sport of Puritan-baiting. *The Knave in Grain New-vampt*, a comedy of a cony-catcher's progress, published in 1640, is prefaced by an address on knaves, including "Hypocriticall, schismaticall, and seperisticall knaves." One of the most repulsive plays of the period, *The Ghost, or the Woman Wears the Breeches,* 1640, goes out of its way to make an issue with the Puritans. In seventeenth-century comedy, the least comic ingredient is that recurrent type, the miserly but amorous oldster, whose senile infirmities of body and brain are set up as an object of mirth. In *The Ghost* such a character appears in the person of Philarchus, whom the author tortures with a venom almost sadistic. In the play occurs this dialogue:

> Amongst my many travels, 'twas my fortune
> To touch upon that preaching island.
>
> England?

> 'Twas call'd so, Sir; 'till another eat it up.
>
> What country, Sir?
>
> They call it Scotland, Sir.
>
> The people too devour'd?
>
> Most of 'um, Sir;
> Some few who clapt hand with the enemy
> Are sav'd, who, for a badge of their conformity
> Unto the victor's will, sharpen'd their ears,
> And 'stead of hair glue'd on their heads the bristles
> Of nasty swine.[7]

Having challenged the citizen critics to do their worst, the author epiloguizes, "What think ye now of plays? Abominable?" to which a just answer in this particular case might have been simply, Yes. There was a growing tendency to augment the unsavoriness of characters like Philarchus and to identify them with the Puritan burghers of London. It is pleasant to compare with the dark and embittered caricature of such plays the good natured and honestly amusing foolery of Davenant's *News from Plymouth*. Here a sea captain, with pretended Puritanical zeal, offers to cut down the mast of his ship simply because it resembles a May-pole.

Two plays of the period particularly rich in political allusion are Suckling's *Brennoralt* and Killigrew's *Parson's Wedding*, yet their reflection of national events lies only in their details. Though *Brennoralt* was written fresh upon Suckling's adventures as a Captain in the Bishops Wars, the play is a romantic fiction and the resemblance between his Polish rebels and the Scotch rebels is purely generic. It is when the characters debate peace, loyalty, rebellion, wise rule, etc., that we perceive the impact of the times upon the author. Menseck, one of the rebels, advises:

> Press much religion,
> For though we dress the scruples for the multitude,
> And for ourselves reserve th' advantages
> (It being much pretext), yet it is necessary;
> For things of faith are so abstruse and nice;
> They will admit dispute eternally.
> So howso'er other demands appear,
> These never can be proved unreasonable.[8]

Such, in Suckling's mind, were the uses of Presbyterianism. In the following speech by a loyal soldier are veiled warnings for King Charles:

> Nor are you, Sir, assur'd of all behind you,
> For though your person in your subjects' hearts
> Stands highly honour'd and belov'd, yet are
> There certain acts of state, which men call grievances,

Abroad; and though they bear them in the times
Of peace, yet will they now perchance seek to
Be free, and throw them off.[9]

One company of Suckling's loyalists gives us our first hint in a drama
of the mood of trooping Cavaliers: they are gay roisterers who display
their virility in hard drinking, bawdy wit, and rounds of boisterous
merriment. Except in the scenes portraying this congenial brotherhood,
Suckling's allusions to the times are solemn and foreboding. Killigrew's, in contrast, are always quite light-hearted. In 1640 or there-
abouts, when *The Parson's Wedding* was written, London swarmed
with the military in consequence of the late frays in the north, and
the first scene of the comedy sets the stage for a duel of wits between a
dissenting clergyman and a captain recently cashiered from the "holy
wars." They are equal rogues, but Killigrew's loyalty was such that
his Royalist soldier triumphs in the end. The play contains many satirical thrusts at the Presbyterian divines,[10] political agitators, and the
Parliament. Says one character:

Now in this age of zeal and ignorance, would I have you four, in old
clothes and demure looks, present a petition in both houses, and say
you are men touched in conscience for your share in that wickedness
which is known to their worships by the pleasure of adultery, and
desire it may be death, and that a law be passed to that purpose.[11]

Oddly enough, before the Puritan Parliament had finished sitting, a
law was passed precisely to that purpose.

On August 22, 1642, the long-threatened war between King and
Parliament began, with the unfurling of Charles's standard upon a hill
at Nottingham. On September 2, Parliament passed a resolution putting down stage plays:

. . . whereas publike Sports doe not well agree with publike Calamities,
nor publike stage-plays with the Seasons of Humiliation, this being an
Exercise of sad and pious solemnity, and the other being Spectacles of
pleasure, too commonly expressing lascivious Mirth and Levitie: It is
therefore thought fit, and Ordeined by the Lords and Commons in this
Parliament assembled, that while these sad Causes and set times of
Humiliation doe continue, publike-Stage-playes shall cease, and be
forborne.[12]

The theatres closed, and the actors left London to fight for the King.
The prohibition of plays remained in effect for nearly eighteen years,
frequent violations giving rise at intervals to strengthening ordinances.
The extent of resistance to the law will be indicated later, but it may
be noted here that innumerable plays published during the Commonwealth period are prefaced by defences of the stage and attacks on
Parliamentary intolerance.[13]

After 1642 plays became an avowed instrument of partisanship and propaganda. Naturally they were on the Cavalier side, the Roundheads disdaining to use a devilish instrument even in a righteous cause. A curious exception to this rule[14] is *Tyrannical Government Anatomized, or a Discourse concerning Evil Councellors,* which the House of Commons itself ordered published on January 30, 1643. The play is a translation of George Buchanan's *Baptistes sive Calumnia,* itself a political allegory wherein Herod had represented Henry VIII, Herod's wife Anne Boleyn, and John the Baptist the persecuted Sir Thomas More. By viewing Herod in a new light as Charles I, Herod's wife as Henrietta Maria, and John as themselves, the Parliamentarians must have considered the play as remarkably apt in 1643. The Insurgents loved to view themselves as voices in the wilderness, their enemies as Philistines. It is Herod's wife who is the chief instigator of persecution in the play, and her sentiments after the death of John must have appealed to the Commons as appropriate to Henrietta Maria:

> Now shall we vindicate
> Our royal dignity, in future times
> To be of none derided; now I'll force
> The stubborn people to speak well of kings,
> Or learn it to their grief, and make them hold
> That all their king's commands, they gladly must
> Bear and obey, though never so unjust.

The committee of publication eschewed the frivolity of blank verse and printed the translation as prose, but the original form has been restored and an excellent case made for John Milton as the translator.[15] One further instance of the Puritans' making use of drama appears in the newsbooks of the period.[16] In 1645 one Colonel Blunt employed two regiments of Parliamentary infantry to divert the folk of Blackheath, Kent, lest they risk Hell-fire in May Day festivities. One regiment represented Roundheads, "who carried it on with care and love, temperance and order, and as much gravity as might be," while the other represented Cavaliers, who "minded drinking and roaring, and disorder, and would bee still playing with the women, and compasse them in . . ." The two sides waged a sham battle, and May-pole dancing and kindred sin were temporarily neglected by the villagers of Blackheath.

It is an oddity of the war plays produced by the Cavaliers that they adhere to the mid-century convention that all comedy should be realistic, all serious drama romantic. Romanticized propaganda creates an impression that is indescribable. In *Cola's Fury, or Lirenda's Misery,* published by an Irish patriot[17] in Kilkenny in 1646, and significantly dedicated to Edward Somerset, the Catholic agent of King Charles in his double-dealing with the Irish rebels, the tone is actually heroic. The gentry of Lirenda (Ireland) plot to strike for their rights in the language of Sicilian princelings, and the Angolean governors and generals plot ruthless suppression in the language of Eastern tyrants. In the series of military encounters which ensue, the rebels are uniformly valorous but unfortunate, their enemies uniformly addicted to treachery, rape, racking, and the massacre of non-combatants. As usual in Irish history appears the figure of the loathsome native informer, but the religious note is not struck: although the native leaders receive ghostly visitations from Heaven and the English leaders from Hell, the supernatural equipage is all borrowed from classical mythology. The historical basis of the piece is obvious despite the romantic atmosphere. Osirus, the Angolean Lieutenant Governor, is Ormonde; and Cola, the chief villain of the play, is Sir Charles Coote; the name "Cola" must derive from Collooney in Connaught where this cruel English colonist held lands. Before the play ends, with an unwelcome twelve-month truce just as the Irish begin to rally for a victory in Stelern (Leinster), Cola is pistolled to death—as was Sir Charles Coote by Irish rebels on May 7, 1642.

Even more highly romantic than *Cola's Fury* is a triumph of absurdity still in manuscript[18] called *The Female Rebellion, c.* 1659, which adumbrates English affairs in the story of a revolt against the Queen of the Amazons. When the policies of Orithya create unrest and the trial of her chief general (Strafford?), one Penthesilia leads a sanctimonious party in revolt. After many shifts of fortune, complicated by the fact that the Trojan consorts of the rebellious ladies are loyal to the Queen, Penthesilia is at last defeated; and the play ends with Orithya, whose nice sense of honor has prevented her from actively combating the rebels, face to face with the ethical problem of whether to marry the King of Scythia or to remain a maid so that a kinswoman will inherit the throne. One might hesitate to call this an historical allegory were it not for allusions to Cromwell, the Rump, the Act of Oblivion, etc., and the author's method of attributing to his party of revolted Amazons all the villainies of the English Roundheads.

The persistence of the conventions of Cavalier romance is illustrated by the detail in one of the most curious and interesting of the war plays, *The Famous Tragedy of King Charles I,* written in a white heat of rancor in the year of the regicide. The subject matter is thus described on the title page:

. . . The severall Combinations and Machinations that brought that incomparable prince to the Block, the overtures hasning at the famous

Seige of Colchester, the Tragicall fals of Sir Charles Lucas and Sir
George Lisle, the just reward of the Leveller Rainsborough, Hamilton
and Bailies Trecheries, In delivering the late scottish Army into the
hands of Cromwell, and the designe the Rebels have to destroy the
Royall posterity.

All this seems so promisingly explicit that one prepares to read a timely
chronicle play, but he soon discovers that the factual element is subor-
dinated to passionate sentiment. The Royalists speak in the heroic
tongue; over the body of Lucas, Sir George Lisle cries out:

> There crack'd the cords of life; Oh noble Lucas!
> Let me breath out my soul upon thy azure lips.

Cromwell rehearses his villainies aloud, like a Senecan villain, and
in his grip writhe the dastardly rebel leaders. Of these only Fairfax is
distinguished by even a modicum of decency. One point the play makes
utterly apparent: every slain Cavalier wings instantly to Heaven, and
every slain Roundhead dives instantly to Hell. The death pangs of one
departing Royalist are pleasantly ameliorated by his reflection that
Heaven will serve as a balcony seat from which he may watch the
rebels burn. The regicide figures again in *The Tragical Actors, or the
Martyrdom of the Late King Charles*,[19] which portrays Cromwell,
Joyce, Vane, Bradshaw, and others changing the great seal, planting
evidence, and plotting to rush their ruler to his doom, but this piece
consists only of a few pages of disjointed scenes and is really no more
than a tract. During the period a number of such political pamphlets
in dialogue appeared, usually anonymous and claiming on their title
pages to be plays, but they can scarcely be classified even as closet
drama and must be omitted from the present survey.[20]

One episode in *The Famous Tragedy of King Charles* not romanticized is an amorous intrigue—including even a bedroom scene—between Cromwell and Madam Lambert, with the Puritan divine, Hugh
Peters, acting as the pander. The Cavaliers loved to compromise Cromwell with Madam Lambert, and to debase Hugh Peters, whose sermons
were as dangerous to the Royal side as a regiment of Ironsides. The
Cromwell-Lambert intrigue is exploited again in *Cromwell's Conspiracy*, published by a "Person of Quality" in 1660. In five short acts
this piece reviews the vile career of Oliver during the entire period of
his power, until he appears, to the obvious satisfaction of the author,
raving on his death-bed. The play ends with the gloriousness of the
convenient General Monk. Since the dramatist has shrouded everything in a conventionally romantic atmosphere and has availed himself of the opportunity to display not only his loyalty but, in almost
every line, his classical erudition as well, the work proves not diverting.

On the whole, the war comedies are more entertaining than the serious plays, and are decidedly better history. Except for John Tatham's *The Rump*, they make little capital of actual national events, but they provide an excellent insight into the character of the Cavalier. Lacy's *Old Troop*, Killigrew's *Thomaso, or the Wanderer*, and Cowley's *Cutter of Coleman Street* deal respectively with young Royalist officers in their wartime barracks, in exile, and in London under the Protectorate.

John Lacy's apprenticeship to the dancing master Ogilby was the first step to a stage career which culminated in his becoming a famous comedian and occasional playwright early in the Restoration. Although *The Old Troop, or Monsieur Raggou* was not written until after 1660, it capitalized experiences gained by the author early in the wars while serving as lieutenant with Colonel Lord Gerard. Judging from this play, Lacy and his fellow junior officers had interests more immediate than that Charles should have his right. The play reveals how an upright Royalist commander, aided by Tom Telltroth, gets the better of a Parliamentary governor and his hypocritical captains, but the major interest lies in the embroilments of the younger lieutenants with Raggou, their scandalous French cook, and with Dol Troop, their still more scandalous camp follower. One episode has a peculiar significance. In order to bring provisions out of hoarding, the Royalist officers pretend that their favorite meat is young children, whereupon the people of the countryside become instantly more amenable. The lieutenants realize their risks: "Though they [the Puritan leaders] know it to be nothing but mirth, they'll preach their parishioners into a real belief in it, on purpose to make us odious."[21] The rumor of cannibalism among Royalists, actually circulated during the wars, may have originated in some such prank as this. *The Old Troop* is one of those plays which derive their appeal almost solely through farcical intrigue and the "business" of comic actors, but it gives an idea of the undisciplined, holiday spirit among the King's troopers, and helps to explain why their final achievements were not consonant with their individual gallantry. All are immersed in their own diversions, and if occasion requires—if Dol Troop, let us say, decides to father upon one of them the most recent fruit of her industry—there is nothing to restrain him from bidding farewell to his Colonel, packing his equipment, and leaving the seat of war for parts remote. The word *desertion* seems not to have occurred in the lexicon of the Royalist subaltern.

When the Cavalier went into exile, he seemed patriotically bent upon proving to foreigners that dour Cromwell and his Latin secretary were not representative Englishmen—or so we should judge from

Thomaso, or the Wanderer, written in 1654 when Thomas Killigrew himself was adventuring on the Continent. A group of Cavaliers headed by the gallant and handsome Thomaso (a fancy-portrait of Killigrew himself) visit Harrigo, the attendant upon the Royalist English ambassador in Madrid. Thomaso woos the wealthy senorita Serulina, but his courtship is so intertwined with a series of riotous misadventures with the courtesans and other notables of Madrid that it requires ten acts of seven or eight scenes each to bring him to the altar. Nothing of political significance appears in the main outline of the story, but the speeches of the characters are full of allusion. Life of Cavaliers in exile is thus described:

The dogs are so muzzled and tied up at home, with constables and [C]romwell, they fight for sport abroad . . . They are as proud of their persecution as the Jews, and brag as vainly of their wants as a Castilian would of his blood; no servants, no money, no clothes, no meat, and always afoot, neither daunts nor dejects them; they beg as confidently in their surly way, and, they think, as meritoriously as Capuchins. By this light, I believe, 'twill be an order in time; they are admitted into the Mendicants already: and those that lov'd the man least call'd their great Charles both saint and martyr.

Henrietta Maria's native land was not lavish in its entertainment of her English court:

France has so cut their combs, the Louvre and the Pale-royal have been sad enchanted castles to them; they have kept a Lazarello's court there: darkness, leanness, and the nest of poverty, but two loaves a day and without fish to work the miracle; yet the gallery was a Christian coney-warren fill'd with Cavaliers of all trades, and unless they fed upon their children, 'tis not visible what they eat . . . They are now remov'd to the Palace Royal . . . where there is not a blade of grass left in the garden, nor a drop of oil in the Madonna's lamps; sacrilege and their salads make it burn dim; they are happy that swim, they dive in the pond and steal the fish. The younger stomachs brouse upon the cops as high as they can reach, they have starved the poor antelope in eating up his commons; their grandees only dine, and that but when fortune smiles . . . there's their Resident too, his arms are up still, but 'tis long since he had the supporters; 'tis thought he eat the unicorn last Passover . . .[22]

Another type of historical high-light is offered in the person of the character Harrigo, who clearly represents Henry Progers. Progers was the ring-leader of the group of Royalists in Madrid who assassinated the Parliamentary envoy, Antony Ascham, believing that thus they were avenging the death of Charles I. One scene in *Thomaso* involves a projected assassination, the details of which are reminiscent of the Ascham episode.[23] Killigrew's Cavaliers abroad are gay, licentious, irresponsible, Bohemian—admirable to a degree that one is not supposed to question.

A less glamorous picture of the Cavalier in his day of decline is furnished in Abraham Cowley's *Cutter of Coleman Street,* adapted in 1661 from the poet's youthful comedy, *The Guardian.* Since *The Guardian* itself has been treated elsewhere,[24] only the element of contemporary satire injected into the altered version need be described here. Cowley's cashiered Cavaliers are dashing enough, but are masquerading vagabonds. Here is a thumb-nail biography of Cavalier Worm, written in Falstaffian vein:

He was a scholar once, and since a merchant, but broke the first half year; after that he serv'd as Justice o' Peace . . .; h'as a pretty smattering too in poetry, and would ha' been my Lady Protectress's poet: He writ once a copy in praise of her beauty, but her Highness gave him for it but an old half-crown piece in gold which she had hoarded up before these troubles, and that discourag'd him from any further applications to the court. Since that, h'as been a little agitator for the Cavalier party, and drew in one of the 'prentices that were hang'd lately. He's a good ingenious fellow, that's the truth on't, and a pleasant Droll when h'as got a cup o'wine in his pate, which your uncle and I supply him with; but for matters that concern the King neither of us trust him. Not that I can say h'as betrayed anybody, but he's so indigent a varlet that I'm afraid he would sell his soul to Oliver for a noble . . .[25]

The most honorable of the crew is Cavalier Jolly, but mark his dearth of joyous idealism in past sacrifices for the Royal cause:

My own estate was sold for being with the King at Oxford. A curse upon an old dunce, that needs must be going to Oxford at my years! My good neighbour, I thank him, Colonel Fear-the-Lord Barebottle, a saint and a soap-boiler bought it, but he'd dead and boiling now himself, that's the best of it; there's a Cavalier's comfort.[26]

When his companion Cavaliers tell him that they fought at Worcester and escaped like their Prince in disguise, Jolly suggests that a disguise as gentlemen would always assure concealment. There is a fine parody of the rumors of Royalist stratagems current among the Malignants during the Protectorate. Jolly's friends bring news garnered from an Irish priest come over disguised as a fishwife—how the King has mustered twenty-five thousand men in Flanders as they saw "in black and white and all in cipher," and how the Emperor of Muscovy has promised to lend ten thousand bears to overrun the country. The author evens the score by turning on the Puritans. The Widow Barebottle tells how the spiritual seekings of her husband were always rewarded; three days after good words in Bucklersbury, "a friend of his that he owed five hundred pounds to was hang'd for a Malignant, and the debt forgiven him by Parliament." Satirists often tried to imitate the pious cant of the Puritans, their delight in visions and prophecies, but none succeeded so well as Cowley. His Cavaliers, in pretending they have been drawn into the fold, converse in this strain:

Cutter. Sister Barebottle, I must not be called Cutter any more, that is a name of Cavalero darkness; the Devil was a cutter from the beginning; my name is now Abednego, I had a vision which whisper'd to me through a keyhole, Go call thyself Abednego.

Tabitha. The wonderful vocation of some Vessels!

Cutter. It is a name that signifies fiery furnaces, and tribulation and martyrdom; I know I shall suffer for the truth.

Tabitha. Not as to death, Brother? if it be his will?

Cutter. As to death, Sister, but I shall gloriously return.

Jolly. What, Brother, after death? that were miraculous.

Cutter. Why the wonder of it is, that it is to be miraculous.

Jolly. But miracles are ceas'd, Brother, in this wicked Age of Cavalerism.

Cutter. They are not ceas'd, Brother, nor shall they cease 'till the Monarchy be establish'd. I say again I am to return, and to return upon a purple dromedary, which signifies magistracy; with an axe in my hand that is called Reformation, and I am to strike with that axe upon the gate of Westminster Hall and cry, Down Babylon, and the building called Westminster Hall is to run away and cast itself into the river, and then Major General Harrison is to come in green sleeves from the north upon a sky-colour'd mule, which signifies heavenly instruction.

Tabitha. Oh the Father! he's as full of mysteries as an egg is of meat.[27]

The comic spirit among the Royalists was not robust enough to permit them to enjoy much laughing at themselves, and for a time *Cutter of Coleman Street* threatened to immerse its author in hot water. It was considered injurious to the Loyal Indigent Officers,[28] and the parody of Revelations was deemed sacrilege. In 1663 Cowley printed the play with a lengthy defense. "Good God! Against the King's party? After having served it twenty years during all the time of their misfortunes, I must be a very rash and imprudent person if I chose out that of their Restitution to begin a quarrel with them . . . We are not, I hope, become such Puritans ourselves as to assume the name of the Congregation of the Spotless." As for sacrilege, he says he has ever been a religious man, and deems it not profane "to deride the hypocrisy of those men whose skulls are not yet bare upon the gates since the public and just punishment of it . . ." Jolly, he explains, is "an ordinary jovial gentleman, commonly called a good fellow," while Cutter and Worm are not Cavaliers at all but "only usurped that name." Better calculated to avoid offense than Cowley's play was *The Committee* of

Sir Robert Howard, which also treats of Cavaliers in the London of the Protectorate. The associates of Mr. Day, Chairman of the Committee of Sequestration, are as venal as Cowley's Puritans, but his Cavaliers, Colonels Blunt and Careless, are bluff, honest gentlemen who prefer relinquishing all their estates to taking the Covenant.

Unique among our war plays in that it was both written and acted in the thick of the events it commemorates is *The Rump*, by John Tatham. Tatham (fl. 1632-64)[29] seems to have been prepared to launch upon a career as a popular playwright when the times closed the theatres, and sent him off to bear arms for the King. Except for *Love Crowns the End*, a conventional little pastoral written for performance by the students of Bingham, Notts, in 1632, Tatham's plays persistently reflect the times, and place all the ills of the land at the door of the hated Scots. *The Distracted State*, 1641, displays in the disjointed fashion of a chronicle play a tragic struggle over succession to a throne. A series of pretenders plot and murder by wholesale in order to rule the state, and despite the locale in Sicily, a Scotch mountebank is dragged in by the heels as a paid assassin: "I an' me countramen ha' peysoned three better kingdoms as this," he proclaims. In *Scots' Figgaries, or a Knot of Knaves*, issued as closet drama in 1652, two Scotch beggars are aided by their military countryman, Scarefool, in imposing as physicians on the people of England. Speaking a villainous Caledonian dialect (which has been repudiated by Tatham's Edinburgh editors), they administer allegorical poisons to country folk, a courtier, a lawyer, a merchant, etc., until they are curbed by Resolution, an English soldier. Tatham's tone is brusque, even churlish, but he writes a brisk colloquial dialogue, and his last comedy is good enough to make us regret that his talents from 1656 onwards were usually sown in the stony earth of the Lord Mayor's pageants. *The Rump* was acted in Dorset Court in the spring of 1660. In the first version of the play some characters were thinly disguised—Lambert, for instance, was christened Bertlam—but this convention may be disregarded. General Lambert plots with wily Secretary Whitelocke to follow up the ousting of Richard Cromwell as Oliver's successor by pricking the political bubble of Richard's brother-in-law, the canting, cautious Fleetwood. The Committee of Safety distribute largess among themselves, Warriston the Scottish Chairman appropriating an especially succulent portion. Lady Lambert is the most vivacious character: she triumphs over the old scold Widow Cromwell, breaks in on a solemn session of the Rump Committee to importune her husband to take over the government at once, and anticipates his elevation by queening it over the other Parliamentary ladies. Milton must have narrowly escaped a place in Tatham's dramatis personæ, for in *The Character of the Rump,* the dramatist's brief prose satire of 1660, the Latin secretary is attacked with particular bitterness. The most accurate historical material in *The Rump* is contained in the scenes displaying the demonstrations of the London apprentices, and, after the desertion of Lambert's army and the declaration of divine General Philargus (Monk) for a free Parliament, the public roasting of rumps of beef. The ending is purely fanciful—with Lady Lambert, Widow Cromwell, and various committee members turned pedlars and hawking pens, turnips, and kitchen ware about the streets. Tatham's comedy is amusing journalism with many touches of reality and hints of true characterization. It is better-natured on the whole than the pro-Royalist plays written in gloomier days.

Various entertainments, some of them written by Thomas Jordan and sponsored by the London guilds, gave General Monk an opportunity to contemplate his unsuspected magnificence. Events moved apace, and soon Charles II was seated on his throne ready to be entertained by the quickly organized companies.

Satire on the Roundheads served as detail in the earliest new plays acted on the stage, and several having no other purpose than to display a retrospective animus toward the fallen enemy appeared on the bookstalls. Several of those already mentioned first appeared in print in these early years of the Restoration. In 1661 were published *Hell's Higher Court of Justice, or the Trial of the three Politic Ghosts, viz. Oliver Cromwell, the King of Sweden, and Cardinal Mazarin,* by J. D., and *The Presbyterian Lash, or Noctroff's Maid Whipped,* by K. F., conjectured on slender evidence to be Francis Kirkman. The political bearing of the first of these, a dull bit of eccentricity peopled largely by the officialdom of Hades, is sufficiently indicated by the title. *The Presbyterian Lash* is dramatized scandal, directed against the Puritan divine Zachary Crofton, here portrayed as a resourceful as well as lecherous knave. His spanking his serving-maid, for entertainment, sets his unfriendly and friendly parishioners at war, but clever roguery clears him in the end.

A crop of usurper plays was a natural aftermath of the fall of the dictatorship and the restoration of the hereditary monarch. Edward Howard's long and dreary *Usurper* of 1664 has a romantic plot, with the true king, "a Lybian born," haunting the court of the tyrant in the guise of a moor, but villainous Damocles and lecherous Hugo de Petra are obviously Cromwell and Peters. The usurper, after his dying speech, is hustled incontinently to Hell. Another play by this lesser Howard, written in 1667 when the new reign had not justified expectations, was less congenial in its political allusions, and King Charles

angrily ordered its suppression.[30] Several of the usurper plays[31] were
inspired by the life of Andronicus Commenus, the vengeful hypocrite
who waded through blood to the Byzantine sceptor: John Wilson's
Andronicus Comnenius (sic), 1664; the anonymous *Andronicus: Impiety's Long Success, or Heaven's late Revenge,* not published until
1661 although written earlier, and *The Unfortunate Usurper,* published
in 1663. To none of these plays, even Wilson's, would one voluntarily
submit himself in the theatre. The last is singularly debased, and it
appears that a rough species of censorship has taken place. In the
only copy available to the present writer, Scene iii, Act V, has been
torn out, only the last few lines remaining intact. A Demon raised by
the conjurer Seth seems to be indulging in some prophecies which
have digressed from Byzantine affairs to those of the English Protectorate:

> . . . Shall with his Tail
> Have tossed up and down the Kingdom's ship,
> Great Charles shall by his prudence safely
> Steer it, and after 't has been floating
> Betwixt the Rump and Lambert,
> (As 'twixt Scylla and Charybdis)
> He'll bring it to the haven
> Of all her former happiness and glory.

That the possessor of the tail was Cromwell, and that he had been furnished with other appurtenances of the Devil seems reasonably certain.
The play which shows the least disposition of all to compromise with
usurpers is *The Subject's Joy for the King's Restoration,* published in
1660. In a foreword, the author explains that, in seeking a subject, he
thought first of the gunpowder plot, then of the defeat of Zedekiah,
then of Zimri and Shallum, but finally selected the treachery of Jeroboam. His play consists of six "shews" ending with Jeroboam in a chair
of state with Hell under him; the usurper laments his treason, and
"with that, the Devil tears him in pieces and throws him into Hell.
Whereupon the party for Abijah clap their hands . . ."

It is a happy circumstance that war propagandists are soon silenced
by the end of hostilities. After the novelty of the Restoration had worn
off, and Royalist hatreds had been purged in the blood of the regi-
cides,[32] dramatists withdrew their whips from the backs of Cromwell,
the Rump, and the Puritan divines. They continued to write political
plays,[33] but upon new subjects. Viewed in the large, the Cavalier war
plays are bitter and hopelessly unfair: religious hypocrisy, cupidity,
and covert lust are charged to every Puritan, and sincerity of purpose
is conceded to not a one. The conviction of the social superiority of
the Cavalier over the Roundhead is implicit in the dramatists' tone of

contempt. Tatham's *The Distracted State* and *The Rump* are almost
identical in theme, but there is a wicked grandeur about his foreign
and fictitious usurpers, while about his native and authentic ones
nothing but meanness and pusillanimity. Parliamentarians to the Royalists were pilfering varlets, among whom only Oliver Cromwell was
conceded the rank of a life-sized villain. But when all is said, these
plays were engendered in blood, and offend no worse than the war
propaganda of all causes in all ages. One entertaining revelation they
bring is that the Cavaliers—perhaps through contagion—were as prone
as the Puritans to mete out Hell-fire and to boil their enemies in antici-
pation.

The Royalist's portrait of himself is more arresting than his portrait
of the enemy. The conception of the Cavalier as a merry, fearless,
improvident goodfellow, morally eclectic but aboveboard withal,
originated in his own age and in his own circle. From the time of Suckling to the time of Lacy the portrait remains substantially the same.
Out of such seeds as exist in these plays grew the congenial figure of
fiction and popular legend. Such plays as *The Committee* were long
read, while *Thomaso* and *The Old Troop* were adapted (and improved)
by Aphra Behn in *The Rover, or the Banished Cavaliers* and *The
Roundheads, or The Good Old Cause,* thus to win wider currency and
appeal. It required only the eighteenth century anecdotist and the
nineteenth century Walter Scott to do the rest. The Cavalier must
surely have possessed a dual personality. That perennial gallant,, wearing with an air his tattered finery, and cracking broad jests with his
penniless comrades, is a character far different from the one we should
conceive after reading the romantic plays in the Cavalier mode.

---

[1] The masques written during the period covered in the present book, and referred
to in the present discussion are Aurelian Townshend's *Albion's Triumph* and *Tempe
Restored,* 1632; Shirley's *Triumph of Peace,* 1634; Carew's *Cælum Britannicum,* 1634;
and Davenant's *Temple of Love* (not political), 1635; *Britannia Triumphans* and
Luminalia, 1638; and *Salmacida Spolia,* 1640. Davenant's *Prince d'Amour,* 1636, and
other masques and entertainments outside the court are treated in the following
chapter on amateur theatricals. The most complete survey of the English masque
is P. Reyher, *Masques Anglais* (1909); for a more recent view see E. Welsford, *Court
Masque* (Cambridge, 1927).

[2] *Cal. State Papers Venetian,* 1626-28, p. 239.

[3] *Court and Times of Charles I,* I, 226.

[4] *Masquerade du Ciel* (1640), dedicated to Henrietta by its author, J. S[adler], is
a "heavenly map" for 1639-40 "shadowing the late commotions between Saturn and
Mercury about the northern Thule." This is a "closet masque," wholly descriptive,
and, one would suspect, allegorizing the Scottish troubles, but to the present writer
its astrological shadowings have proved incomprehensible.

[5] See P. Reyher, *op. cit.*, pp. 308-309.—A tract in dramatic form discussing ship-money and condemning the judges who supported it is Richard Brathwait's *Mercurius Britannicus*, published in Latin, but translated into English in 1641. For a description, see M. Black, *Richard Brathwait*, Univ. of Penna. diss. (1928), pp. 75-78.

[6] Pp. 13-31.

[7] Act iv.

[8] Act ii.

[9] Act iii.

[10] Stephen Marshall, Thomas Case, etc. are mentioned by name; cf. Act v, Scene ii.

[11] Act iv, Scene i.

[12] This resolution by the Commons is reproduced from the B. M. document in facsimile in Joseph Knight's ed. of Downe's *Roscius Anglicanus*, 1886.

[13] A number are quoted by T. S. Graves, "Notes on Puritanism and the Stage," *SP*, xviii (1921).

[14] See also *Canterbury his Change of Diet*, and *Read and Wonder*, both of 1641, pamphlets in dialogue satirizing Archbishop Laud.

[15] See edition of J. T. T. Brown, pp. 61-173, in *George Buchanan Glasgow Quatercentenary Studies* (Glasgow, 1907).

[16] See L. Hotson, *Commonwealth and Restoration Stage* (1928), p. 16.

[17] Henry Burkhead, of whom nothing is known save through Wood's dubious comment that he was a Bristol merchant.

[18] MS. Tanner, 466, fols. 174-199.—This play was printed from a Hunterian manuscript and mistakenly dated 1680 by Alexander Smith (Glasgow, 1872); later it was assigned to Sir Thomas Browne; see *N&Q*, Fifth Series, iii, 341, 398, 489. The Bodleian Copy is initialed "H. B." and ascribed in a coeval hand to Henry Birkhead, who, possibly on the evidence of the name alone, has been identified as the Oxford philologist and Latin poet who followed a deviation to Romanism in his youth by becoming a fellow of All Souls, and later a Royalist lawyer. (*DNB*, v, 83.) The author, however, may have been the Henry Burkhead who wrote *Cola's Fury*. I should suspect neither of these plays to be written by an Oxford scholar. For a more detailed note on the subject, see my communication to *LTLS*, Nov. 8, 1934.

[19] No date, but B. M. copy bears "March 30, 1660" in a coeval hand.

[20] The following list, given with abbreviated titles, may be incomplete: S. Sheppard, *Committee Man Curried*, 2 parts, 1647; Mercurius Pragmaticus [M. Nedham], *Levellers Levell'd*, 1647; *Scottish Politic Presbyter*, 1647; *A Key to the Cabinet of Parliament*, 1648; *Cuckows Nest at Westminster*, 1648; *Women will have their Will*, 1648; *Crafty Cromwell*, 1648; *Kentish Fair, or the Parliament Sold to their Best Worth*, 1648; *Mistress Parliament her Gossipping*, 1648; *A New Bull Baiting*, 1649; *New Market Fair*, 2 parts, 1649; *A Bartholomew Fairing*, 1649; *The Disease of the House*, 1649; *Jovial Crew, or the Devil Turned Ranter*, 1651; Henry Neville, *Shuffling, Cutting, and Dealing*, 1659; *A Fanatic Play*, 1660; *The Famous Tragedy of the Life and Death of Mrs. Rump*, 1660; *Hewson Reduc'd, or The Shoemaker Return'd to his Trade*, 1661; *Robinhood and his Crew of Soldiers*, 1661. Professor Rollins believes some of these playlets may have been performed for the Royalists; cf. *SP*, xviii (1921), 299.

[21] Act iii, Scene i.

[22] Part I, Act iii, Scene i.

[23] A. Harbage, *Thomas Killigrew*, pp. 227-28.

[24] See above, pp. 72-74.

[25] Act i, Scene vi.

[26] Act I, Scene iv.

[27] Act III, Scene xii.

[28] John Downes, *Roscius Anglicanus*, p. 25.

[29] Biographical memoirs of Tatham, Lacy, and Wilson, all mentioned in this chapter, appear in Maidment and Logan's edition of their works; the best life of Wilson is prefixed to M. Nahm's edition of *The Cheats* (Oxford, 1935).

[30] Called *The Change of Crowns*, cf. *Pepys Diary*, April 15, 1667.

[31] Accounts of the cruelties of Andronicus were available to dramatists in Heylin's *Cosmography*, and Fuller's *Holy State*.

[32] A Latin play treating of the trial and execution of the King's judges is R. Brathwait's *Regicidium*, 1665, described by M. Black, *op. cit.*, pp. 78-80. Two French plays on the English troubles survive in manuscript: E. Aigrot's *Charles Stuardt, Tragedie, or La Mort du Roy d'Angleterre*, 1660, Brit. Mus., Add. MS. 20,049; and Euvertre Jollyvet d'Orleans's *Tragicomedie sur les derniers troubles d'Angleterre*, Bodleian, MS. Rawl. poet. 7.

[33] See A. Nicoll, "Political Plays of the Restoration," *MLR*, XVI (1921), 224-42.

V

CAROLINE AND COMMONWEALTH PRIVATE THEATRICALS

MEMBERS of the Cavalier generation, as we observed at the outset, showed their fondness for drama by acting in plays. The enthusiasm for private theatricals, mounting during the Caroline reign, continued through the Interregnum. The extent to which plays were acted between 1642 and 1660 privately and by amateurs can only be guessed at, but enough evidence survives to suggest that the custom was prevalent, and that young playwrights of the early Restoration— recruited chiefly among the wealthy and well-born—became familiar with play-production elsewhere than abroad or in the harassed public theatres of Cromwell's England.

The English gentry had not awaited, of course, the accession of King Charles I before producing and enacting plays. Students at the universities and inns of court had never been averse to testing their quality as actors. Masques elsewhere than at court, barriers, entertainments, and festival mummery and recitation had also been common. Let us note, however, that acting by genteel amateurs other than students seems to have experienced the same falling off during later Elizabethan and earlier Jacobean times as had practicable play writing in this group. In Jonson's masques written for Queen Anne, professional actors were called on to take the speaking parts, the courtiers confining their participation to the stately and decorative motions of the dance.[1]

A greater relaxation is apparent after the rise of Buckingham as arbiter of courtly fashion, but the activities of the more dashing courtiers late in the reign of James were considered rashly unconventional. In 1618 "neither the Queen nor King did like or allow" a masque in which Lady Hay and eight others were to appear as Amazons.[2] In January of this year a group of gallants, including Sir Thomas Dutton, Sir George Goring, and others, acted an interlude of "Tom of Bedlam" before King James at Theobalds, but James frowned, and Chamberlain marvelled that "amongst so many, none had the judgment to see how unfit it was to bring such beastly gear in public places before a prince."[3] The court favorite was a lover of dancing. In January, 1620, James was entertained at court by a masque in which Prince Charles and Buckingham contended for honors,[4] and at Lord Doncaster's with a "running ballet" (an informal and improvised masque),[5] and again shortly afterwards at Sir John Crofts, near Newmarket when the ladies invited the court to a masque of their own invention.[6] Buckingham and his circle refused to confine themselves to mere masquing, and began to follow the French fashion for nobles to take character parts and to speak lines. At Salisbury, August 5, 1620, Buckingham spoke the lines of an Irish footman in an entertainment in which the Marquis Hamilton was a pirate and Sir William Fielding a Puritan "that marred the play."[7] The royal favorite began looking elsewhere than to professional writers for texts, Sir John Maynard[8] furnishing him with a masque presented at York House, November 18, 1623, and another performed at Burley-on-the-Hill August 5, 1624; visiting ambassadors dignified both occasions with their presence, but Maynard's offerings seem not to have met with great success.

None of the interludes or masques emanating from Buckingham's circle have survived. The tendency of the courtiers to appear in them so conspicuously was the ostentation of a privileged clique, and was neither highly approved nor widely imitated. We have already described how Queen Henrietta's appearance as an actress in a French pastoral privately performed by her maids in 1625 aroused distinct disapproval even about the court itself.[9] In editing Sir John Beaumont's *Theatre of Apollo*, a show designed for presentation at court in the year of King James's death, W. W. Greg[10] speculates on whether the tableau featuring James, Prince Charles, and Elizabeth of Bohemia was to be effected by waxwork figures or by actors appropriately costumed. He assumes that royalty itself would not condescend to appear in the flesh in such a display. Had the production been designed a decade later, however, such a possibility could not have been disregarded, for in the interim the attitude toward acting in private theatricals had changed.

Amateur acting among the gentility flourished after Henrietta had appeared as Bellesa in Montague's *Shepherd's Paradise*, and Prynne's animadversions upon "woman actors" had established approval of the Queen's conduct as an article of Royalist faith. To be sure, those most pleased originally by her Majesty's interest in amateur acting were the ones who had been converted earlier by Buckingham's example. Taking the part[11] in Montague's play second in importance to that of the Queen herself was Mary Hamilton, wife of the Marquis who had been Buckingham's rival in dancing and acting. In the rôle of third importance was Cecilia Crofts, daughter of Sir John Crofts at whose estate the masque invented by ladies had been performed in 1620. The fiancé of Cecilia Crofts, Thomas Killigrew (whose sister Mrs. Kirke was also a fellow actress with the Queen), had taken the part of Circe's captive in Aurelian Townshend's *Tempe Restored,* the Queen's masque of a previous year. The Caroline conception of the attire of this classical figure encompassed "a doubtlet of white satin, breeches of carnation satin, cloake of the same coloured satin, lined with carnation coloured plush, trimmed with silver lace: silke stockins of pearl colour, white shooes, roses and garters of carnation, a hatt & a feather, a falling band with lace of the newest fashion, gloves, girdle & points sutable . . ."[12] More essential is the fact that here we have a page of honor to the King replacing the professional actor by taking the chief speaking part in the masque.

In the court masques subsequent to 1633 courtiers do not seem to have replaced the professional actors altogether, but there was a tendency for them to participate elsewhere than in the figure dance alone. The King and Queen spoke no lines, but appeared spectacularly as characters in the fables. Davenant's antimasques consisted usually of long sequences of comic pantomimes and eccentric dances, and here the performers ranged from Jeffrey Hudson, the court dwarf, to the grooms of their majesties' bedchambers.

Among regular plays written and performed at court, Habington's *Queen of Aragon* and probably Henry Killigrew's *Pallantus and Eudora* as well as Montague's *Shepherd's Paradise* were originally performed by amateurs. *The Pastoral of Florimene,* and other plays which we know only by allusion, were acted by the Queen's maids. In most cases there is no means for us to determine whether the original casts of the plays written by courtiers were composed of professionals or amateurs. There was certainly a tendency to view the latter as rivals in merit to the former. *The Royal Slave* was reenacted at Hampton Court so that the Queen might determine whether the regular players could "do it as well" as the students—"but by all men's confessions, the players came short of the university actors."[13]

Since the court as such was banished during the Interregnum and could perpetuate neither its administrative functions nor its amusements, whereas the county seats of the nobility remained, frequently as populous hotbeds of "malignancy," it is important for us to trace the vogue of amateur theatricals as it spread beyond Westminster. After January, 1633, play acting became increasingly common at English manor houses. In May of this year, King Charles on his way to Scotland was entertained by the Marquis of Newcastle at Welbeck in Nottinghamshire with a show written by Ben Jonson. Although now rejected as the author of the court masques, Jonson composed speeches of welcome and eulogy which lack nothing of warmth. The humorous dialogue and mock-tilting or quintain with which this dramatically slight entertainment was rounded out was evidently presented by the local gentry, provided with what must have been extremely lavish equipment. Charles was so well pleased that he offered Newcastle the opportunity to entertain him again, and in July, 1634, both he and Queen Henrietta were welcomed in the neighboring seat at Bolsover with a second entertainment by Jonson. This time the song of welcome, the dance by mechanics, the contest between Eros and Anteros, and the concluding laudation of the royal pair offered little of novelty except in the rugged author's brave persistance in gibbeting "Iniquo Vitruvius," his ancient enemy Inigo Jones. Lady Newcastle asserted that the first entertainment cost her lord four or five thousand pounds, the second fourteen or fifteen thousand, a claim corroborated by Edward Hyde, who wrote that the entertainment at Welbeck "would still be thought very prodigous if the same noble person had not, within a year or two afterward, made the King and Queen a more stupendous entertainment, which God be thanked . . . no man ever after imitated."[14] Hyde himself was one of the committee in charge of the great inns of court masque, *The Triumph of Peace*. Newcastle's offerings may be viewed as part of the series including this and Carew's *Cœlum Britannicum*. King Charles was craving these visible manifestations of the loyalty of his subjects and the splendor of himself.

It is odd that the name of John Milton should appear in a discussion of the flurry in amateur theatricals stimulated by Henrietta's advent as an actress and the indignation provoked by the expressions of distaste from the Puritan Prynne. Milton and Prynne, however, were Puritans of a different water. Among the "young lords and noblemen's sons" participating with their elders in Carew's *Cœlum Britannicum* were Viscount Brackley and Mr. Thomas Egerton, the two youngest sons of the Earl of Bridgewater. When the Egertons decided upon family theatricals of their own, Milton, no doubt through the agency of Henry Lawes, was commissioned as the poet. About 1633 he wrote the three songs and the eulogistic speech which compose *Arcades*, the gracious little formality with which the Egertons and other relatives celebrated a visit in pastoral attire to Harefield and the Countess Dowager of Derby, who was at once Bridgewater's stepmother and mother-in-law.[15] Then to celebrate a family reunion of the Egertons at Ludlow Castle in Shropshire, and as part of the ceremonies attendant on the Earl of Bridgewater's installation there as Lord President of Wales, Milton again collaborated with Lawes, this time on the masque since known as *Comus*.[16] On September 29, 1634, the performance was given in the council chamber of the castle, on a stage probably improvised but certainly provided with painted scenery, before an assembly of the President's household, his resident councillors, and the neighboring gentry. Lawes and probably two other professional musicians, and three of Bridgewater's children, filled the important rôles; Lady Alice Egerton was no more than fifteen years old, and her two brothers, Mr. Thomas Egerton and Lord Brackley, were respectively about twelve and thirteen. There is no need here to describe *Comus,* or to expatiate upon its quality. The Bridgewater children might not have acted in it—indeed it might never have been written at all—except for the revived taste for private theatricals spreading outward from the court; it belongs properly to a discussion of one phase of Cavalier drama, and its existence dignifies a movement which can boast too few artistic justifications. *Comus* has frequently been termed undramatic, but it is in fact somewhat more dramatic than most members of its class. It is not isolated in type, for entertainments, part morality and part masque, as has already been pointed out, were not uncommon.

The young Egertons were not the only noble children given the opportunity to shine as actors. Lord Buckhurst and Mr. Edward Sackville, the sons of Henrietta's chamberlain the Earl of Dorset, and the reputed assistants of their tutor Joseph Rutter in translating *Le Cid,*[17] took speaking parts in *The King and Queen's Entertainment at Richmond,* an improvised masque presented September 12, 1636, expressly to satisfy the Queen's desire to see her little Prince Charles dance in a masque. According to a "Note to the Reader," one Simon Hopper was required to devise some country dances such as would best set off the Prince, and "now of necessity a body [of dialogue] was to be fitted to their garment . . . and because most of the Interlocutors were Wiltshire men, that country Dialect was chosen, and thus every man fitted his part to his owne fancy, and the constitution of the whole tending to a greater bulke, it came to be what it is, without any designe, but rather out of a kind of necessity urging it." The entertainment begins with a bumpkin entering to present the gift of a melon to the Queen who has taken her seat among the spectators. After he has failed to pick her out from the company of ladies, Mr. Edward Sackville bursts into blank verse,

> Away you asse,
> Dost thou not see a light outshine the rest,
> Two stars that sparkle in a milky way,
> Dimming the shine of Ariadne's crown . . .

The bumpkin is joined by several kindred spirits, who after indulging in some rather broad humor, fall into a rustic dance. After a song in

parts by a shepherd and a shepherdess, the scene changes to a camp
where a Druid and a British Captain [the Sackville brothers] engage
in conversation. Pacifism is advocated, and the Queen is described as
a tamer of soldiers. Following this, the arrival of Britomart is an-
nounced, and the Prince with six peers dance their figures. A song to
the Queen concludes this incoherent but interesting production:

Then was the Curtain let fall, and this folly (as others doe) had con-
sum'd it selfe, and left no impression on the spectators, or hearers, had
it not bin that much admiration was conceau'd at the great quicknesse
and aptnesse of the Prince, who varying figures so often was so farre
from being out, that he was able to lead the rest. The speaking and
action (which grac'd the words) perform'd by my Lord of Buckhurst
and M. Edward Sackvile, shew'd that genuine action was not so much
confin'd to the stage, but a Gentleman might reach it, if not tran-
scend it . . .

On Twelfth Night, 1640, the two children of Philip Stanhope, first
Earl of Chesterfield, spoke lines in a masque performed at Bretby in
Derbyshire written by the Earl's kinsman, Aston Cokain. After Lars
Familiaris instructs a satyr in the superiority of civilized life over that
in the greenwood, the two boys of the house (probably Alexander and
George, Chesterfield's children by his second wife) burst in and salute
their parents. Then follows an interesting reminiscence of *Comus:*

First Boy
He would outrun me, and be kissed before me.

Second Boy
And he leave me among these dreadful Satyrs.

Lars Familiaris
Whence come you?

First Boy
We both were left i' th' woods, and tempted by
Such things as these to live abroad with them.

The boys are kissed by their parents, and after an antimasque of satyrs,
the figure dancing begins. A few songs, one of which displays the essentially imitative nature of Cokain's art with a refrain suggested by
Spenser,

And let us sing
Till hills and dales with echoes ring,

and a speech of good night concludes the entertainment.

A somewhat livelier Twelfth Night production was devised by Sir
Thomas Salisbury[18] and performed in 1641 at Knowsley, the country

seat of James, Lord Strange, later seventh Earl of Derby. Christmas is warned by Dr. Almanack that his time is short and he should make his will. The Holidays are borne out on the backs of the "leane ghost-like Apparisions of fastinge days," and after Christmas makes a humorous disposition of his estate, he likewise is carried away. Two anti-masques punctuate these preliminary jollities. Then the scene changes to a temple, and New Year with his twelve attendant months, six wintry men and six summery women, crown the entertainment with singing, speech-making, and dancing. Charles Stanley, the son and heir of Lord Strange, acted the part of New Year; and Viscount Molineux and his child wife, the eleven year old daughter of Lord Strange, spoke the lines respectively of February and April.[19]

Poetical addresses from a similar entertainment of 1634 at Chirke Castle, the seat of Sir Thomas Middleton, survive in manuscript.[20] The services of professional playwrights were sometimes called upon for these private shows. Thomas Heywood seems to have prepared an entertainment given on New Year's day, 1637,[21] at the estate of Henry Carey, fourth Lord Hunsdon and Earl of Dover, the grandson of Queen Elizabeth's lord chamberlain. Among the works of Thomas Nabbes is *The Spring's Glory*, c. 1637, an entertainment in which Ceres and Venus, with their seconds Bacchus and Cupid, indulge in a dispute. That this too was prepared for a pre-Lenten festivity is indicated by the fact that Christmas, Shrovetide, and Lent become involved in the quarrel, which is finally resolved by the arbitrator Spring, who makes a preachment in the cause of platonic love! Also by Nabbes is the very slight piece, *A Presentation intended for the Prince his Highness on his Birthday, the 29 of May, 1638*, wherein Time squabbles with the Almanack Makers, and, together with May, compliments the Prince in songs and speeches, following which a dance is performed by eight princes of Wales. Prince Charles, his brother James, and sister Mary had previously been privately entertained, February 27, 1636, by *Corona Minervæ*, a show prepared by Sir Francis Kynaston to celebrate their visit to his newly opened academy, Museum Minervæ, where the sons of the nobility and gentry were invited to take a three or seven year course in such essential branches of learning as dancing, heraldry, numismatics, and the like. Kynaston[22] was an esquire of the body to King Charles, who contributed £100 and a patent to the venture, possibly reassured by his courtier's guarantee that no rivalry to Oxford, Cambridge, or the inns of court was intended. The entertainment of the royal children begins with speeches of welcome by Minerva and Time. Then the four seasons quarrel for precedence, until amity is settled among them and they combine in making verbal offerings of their riches to the visitors. The academy is described, and learned books are offered the children. These prove to contain the refreshments: Suetonius is filled with sweets, Gellius with jellies, Friar Bacon with meat, Apuleius with apples, etc. Nothing was spared in the way of setting; cherubs suspended from the ceiling acted as chandeliers. Probably Kynaston and his assistant educators spoke the lines. It is surprising that this monstrous conceit is not badly written.

It is in the nature of things that the texts of private theatricals should have only the slightest chance of survival, and the number of those at hand is the more impressive since it can represent only a fraction of the original total. The survey of the shows privately produced and acted before 1642 may well conclude with an account of a series which has lain in manuscript,[23] undisturbed until the present time. At Apthorpe in Northamptonshire still stands an impressive old mansion, parts of which date back to about the year 1500.[24] During the reign of Charles I, this was the country seat of Mildmay Fane, Earl of Westmoreland (d. 1665), whom we must add to the list of Caroline playwrights. The Earl[25] was born near the beginning of the century, took his M.A. at Cambridge in 1619, entered Lincoln's Inn in 1622, and followed a subsequent career normal to his station. His first wife dying in April, 1640, he promptly wedded the widow of Sir Roger Townshend who brought him several children by her first marriage. At the outbreak of the Civil Wars, Fane espoused the Royal cause, but was arrested as a delinquent before hostilities were well under way. He was paroled from the Tower to his home in Bartholomew Close in 1643, and in the following year was rewarded for taking the covenant by receiving full liberty and the discharge of his sequestered estates. At the Restoration, he was forgiven his capitulation to Parliament and remained in good repute until his death in 1665. For several years following 1640 Apthorpe was the scene of annual entertainments, composed by its noble proprietor and acted by members of his household, and his neighbors and guests.

The first of Fane's plays in point of date is *Raguaillo D'Oceano*. In the words of the author, "This Show was written & prepared to be acted in Añ. 1640." The words "prepared to be acted" are characteristic phraseology of the day, and do not signify that the performance failed to take place. The title leaf of *Raguaillo D'Oceano* contains, besides the date, a statement of the theme: "The drift or plot to shew the insatiate desires that posess the mind & make it search after novelties even to impossebilety"; and a very rough sketch of the ground plan of the stage. In the background is "Antarctacus," a "scene of hills & craggy rocks all covered with snow." Disposed about the stage, evidently as permanent adjuncts of the setting, are the Princess Terra Australis Incognita in the center framed by phoenixes and a unicorn's horn, and, at either side, "six yong ladies in various colours" and "six yong gallants whiffing tobacco." Subsequently, costumes are described in considerable detail. The entertainment itself is more purely a masque than any of Fane's later works, but it departs from the type in its great length, and in its tendency to make song and dance subsidiary to prolonged allegorical dialogues. The central character, Oceanus, interviews the various rivers of the world, and questions and repels a succession of would-be visitors to Terra Incognita. There are fourteen of these, each representing one of the nations of Europe, Asia, Africa, and America. The action, of course, was suggested by the rumors incident to the early seventeenth-century activities of Portuguese, Spanish, and Dutch seamen in skirting the coast of Australia. No Englishman put foot on the island until 1688, but Fane placed an Englishman in his show—as well as a Gypsy, a Brazilian, and an Amazon. The interlopers are permitted only a glimpse of what they seek before they are banished; then Oceanus himself weds the Princess Terra Incognita, whose "chastity" he has preserved.

Second in the series is *Candy Restored,* "Presented in a show at Apthorpe in the 12th of ffebruary 1640 to the Lord and Lady of that place, by some of their owne children and famelie." The year is evidently recorded in the old style, and should read 1641, since the play must have been presented after Fane's second marriage: the actors referred to as "their own children" were Fane's stepsons, Sir Roger and Horatio Townshend. The elaborate scenery used in the production is described in the manuscript, and the members of the cast, upward of thirty in number, are all listed, including "Mr. Stapleton" and "Mr. Waller." From the fact that in the case of these two only are the first names omitted, we may guess that they were considered notables, and were probably the poets. Mr. Waller took the part of Captain Laroles, master of the bark. The play itself is a political allegory. To Candy, once a land of pastoral peace and plenty, turbulence and distress have come since the banishment of the great sage and physician, Dr. Synedarke. We see discontented citizens and tattered groups of pressed soldiers. We hear Mr. Downright and Tom Telltroth complain of the heavy taxation, disorder, and mismanagement. Prayers are offered to Diana, and a company of sailors appears bringing Dr. Synedarke back to the realm. Synedarke's helper, Rhodakin, procures for him the urinals of the three daughters of Cosmus: Albinia, Ibernia, and Calledonia. Analyzed with astrological guidance, these prove the source of the ills of Candy, Albinia,

> hath beene very active in all kindes
> Of late, to serve and suite herselfe to the fashion
> Of other countries, dresse as they do dresse,
> Use the like foode, like speech, and to be one
> With them in all, halfe turn devotion
> To their key, halting between two opinions . . .

Ibernia, suffering sympathetic ailments, has turned consumptive. Calledonia's disease has resulted from self-assertion and ambition. After purges, emetics, and bleeding have been properly administered through the prescription of Dr. Synedarke, the three daughters of Cosmus are cured, and Candy is restored to its former blissful state. It is not difficult to relate the action of the play to conditions in England subsequent to the Bishops Wars.

The restoration of Candy to peaceful felicity represented only a wish-fulfillment on the part of Mildmay Fane. His next play, *Time's Trick upon the Cards,* "prepared to be represented at Apthorpe by the youth and servants their the 22nd of ffebruary—1641" [i.e. 1642], reverts to its predecessor in the prologue:

> Though Candy be restor'd as wee suppose,
> Tis sayd two words to every bargain goes;
> And thus a sunshine day admitts a cloud
> Least constand splendor make the climat proud.

The play is a moral allegory, consisting of an all but unintelligible succession of dialogues and encounters, first at Æstopolis [Inconstancy], than at Agape [Love or Charity], the latter a town sacked by appropriately symbolical pirates. It is not necessary here to outline the adventures of Blanducio [Flattery], her governess Cronostia [Time-past], and the several score additional personifications which compose the dramatis personæ. Fortunately a key is provided to indicate the identity of each quality represented by the characters, and we are able to appreciate the final downfall of Malice and his ilk, and the triumph of Sincerity. The piece is crowned by an interlude in which Nike lays his trophies at the feet of Eyrene and Symphonia.

There is nothing to indicate that Fane's remaining plays, or "shows" as he perspicaciously chose to call them, were acted. *The Change,* dated December 1642, and provided with a prologue and epilogue by the author in the rôle of a prisoner, was written when Fane was cogitating his Royalist sins while lodged in the Tower as a captive of Parliament. The piece consists of a succession of dialogues, full of elaborate symbolism, in which two merchants and three ladies, "great reformers or rather deformers of state government," project a new topsy-turvy world in which everything is to be wrenched out of square and made round. A mock trial is held to try "the old felonious world," and the interlude ends with veiled preachments against change and innovation. *Virtue's Triumph* "writt in Ann—1644" is a formidable moral allegory in which the tyrant Ambition and his concubine Malice succeed for a time in raising their dominion above the other qualities, and the Vices triumph over the Virtues. Nature, the wild, stubborn son of Lord Earth, disdains his tutor Reason, misled by Custom and Will. But he is at last reclaimed, Nobility and Truth emerge from disgrace, and the miscreants are punished "only Ignorance excus'd." The play, with its minimum of action and maximum of homiletic dialogue is anything but absorbing. A moral allegory which may be by Fane, although it exists in a manuscript separate from those certainly his,[26] is dated August 15, 1643, and has been given the title *Time's Triumph*. In Arcadia, where Juno is condescending to act for a time as a sort of Bonus Genius, there is a typical imbroglio among the Vices and Virtues, and a tendency toward misalliance even among the Virtues themselves, but at last right prevails and Desert is properly wedded to Will, Virtue to Judgment, Honor to Age, and Love to Fortune. A few songs and dances are interpolated, but for the most part all is allegorical action and dialogue quite in the manner of Fane's *Virtue's Triumph*.

Fane's last extant play is more interesting than either of those just described, although it too is a moral allegory. *De Pugna Animi,* dated 1650, resembles in theme Nabbes's "moral masque" *Microcosmus,* concerning as it does the anarchous revolt but final subjugation of the five Senses; in fact the scene specified is the island Microcosmus, "that little world of man." On the island the Senses rule in the licentious company of depraved companions, until Mind, represented as a German Rhinegrave, and his faithful aides, Captain Prudence and Admiral Reason, muster their forces and, through a series of physical attacks, abetted by dissension among the sensual rebels themselves, obtain a victory. The repentant Senses present Virtue, Queen of the Isle of Providence, whom they have been holding in thrall, to Mind as his bride, "& so ends the comedy with matrimony—accordinge to custome." There is some action in the play, and fairly lively dialogue.

One play by Fane seems to have disappeared, *Ladrones or The Robbers' Island,* "an Opera in a Romansike way," a manuscript on sale at Sotheby's, July 17, 1888.[27] The names of Magellan, Drake, and Cavendish figured in the dramatis personæ, so it seems probable that it was written in imitation of Sir William Davenant's Commonwealth entertainments. It is entirely possible that there was an attempt to present at Apthorpe even such plays as *The Change, Virtue's Triumph* and *De Pugna Animi* during the Interregnum; as in the case of his

earlier entertainments Fane appears to have written for purposes other
than publication.

Nothing can be claimed for the Earl of Westmoreland as a poet or a
dramatist, but his works, though in most instances of an admittedly
dull variety, are literate and readable. He wrote in mingled rimed and
blank verse, achieving the greater success in the latter, which is fairly
regular for its time and contains a number of good lines—as well as a
few bald plagiarisms. An interpretation of his political allegory would
prove interesting, since his opinions were so typical of a large class of
the Cavaliers. He hated the thought of change, craving only quiet and
stability, a drowsing government in London and festivities at Apthorpe.
No doubt he would have wished nothing better than for King Charles
to arbitrate with the Commons. His plays are most interesting to us
as further illustration of the vogue of private theatricals, and of the
ease with which activity of this class can evade for centuries the search-
light of scholarship.

Fane's later plays have carried us well into the period of the Interregnum. Long days of suspense and idleness were the lot of the suspect
Royalists after hostilities had ceased, and among the majority of them,
who had returned to London or their country estates after compound-
ing with Parliament, conditions were favorable for the revival of private theatricals. Now,

> . . . the more Generous race of men revives
> This Lampe of Knowledge, and like Primitives
> In Caves, fearless of Martyrdom, rehearse
> The almost breathless, now, Dramatick verse.[28]

In publishing Quarles's *Virgin Widow* in 1649, the printer tells us
that the play had been performed at Chelsey "privately acted by a
company of young gentlemen with good approvement." Thomas Jordan wrote a prologue for a play, no longer extant, *The Florentine
Ladies,* "played in the night by gentlemen."[29] In his preface to his
Cutter of Coleman Street, Cowley refers to its original form as *The
Guardian,* which was several times privately acted during the "troubles."

In her letters to Sir William Temple, the delightful Dorothy Osborne
affords us a glimpse into a typical Cavalier household.[30] In the Spring
of 1654 she travelled into Kent to visit at the home of her kinsman
Sir Thomas Peyton. Here, in "a house the most filled of any since the
Ark," she found life different from that at Chicksands "where you
might finish a romance of ten tomes before anybody interrupted you."
Writes she, "We go abroad all day and play all night, and say our
prayers when we have time. Well, in sober earnest now, I could not

live thus a twelvemonth to gain all that the King has lost, unless it were to give it to him again." On July 20, she complained to Temple, "I leave you to judge the constraint I live in, what alarms my thoughts give me, and how unconcerned this company requires I should be; they will have me at my part in a play, *The Lost Lady*, it is, and I am she. Pray God it be not an ill omen!" Dorothy mentions the play in none of her subsequent letters, her general attitude indicating that such an amateur production was nothing unusual. An entertaining passage appears in a letter penned later in the year. After a romantic description of one whom she claims to be a fellow guest, a sadly tender gentleman bereaved of his sweetheart in youth, the writer concludes: "You will not be jealous though I say I like him very much. If you were not secure in me, you might be so in him. He would expect his mistress should rise again to reproach his inconstancy if he made court to anything but her memory." Dorothy was not above giving William something to worry about. As Milesia in Berkeley's *Lost Lady*, her lover had been Prince Lysicles, and it is the latter whom she seems to be describing. She herself as the "lost lady," supposedly deceased, has arisen to reproach Lysicles, supposedly inconstant.

A few school plays survive to prove that the student actor did not entirely disappear during the Interregnum. *Titus, or The Palm of Christian Courage*, "exhibited" and printed in 1644, illustrates, what we might have suspected, that the Parliamentary loathing for the drama did not extend its influence to the scholars of the Society of Jesus in Kilkenny. On December 21, 1647, the school boys taught by John Mason in Surrey acted his *Combat of Caps*,[31] a series of academic scenes and disputations full of scholastic and heraldic allegory. The inns of court still enjoyed occasional entertainments. A masque at the Middle Temple was given in 1651, and in 1657 the musicians of the Inner Temple were rewarded for acting *The Countryman* before the residents.[32] In the universities, uniformly at Cambridge, and, after the King's expulsion, at Oxford also, student acting was effectively discouraged. It was not until the very end of the period that the students at Trinity College, Oxford, performed *The Christmas Ordinary*,[33] a festival show containing, besides the usual speeches of the Seasons and kindred abstractions, a skit in which an apprentice, a religious hermit, a student astronomer, and a town blade, riot in an ordinary, and crack the usual anti-Puritan jests. Shortly after the Restoration, Robert Neville, with nostalgic allusions to the past glories of such gownsmen as Randolph, tried to revive academic comedy at Cambridge with *The Poor Scholar*, an old-fashioned comedy of student life, love intrigue, and youths outwitting their elders.

If dramatic festivity drooped at the closely supervised traditional seats of learning, it enjoyed a happier fate at the "select academy," the finishing school for the sons of the nobility and gentry. Musarum Minervæ seems to have expired with the entrepreneur Kynaston in 1642. But a similar academy was organized by Sir Balthazar Gerbier in 1649. Among the subjects to be taught the privileged patrons was the art of perspective and architecture; not only for great houses but also for the "Secret Motions of Sceanes." Mock tournaments, dancing, musical entertainments, and "representations in scenes"—sometimes, to be sure, of a deprecatingly pious cast—were among the diversions available to Gerbier's students, their relatives and friends.[34] In 1654 Thomas Jordan wrote an entertainment, which survives in manuscript, *Cupid his Coronation*, "a Mask as it was Presented with good Approbation at the Spittle diverse tymes by Masters and yong Ladyes who were theyre Scholers . . ."[35] At first glance, owing perhaps to the reference to ladies in the unladylike region of the Spittle, one suspects the work to be satirical, but such proves not the case: the entertainment must actually have been given at a girls' school. "A curtain riseth, admitting the discovery of a Frontispiece formed piramidically, beautified with the figures of Peace on the right hand, Plenty on the left, and Love more eminently placed in the medium . . ." The only speaker is a young priest of Apollo, who guarantees at the outset that there is to follow "only art and innocence." Performers representing the figures painted on the proscenium sing and dance in a group. Symphonies are played, and six "Vinitorians" move in a figure dance. Representatives of the various nationalities appear and are described; these dance singly, then in chorus, after which a quarrel among them is ended by Love. With a final song, and a speech promising that the "little Ladies" intend to have more masques, the entertainment ends. It is not hard to picture the rows of fond parents viewing this music and dancing school concert of a bygone age.

Jordan provided the librettos for other amateur theatricals. *Fancy's Festivals,* published in 1657, was a masque which had been "privately presented by many civil persons of quality . . . in the presence of persons numerous and noble . . . being much advantaged with the illustrative faculties of Musick, Painting, and Dancing." Again there is a prologue promising only art and innocence. After an induction in which Fancy is shown giving birth to the entertainment, four interludes or contentions, each diversified with song and dance, lead up to a grand masque of heroes of the late war. The first of the four interludes is a rewriting of *Cupid his Coronation* (Jordan, as usual, making double use of his efforts), the second an encounter between Power and Policy, the third an exchange of persiflage between Mr. Frolick and Mrs. Friendly ending in a tavern jollification, the fourth an encounter between Sleep and Watch who are soon supplanted by their kinsmen Death and Life. Here we observe the familiar mid-century predilection for moral allegory, but little of literary interest besides, despite Jordan's boast that his characters speak rather "properly then highly, since . . . aptitude is more commendable then altitude"—a shaft probably directed against the contemporary dramatic offerings of Sir William Davenant.

Although it is scarcely fair to bracket him thus with Jordan, James Shirley likewise supplied entertainments for amateur actors of the Interregnum, possibly for the students of his own grammar school. These late works have usually been belittled or ignored, and two of them have been incorrectly dated before 1642.[36] *The Triumph of Beauty* "As it was personated by some young Gentlemen for whom it was intended at a private Recreation" appeared in 1646, a date probably very near to that of its original production. From twenty to thirty performers must have taken part in this interesting piece. It begins with Bottle and a company of rude shepherds preparing to act the story of Jason and the Golden Fleece in order to cheer Paris, who dwells sadly alone upon Mount Ida. They quarrel over parts, and substitute for their play a country dance. Paris falls asleep to the tune of a soothing song, and Mercury descends with a golden ball. Then follows the contest of the three goddesses. Venus, happy in her victory, entertains Paris—with a song in parts by Hymen and Delight, and a dance by the Graces and the Hours. The entire entertainment is graceful, pleasing, and excellently written—notably the speeches of the contending goddesses. The comic induction imitates but does not plagiarize Bottom's rehearsal of the Pyramis and Thisbe play in *Midsummer Night's Dream;* the Paris legend itself has never been more graciously treated. Shirley was certainly not "written out" though the dramatic career, cut short four years before, had been so prolific, and though he was now reduced to the station of a literary hack.

Printed with a second of Shirley's Commonwealth entertainments, *Cupid and Death* "Presented before his Excellence the Embassadour of Portugal, upon the 26 of March, 1653," is an explanatory note informing us that the masque was "born without ambition of more than to make good a private entertainment," but that it surprised its author by meeting favorable reception when presented before the foreign envoy by Mr. Luke Channen and others. There were elegant scenes (evidently painted backdrops, three in number), and "for the gentlemen that

performed the dances, this much the author did affirm upon sight of
their practice, that they showed themselves master of their quality."
Concerning Luke Channen the present writer has discovered nothing
save that his surname was that of a family of Royalist malignants. The
Portuguese Ambassador was the nobleman Joao Rodriguez de Sa e
Menezes, who, though he was eagerly negotiating a peace treaty with
Cromwell, might very readily have accepted hospitality in a Royalist
household.[37] His legation specialized in diplomatic unorthodoxy. The
Ambassador's own brother murdered several Englishmen in a quasi-
political brawl, and in July, 1654, just after the treaty between the two
nations had been signed, he paid the penalty on an English scaffold,
the inflexible Protector refusing leniency.[38] *Cupid and Death* is a
"moral masque" which retains a dramatic quality though peopled with
abstractions. It retells the old fable of the exchange of weapons by the
two ancient enemies, and the consequent disaster. Mercury descends to
prevent perpetual tragedy; and after their proper weapons are restored,
Cupid is forbidden palaces and "confin'd to cottages, to poor and humble cells," while Death is commanded to shoot no more where "marks
of art or honour shine." The conclusion is a grand masque of dead
lovers in Elysium. Several excellent songs, and some scenes of diverting
comedy, relieve the moral burden of this forceful allegory.

In 1659 appeared in print *The Contention of Ajax and Ulysses* "as
it was nobly represented by young Gentlemen of Quality, at a private
Entertainment by some persons of Honour." This is no more than an
interlude, a debate before the Greek chieftains by Ajax and Ulysses,
written with an admirable distinction between the grim bluntness of
the one and the subtle eloquence of the other. Vanquished, Ajax runs
and slays himself, whereupon the entertainment ends with that splendid
dirge, "The glories of our blood and state."

. . . .
The garlands wither on your brow,
    Then boast no more your mighty deeds;
Upon Death's purple altar now
    See, where the victor-victim bleeds:
        Your heads must come
        To the cold tomb,
    Only the actions of the just
    Smell sweet, and blossom in their dust.

With this grand valediction, the dramatic activity of James Shirley, a
poet still inspired after all his lean and struggling years, came fittingly
to a close.[39]

Were fuller information available, our survey of private theatricals
among the English during the Interregnum would certainly take us

outside the country. Except in the very bleakest years, Royalty had to have its pleasures, even though banished from London or from England itself. In 1643, and again in 1646, the court was entertained by plays at Oxford,[40] sometimes by amateurs, although in the earlier period plays were also presented by the Blackfriars actors, then enlisted in the royal army. The army had also its dramatic authors; some of the plays of Major Cosmo Manuche have survived,[41] and *The Enchanted Grove*, a masque in two parts, was written by Samuel Holland, possibly for amateur performance. It was dedicated to the Earl of Northampton, in whose regiment Holland, as well as Manuche, evidently served.[42] The members of the royal family living in Paris were regaled with masques on festival days, a description of one given New Year's Eve, 1647, indicating that the traditional characters of Christmas, Time, etc., were preserved, together with the usual assortment of "conceited dances" or antimasques.[43] In 1654 James Howell published the translation of a "Great Royall Ball," *The Nuptials of Peleus and Thetis*, acted in Paris six times. In this, three members of the English royal family, Charles II, James, and Princess Henrietta, had taken speaking parts side by side with members of the French nobility.

While their husbands or fathers were junketing about Europe in the games of war and diplomacy, lady exiles were forced to seek refuge in friendly households on the Continent, frequently at the Hague. The Duchess of Newcastle, and two Stuarts, the Queen of Bohemia and Princess Mary of Orange, gave asylum to many, and it is nearly certain that among these groups theatricals helped to while away the days of separation and waiting. It is possible, though there is no proof in the matter, that some of Sir William Lower's work,[44] produced while he was at the Hague between 1654 and 1660, was acted. Both Elizabeth and Mary seem to have been familiar with his plays before they were in print. In dedicating to Mary the *Amorous Fantasme* (which itself is supplied with a prologue and epilogue "to the court"), Lower expresses the hope "to introduce some thing with the New Yeere which may give you the least satisfaction."

Richard Flecknoe, lutenist and literary trifler, won for himself quite a reputation abroad with a succession of noble patronesses, including the Duchess of Newcastle, because of his dexterity in devising "sports of wit"—games, such as charades, interpreting dreams and oracles, "wonders," "wishes," "lotteries," and the like.[45] Between 1650 and 1651 Mlle. de Beauvais and the Duchess of Lorraine contended bitterly for his services as *maître de plaisir*. At Berseel in Flanders, *Love in its Infancy*, an earlier version of *Love's Dominion*, was performed while Flecknoe was the guest of the Duchess of Lorraine. In *Relation of Ten*

Years Travels, Letter L, written about 1650, describes to a female correspondent the design for a play which is to deal with the magnificent exploits of Amazons and "love stript from suspition of Harm." The plan provides for "representing it by Ladies, after the like example of the Queen [Henrietta] and her Ladies here formerly." Flecknoe, too, was the author of a Commonwealth masque, *The Marriage of Oceanus and Britannia,* printed in 1659; no copy of this have I been able to trace. His surviving plays will be discussed as part of Interregnum closet drama.

Toward the end of the Commonwealth period, private theatricals subtly transformed themselves into public theatricals, and with an account of Davenant's entertainments and "operas" at Rutland House and elsewhere, the present survey may well conclude. First we must note that Puritan restrictions on popular pleasures had been in constant danger of dissolution. The normal activities of a freedom-loving people cannot easily be checked; suppressions in one direction will only lead to effervescences in a dozen others. Cromwell, though surrounded by impractical zealots, was quite aware of this and of the necessity for compromise; his own capacity embraced the ability both to see holy visions and to relish fun. The London of his time was not the fen of miasmic gloom it is frequently supposed to have been. Ladies and gentlemen of the town had a fairly good time, with receptions, dances, and outings in Hyde Park and the New Spring Gardens. There were vernal stirrings even among the burghers. In 1655, after an interval of sixteen years, city pageantry was restored with *Charity Triumphant, or The Virgin-shew,* written by Edmund Gayton and presented by the Mercer's Company upon the mayoralty of Sir John Dethick. In printing his pamphlet, Gayton addressed the right honorable aldermen in politic vein: "The severest and, in other matters, the most rigid policies of Commonwealths (to wit, the Spartan, and Lacedemonian, and Athenian) smooth'd the rugged front of their power . . . to let the people spend their own time, and some of their money, where they pleas'd, especially in innocent and delightful diversions . . ." Gayton's economic arguments in favor of entertainment remind us of Davenant's, which urged that "money should at home be continually spending."[46] In 1656 the lord mayor's show was written by one "J. B.," for the eight subsequent years by John Tatham, and, after an interruption caused by the fire and plague, for the eleven years following 1671 by Thomas Jordan. The moral allegory of the pageants had ceased to be old-fashioned in 1655; we have witnessed a reversion to the type in theatricals elsewhere.

At the regular theatres, supposedly padlocked, the professional actors displayed an amazing persistence in waging guerilla warfare with the

Puritan constabulary.[47] Salisbury Court, the Phœnix, and the Fortune witnessed numerous surreptitious performances, often diversified with disastrous raids, especially in 1647 and 1648, years of especially severe anti-theatrical ordinances.[48] After 1649 when the interiors of the other theatres were torn down, the torch continued to smoulder at the old Red Bull, and the coaches of the gentry could often be seen lined up in the neighborhood of this once disreputable theatre. Of course the actors found their chief comfort and safety with the Quality. James Wright tells us:

. . . in Oliver's time, they used to act privately, three or four miles, or more, out of town, now here, now there: sometimes in noblemen's houses, in particular Holland House at Kensington, where the nobility and the gentry who met (but in no great numbers) used to make a sum for them, each giving a broad piece, or the like. And Alexander Goffe, the woman-actor at Blackfriars (who had made himself known to persons of quality), used to be the jackal, and give notice of time and place . . .[49]

Since players as a rule acted old stock plays, few new texts are furnished us by the professional stage of the Commonwealth. An exception may be made, however, in the case of the "Drolls," abbreviated entertainments adapted to the omnipresent possibility of interruption:

. . . sundry times acted in publique and private, in London at Bartholomew, in the country at other fairs, in halls and taverns, on several mountebancks stages, at Charing Cross, Lincolns-Inn-Fields, and other places; by several strolling players, fools and fidlers, and mountebancks zanies, with loud laughter and great applause; written I know not when, by several persons I know not who . . .[50]

Although most drolls are no more than the condensed comic underplots of the plays of Shakespeare and his successors, some of them first appear in print in Commonwealth booklets or in Kirkman's collections, and have an antiquarian interest. A few, such as *King Solomon's Wisdom* and *King Ahasuerus and Queen Esther,* are brief biblical dialogues which may have been used originally in puppet shows. Others, *Actæon and Diana, Œnone, Diphilo and Granida, Philetis and Constantia, Venus and Adonis,* are debased little pastorals or sentimental love scenes in rime. Most interesting among this fragment drama are the farcial jigs and interludes such as *Simpleton the Smith, Singing Simkin, John Swabber the Seaman,* and *The Black Man.* Here we have horseplay, contests in wits between "gentlemen" and clowns, and ribald little domestic scenes involving interlopers with wives and sweethearts. We are reminded of the old process of absorption of the fabliau into the interlude. Kirkman's editorial comment that these pieces were generally known and "very ancient" may be more than figuratively correct.[51] Chief adapter, actor, and (before Kirkman's time) publisher of drolls was Robert Cox, who was fined for playing the Swabber two years before his death in 1655;[52] Cox enjoyed considerable reputation for his comic prowess.

Several additional playlets slightly more ambitious than drolls, and possibly produced during the Interregnum, are *The Gossips Brawl, or The Women Wear the Breeches,* 1651 or 1655,[53] an exposition of Billingsgate, wherein several slum women gather in an ale-house to drink, smoke, and abuse the hostess Bess Bunghole; and *The London Chanticleers,* 1659, a series of fourteen scenes in which the city pedlars, male and female, foregather in homely wise to entertain us with quaint and harmless mirth. The prologue of this pleasant diversion suggests a performance before Royalists expelled from London,

> Your welcome then to London, which our show,
> Since you mayn't go to that, has brought to you.[54]

Money is an Ass, a short piece half morality and half comedy of love intrigue, written by the ubiquitous Thomas Jordan, seems also, judging from intimations in its prologue, to have been acted in the time of prohibition.[55] Among the seven youths who, with Jordan himself, acted the play, having "never had more tutor then the poet," were Wal. Williams, Thomas Loveday, and Thomas Lovel, who became professional actors of the Restoration.

We have journeyed momentarily afield from the subject of private or uncommercialized theatricals, but an awareness of the professional as well as the amateur activity during the Commonwealth is necessary to an appreciation of the methods of Sir William Davenant, whose ventures partook of the nature of both.[56] In 1654 Davenant was released from the Tower after a long imprisonment which had come as the climax to hectic years of service in the Royal cause at home and in exile. Except for his knighthood, his years of travail had netted him no material gain. With his fortunes to repair, he turned naturally to the drama, which had spelled his rise to success before 1642. After unlucky experiences as a theatrical entrepreneur in the playhouses already existing, and with a new one which he designed to build, he hit upon the idea of providing entertainment in his own home, inspired no doubt by the vogue for private shows in the great halls of the nobility. Shrewdly enough, he leased Rutland House, a former nobleman's mansion on upper Aldersgate Street. Then he gathered about himself a few scene-painters and some of the former court musicians, including Henry Lawes and the Coleman family, the most respectable kind of professional entertainers. Thus he prepared to give musical entertainments and "moral representations with scenes"—private theatricals, with this slight difference that his fashionable guests would be expected to express their gratitude for his hospitality with an entrance fee. The new word "opera" was studiously substituted for the words "theatre" and "play."

On May 23, 1656, came the formal opening. About one hundred and fifty visitors—who had paid the considerable sum of five shillings apiece—, and the inevitable government spy, composed the audience. Performed upon a narrow stage provided with a curtain and a few ornamental accessories, was *The First Day's Entertainment at Rutland House,* a set of contentions, not unlike those we have come upon elsewhere, between Diogenes and Aristophanes, and between a Parisian and a Londoner, the whole supplemented by concert music and concluded by several songs, one in praise of the Protector. The speech by Aristophanes was propaganda in the cause of entertainment. Unmolested in his initial venture, Davenant proceeded, probably after a few similar non-dramatic entertainments, to more ambitious things. In September, 1656, he produced the first part of *The Siege of Rhodes,* the dramatic character of which was only partially disguised by the quasi-operatic device of rimed lines chanted in *stilo recitativo.* Henry Lawes and possibly Henry Purcell[57] the elder helped to compose the music; John Webb, the protégé of Inigo Jones, designed the scenery; and Mrs. Coleman made theatrical history by filling the leading female rôle.

There is no need to detail the official stirrings at Davenant's audacity, his diplomatic overtures to the more friendly government authorities, nor the outcrop of public praise and ridicule which greeted his endeavors. His technique throughout was admirable. By July, 1658, he had escaped from the cramping confines of Rutland House, and was presenting "daily at the Cockpit in Drury-Lane, at Three after noone punctually," with admission charges ranging upward from one shilling, *The Cruelty of the Spaniards in Peru. Exprest by Instrumentall and Vocall Musick, and by Art of Perspective in Scenes, &c.* Here, a set of painted backdrops supplement speeches, songs, and dances, in providing a panorama of the life of the Incas, the atrocities of the Spanish, and the magnanimity of the English. A tight-rope dance by two mimic apes, and acrobatic feats by an irrelevant attendant upon an Incas priest diversify this peculiar compound; however it is little more eccentric than other Commonwealth entertainments, fathered, as we have seen, by masques, moralities, and what not. As a sequel to *The Cruelty of the Spaniards in Peru,* came *The History of Sir Francis Drake,* dram-

atizing older historical material of the same locale, and resembling in
type, despite its more episodic and operatic quality, the first part of
The Siege of Rhodes. Drake Senior, Drake Junior, and Captain Rouse
penetrate Peru; climb a high tree to a perch affording a glimpse of both
the Atlantic and the Pacific; befriend the native Symerones; and vic-
timize the colonizing Spaniards, one of whose mule trains of gold they
plunder, and one of whose women they treat with the most exemplary
courtesy. Both mule train and Spanish woman were represented in the
cast only by painted figures on the scene. It is probable that Davenant
produced the more notable, second part of *The Siege of Rhodes* also
during the Commonwealth. In the two parts of *The Siege of Rhodes* we
observe the tone and materials of the Cavalier mode in the process of
mutation; a discussion of this important play, with its formal innovations, has already figured in our treatment of the genesis of the Restoration heroic play. Davenant's employment of scenery and actresses in
his Commonwealth "opera" forms a natural link between the practices
in private theatricals before 1642 and in professional theatricals after
1660.

[1] See above, p. 25; and F. E. Schelling, *Elizabethan Drama*, II, 94.

[2] Letter from Chamberlain to Carleton; cf. Nichols, *Progresses James*, III, 454.

[3] *Court and Times of James I*, 2 vols. (London, 1848), I, 455, II, 57-58.

[4] *Cal. State Papers Venetian*, 1619-1621, p. 138.

[5] *Cal. State Papers Domestic*, 1619-1623, p. 112.

[6] *Progresses James*, III, 587.

[7] *Cal. State Papers Venetian*, 1619-1621, p. 390.

[8] *Progresses James*, IV, 941.

[9] See above, p. 12.—The performance by amateurs of a play, possibly *Midsummer
Night's Dream*, in the house of John Williams, Bishop of Lincoln, Sept. 27, 1631,
also caused great distaste, but chiefly among the Puritan clergy; see E. K. Chambers'
edition of *Midsummer Night's Dream*, The Arden Shakespeare (1916), p. x.

[10] London, 1926.

[11] Other parts were taken by Lady Ann Feilding, Sophia and Victoria Carew, etc.
A complete caste is given in B. M. MS. Stowe 976.

[12] P. Reyher, *Masque Anglais* (1909), p. 511.

[13] Anthony à Wood, *Hist. and Antiquities of Oxford*, II, 413.

[14] For a description of these visits, see Herford and Simpson's *Ben Jonson*, II
(1925), 332-334.

[15] D. Masson, *Life of Milton*, I (1881), 590.

[16] *Ibid.*, I, 604-611.

[17] See above, p. 117.

[18] Mention of Salisbury as an author, but without mention of this entertainment
appears in *DNB*, L, 195. *The Masque at Knowsley* was reprinted by R. J. Broadbent
from *Transactions of the Historic Society of Lancashire and Chesire* (1926).

[19] Among the poems of Bishop Samuel Rutter appears "On ye New Yeare, in a
Masque by ye Lord Strange," cf. *LTLS*, 1923, p. 536.

[20] B. M., MS. Egerton, 2623, fol. 22.

[21] Cf. Thomas Heywood, *Pleasant Dialogues and Dramas*, 1637, pp. 243, 245-247.

[22] *DNB*, XXXI, 356.

[23] British Museum Add. MS. 34221.

[24] *Victoria History*, "Northamptonshire," III, 544-547.

[25] This account of Fane is a condensation of the present author's "An Unnoted Caroline Dramatist," *SP*, XXXI (1934), where a sample of Fane's dialogue is given. At least one more Fane play is extant, *Don Phœba's Triumph;* cf. Huntington Library, MS. H M 770. For additional materials for the study of Fane, see his autobiography, B. M. Add. MS. 34220; and his "Fugitive Verses," *Historical MSS Commission*, Vol. XIII.

[26] B. M., MS. Egerton, 1994, fols. 212-223. Bullen has noted plagiarisms from Chapman in this masque (*Old English Plays*, Vol. II, 1883), and an article on the subject by J. D. Jump appears in *RES*, XI (1935), 186-191.

[27] W. C. Hazlitt, *Manual for the Collector & Amateur of Old English Plays*, p. 127.

[28] Cf. commendatory verses by T. C. to Alexander Gough for publishing *The Queen, or The Excellency of her Sex*, 1653. For Puritan allusions to heaven-sent disasters of private performers, see H. Rollins, *SP*, XVIII (1921), pp. 317, 333.

[29] Printed in Jordan's *Nursery of Novelties*, 1660.

[30] *Dorothy Osborne's Letters*, E. A. Parry, ed. (1888), pp. 299, 304, 307.

[31] Described by C. S. Northrup, "On a School Play of 1648," *ESt.*, XLV (1911), p. 156.

[32] A. W. Ward, *English Dramatic Literature*, III, 279, note 5; and *Calendar of Inner Temple Records*, II, 328. *The Countryman* was probably a droll fashioned from Davenant's *The Wits*.

[33] Not printed until 1683, but written "half an age ago" and acted at a gentleman's house. For date and university performance, see Hazlitt's *Manual*, p. 40.

[34] L. Hotson, *op. cit.*, pp. 133-136.

[35] Bodl. MS. Rawl. B. 165, fols. 107-114.

[36] F. G. Fleay, *Biographical Chronicle*, II, 244, 247, places *The Triumph of Beauty* in 1640 because of its fancied attack on Heywood, and conjectures that *The Contention of Ajax and Ulysses* belongs to the same year. But the texts of amateur theatricals, when printed at all, were usually printed close upon their performance; and about the title pages of Shirley's there is a politic vagueness suggesting Interregnum production.

[37] In reply to a note by Clifford Leech on Jordan's *Cupid his Coronation* (*LTLS*, April 12, 1934, p. 262), Percy A. Scholes (*LTLS*, June 14, p. 424) cites the "official" performance of Shirley's *Cupid and Death* in support of his contention that the Puritans objected to the abuses of drama but not to drama as such. But what is true of the earlier Puritans and a few of the later ones is not true of the rank and file of the petty officials of the Commonwealth. These did object to drama *as such*. I do not believe that the 1653 performance of *Cupid and Death* was official or that it took place at Whitehall, as conjectured by R. G. Howarth, *LTLS*, Nov. 15, 1934, p. 795. If so the printer would have made much of the fact. Mr. Howarth's note contributes the information that the music for the piece by Locke and Gibbons was written for the second performance, which took place under unknown auspices "att the Military Ground in Lescester fields 1659."

[38] *Cal. State Papers Venetian*, 1653-1654, *passim*.

[39] *Ajax and Ulysses* was probably Shirley's last dramatic work. In the address to his revised version of *A Contention for Honor and Riches*, 1631, published as *Honoria and Mammon* with the present entertainment in 1659, he says, "nothing of this

nature shall, after this, engage either my pen or invention."

[40] L. Hotson, *Commonwealth and Restoration Stage* (Harvard Univ. Press, 1928), pp. 9, 13. English strollers also entertained the court abroad; *Ibid.*, p. 21 *et passim*.

[41] See below, pp. 226-228.

[42] A Watkin-Jones, *LTLS*, November 15, 1934, p. 795. See also below, p. 217.

[43] L. Hotson, *op. cit.*, pp. 22-23.

[44] See above, pp. 135-137.

[45] P. H. Doney, *Life and Works of Richard Flecknoe*, MS. Diss., Harvard Univ. (1928), pp. 67-76, 362-364, 378.

[46] Davenant's petition to the government, printed by C. H. Firth, "Sir William Davenant and the Revival of Drama during the Protectorate," *Eng. Hist. Review*, XVIII (1903), 320.

[47] Treated in detail by H. Rollins, "Contribution to the History of the English Commonwealth Drama," *SP*, XVIII (1921); XX (1923); and by L. Hotson, *op. cit.*, Chapter 1.

[48] L. Hotson, *op. cit.*, Chapter I, *passim*.

[49] *Historia Histrionica*, 1699; cf. Hazlitt's *Dodsley*, XV (1874), 410.

[50] *The Wits or Sport upon Sport*, title-page of 1673.

[51] Charles R. Baskervill, *The Elizabethan Jig* (Univ. of Chicago Press, 1929), pp. 234-238, believed *Singing Simpkin* may possibly have been written by Tarlton. J. J. Elson in the introduction to his edition of *The Wits or Sport upon Sport* (Cornell Univ. Press, 1932), conjectures that the adaptations of the comic plots of older plays were made by Francis Kirkman simply as a publishing venture.

[52] H. Rollins, *op. cit.* (*SP*, XX [1923], 58.)

[53] Date of title-page corrected in a coeval hand from 1651 to Jan. 30, 1654 (1655?). For other interludes which may have been acted, see below, p. 236.

[54] Suggested by F. G. Fleay, *Biographical Chronicle*, II, 340, to refer to performance during the plague of 1636-37; however, allusions to the second part of Mother Shipton's prophecies (published after the closing of the theatres) indicate Commonwealth production.

[55] A title-page and address especially printed for a copy of this play, dedicated to John Philips in 1668, informs the reader that Jordan was "scarce 15" when he composed the work; see G. Thorn-Drury, *RES*, I (1925), 219. The statement is probably mendacious, but suggests at least a pre-Restoration date.

[56] L. Hotson, *op. cit.*, Chapter III, treats Davenant's opera *in extenso*. My *Sir William Davenant* (University of Pennsylvania Press, 1935), pp. 119-130, emphasizes its biographical interest.

[57] *Grove's Dictionary of Music and Musicians*, IV, 285.

VI

CLOSET DRAMA OF THE COMMONWEALTH

THE official classification of drama as a gin of the Devil did not prevent the stubborn survival of a love of plays. Private theatricals and surreptitious professional performances were not the only means of indulging this love, since plays could still be read. Old stock plays were made available in print, and others already available were issued in new editions. A surprising number of new plays were written, either to supply the reading demand, or simply to satisfy the personal cravings of the authors. Some of these closet dramas we have already examined. A number of the civil war plays belong to this class, as presumably do the later works of Thomas Killigrew, William Lower, and Mildmay Fane.[1] With each of these three, his Commonwealth products show a falling off in merit from standards originally none too high. The decline is to be expected; playwrights need the incentive and discipline of a stage.

Those who consider closet drama deplorable as a class will find countenance for their prejudice in the plays written between 1642 and 1660. The writers deserve credit for their persistence, but rarely for anything else: the quality of their work represents the ebb-tide in English drama. It is odd that between the best and the worst of English playwrights—between Shakespeare at his height and Thomas Meriton—intervenes a period of only fifty years. But though Commonwealth plays are prevailingly bad, there is this much to cheer the explorer of the wastelands: bad plays, if bad enough, can be entertaining, while the occasional readable play in such surroundings wears a positive luster. And in this period so long neglected by historians of drama, there is always the chance of discoveries.[2]

It will suffice to mention briefly the group of plays made available to English readers through translation. We have already noticed the inferiority of Lower's versions of popular French plays at this period,[3] and though few of his contemporaries were as inept as Lower, most Commonwealth translations are indeed literal and uninspired. The dramatic fields exploited included the classical. Christopher Wase, fresh from his Greek studies at Puritan Cambridge, but an ardent Royalist nevertheless, translated and dedicated to Princess Elizabeth the *Electra* of Sophocles. The year was 1649, when the fate of Charles I left another "murder" of a royal father to be avenged. In his *History of Philosophy*, 1655, Thomas Stanley, wealthy amateur and patron of letters, included a translation of *The Clouds*[4] of Aristophanes to illustrate the life of Socrates. Another comedy by Aristophanes was Englished by H. H. B. and issued in 1659 with the title *The World's Idol, or Plutus the God of Wealth*. There was also the usual crop of Senecan translations: *Medea* by Sir Edward Sherburne, 1648; *Hippolytus* by E. Prestwich, 1651; and *Troades* by Samuel Pordage, 1660. *Medea* and *Hippolytus* are in rime. Sherburne and Pordage lent further scholarly service to drama during the Restoration. In 1652 Francis Goldsmith published *Sophompaneas, or Joseph*, translated with annotations from the Latin of Hugo Grotius. Judging from their exchange of complimentary verses, these translators from the classical tongues were acquainted with each other, usually through association about the inns of court; several were friendly with James Shirley, and evidently all were Royalists.

Italian pastoral drama also remained popular. Tasso's *Aminta* appeared in an anonymous translation, Oxford, 1650,[5] and in a version by John Dancer, 1660. Jonathon Sidnam, who in 1630 had Englished Guarini's *Il Pastor Fido*, is the probable author of the translation of Bonarelli's *Filli di Sciro* appearing as by "J. S." in 1655.[6] *Filli di Sciro* was also translated by Sir Gilbert Talbot in 1657, his version with a dedication to Charles II still remaining in manuscript.[7] The most important Commonwealth translation of an Italian pastoral, in fact one of the most important translations of the century, is Sir Richard Fanshawe's *The Faithful Shepherd*, 1647, freely rendered from Guarini's *Il Pastor Fido*.[8]

Sir Richard Fanshawe (1608-1666), Royalist quixote and married lover, was an outstanding personality even in a period rich in extravagant types. As soldier, diplomat, and peregrinating courtier, he seems to have held the Royalist record for adventures and adversities, yet was so persistently domestic as to become the father of sixteen children in the midst of his wanderings.[9] Fanshawe brought to translation both greater linguistic and greater literary skill than his fellows, *The Faithful Shepherd* by precept and example teaching later translators not to sacrifice distinction of style and freedom of their native idiom. Fan-shawe also made a unique move toward a balance of trade in translation by turning an English play into Latin, selecting Fletcher's *Faithful Shepherdess* for his experiment; *La Fida Pastora: Comœdia Pastoralis* appeared in 1658. His versatility is further evidenced by *To Love only for Love's Sake*, a paraphrase of Mendoza's *Querer por solo Querer*, which, though it first appeared in print in 1670, was also a Commonwealth product, having been rendered from the Spanish in 1654.[10]

It is curious that there were not more French plays translated, that so little intervened between the late Caroline translations of Joseph Rutter and the late Commonwealth translations of William Lower. It was not until the Restoration that the full tide of translation from the French set in, a number of the linguists enumerated above then joining with new writers to supply the demand. Perhaps familiarity with the French tongue on the part of the play-reading class of Englishmen explains the delay. On the other hand, the new French heroic romances, although widely read in the original, were rapidly translated into English. Charlel Sorel's mock romance *Lysis* was translated by John Davies and published in 1653. In the following year one T. R. published *The Extravagant Shepherd,* a translation of Thomas Corneille's dramatization of Sorel's romance. *The Extravagant Shepherd* is not only an exception to the rule of neglect in translating French plays, but it is also one of the more skillful and entertaining products of the period. In 1660 Samuel Holland published *Romanciomastix,* a native English mock romance, in which was incorporated an earlier product of the author, *Venus and Adonis,* 1656, a coarse and slapstick but amusing burlesque masque.[11]

The type of play which suffers least in exile from the theatre is the pastoral. A few of the Commonwealth closet dramatists took advantage of the fact and cast their work in this mould. However, the tendency was to imitate the pseudo-pastoral like those popular among courtly writers and developed to absurdity in Peaps's *Love in its Ecstasy.* Several plays of this type belong to the Commonwealth period, as do a number more that are purely romances in the Cavalier mode. A few plays defy classification altogether.

The Shepherd's Holiday, dedicated by its author William Denny to Lady Kemp and Mrs. Thornton, June 1, 1651,[12] is a mixture of pastoral, masque, and morality, and illustrates the fact that among county ladies the interest in platonic love was still much alive. A band of shepherds and shepherdesses on a holiday have a poetical, musical, anagrammatical contest to decide the relative merits of marriage and virginity. When their oracle decides the matter in favor of marriage, two of their number are expeditiously joined. The current interest in character abstractions is reflected in the *dramatis personæ,* which includes not only Vida (Experience) and Vota (Virginity), but also Alpha, a father, Beta, a mother, and their family, in which the children are vowels, the servants consonants. Despite such ludicrousness, the piece is not among the worst of its time, the language, usually in rime, possessing a degree of merit. The following is an example of Denny's fragile prettiness:

> The feather'd snow so white
> When touch'd its candour fades away;
> The ruddy blushes of the morning's light
> Like not bold looks of the broad faced day;
> Rose sweets in buds are dight
> Then where does lie
> Whiteness, beauty, sweetness, but in Virginity?

Contrasting with Denny's pastoral, which is near akin to the eclogue, is Leonard Willan's *Astrea, or True Love's Mirror,* 1651, a dramatization of D'Urfé's famous pastoral romance. In prosaical rimed couplets, Celadon pines for Astrea, Sylvander expounds platonic love, and Hylas is skeptical and fleshly in a gentle way. The succession of impasses in courtship, confusing oracles, and baffling disguises terminate in a happy ending celebrated by a masque. This operatic conclusion, the opening description of the scene, the narrative stage directions, the couplets, and the dialogues in song, make the play historically interesting despite its lack of literary merit.

The dedication of *Astrea* to the Duchess of Richmond and the dedication of *Orgula, or The Fatal Error,* 1658, a tragic romance, to Lady Francis Wildegoss are written in the same turgidly unintelligible style; otherwise the latter play, written in blank verse, gives few stylistic clues as to authorship, but the "L. W." of the title page is probably identifiable as Willan. In *Orgula,* Sinevero, with the suggestive title "Lord Protector," is the villain. He persecutes Eumena, his ward and future regent, and her lover Ludaster, son of an ancient rival. Orgula, the betrothed of Sinevero, is in love with another, and plots with her slave Mundolo to drug Sinevero on their wedding night, so that her lover may take the place of her husband in the bridal bed. Mundolo, unable to effect the assignation, himself substitutes for the drugged husband. Upon discovering the imposture, Orgula slays Sinevero in mistake for Mundolo, then goes spectacularly insane. In this major action the play resembles debased Fletcherian tragedy, the plot reminding us of the much superior *Albovine* by Sir William Davenant. But the main plot is the merest fraction of this play. There is something of everything: a disguised girl page, romantic wanderings and encounters in a wood, heroic friends embroiled by a misunderstanding, and other trappings of romance. The inchoate sequence of incidents resulting from disguise, mistaken identity, and mixed letters and tokens reminds us, as do the incredible bathos and bombast of the language, of Killigrew's contemporary closet dramas, *Cicilia and Clorinda* and *Bellamira her Dream.* But unlike Killigrew, Willan lets all end tragically. Except for those who die of a spontaneous combustion of grief, nearly everyone in the play is slain in mistake for someone else. At the end, Gratiano of Ludaster's faction, one of the few besides the lucky author to survive the action, "pulls his hat sadly over his eyes and marcheth out with the bodies."

More interesting in its literary associations than *Orgula* is Gilbert Swinhoe's tragedy, *The Unhappy Fair Irene,* carelessly hustled into print in 1658. The play opens amidst the sack of Hadrianopolis by Mahomet, Sultan of the Turks. A beautiful captive about to be ravished by a common soldier is rescued and delivered to the Sultan. Her lover, Lord Pæologus, manages to see her long enough to arrange a tryst for when he shall return with the Turk's Hungarian enemies. Mahomet becomes enamored of his captive, and languishes in love while all his conquests are lost through his indifference. His warlike bashaws protest, but he ignores them, banishing one Natolia for his officiousness. Finally, when a revolt of his Janissaries forces his hand, he forestalls their blood-lust by slaying Irene himself. Pæologus, returning too late, commits self-slaughter, together with his ever faithful servant. Obviously this is the familiar story of the Sultan Mahomet's sacrifice of the fair Grecian maid taken captive at Constantinople in 1453, told by Bandello, Belleforest, and Painter, and by Richard Knolles in his *General History of the Turks.* An English dramatization of the story had appeared as early as *c.* 1588 in Peele's *The Turkish Mahomet and Hiren the Fair Greek.* Swinhoe's variations upon the original tale were such as might have been predicted in an author of his period. In providing Irene with a heroic lover, he may have followed a suggestion in Lodowick Carlell's *Osmond the Great Turk,* but the device would have occurred to any of the courtly playwrights or their imitators. *The Unhappy Fair Irene* is in rudimentary form, lacking division into acts and scenes, and versified in short lines of constantly varying length, but its tone combines the sentimental and heroical in an arresting way.[13] A closet drama on the same theme, *Irena,* published anonymously in 1664, retains some of Swinhoe's refinements, but ends happily with the heroine slain only by proxy and permitted to bestow herself upon her true love by a very genteel and sensitive Sultan. To a much greater extent than Swinhoe's play *Irena* is a rendering of the old story with Platonic embellishment.

One of the few dramatic romances of this Commonwealth period that have been edited in our times is *Love's Victory,* 1658, by William Chamberlaine, the Dorset physician and Royalist soldier who composed *Pharonnida,* so-called chief of the heroic poems.[14] Adapting the material

of the Greek romances in about the same manner as did Carlell and Cartwright, Chamberlaine displays how Oroandes conquers the rebel Zannazarro, and then, with the aid of heavenly portents, rescues from the
sacrificial altar both Zannazarro and this rebel's sister Eurione. In
rivalry for Eurione's love, Oroandes and his liege, the King of Sicily,
fight a duel wherein the latter is apparently slain. Oroandes later con-
fesses his deed and is about to take his own life when the King reappears
alive, in a forgiving mood, and with passion renewed for his former
loved one, Heroina. Since Zannazarro has long loved Oroandes' sister
Glorianda, the way is now paved for three reconciliatory marriages. A
comic underplot, unusual in this type of play, concerns the pretensions
of the rich clown Buffonie to the hand of the maiden Theocrine. Saintsbury and others have spoken well of the "poetic moments" of *Love's
Victory,* but these moments are very few and very brief.

Another play called *Love's Victory,* an anonymous pastoral in couplets, may also belong to the Commonwealth period although the manuscript in which it survives is undated.[15] The verse has little distinction,
and the plot, save that Venus is portrayed as a benign deity while her
son Cupid is the cause of all the trouble, offers little new to the theme
of the eternal difficulties of all shepherds and shepherdesses who aspire
to reach the altar with their true loves in the vicinity of Arcadia.

A romance at least as good as that of William Chamberlaine is *Love's
Labyrinth, or The Royal Shepherdess,* 1660, by Thomas Forde, "Phila-
thal," a bookseller's studious workman, and sincere lover of literature
and the Royal cause. The play is a successful adaptation of Greene's
Menaphon, whence the plot, the characters, and even some of the language are drawn.[16] Although Forde at times followed the lead of his
predecessor a little too closely to comply with modern ethics in such
matters, he was capable of good lines of his own, and both the blank
verse and the lyrics of *Love's Labyrinth* are considerably above the average of the day.

Dramatic versions of prose romances were provided not only in
Willan's *Astrea* and Forde's *Love's Labyrinth,* but in two anonymous
manuscripts, the date of which is probably the period of the Commonwealth. One of these, *Love's Changelings Change,* is a very long and very
dull treatment of Sidney's *Arcadia.*[17] The other, *The White Ethiopian,*[18] is an amateurish but historically interesting treatment of Heliodorus's *Æthiopica. The White Ethiopian* invites attention not only
because it dramatizes one of those Greek tales which form the original
fount of Cavalier dramatic romance, but because it impregnates with
précieuse sensibilities material which on a previous occasion (in Gough's
Strange Discovery) had been utilized in a play of mere intrigue and

adventure; also because it is written throughout in rimed couplets.[19]

A play which, like *Love's Labyrinth*, resembles Cavalier romance more than pastoral despite its setting in Arcadia is *The Rewards of Virtue* by John Fountain. Urania, a lovely cottage girl, has been taken into the court of King Basilius to attend the Princess; and the King, his son Theander, and the poor Lord Endymion all become enamoured of her. The King is shamed from his lustful love by a ruse of the Queen, so that Endymion's suit seems about to prosper; then suddenly it is revealed that Urania has already wedded Prince Theander and has just borne him a premature child. Outraged by the inferiority in rank of his new daughter-in-law, the King orders her death. Urania's head is actually on the block, when her mother reveals herself to be no humble cottager, but an unfortunate queen. While felicity is in order, the King's daughter is permitted to marry beneath her to Endymion whom she has long adored. The chief themes are the all-conquering force of virtue, and the unfairness of permitting disparity of birth to throw its barrier athwart the pathway of love. Surprisingly enough, there is a substratum of common sense underlying the discourses of the characters. The blank verse is clear and fairly regular and the play readable, despite the lengthiness of the speeches and the awkwardness of the plotting. An odd refinement of sentiment allows certain characters to pity others for pains which they themselves have inflicted.

Although *The Rewards of Virtue* was not published until 1661, it was probably written before the opening of the theatres; its Restoration adapter[20] commented on its unsuitability for the stage. Another play not published until 1661, but "penn'd many years ago,"[21] is *The Heroic Lover*, a romance in couplets dedicated by its author George Cartwright to the restored King Charles. The verse is flat and mechanical, and the play as a whole spiritless, so that it is difficult to take much interest in the traditional Cavalier theme of involved love affairs among friends and relatives. The central episode is the heroic self-sacrifice of Nonantious (perilously suggestive name) in wooing his sweetheart Francinia for his friend the Prince of Poland, who prefers her to his own predestined bride, the Infanta of Spain. Francinia at last retires to a nunnery, joining there the sorrowing sweetheart of her own long-lost brother. A rebellion among the Polish citizenry hints dimly at the civil strife in Cartwright's England.

The authors thus far enumerated, with the possible exception of Leonard Willan, confined their efforts to a single pastoral or dramatic romance. One of their co-workers in the mode was a little more persistent. When Kirkman, bookseller, and collector, printed his second catalogue of English plays,[22] he appended a note on dramatic publication: "I . . . will conclude thus; that as John Heywood was the first English play-writer, so in my opinion, one Thomas Meriton, who writ two pamphlets, which he calls playes, viz. *Love and War,* and the *Wandring Lover,* was the worst." Although the student of Commonwealth drama could suggest several alternate candidates for the distinction here accorded Meriton, he would not be seriously inclined to dispute Kirkman's decision. Meriton (b. 1638) was a younger son in a genteel family of some slight literary and clerical note. His plays are partially excusable on the basis of their author's youth, since he had not passed twenty when he wrote them; he lived them down, entered St. John's College, Cambridge, at twenty-four, and became rector of Normanton, Lincolnshire.[23] *The Wandering Lover,* 1658, is introduced by a prologue, promising,

> You must expect no great tologies
> Nor Nector's drum, nor no ambrosian phrase . . .
> But mother-like tongue plainly writ and spoke.

But as we read of Greceana's kidnapping by three Thessalians, and her recovery, after many vicissitudes, by her "germane" lover Euphrates, we look in vain for the mother-like tongue. We may quote one of Meriton's characters as he says "Yes," and another as he replies "Thank you." Euphrates has asked Drosanus if Pecor is one of the kidnappers:

Drosanus. Worthy friend, I shall venture so far upon the brinks of liberty as I can pass without mendation or fabulating unto you, for this I can affirm for a truth both by prospect and likewise by a most pensive report, that Pecor was one malefactor in the same illitable enterprise, in exhausting the only diadem and splendent lustre of chaste virgins to that place of deprived liberty.

Euphrates. For answering me this query in one respect, for uttering the utmost of your knowledge, therein hath link't me to you with the chain of everlasting amity; and, contrary, hath pin'd me with the bolt of tetrissity from you for hearing of such penetrating and poisonous sentence;

> But this I am resolv'd before
> Those resplendent eyes I see no more, etc.

The entire piece—no pamphlet, but a full length play—is written in rimed octosyllables and in this same monstrous prose. The strange pedantry in diction marks the style of several Commonwealth writers.

Two of the characters in Meriton's second play, *Love and War,* 1658, are named appropriately "Hollarro" and "Histerica." Hollarro, Prince of Bruzantia, is tremendous in the conquest of Numeria. His captives are delivered to his mother, whose blood-lust is so great that after she gloatingly beheads the Numerians, she turns to domestic sources for similar entertainment. On Hollarro's wedding day, a Numerian army led by the Prince's erstwhile rival for the hand of the bride invades the capital and almost exterminates the Bruzantians. Most of the leading personages commit suicide, but when Hollarro tries to do so, his sword will not enter him: he is of royal lineage and, after all, has not shared the barbaric guilt of his family. So he wanders sadly off; and the last line of this idiotic play, with consistent illogicality, expresses the Royalist sentiment, "I wish all native Princes had their right." The influence of the prose romances is apparent, not only in the heroic and pathetic orations of the characters, but in the nature of the armies, fighting under romantic insignia and causing casualties normally in the millions. There are many classical and historical allusions, including one to Julius Cæsar's conquest of Troy. If the play reveals anything, it is the tendency of Cavalier dramatic romance to merge into heroic tragedy. Heroic couplets are frequently employed, and the example of *The Siege of Rhodes,* Part One, is followed in the songs which chorus the action after each act.

In Meriton's dedication to *The Wandering Lover,* he mentioned the fact that he had written *The Chaste Virgin,* a romance, and *The Several Affairs,* a comedy; but these were pocket-companions and shown only to his private friends. "Happy certainly were those men," said Langbaine in his *English Dramatick Poets,* "who were not reckoned in the number of his friends."[24]

The original plays thus far discussed extend the tradition of the Cavalier mode. Other Commonwealth closet dramas are cast in different moulds. Fletcherian tragedies of court intrigue were popular, especially those which treated of rebellion and usurpation; and several authors directed their attention to the time-honored practice of dramatizing history. One of these was Robert Baron (b. 1630), son of a Norwich alderman, and student at Cambridge and Gray's Inn.[25] Baron began publishing books at the age of seventeen, freely ornamenting his early efforts with lines filched from Webster, Milton, Lovelace, Suckling, and Waller; consequently he has won some notoriety as a plagiarist,[26] though his crime was really no more than the awkward cribbing of a boy. His first book, *The Cyprian Academy,* 1647, is a prose romance, ornamented with an engraving of the author and commended by Oxford, Cambridge, and Gray's Inn students, some of whom must have written with tongue in cheek. Baron's opening epistle is addressed to James Howell, his kinsman and literary mentor,

As I did frequently take fresh aire in your Dodonean grove attending the articulate and intelligible susurrations of your ever verdant vegitals (to which former ages have nothing in that kind to assimilate, neither shall future times be able to parallel) from these Appollinean plants of yours, I have shifted here a twig and there a sprig . . .

In the romance is incorporated a pastoral play acted by the characters and called *Gripus and Hegio, or The Passionate Lovers.* The seeker after literary curiosities will find in this pastoral lines he would not willingly let die. Gripus in a lyrical lament upon his thwarted love suspires,

> My head of late was thatch't with yellow straw;
> Now it is perriwig'd with winter's gray.

Later in the romance appears *Deorum Dona*, a rudimentary masque performed before the King and Queen of Cyprus, and as deplorable on the whole as the pastoral.

Baron was capable of better work, and in 1655,[27] when his "green muse" (in Howell's phrase) had ripened somewhat, he produced his historical tragedy *Mirza*. This makes capital of the same episode in recent Persian history that Denham had dramatized in *The Sophy*. Baron tells us he was unfamiliar with Denham's play until three of his own acts were finished—"nor was he then discouraged." He comments on Denham's inaccuracy in historical fact and promises a more faithful treatment of the material. His play, frankly intended for reading, is a conscientious reconstruction of history, enough so at times as to be prosy and artistically meaningless. The annotations, historical, topographical, etc., almost equal the play in length. Yet the silliness and pedantry of Baron's earlier work have disappeared, and his tragedy is dignified and readable. Nor does it plagiarize Jonson's *Catiline*, as those preconvinced of the author's perfidy in such matters have stated; the few suggestions in the plot taken from Catiline are duly acknowledged in the copious notes.

An even more recent episode in foreign history than the tragic clash between the Persian monarch and his son was dramatized in *The Rebellion of Naples, or The Tragedy of Massenello*, 1649, by T. B., "a gentleman who was an eye witness where this was really acted upon that bloody stage, the streets of Naples, anno domini MDCXLVII." The play is an interesting though brutalized and entirely sub-literary treatment of the usurpation of power by the Neapolitan general Tomaso Aniello di Malfi, his horrid tyrannies, his licentiousness and greed, and the blood curdling atrocities within his family circle. A counter-rebellion at last throws him from power, but he saves his life by means of a clever ruse. Although an address to the reader cautions that the play is not to be mistaken as English allegory, some of its preachments leave no other alternative. It is anti-democratic in spirit, and in the equivocal fashion of Royalist English sentiment of the day, it condemns both tyranny and rebellion against tyranny.

The most congenial of these historical plays of the Commonwealth returns to an older, fresher day, and to a native English scene. R. Kirkham's *Alfred, or Right Reenthroned*, 1659, was suffered to remain in manuscript[28] though it deserved printing more than most plays of its time. The action begins with the defeat of the English by Danish King Gothurnus, the flight of the court, and the separation of Alfred from his family. We follow the good King as he takes refuge among simple country folk, penetrates into the Danish camp as a musician, and at last rallies his forces to victory. Alfred's officers and children rival him in virtue, the entire play being permeated by a wholesome spirit of valor and Christian piety. Although the numerous comic interludes are only moderately successful, and the language never achieves poetry, the rapid variety of incidents is arresting, and the play as a whole sane and refreshing. St. Cuthbert acts as a sort of chorus and as guardian angel of King Alfred, the element of the miraculous and other devices from the old chronicles uniting interestingly with heroic tone and features of plot borrowed from the more recent dramatic romances.

Another play still in manuscript is *The Governor*,[29] not an historical drama but a Fletcherian tragicomedy of amatory and other intrigue. A play of this title was presented at court, February 17, 1637, and was entered as by Sir Cornelius Formido in the *Stationers' Register*, September 9, 1653;[30] however it remained unprinted and the manuscript was among those destroyed by Warburton's cook. The existence of the present play, on which someone has noted that it formerly belonged to the Somerset herald, has led to the error that Formido's play escaped the Warburton holocaust,[31] but an examination of the manuscript sets the matter at rest. Although in type the play is not unlike several written about 1637, the title leaf is dated 1656, and there remains legible the first name of the author, which was not Cornelius but Samuel. In any case, the surviving *Governor* is scarcely worth a controversy. It concerns the nefarious devices of Nicholaio, Governor of Barcelona, to ruin his poor neighbor Vigetto, and to seduce Sabina, the wife of the upright citizen Facundo. Sabina vacillates at first, but before action succeeds to inclination, she is won to tearful penitence by the example of her virtuous husband. Nicholaio is a heavy, cumbersome plotter, employing not only the usual bawdish nurse but a plethora of other villainous agents besides. At last the ingenuity of Facundo's brother Strenuo brings the fantastically reared structure of imposture crashing about the builder's own ears. It is a poor, dull play, gratifying only in the fact that its dragging, complicated story does finally end.

Fully as bad is another play suggestive of Fletcherian antecedents, George Gerbier D'Ouvilley's *The False Favorite Disgraced and The Reward of Loyalty,* 1657, a tragicomedy of court intrigue. Ransacking all the old situations, the author portrays the multiple double-dealings of Hippolito in the court of Florence, until the Duke, taking a leaf from the book of his compeer in *Measure for Measure,* surprises the villainies of his favorite by assuming the disguise of a friar. D'Ouvilley's offenses are chiefly in his language—remarkable for its unskilled bombast, childish alliterations, and Latinical word coinages. Can Diana, asks one character, allow disease

> T'enthrone himself in the majestic seat
> Of my fair's rosy-excellence, and there
> (With a tyrannic quatefaction) threat
> The sudden dissolution of so pure
> A vivid temple . . . ?

The only apology possible from a commentator is that D'Ouvilley was an Anglicized Dutchman.[32]

These plays which for convenience in distinction have been roughly classified as Fletcherian are no better on the whole than those in the Cavalier mode. However, Major Cosmo Manuche (fl. 1652-66), chief Commonwealth practitioner in the Fletcherian type of play, was a person of much greater capacity than Thomas Meriton. Writing in a period more favorable to dramatic authorship, Major Manuche would have made a lesser William Davenant. He wrote upward of a dozen plays in all, though only a few of these are at present accessible. As the name indicates, Major Manuche[33] was of Italian extraction, but he probably spent his entire life in an English environment, his father having been in the service of an English nobleman. He himself became attached to the household of James Compton, third Earl of Northampton, and during the wars served as an officer of foot both in England and Ireland. During the Protectorate he lived a precarious life in London, teaching, writing, and, as is suspected, even trying to collect money by conveying information to the Roundheads. Northumberland patronized his literary efforts, and gave him practical assistance after the Restoration.

The Major's first play is a tragicomedy called *The Just General.* Amasius, the youthful King of Sicily, is in love with the subject Aurelia. To escape the murderous plots of Amasius's self-appointed mistress Artesia, and the latter's enamoured tool Delirus, Aurelia flees to the shepherd folk. Amasius, thinking she has been spirited off by Bellicosus, the great general of Sicily, also leaves the court, later finding and tenderly recognizing his lost love. General Bellicosus accepts the Sicilian crown during the absence of Amasius, and prepares to punish the treachery of Artesia and Delirus, who, by the way, is his own son. But these have made some amends by falling truly in love with each other. When Amasius and Aurelia return to the court, the repentant lovers are reprieved, while the just Bellicosus promptly restores the crown to its rightful owner. An underplot portrays the devices by which Snap preys on the worldly goods of Goldcalf, whose father had defrauded Snap's father of his fortune. The blank verse of this play is barely distinguishable from prose, but the language is clear and relatively free from excesses. Though the plot creaks at times, and characterization yields too obviously to its exigencies, the play on the whole is competent, and pleases the reader with the unusual feature of characters turning out better than expected.

An allusion to "this sanctified ten years"[34] suggests that Manuche's next play, *The Loyal Lovers,* was written in the year of its publication, 1652. The play concerns the romantic adventures of Adrastus, a Royalist ex-officer, and Letesia, daughter of a "committee-man" but herself a Royalist at heart. Their elopement, their flight to a coast-town, where Adrastus wounds a lieutenant of the garrison and Letesia is threatened with violation by the governor, their happy salvation, and the conversion of Letesia's father to Royalism, involve a host of complexly plotted situations which combine the real and the romantic in interesting fashion. The thin disguise of a locale in Amsterdam does not obscure the obvious fact that Manuche is romancing about conditions in Commonwealth England. Though the verse is even more formless than that of *The Just General,* the play repays reading. Most amazing is the fashion in which this work, openly acknowledged both by author and publisher, proclaims Royalist allegiance and caricatures the Puritans—in such characters as Phanaticus, Gripeman, and Sodome!

A third play, *The Bastard,* was issued in the same year and by the same publishers as the two plays just discussed, and contemporary and later bibliographers have attributed it to Manuche.[35] His name does not appear on the title page, an absence hard to explain, if he is truly the author, in view of his willingness to acknowledge such a play as *The Loyal Lovers.* The style too is vastly different from that of the plays indubitably his. In *The Bastard,* the blank verse is truly verse, the language vigorous and richly, in fact excessively, figurative and allusive—on the whole, of a literary quality of which one would not suspect Manuche capable. The prologue implies that the play is a translation from the Spanish, but since its formal characteristics render this plainly impossible, perhaps no more is intended than that the plot derived from a Spanish source.[36] *The Bastard* is a tragedy, powerful at moments, but with an atmosphere so dark and action so bloody as to convey us over into the realm of delirium. Gaspar, the factor of Alonzo, merchant of Seville, has been encouraged as the suitor of his master's daughter Mariana during a time of adversity, but with the return of better times he is spurned because of his bastardy and is reviled even for mentioning his claim. Thus he is converted into a fiend—lustful, vengeful, but, withal, patient and calculating. Alonzo's designs to wed Mariana, and his ward Varino, to wealthy but unwanted suitors gives Gaspar his opportunities. When Mariana weds her own choice of a husband, then commits adultery with another, Gaspar connives at her offense, sure that it will betray her into his power at last. The affairs of Mariana with her secret husband and secret lover, of Varino with her own suitor Rodriguez, and of the wealthy candidates for marriage favored by Alonzo, are all controlled by the hand of the Bastard. When the skeins become too tangled even for him, he has to multiply his original murderous intentions, so that the play ends in one of the most thorough debacles in literature, the Bastard, of course, perishing with his victims.

In 1770 Bishop Percy discovered at the Marquis of Northampton's library at Ashby manuscripts of seven or eight additional plays by Manuche: *The Banished Shepherdess, The Feast, The Mandrake, Agamemnon, Leontius King of Cyprus, The Captives, Mariamne,* and certain fragments. Several of these seem to be translations or adaptations, the rest original. The present whereabouts of some of these manuscripts is in doubt.[37] If they could be recovered, Manuche, especially if he were proved the author of *The Bastard,* would make the subject of an interesting study.

Several closet dramatists of the Commonwealth were ladies, the Marquis of Newcastle being punished for his condescensions to drama when the women of his family caught the fever and began to deluge him with their literary offerings. When Newcastle retreated to the continent after the disaster of Marston Moor in 1644, he left behind the three daughters of his first wife, who had died in the previous year. The eldest of these, Lady Jane Cavendish, who was twenty-three at the time of her father's departure, dwelled at Welbeck and, at intervals perhaps, at Bolsover while these country estates of her father were garrisoned successively by Royalist and Parliamentary forces in 1644 and 1645. At this period, or a year or so later when she may have retired to the estate of her brother-in-law at Ashbridge in Hertfordshire, she collaborated in several dramatic compositions with her younger sister, Elizabeth, who in 1642 had wedded Lord Brackley, one of the brothers who had performed in Milton's *Comus.* Dedicatory epistles indicate that the plays of the sisters were intended primarily to please their noble father, the rumors of whose impending marriage to a youthful second wife must have proved disturbing.

One of these plays, called simply *A Pastoral*, is still in manuscript[38] with each page carefully initialled by the respective partner in the enterprise. It is a brief and faded little piece in which shepherds and shepherdesses in pairs converse quaintly of love, and chiefly devoted to intimations of the devotion and yearning of three "sad sister shepherdesses" for the lord their father who is in France. A few preliminary dialogues called antimasques, though meaningless in relation to the piece as a whole, have some slight interest: one portrays witches brewing mischief; another, townswomen talking of a visit with the gift of a pig to young ladies in their garrisoned estate; and another, countrymen innocently discussing the invasion of the neighborhood by satyrs.

A more ambitious effort by the Cavendish sisters is *The Concealed Fancies,* a comedy of courtship probably autobiographical in its inspiration.[39] Lucenay and Tattiney, daughters of Monsieur Calsindow, are wooed by Courtly and Presumption, and, after a proper interval of haughtiness, are won, whereupon the traits of character indicated by the names of their suitors are reversed. The play, besides, contains a sketchy treatment of the events of a siege, and of the designs of flirtatious Lady Tranquillity upon the attentions of Calsindow. At last Lady Tranquillity weds one Corpolant for his money, and Calsindow is narrowly saved by an "Angel" from a misalliance with Toy, a coquettish lady's maid. It seems likely that the Cavendish family is represented in disguise by the main characters of this play, and that a timid resentment toward Margaret Lucas, Newcastle's new love, may have inspired the portrait of Lady Tranquillity.[40] The play is an oddly formalized succession of dialogues of courtship, feminine intrigue, and domestic affairs. The sad sister authoresses essayed no further plays, but left many manuscript evidences of their literary aspirations in other directions.

Margaret Lucas (1623-73) wedded no "Corpolant" but Newcastle himself in 1645, in spite of opposition from the Earl's friends, and from Margaret's mistress at the exiled court, Queen Henrietta Maria herself. Thereafter she proceeded to make herself the literary wife of a literary husband, and to create a prodigious body of works, lyrical, scientific, philosophical, biographical, miscellaneous, and dramatic. Her first publication was *Poems and Fancies,* 1653. Dorothy Osborne asked William Temple to send her this book, but before he could do so, the alert young lady procured it for herself: "You need not send me Lady Newcastle's book at all, for I have seen it, and am satisfied that there are many soberer people in Bedlam. I'll swear her friends are much to blame to let her go abroad."[41] Later commentators have dissented slightly from this snap judgment, but in the main Lady Newcastle has achieved notoriety as an eccentric. Charles Lamb accorded her his tender sympathies, and Monsieur Jusserand excused her with Gallic courtliness for the sake of her beauty.[42] We will not dispute her right to immunity on this score, although her portrait produces mixed impressions. More recently, Margaret has received tribute in a kindly work of scholarship.[43]

Lady Newcastle wrote in all nineteen plays, seven of which are in two parts. Although they were not printed until the Restoration (in folios dated respectively 1662 and 1668), it is evident from the author's own comment that most of them were written during the Commonwealth period. The folio of 1662, containing three-fourths of the dramatic work in point, opens with a long succession of dedications and epistles to the reader. Lady Newcastle concedes the superior worth of her husband's plays, admits that he wrote the best parts of her own, and regrets that she had no professional play-maker to help her "tie together" her scenes. She observes that her plays can't be acted since the theatres in England are closed. She doubts if plays will be acted for many years in view of the disappearance of trained actors; incidentally she considers it no "debasement for the nobler sort to act playes." She is at her best when she comes to discuss the playwright's craft. Her theories are original, prophetic; perhaps she was an impressionist, the Gertrude Stein of her day. Plays, she thought, should be as diffuse as life itself:

I do not perceive any reason why that the several persons presented should be all of acquaintance . . . or have a relationship to each other . . . likewise some of my scenes have no acquaintance or relation to the rest of the scenes, although in one and the same play, which is the reason many of my plays will not end as other playes do.

Her plays, she remarks, are written without strict attention to the rules of grammar, without plot, and without limits as to time, space, or topic. In the 1668 folio she announces that she is indifferent whether anyone reads her plays or not, since she regards "not so much the present as future ages, for which she intends all her books"; and concludes the volume with her crowning achievement—a cast of characters for a play which she had neglected to write.

One is astonished to find that Lady Newcastle's plays are exactly as she describes them. Each is a collection of scenes, often entirely disassociated from each other and rarely making any attempt to tell a coherent story. Various characters, usually personified abstractions, meet and engage in endless conversations. Incidents occur sometimes; but usually, to put it in her own way, Lady Newcastle's brain is the stage, her thoughts are acting. The absence of plots and the uniformity in the nature of the plays relieves one of the necessity of writing synopses, but for completeness of record the titles may be enumerated. In the 1662 folio appear in order: *Love's Adventures, The Several Wits, Youth's Glory and Death's Banquet, The Lady Contemplation, The Wits' Cabal, The Unnatural Tragedy, The Public Wooing, The Matrimony Trouble, Nature's Three Daughters Beauty, Love and Wit, The Religious, The Comical Hash, Bell in Campo, The Apocryphal Ladies,* and *The Female Academy.* The 1668 folio adds to the list: *The Sociable Companions, The Presence* (together with a host of scenes to be "added" to it), *The Bridals, The Convent of Pleasure,* and the uncompleted *Blazing World.* If some of these titles seem promising, the reader should not be misled; frequently there is no connection whatever between title and play. A few, such as *The Unnatural Tragedy* and *The Sociable Companions,* do, it must be confessed, make a slightly greater effort than the rest to tell a story, but for the most part all is declamation, disputation, and wit combats, skirmishing with every subject from the proper method of rearing children to the nature of absolute truth. Characters often appear in pairs of opposites and in schematic groupings. *The Female Academy* consists almost exclusively of a discourse by Lady Speaker, who defines "wit," "virtue," "female behavior," etc., before her lady pupils, while a group of males, silent and mysterious, hover outside the grill.

It has been said that "The fastidious Duchess of Newcastle gives us only the smooth surfaces of *précieuse* society,"[44] but such is scarcely the case. The Marchioness was not the ordinary *précieuse. The Unnatural Tragedy* is a quite calm treatment of the theme of incest. In *The Lady Contemplation,* Part I, Scene 19, there is a thoroughgoing discussion of pimps and bawds. Incidentally the subsequent scene pictures realistically the seduction of Moll Meanbred by Sir Effeminate Lovely, and was written by the Marquis, the lady intimating that she could not be expected to have experience in such matters. Margaret sometimes startles us with trenchant realties, much too indelicate to come from a *précieuse.* Observe these lines from Act I, Scene i, of *The Several Wits:*

Maid. Madam, Monsieur Importunate is come to visit you.
Madam Caprice. Did not I tell you I would receive no visits today!
Maid. I did tell him that you desired to be excused, but he said he would not excuse you, for he must see you.
Madam Caprice. Go tell him I have taken physic.

Maid. I did tell him so, but he said he would stay until it had done working.

Madam Caprice. I would it were working in his belly.

Passages equally startling occur elsewhere.

Lady Newcastle was a pioneer and could claim to the hilt the virtue of originality. The fact that her plays belong to no literary development, Cavalier or otherwise, that so far as she had any dramatic mentor at all it was Ben Jonson, makes her a somewhat extraneous element in the present history—except that she further illustrates the Commonwealth's resort to closet drama, and the tendency for the field of dramatic authorship to expand to include the fashionable and highborn. As a woman author who habitually gave books to the press, she beat a path for later members of her sex. If we think of that division of her works just discussed not as drama but as a kind of commonplace book in dialogue, we are likely, even though recognizing that there was no excuse for publication, to feel more charitably disposed toward it. The ideas expressed are not good; in fact when not fantastic, they are usually old and motheaten; but they indicate a sense of obligation to think and to enjoy thinking. Lady Newcastle had no specific information nor orderly opinions about anything; a social historian should be interested in her active but empty mind. More can be said for her language than for her material. When she is not striving for "Wit," or ingenuity of thought and expression, she writes a good conversational prose. There is often reality about her lengthy dialogues, a plausibility resulting from the very fact that they preserve the trivialities and banalities of actual conversation. The best quality of Lady Newcastle—probably that which commended her to Charles Lamb—issued not from the head but from the heart. She was an amiable and good-natured woman. She was at bottom quite humble about her offerings—was only too ready to admit her failings in all things save in her possession of the most perfect of all husbands. About the multiple addresses and the dedications to her plays there is an air of hesitant decision, a mixture of timidity and nervous assurance that is delightfully feminine.

Before taking final leave of Lady Newcastle, one must mention the peculiar play called *Lady Alimony, or The Alimony Lady,* printed in 1659, assigned by seventeenth century bibliographers to Lodge and Greene (!), and by its modern editor to an anonymous author writing before the closing of the theatres.[45] That it was actually written shortly before its publication is indicated by allusions in Act I, Scenes ii, to "a monkey dancing his tricotee on a rope for want of strong lines from the poet's pen" and "the sad presentment of a roasted savage," obvious allusions to Davenant's *Cruelty of the Spaniards in Peru.* Frequently in this first act, the whole of which forms a sort of Induction, there are satirical thrusts at Davenant and theatrical activities of the Commonwealth, which would repay examination by historians of the stage. The play itself is frankly closet drama, with a schematization in the design of its scenes like nothing in English drama outside of the works of Lady Newcastle. It deals with six ladies, concupiscent dames, who are living on alimony from their divorced husbands, six knights who failed to satisfy. They are attended by six courtly platonics—"platonick" here being a polite synonym for lecher. In one scene the ladies plead their case against their husbands most indelicately at court, but the husbands triumph in the end by disguising as gallants, snubbing the ladies, and ousting the platonics. One wonders if the Marquis of Newcastle, or perhaps some bookseller's hack might not have produced this play, working upon material originally drafted by the Marchioness, naturally concealing the authorship because of the riggish theme.[46]

The remaining Commonwealth closet dramas were written by authors who, like Lady Newcastle herself, continued to write plays during the Restoration. One of these authors, Richard Flecknoe (d. 1678?), could boast that her Ladyship had been one of his numerous genteel patronesses. Flecknoe's way of life during the Commonwealth period has already been described,[47] and there is no need to deal further with the life-history of this time-serving lay-priest and Restoration bore. In 1654 he published *Love's Dominion,* a tragicomedy "full of excellent morality . . . written as a pattern for the reformed stage." The preface asserts that the play is noteworthy not only for its purity but for its happy union of English complexity and French simplicity in play-making. However, the work itself gives little evidence of the excellences claimed. In the pastoral environs of Cyprus, Bellinda, knowing that her true love Philander is present in disguise, swears that she loves someone in the realm, thus complying with the amatory statutes by which it is governed. She is tried for perjury, but when the identity of Philander is revealed, the troubles of herself and the other love-entangled principals are automatically ironed out. A sub-plot pictures lustful Pamphilus humiliated by Cyprian nymphs. The piece, dogmatizing against both fleshly and platonic love, is written in execrable blank verse, with here and there an eddy of felicitous language. Descriptions of scenes and costumes and a number of songs and masques diversify the reading. Revised as *Love's Kingdom,* the play was acted at Lincoln's Inn Fields in the early days of the Restoration; but it failed, and Flecknoe never afterward forgave the playhouse manager, Sir William Davenant, whose admirer he had formerly been.[48] In 1664 he published the revised version "not as it was acted . . . but as it was written," together with his *Short Treatise of the English Stage*, one of the few truly interesting works that Flecknoe is known to have written.

In 1661 Flecknoe published *Erminia, or The Fair and Virtuous Lady*, certainly designed as a closet drama though possibly composed after the reopening of the theatres. It had been written at Westham in the home of Lady Southcot, whom the author proclaimed as the prototype of his heroine—"chaste as white ermine." A supercilious prologue condemns theatrical managers and gives aids to the reader in visualizing the play—including the names of such actors as might have proved worthy to take parts. The play is a long and involved romance of over forty scenes in verse and prose. Erminia, whose chastity is fruitlessly beset by the Duke of Missena and others convinces her husband of her probity when Aurindo, her suspect page whose charms have set all the other court ladies agog, turns out to be a woman. To spy upon her affairs (and to provide incidental mirth), Erminia's husband goes about in the disguise of a blackamoor; but this blackamoor, although obviously not what he seems, never evokes the slightest curiosity in the reader.

The plays just described, and the lost entertainments previously mentioned, comprise Flecknoe's dramatic works—except the distinctly Restoration product, *The Damoiselles a la Mode*, 1667, a comedy compounded of *Les Précieuses Ridicules*, *L'École des Maris*, and other pieces by Molière.[49] This play, also a failure on the stage, is remarkable only for its author's effrontery in Englishing a satire of *préciosité*—on the professors of which he himself had so successfully battened. It is hard to be patient with Flecknoe, he himself is so ill-natured, and—without the slightest justification—so pretentious. His surviving original plays should be considered in the line of Commonwealth compositions preserving the Cavalier mode, and must be conceded some slight historical interest for their early employment of rime, and their critical prefaces.

The few additional authors who essayed closet drama during the Commonwealth had best be considered along with writers of the early Restoration, at which time they come into more literary prominence. A tragicomedy called *The Royal Choice*, by Sir Robert Stapylton, was entered in the *Stationers' Register*, November 29, 1653, and in 1656 the words "Pastor Stapilton" occur in the list of plays published with *The Careless Shepherdess* by Rogers and Ley; so it is evident that at least one play (possibly two), now lost, was produced by this author before the opening of the theatres stimulated him to practical play writing. Sir Robert Howard's little known *Blind Lady* was actually in print by

CLOSET DRAMA OF THE COMMONWEALTH 235

1660, and such promptitude, together with the type of play it is, indicates that Howard's dramatic activities also had anticipated the restoration of the stage. Even so important a play as Etherege's *Comical Revenge* may have been adapted from a dramatic romance written, as numerous allusions suggest, during the Commonwealth.

But even without these, the Commonwealth playwrights are numerous enough; and offer ample illustration that, both in their social foregatherings and in the privacy of their closets, those not of Oliver's faction had kept the interest in native English drama alive, and had preserved the Cavalier mode.

---

[1] See above, pp. 107-109, 136-137, 181-183, 198-202.
[2] *The Bastard*, 1652, *The Hectors*, 1656, and several other Commonwealth plays deserve an editor.
[3] See above, p. 136.
[4] Part II, p. 67 *seq.*; for Stanley, cf. *DNB*, LIV, 79.
[5] This work, which I have not seen, is listed by Ernest Grillo in his edition of *Aminta* (1924).
[6] W. W. Greg, *Pastoral Poetry and Pastoral Drama* (1906), p. 249.
[7] MS. Rawl., poet., 130; B. M. Add. MSS. 12128.
[8] A translation by "Gent, T. S.," 1655, is listed by Ernest Grillo, *op. cit.*
[9] *DNB*, XVIII, 184 seq.; Fanshawe would make the subject of a fascinating biography.
[10] A manuscript copy exists, B. M. Add. MS. 32133.
[11] *Romanciomastix* was otherwise titled *Don Zara del Fogo*; *Venus and Adonis* (first published in 1656) is supplied with an epilogue promising the press *Cupid and Psyche*, a second burlesque masque.
[12] Printed in the rare *Huth's Inedited Poetical Miscellanies, 1584-1700*, W. C. Hazlitt, Ed. (1870).
[13] Quoted above, p. 59.
[14] The play was altered as *Wits led by the Nose* and acted at Drury Lane, 1677 (published 1678); reprinted with *Pharonnida* by S. W. Singer, 1820; and edited as a Univ. of Penna. thesis by C. K. Meschter, 1914. For Chamberlaine, cf. *DNB*, X, 10, and G. Saintsbury's introduction to *Pharonnida* in *Caroline Poets*, I, 3-13.
[15] Printed in part in *Brief Descriptions of the Ancient and Modern Manuscripts Preserved in the Public Library, Plymouth*, J. O. Halliwell, Ed. (London, 1853).
[16] For a discussion of the sources of *Love's Labyrinth*, see the essay by J. Q. Adams cited above, p. 46.
[17] See above, p. 171.
[18] Harl. MS. 7313.
[19] Examples of these are quoted above, pp. 63-64.
[20] Adapted for the stage as *The Royal Shepherdess* by Shadwell, and printed in 1669.
[21] Dedication to King Charles.
[22] Published with *Nicomede*, J. Dancer, tr. 1671.
[23] *DNB*, XXXVII, 280; *Alumni Cantabrigienses*, I, III, 177.
[24] P. 369.

[25] A corrective account of Baron by G. C. Moore Smith appears in *N&Q*, Series XI, I (1914), 22, 43, 61, 206.

[26] The account by Langbaine (*English Dramatick Poets*, pp. 13-14) is quite fair.

[27] Dated by Moore Smith, *op. cit.*, p. 61.

[28] MS. Rawl. Poet. 80 (Bodl.). Dedicated to Lady Blount by her brother "R.K."

[29] B. M. Add. MS. 10419

[30] See above, p. 117.

[31] *Dramatic Records of Sir Henry Herbert*, p. 58, note 3.

[32] *DNB*, xv, 376.

[33] *DNB*, First Supplement, III, 138-139.

[34] Act I (page 11 in the quarto).

[35] Archer's playlist, 1656, assigns it to Manuche.

[36] *Poema tragico del Español Gerardo* by de Céspedes y Meneses, translated as *Gerardo the Unfortunate Spaniard* by Leonard Digges in 1622. Langbaine also suggests *The English Lovers* as the source; see *English Dramatick Poets*, p. 527.

[37] Since writing this, I have learned that a copy of *The Banished Shepherdess* is at the Huntington Library (MS. E. L. 8395), and of *The Feast* at Worcester College, Oxford. *DNB*, First Supplement, III, 138-139, implies that the plays are still at Ashby, but the *Index and Epitome*, p. 837, states that only one is now known there. This one is evidently a copy of *The Feast*. B. M. Wagner (*LTLS*, Oct. 4, 1934) dates this play after 1664, and indicates that the other plays are at Ashby. My inquiries on the subject have elicited no reply, but see A. Watkin-Jones, *LTLS*, Nov. 15, 1934, p. 795.

[38] MS. Rawl. Poet. 16.

[39] Edited from MS. Rawl. Poet. 16 by N. C. Starr, *PMLA*, XLVI (1931), 802-838.

[40] Cf. N. C. Starr, *op. cit.*, pp. 836-838.

[41] *Dorothy Osborne's Letters*, E. A. Parry, ed. (London, 1888), p. 111.

[42] J. Jusserand, *English Novel in the Time of Shakespeare* (1890), p. 377.

[43] H. T. E. Perry, *The First Duchess of Newcastle and Her Husband* (Cambridge, 1921).

[44] K. M. Lynch, *The Social Mode of Restoration Comedy*, Univ. of Michigan Pub., III (1926), 130.

[45] W. C. Hazlitt, *Dodsley*, XIV (1875), 274-367.

[46] Act IV, Scene vii, for instance, is precisely in the manner of Lady Newcastle. Few other writers of the period wrote comedy. Scarcely classifiable as closet drama are the scattered comic pamphlets in dialogue: *News out of the West, or the Character of a Mountebank*, 1647; *The Prince of Priggs Revels, or the Practices of that Grand Thief Captain James Hind* (containing allusions to the escape of Prince Charles at Worcester), 1651; and *The New Brawl*, 1654. Thomas Brewer's *A Knot of Fools*, 1657, seems to be an adaptation of an early droll; cf. H. Rollins, *SP*, XVIII (1921), p. 325. *The Cyprian Conqueror* (Sloane MS. 3709), a crude comic treatment of Petronius Arbiter's tale of the Roman matron, is supplied with a prefatory defense of drama suggesting Commonwealth composition. In a note upon this play (*MLN*, XXIII (1908) Joseph Q. Adams conjectures that it was written during the reign of Charles I.

[47] See above, pp. 207-208.

[48] A. Harbage, *Sir William Davenant, Poet Venturer* (Univ. of Penna. Press, 1935), p. 156.

[49] Flecknoe seems also to have adapted Molière's *Le Médecin Malgré Lui*, but only the Prologue survives.

VII

THE LAST OF THE CAVALIER PLAYWRIGHTS

IT has been remarked that "for four complete years of the reign of Charles II . . . the English theatre was the theatre of Charles I restored";[1] and such was the case—with this distinction: that the Beestons and the Bromes, the older type of theatrical guildsmen, were erased from the picture; and in their stead were the Killigrews and the Howards, courtly gentlemen exercising a virtual monopoly of theatrical management and authorship. Except in the capacity of actors, the ungenteel were discouraged from intercourse with the stage. Those entrepreneurs who had organized companies at the Phoenix, the Red Bull, and Salisbury Court at the dawn of the new reign were suppressed,[2] and control of all theatrical entertainment was placed in the hands of two royal patentees and the Master of the Revels. Thomas Killigrew, Sir William Davenant, and Sir Henry Herbert became a dictatorial triumvirate supported by the King himself, and though they quarreled for precedence among themselves, they united to resist the encroachment of outsiders: witness the conspiracy of Killigrew and Davenant to prevent the erection of a third and competing playhouse by stalwart George Jolly, the strolling actor-manager.[3] No plebian showmen, of the type of John Tatham and Thomas Jordan, but grooms of his Majesty's bedchamber governed the theatres and determined their repertories. Tatham, Jordan, and Shirley—survivors of the popular stage before 1642[4]—were discouraged even from writing for the King's and the Duke's Men. At first the two managers were content to revive old plays, their own conspicuously included, and when they began to accept new plays, they favored the work of men of quality: the Howards, the Digbys, the Tukes, the Stapyltons, and Orrerys. Others had usually to be content with printing their plays, and loud and dolorous were their introductory laments at the cruelty of theatre managers.

Here is the apex of a cycle. Nothing gives greater significance to the courtly invasion of the theatre after 1633 than the courtly conquest of the theatre after 1660. It is not our purpose to chronicle the work of all the *élite* after 1660; we shall confine our view to those who were truly of the Cavalier generation; but we must remember that all, Etherege, Wycherley, Rochester, Buckingham, Sedley, and the rest, follow the lead of Montague, Suckling, Carlell and those polite dramatists of the earlier reign. The courtiers of Charles II pass through the breach made by the courtiers of Charles I. The lady dramatist also passes through the breach, following the valiant Duchess of Newcastle, so that by the end of the century the Mistresses Phillips, Boothby, Behn, Trotter, Pix, and Manley have swelled the female contingent of our English playwrights. To be sure, it was only during the earliest years of the new period that the courtier playwright was supreme. Through Lacy, Betterton, and Medbourne the actor-playwright regained a foothold: and in Thomas Shadwell emerged a contender for laurels with no glittering social background to lend his plays prestige. Toward the end of the century, gentlemen playwrights were somewhat uneasy, and William Congreve was not quite certain that writing plays was the best of form.

It is common to think of Restoration drama in terms of licentious comedy. It is also common to attribute this licentious comedy to war-weariness and reaction against Puritan bigotry. Without cavilling at the application of the term "Restoration" to drama written after the restored king had died and his successor had been banished by a second revolution, we must insist that the drama of the first years of Charles the Second's reign—literally the years of the Restoration—was not remarkable for licentious comedy but for serious romantic plays, highly moral and elevated, of the same general tone as those written by the courtiers in the circle of Henrietta Maria. The documents authorizing the revival of drama and licensing the companies were almost pietistic in tone.[5] And the authors of these plays and of these documents were the Cavaliers—the men who had fought in the great rebellion, suffered imprisonment and the sequestration of estates, and had therefore, one would suppose, the chief reason to be war-weary and to react against Puritan bigotry. Vanbrugh, Congreve, and Farquhar were not yet born.

One body of early Restoration dramas may be briefly disposed of. A group of authors encouraged to dramatic composition by a tradition already established in their circle and by the recent institution of theatres in which the royal box rivaled the stage itself in glamorous appeal, yet inexperienced in conceiving and constructing plays, found that they could shine with reflected light by producing translations. Lodowick Carlell himself, evidently feeling that his creative days were past, was contented to render Corneille.[6] In Ireland the King's Lord Justice encouraged Catherine Phillips[7] to translate Corneille's *Pompée*, and her skillful rimed redaction was acted with éclat at Smock Alley in Dublin, February, 1663, garnished with a prologue by Lord Roscommon and an epilogue by Sir Edward Deering. Her second translation from Corneille, *Horace,* was left incomplete, but Sir John Denham supplied the conclusion and the play was performed by the King's Men. This authoress had been a girl in her teens during the first Civil War; and later, as *Orinda*—she herself did not claim to be *Matchless*—, had formed the center of a group of English *précieuses.* In 1664 appeared a more widely heralded version of *Pompée,* the communal effort of a perfect brood of courtiers old and young, including Godolphin, Sackville, Sedley, and Waller. This collaboration gives Waller, so prominent among Cavalier poets, at least a slender association with drama. Waller seems also to have operated upon the ending of Beaumont and Fletcher's most famous play so that the *Maid's Tragedy* became a tragicomedy.[8] Nearly all the Cavalier poets can be claimed as Cavalier playwrights. Charles Cotton published an augmentation of Corneille's *Horace;* and even John Evelyn, who had felt a Puritanical tremor at his sin in attending a performance at Davenant's Commonwealth theatre,[9] fell into line and wrote plays: "Very good," said his fellow diarist Pepys, "but not as he conceits them, I think, to be."[10]

Several of the Cavaliers adapted Spanish plays. George Digby, Earl of Bristol, and Sir Samuel Tuke, both middle-aged men who had fought in the cause of the first Charles, worked this vein, with royal encouragement. Digby's *'Tis Better than it Was, Worse and Worse,* and *Elvira, or The Worst not always True* all seem to stem from Calderón.[11] Only the last, acted about 1663, is extant, and though mechanical, and irksomely overplotted, its flaws are not licentiousness and cynicism as the flaws in a play by a war-worn Cavalier supposedly should be. Much better than *Elvira,* although Downes[12] informs us that Digby had a hand in its production, is Tuke's *Adventures of Five Hours,* suggested by Cœllo's *Los Empeños de Seis Horas.* Tuke may claim a large measure of originality in the composition of this play, which is bright and entertaining, even though its contemporary fame and thirteen-day run in January, 1663, leaves the modern reader slightly bewildered. Pepys was moved to admiration at this "famous new play," which he pronounced marvellously unified and "without one word of ribaldry."[13]

Without one word of ribaldry likewise are the more purely original plays of the Cavaliers making their last stand during these first years of the Restoration. One of these Cavaliers was Sir Robert Stapylton (c. 1604-1669), a man approaching sixty before he had a play produced upon the stage. Stapylton, however, had been interested in drama before the closing of the theatres,[14] and had entered upon dramatic authorship at the latest by 1653.[15] His career is curious, and typical of his age in its peculiar fluctuations.[16] Educated at Douay and confirmed a monk in the year of the accession of Charles I, he proved "too gay and poetical to be confined within a cloyster," and established himself at London to move in the society to which his gentle birth admitted him. After renouncing Romanism, he became a gentleman of the privy-chamber to Prince Charles, and was among the first to stand in arms for the King. He was knighted at Nottingham, and was given a chance to prove his knightly prowess at the Battle of Edgehill. Following his king to Oxford, he secured one of the academic degrees so liberally distributed there among the Royalist officers. When Oxford fell into the power of Parliament, he imitated many another by making himself prudently inconspicuous, and for the remainder of the Commonwealth period he busied himself with study and translation. At the Restoration he was appointed a gentleman usher by the Stuart in whose privy-chamber he had served before the wars, and upon his death was deemed worthy of a corner in Westminster Abbey.

The first mention of Stapylton as a playwright of the new period occurs February 23, 1663, when Pepys saw *The Slighted Maid* and noted in his diary that the girl who danced in boy's apparel had fine legs, but the play itself had "little good in it." To the second of these judgments we are in a position regretfully to subscribe, conceding at the same time the worthiness of the author's avowed moral purpose. The play telescopes two stories, suggestive of romantic prose fiction but developed somewhat in the manner of the currently popular Spanish drama of cloak and sword. One plot, utilizing a background of war and ancient political conspiracies, displays how Filomarini saves his son and nephew from their philandering, and weds them to a pair of Bulgarian princesses, an achievement which involves the outwitting of Menanthe, a Greek impostress, and Peralta, an ex-pirate. The other plot gives the play its title. Ericina disguises herself as a man and wins a promise of marriage from the new mistress of her former lover. Having thus revenged herself for the jilting she has received, she reveals her identity, lets the couple marry, and finds herself a consolation husband elsewhere. Written in formless blank verse diversified with occasional couplets, the play aims at an absorbing intricacy but hits only mystification. To meet the requirements of the latest theatrical fashion, a number of musical interludes are provided, but never has *divertissement* been introduced less appropriately.

Stapylton's next play, *The Stepmother,* produced in the latter months of 1663, is an episodic romance, the fable of which may have given Dryden suggestions for his *Indian Emperor.* It repays reading for this reason, and is, besides, a less abortive effort than *The Slighted Maid;* the plotting is more coherent, and the musical entertainment is inserted with more show of reason. The material of the play is sophisticated British history. Sylvanus, king of the principality of Verulam, is dominated by his second wife, Pontia of Malden, a woman of barbaric wilfulness. Sylvanus and Pontia have each a son and daughter by a previous marriage, and among these four paragons develop idealistic love affairs. With Pontia as the villainness of the piece, the young people make heroic sacrifices for each other and for the King. The Queen is at last reclaimed, the proof of her conversion appearing in her display of justice after her faithful general has placed in her hands full power over the realm. Love, honor, friendship, and heroic disinterestedness form the refrain; and though there is less exposition of *préciosité* than display of romantic adventure, the play is quite in the Cavalier mode and might have been written twenty years before. Few of its exotic situations will appear novel to one who has read Carlell and Killigrew.

Stapylton's final play was never acted. In 1669, the year of his death, he published a complicated dramatic version of the Greek poem of Musæus, which he had translated and published at Oxford in 1645. In transposing his *Loves of Hero and Leander* into his play, *The Tragedy of Hero and Leander,* he persisted in the Cavalier technique, and except for certain peaks of the dialogue which he managed to beat into couplets, he wrote in his customary boneless blank verse. He seems to have felt that his poetic era had passed, and not to have recognized that the present one, with its brilliant heroic plays, was its child. A note of repining sounds in his dedication to the Duchess of Monmouth: "Love and Honour (theams of former ages) are turned into bourlesque on modern stages, and puppets play mock-Hero and Leander." Literature could well have spared Stapylton, would have lost little if he had decided to distinguish himself, let us say, in heraldry or numismatics; but he deserves our interest as a survival, and our respect as one of those whose idealism had survived a disillusioning age.

Of about the same type as Stapylton, though a more interesting figure, was his friend and comrade in arms, Sir William Killigrew (1606-95). These two were equal in age, and had received together their degree in Civil Laws from the beleagured King at Oxford. Stapylton wrote commendatory verses "To Envy" when Killigrew published his plays. The oldsters of the court lent each other support. Carlell, also, commended Killigrew's plays, tracing their inspiration to the Queen Mother Henrietta Maria:

> You reach what was your highest end,
> To show her power, on whom you now depend . . .

Carlell had just written his own *Heraclius* to please Henrietta, and it is interesting to see this revival of her influence upon the survivors of that generation of courtiers which she had spurred to authorship a quarter of a century before. Sir William's younger brothers, Thomas and Henry, had written then, and now he belatedly entered the lists, wearing dramatic insignia identical with theirs.

Sir William's plays, though scarcely to be described as buoyant, are surprisingly youthful in spirit considering the frustrations he had known. Long before the wars, his life had been filled with strenuous activity, as a student at Oxford, as a traveller abroad, as belligerent Governor of Pendennis Castle, as a business speculator, and as a gentleman-usher to King Charles I.[17] During the wars he captained one of the troops of horse guarding His Majesty's person at Oxford. The loss of the Royal cause plunged him into absolute penury; his family fortune he had invested in a project to drain the fens of Lincolnshire, and with the sitting of the Committee of Sequestration such Royalist investments were at a cruel discount. This Cavalier, once so proudly militant and full of business, was reduced to begging small favors of his friends, so that for him even more than for the average Royalist the return of a Stuart king was the return of springtime. He wrote a long letter[18] to the awaited Charles II, urging in his own behalf "no perticular sute" but asking "only to share in the general good of the nation," and enclosed his greatest treasure—a letter in which Charles the Martyr had thanked him for sacrificing his own advantage to the good of the Crown. There is something of pathos in Sir William's letter, with its long paragraphs of solemn counsel and stale sagacity. Such discourse, said he, "I have often entertained the Kinge your father with in the garden at Oxford, when every body wondered what he could find to talke so much alone with me about." The new King, no doubt through the intercession of Henrietta Maria, awarded him the minor court offices which Killigrews had filled for a hundred years, and the remainder of his long life passed in security though never in affluence. The record of Sir William's private enterprises reveals him to have been more vigorous than wise, and at times a strenuous self-seeker; but there is nothing discreditable in this record, nothing to make one skeptical about the intense piety of his last years. He was an earnest, old-fashioned gentleman who lived a futile life, sinking his noblest impulses and his best years into the sand-pit of the Stuart cause.

Five plays were the fruit of Sir William's tardy advertence to literature, but only for the first two of these, *Pandora, or the Converts* and *Selindra,* and the last, *The Imperial Tragedy,* is there good evidence of stage performance.[19] That *Pandora,* c. 1662, was given a trial on the stage appears from Waller's commendatory verses which remark that it had been changed to a comedy after having failed as a tragedy. It remains a fairly serious play in its revised form, few of its scenes being mirth-provoking even in intent. A group of self-consciously virtuous ladies and gentlemen, some sprightly but others very solemn and didactic, succeed in making a match between the major characters, Clearcus and Pandora. Pandora has to be converted from her aversion to marriage, and Clearcus from his rakishness and paradoxical resolve never to marry a woman who will consent to have him. A few subsidiary love affairs and a dash of state intrigue round out the play, but it is basically a drama of matrimonial debate revolving about Pandora's manners and Clearcus's morals. There is much conversation, little action: a re-claimed rake sermonizes; a chaste lover appears as a pattern of be-havior; a witty damsel self-illustrates her thesis that the charms of the pure woman are superior to those of the lewd. We are swept backward to the days of Davenant's *Platonic Lovers* and Henrietta's maids por-ing over their volumes of D'Urfé. We can only hope that the younger courtiers of the restored King did not mock too openly this prodigiously guileless play.

In *Selindra,* which was given a lukewarm reception when staged by his brother at the Theatre Royal in March, 1662,[20] Sir William wrote of chivalric adventure and produced a better plotted and more effective play. Prince Phillocles of Greece returns from conquests in the north, sadly believing that he is responsible for the death of his friend, the Hungarian Prince Pollinesso. No sooner has he been welcomed home than he falls in love with Selindra, a lady attending upon his sis-ter. She repulses him, for reasons unknown, but he becomes her heroic protector from a succession of lustful assailants. Imprisonments, flights, and conflicts follow in strenuous succession, until Phillocles finds an ally in the person of the wanderer Pollidor. After the appearance of Pollidor, Selindra grows more tender toward her champion, but incites his jealousy by showing an equal tenderness for the stranger. All is well, however, for Pollidor proves to be the supposedly deceased Pol-linesso, and Selindra proves to be his devoted sister Astella. A Hun-garian army is in the field, all ready to attack the Greeks, when a revelation of identities and a contract of marriage effects a joyful amnesty. There is no need for discussion: here is the old Cavalier formula, followed in the old Cavalier way.

The successor to the two plays described, *Ormasdes, or Love and Friendship,* though an oddly disjointed product, has a special interest because much of it is written in couplets, and its leading character is an even nearer kinsman to Montezuma and Almanzor than is the average Cavalier hero. The play was printed in 1664, so that its period of composition must have been close to that of *The Indian Queen*. Ormasdes, all-conquering General of the Queen of Sitherea, has been ever ready to place his sword at the disposal of fair ladies, but has never fallen in love. Mere valor, however, proves insufficient to relieve the distresses of Mariana, a local Princess, for she falls so violently in love with her champion that she is ready to expire of her passion. Having saved her from dangers without, Ormasdes deems it equitable to save her from dangers within. His pretended reciprocation of love turns genuine; and a play which begins with conquest and high heroism ends tamely in the creation of a Benedict.

Killigrew's best play remains to be described. It was succeeded by possibly his poorest, but the latter may be dismissed with mention: *The Imperial Tragedy*, 1669, is admittedly a translation, evidently of some academic Latin tragedy, and treats of the tyrannies of the Emperor Zeno; its waxwork horrors are less convincing even than the average of their class, and the authorship of the translation was not publicly acknowledged.[21] *The Siege of Urbin*, c. 1665, on the other hand, will afford genuine pleasure to an understanding reader in the proper mood. Princess Celestina of Pisa, preferring death to the marriage of convenience urged by her father, disguises herself as a man, takes the name Florio, and volunteers her service to the besieged Duke of Urbin. She unites in a pact of friendship with a fellow volunteer, Fernando, and these two prove so mighty in arms that they are created commanders. Native Urbinites grow jealous, and the friends find themselves imperilled by the besieged as well as the besiegers. But the Duke of Urbin himself grows strangely tender toward Florio, especially after this gracious volunteer saves his life at the cost of deadly wounds. Picture his rejoicing then, when Florio recovers and proves to be not only a woman but an eligible Princess. Fernando is discovered to be her cousin—an ideal suitor to the Duke's sister Silviana. This ending is made all the more joyous by the misunderstandings, jealousies, intrigues, and misplaced attachments that have gone before.

The Siege of Urbin works adroit variations upon ancient characters and situations, and is as good a romance of its kind as one may find. Although its coincidences and disguisings risk the ludicrous, epecially since the author shared the Killigrew family penchant for clapping eye-patches and periwigs on handsome princes and princesses, there is nothing forced or ungraceful about the piece as a whole. Rather, one finds charm in its fluent prose, interest in its episode and movement. Of his own work, Sir William wrote,

What you'll see here is natural, all pretense
He disavows to wit or eloquence . . .
With Friendship he presents you and with Love,
Such as are wont in his free breast to move;
Such passions as he feels our Author writes . . .[22]

And one may accept the avowal as almost literally true. This sixty-year old veteran of private misfortunes and public catastrophes, now moving in the disenchanting company of Sedley, Rochester, Buckingham, and Old Rowley, was unswervingly romantic—still devoted to his champions of honor, his fair princesses in disguise.

The record of the Killigrew family, with three play-writing brothers, was surpassed by the Howard family, with four. Among the numerous sons of the Earl of Berkshire, Edward, Henry, Robert, and James all wrote plays, and, with the probable exception of James, all were Cavaliers—that is, they had been old enough to bear arms at the time of the Civil Wars. Although they began to write after the Restoration, the mark of the former age is in their work. This fact, and a certain pomposity in the efforts of Edward and Robert to dictate dramatic laws, account for the amusement with which they were viewed by the younger wits of the court of Charles II. James was the youngest, and the most adroit in escaping ridicule, but the serious plot of his *All Mistaken, or The Mad Couple,* 1667, is reminiscent of Caroline courtly drama. Here figure the usual artificially created barriers to love, and the usual method for removing the chief barrier: Artabella, fiancée of Duke Archemedos, is proved to be his sister, and thus he is freed to wed his true affinity, Amphelia. James's *English Monsieur,* 1663, and his adaptation of *Romeo and Juliet, c.* 1664, are mentioned elsewhere.[23] The only known play of Henry Howard, *The United Kingdoms, c.* 1663, is lost, but we know that it began with a funeral, had two kings in it, and affected the risibilities of the Duke of Buckingham.[24]

Edward Howard (b. 1624) seems to have struck his contemporaries as the epitome of the literary fop,[25] and such of his plays as have survived will incline no one to leap to his defense. *The Usurper,* 1664, and *The Change of Crowns,* 1667, have been noticed in our survey of political plays.[26] *The London Gentleman, c.* 1667, was entered in the *Stationers' Register,*[27] but apparently not printed. In *The Women's Conquest,* a tragicomedy of 1670, Queen Mandana, a heroic bluestocking who resents the kind of divorce laws in effect in neighboring Scythia, leads her army of Amazons in a holy war. Her wrath is appeased when Bassanes, a Scythian general, reverses her earlier victories but succumbs to her charms. The divorce laws of Scythia are properly amended. The action of the play reminds us slightly of Jasper Mayne's *Amorous War*, but the author's tone, unlike Mayne's, is deadly earnest. The theme, to be well treated, needed a light and whimsical touch, not Edward's heavy hand. Later the dramatist composed two miserable comedies.[28]

Not so likely as his brothers, or as Stapylton and the Killigrews, to be brushed aside by historians of drama is Sir Robert Howard (1626-98), for he had the luck to collaborate with Dryden on a famous play and then to engage with Dryden in a famous controversy. Were it not for these contacts with Dryden, Sir Robert would share the obscurity of the other Cavalier dramatists, even though his abilities were somewhat superior to theirs. His life was an interesting one.[29] As a youth he had fought in the first Civil War, and had fought valiantly. Having saved the life of Lord Wilmot at Cropredy Bridge, he was knighted for the deed in the field of Newbury. Then he suffered for allegiance to the Royal cause through a long Parliamentary imprisonment. Howard was young enough and vigorous enough to become a person of social and political importance during the Restoration, yet old enough to have acquired the mannerisms of the former age. He considered that matters of state rather than the fashioning of epigrams was the proper business of the descendant of Lord Burghley and the Earl of Berkshire, and remaining dignified and aloof amidst a society which affected a careless informality, he acquired a reputation for superciliousness. It is doubtful if there was much more provocation than nonconformity behind the cruel caricature of Sir Robert as Sir Positive At-all in Shadwell's *Sullen Lovers*. Posterity has tended to accept the appraisal of his contemporaries in estimating Howard's personality, largely because of the air of condescension with which he prosecuted his literary dispute with Dryden, but, after all, Sir Robert was in no position to recognize Dryden as one of the future great.

Howard's *début* as a dramatist was inauspicious. In his collection of poems published in 1660 appeared *The Blind Lady*. In this rare and justly neglected play, the love rivalry of Phylanter and Miranault expresses itself, as usual in Cavalier romance, in armed combat more than in addresses to the loved one; the rivalry ends, also as usual, when Phylanter falls in love with Miranault's sister. The title of the play derives from comic scenes which follow Miranault's retreat to the home of Cæca, an aged blind woman; we say "comic" but the manner in which Cæca's infirmities are made subject of jest seems ugly and callous unless we consider her no more than a symbol of jade Fortune. Like most plays written during the close of the theatres, *The Blind Lady* is wretchedly executed; yet it is worth notice as placing Howard immediately in the Cavalier tradition. The characters are given to typical refinement of sentiment and loquaciousness. Miranault shows unusual restraint when he pauses on the brink of a martial sally and says,

> Oh what a speech could I now make
> of this frail world. But however
> I'll not stay now to do it.

Perhaps Sir Robert was very young when he wrote this play, or was enfeebled by his incarceration at Windsor.

Slightly superior to *The Blind Lady* is *The Surprisal,* Howard's first play to appear on the Restoration stage. Although technically a comedy, the atmosphere of *The Surprisal* is prevailingly serious. The play conforms in type with such bourgeois drama of intrigue as Davenant's *Just Italian,* and might have appeared at Blackfrairs in 1622 just as well as at the Theatre Royal in 1662 as it actually did. Emilia and Samira, about to be married off to wealthy undesirables, find true lovers in the persons of Miranzo and Cialto. The young men incur the hazard of assassination, the young women the hazard of rapine, but happy marriages and affluence reward the final passage of these four through the fens of villainy and greed. Little can be said of this play, save that it is mightily tiresome, and follows a tradition established on the popular stage not one but several generations before. When the author turned to realistic comedy in *The Committee,*[30] also acted in 1662, he was much more successful.

Howard's *Vestal Virgin, or The Roman Ladies,* 1664, has a little of the merit of his *Committee,* although its antithesis in type. The Princes Tiridates and Artabaces, Armenian brothers captive in Rome, fall in love respectively with Hersilia and Verginia, sisters of course, and the latter a vestal virgin. Tiridates finds a friend and noble rival in the Roman general Sertorius. The brother of Sertorius is the lustful villain of the tale. The complicated plotting and violent action defy retelling, but end at last in wholesale slaughter. That is, in one version: an alternate ending was provided in which virtue triumphs to the tune of a triple wedding. Such reversible endings are a tribute to the influence of Suckling and his *Aglaura;* we have already noticed several instances of the device in these first years of the Restoration, and to the list may be added *Romeo and Juliet,* which was provided with a happy ending by Sir Robert's brother James, so that audiences could smile and weep on alternate days.[31]

The Vestal Virgin is not only a Cavalier dramatic romance, but its materials were provided by an earlier one, by Thomas Killigrew's *Cicilia and Clorinda,* written in 1650 and printed just before Howard composed his play. That this relationship has escaped notice is per-

haps due to the silence of Langbaine, who was as partial toward Howard as he was unfriendly toward Dryden, and dismissed the former's
sources with an odd bit of special pleading: "Some readers, who are
strangers to the excellent talents of Sir Robert, might expect from me
some discoveries of what he has borrowed; but I am to inform them
that this admirable poet has too great a stock of wit of his own, to
be necessitated to borrow from others."³² Howard's reputation was
otherwise; and when he published his *Duke of Lerma,* he was forced to
admit that it was an adaptation of a manuscript play submitted to him
for revision by Mr. Hart, the actor. It is possible, in the case of the present
play, that Howard went directly to Killigrew's sources in La Calprenède
and Scudéry, but if so, the two dramatists showed a remarkable unanim-
ity in the selection of details. Howard has improved considerably upon his source if it was *Cicilia and Clorinda;* in fact *The Vestal Virgin*
is better balanced, more skillfully plotted, than most of its predecessors
in the type. The language is felicitous, especially where unrimed, and
many scenes illustrate that the author has retained the interest of his
generation in *précieuse* dialectics. The weakness of the play is the weakness of all the plays of love, friendship and honor in the Cavalier mode
—a fantastically unreal background, and an ethical and emotional basis
of conduct so artificially formalized as to result in a rudimentary or
totally absent psychology.

 The Indian Queen, one of several plays which have been accorded
distinction as the "first" Restoration rimed heroic play, has been
described elsewhere.³³ It was acted in January, 1664, and published, not
as a work of collaboration but as Howard's own in 1665. Dryden's
comment, ". . . *The Indian Queen,* (part of which poem was writ by
me) . . . ,"³⁴ led Scott, who was quite partisan in questions involving
Howard and Dryden, to claim the play almost exclusively for the latter. However, if we reckon with the type of drama produced by the
two men before, rather than after, the time of *The Indian Queen,* we
will admit the possibility of Howard's major claim. It may be that
Dryden lent to the enterprise little more than his technical skill in
heroic versification.

 Better worth reading than *The Indian Queen* is Howard's last extant play,³⁵ *The Duke of Lerma,* 1668. This is a tragicomedy in blank
verse, strongly resembling the romantic drama of John Ford, and
stands apart not only from the heroic plays of its time but also from such
Cavalier romances as the author's own *Blind Lady,* and *The Vestal
Virgin.* It bears about the same relationship to Howard's earlier romantic plays that *Aureng-zebe* bears to Dryden's earlier rimed plays. The
semi-historical story of the Duke of Lerma's design to retrieve his

political fortunes by prostituting his daughter Maria to young King Philip of Spain is developed with dignity and dramatic effectiveness. In this play alone do Howard's characters invite attention as human beings. These characters, to be sure, are strangely warped: Charles is tenderly aware of the charms of his daughter,

> . . . sweeter than the spring wreath'd in the armes
> Of budding flowers . . .;

yet he suffers few qualms of conscience. Maria, who is all self-abnegating love for Philip and devotion to her unworthy father, possesses a virtue that is more real, less purely pictorial, than that of the ordinary heroic damsel. When Medina, the King's honest counsellor, makes her weep with a mistaken charge of unchastity, she saves him from the King's displeasure:

> Think how the world would curse me, when they hear
> Medina's love to virtue lost his life.

The lines that follow have a fine simplicity:

> He talkt to me of nothing but of goodness,
> And when he spoke of that, (as he must needs)
> He named my mother, and by chance I wept.

King Philip's love for Maria proves to be true love, and he makes her his lawful Queen. Duke Charles reforms—at least such is the hint in the play's rather vacillating conclusion—, but not until his villainies have taken such an ingenious twist as to become almost admirable in themselves. Throughout, the play is marred by inconsistencies, but it has moments of power, moments even of poetry.

The Duke of Lerma is Sir Robert Howard's testimonial of allegiance to the drama of the past. His loyalties were largely retrospective. In his controversy with Dryden[36] (wherein he had the truth while Dryden had the logic, the learning, and the brilliance), he defended blank verse as the medium of serious plays and attacked the tyranny of the dramatic unities—as we should expect a partisan of the former age to do. Yet certain features of his *Committee* pointed forward to the new comedy of manners; and his *Indian Queen* was among the earlier works which invested dramatic romance with those formal characteristics frequently regarded as the *sine qua non* of the Restoration heroic play. He was then, like Sir William Davenant, and like the Killigrews, Stapylton, and others in less degree, a living link between the drama of the former and the latter age.

Sir William Davenant himself was too busy as a theatre manager, too willing to rest on the laurels he was winning as author of *The*

Siege of Rhodes, and perhaps too "written out" to produce much
original work after 1660. He compounded his *Law Against Lovers* out
of *Measure for Measure* and *Much Ado about Nothing* in 1662, pieced
out his "Peruvian" entertainments of the Commonwealth with some
farcical interludes and presented them as *The Playhouse to be Let* in
1663, adapted *Macbeth* in the same year, and converted *The Two Noble Kinsmen* into *The Rivals* about 1664. He returned to Shakespearean adaptation later on, once—in the case of *The Tempest*—
collaborating with Dryden. Critics have been humorlessly severe with
Davenant for his bungling, failing to see that a man might deserve
credit for trying to make Shakespeare palatable to an unsympathetic
age even though incapable of improving upon the master. Although
he wrote no wholly original plays after the reopening of the theatres,
Davenant exerted considerable influence on those around him, including Dryden, and deserves A. W. Ward's commendation as a Restoration touchstone of the old theatrical tradition.[37]

Among those encouraged by Davenant was Thomas Porter (1636-
80), son of that engaging old courtier Endymion, who had befriended
Davenant in his youth and had secured him his opening at the court
of Charles and Henrietta. Porter's plays may be briefly noticed here
though their author was scarcely of the Cavalier generation. He was
nineteen years old in 1655—and at odds with the law on two distinct
counts, murder and abduction;[38] although his offenses were actually
milder than these charges would imply, he was indeed pretty much
of a blade. So also, by the way, were the sons of Thomas Killigrew
and of Davenant himself. Not the Cavaliers, even the younger ones
like Sir Robert Howard, but the sons of the Cavaliers—those who
had been children in the days of the Wars—were the rake-hells of the
Restoration.[39] Porter's first play, acted at Davenant's theatre in 1662,
was *The Villain.* It is a voluble tragedy, full of Elizabethan reminiscences; and the villainies of "honest" Maligni, with the fatal misunderstandings among a group of regimental officers and their loves, would
be totally uninteresting were it not for several scenes of realism which
take us directly into the military barracks of the seventeenth century.
The Carnival, acted about 1664, is filled with romantic intrigue certainly derived from some Spanish drama of cloak and sword, possibly
the same that had suggested Davenant's *Spanish Lovers* of 1639. Two
additional plays have been attributed to Porter on the strength of the
initials "T. P." on their title pages: *A Witty Combat,*[40] printed in
1663, and *The French Conjuror,* acted about 1677,—that is, far beyond
the period of the present survey. By 1677 the restraint notable during
the early years of the Restoration had long dissipated, and *The French*

Conjuror, like many minor comedies of its day, is nasty without compensating wit and good manners.

Two of Porter's three plays written by 1664 are serious in tone, and though not of the courtly type, are in harmony with the romantic and high-minded ideal to which most of the earlier Restoration writers were committed. A scattering of additional early plays have a similarly elevated and serious cast. William Clerke's *Marciano, or The Discovery,* presented by the author and other gentlemen actors at Holyrood House, Edinburgh, on St. John's night 1662, before the King's High Commissioner the Earl of Rothes, is a hectic tragicomedy of the intermingled loves and politics of Florence. Viscount Falkland's *Marriage Night,* probably acted at Davenant's theatre in 1664, is, like Porter's *Villain,* a bloody tragedy of Elizabethan inspiration. Thomas Southland's⁴¹ *Ungrateful Favorite,* printed in 1664, is also old-fashioned, a tragedy of court intrigue full of violence and spectacularity. All three plays are awkwardly constructed. Clerke, Falkland, and Southland were young amateurs of social standing. The sober hue of the reawakening drama was emphasized by such plays as George Cartwright's *Heroic Lover,* Forde's *Love's Labyrinth,* and Fountain's *Rewards of Virtue,* all first printed in 1661 although probably written earlier.⁴² Flecknoe's *Erminia* and *Love's Kingdom* were additional exemplars of the school of noble elevation. Etherege's *Comical Revenge* itself has its "heroic" moments.

Among the original plays produced during the first few years of the Restoration, the dominant types are: dramatic romances of the Cavalier mode, drama of Spanish intrigue, and Elizabethan tragedy and tragicomedy. We may observe that the first type was chiefly produced by the older writers, the surviving Cavaliers themselves; the last type by the younger writers, directly influenced by their reading and by the revivals of Shakespeare, Fletcher, and their fellows at the Duke's House and the Theatre Royal. The sprinkling of comedies written during these years has already been described.⁴³

Roger Boyle,⁴⁴ Earl of Orrery, was himself one of the last of the Cavaliers. He reached his majority before the outbreak of the wars. He fought effectively in the Irish phase of the Troubles, finding, in one of the most freakish political alignments of the epoch, a means of serving faithfully under Oliver Cromwell and yet remaining essentially loyal to the Stuart cause. He was friendly with Davenant, and was related by marriage to the Killigrews and the Howards. Like all the Restoration heroic plays his have much in common with the dramatic romances of the Caroline courtiers. Only for two factors, that he wrote persistently in rime, and that his social and political prestige was such that the performances of his plays were theatrical events (until their monotony grew wearisome), Boyle would occupy in dramatic history about the same position as Sir William Killigrew. As it is his historical importance in the development of Restoration dramatic types has been somewhat overemphasized.

John Dryden himself is linked remarkably with the playwrights of the Cavalier generation. He was considerably older than the Restoration playwrights with whom he is usually associated. He was patronized by Boyle, and was related by marriage to Sir Robert Howard, with whom he dwelled for a time in 1663.[45] He collaborated not only with Howard but also with Davenant, whom he remembered with veneration and of whom he was willing to be considered the disciple.[46] He collaborated also with that veteran, the Earl of Newcastle,[47] who alone of the Cavaliers had preferred comedy to romance. It is well to remember such contacts when distinguishing between Dryden's comedy and that of Etherege and Wycherley, who were more isolated from the past, and when debating the origin of his heroic plays.

The tradition of Cavalier Drama might have died with Boyle had not Dryden taken it up.[48] Though romantic and elevated plays prevailed during the first years of the Restoration, they were not in tune with the spirit of the age, or—its equivalent for drama—the court of Charles II. Few of the plays discussed in the present chapter were well received. Audiences were craving spicier fare. In lamenting the failure of *Love's Kingdom,* Flecknoe complained that "love without lust was as meat without sauce."[49] to the theatregoers of the new day. Sauce enough was provided when the manager of the King's House in October, 1664, served up his ribald *Parson's Wedding* cast entirely with women. After such diversion, the ethical perplexities of Sicilian princesses must have seemed decidedly tepid. One "T. L." praised Sir William Killigrew's collected plays in the following terms:

> That thy wise and modest muse
> Flees the stage's looser use;
> Not bawdy wit does falsely name
> And to move laughter put off shame.
>
> That thy theatre's loud noise
> May be virgin's chaste applause;
> And the stoled matron, grave divine,
> Their lectures done, may tend to thine.

But in glancing over their audiences, the theatre managers saw too few virgins, stoled matrons, and grave divines to feel justified in encouraging Sir William to further efforts.

The best cue to the barriers thrown up against the old ideology is provided by an entry in *Pepys Diary*. In the same month that *The Parson's Wedding* was revived with its feminine cast, the diarist attended a performance of Orrery's *The General:*

I happened to sit near to Sir Charles Sidly; who I find a very witty man, and he did at every line take notice of the dullness of the poet and badness of the action; which I was mightily taken with; and among others where by Altemire's command Clarimont, the general, is commanded to rescue his Rivall, whom she loved, Lucidor, he, after a great deal of demurre, broke out, "Well, I'll save my Rivall and make her confess,/ That I deserve while he do but possesse." "Why, what, pox," said Sir Charles Sydley, "would he have him have more, or what is there more to be had of a woman than the possessing her?"[50]

Such blasts would have spelled quietus for the plays of love and honor had not Dryden furnished them with a technical brilliance which made susceptibility to their message unnecessary.

---

[1] John Palmer, *The Comedy of Manners* (1913), p. 3.

[2] Leslie Hotson, *Commonwealth and Restoration Stage* (1928), p. 197 ff.

[3] *Ibid.*, Chapter IV.

[4] Shirley wrote nothing at all, unless he "assisted" others, although he lived until 1666. Jordan wrote a few interludes, and he and Tatham wrote the civic pageants. Others who produced drama in some form both before 1642 and after 1660 were mostly amateurs: the list includes, besides Davenant, Cokain, Denham, Lower, Milton, Cowley, Carlell, Newcastle, and possibly Stapylton. Fane and T. Killigrew, as well as Shirley, had continued writing after 1642 but had ceased before 1660.

[5] See for instance Davenant's preliminary draft of the King's grant of monopoly; *Dramatic Records of Sir Henry Herbert*, pp. 87-88.

[6] See above, p. 103.

[7] P. W. Souers, *The Matchless Orinda* (Harvard Univ. Press, 1931).

[8] The adaptation is attributed to him and printed with his poetic remains in 1690.

[9] *Evelyn's Diary*, May 5, 1659.

[10] Nov. 5, 1665.—From Evelyn's correspondence it appears that the title of one of his plays was "Thyrsander."

[11] A. Nicoll, *Restoration Drama* (1928), p. 180.

[12] John Downes, *Roscius Anglicanus*, p. 22.

[13] Jan. 8, 1663.

[14] See his commendatory verses in Harding's *Sicily and Naples*, 1640.

[15] See above, pp. 234-235.

[16] *DNB*, LIV, 100.

[17] A. Harbage, *Thomas Killigrew* (1930), pp. 29-34.

[18] Printed in full by Bliss in Wood's *Athenæ Oxonienses*, IV, 694.

[19] W. J. Lawrence, "Sir William Killigrew's Plays," *LTLS*, Oct. 18, 1928, p. 755, suggests that *Ormasdes* and *The Siege of Urbin* may also have been acted, but this remains doubtful. A manuscript copy of *The Siege of Urbin* (MS. Rawl. Poet. 29) contains on folio 71 a partial list of actors, but the author may have been fancying those *qualified* to act in his play—in the manner of Flecknoe when he published his unacted *Erminia*.

[20] See the criticism by a contemporary rimester quoted by L. Hotson, *op. cit.*, pp. 246-247.

[21] Though publication was anonymous, Sir William's authorship is established by a presentation copy to the Earl of Anglesey, cf. Hazlitt's *Manual*, p. 118. The play was acted at the theatrical nursery in the Barbicon. Since the present study was completed, the play translated has been identified as Joseph Simeon's *Zeno* (Rome, 1648); cf. M. Summers *Playhouse of Pepys* (1935), p. 257.

[22] Verses printed with *Pandora*, 1664.

[23] See p. 247.

[24] M. Summers edition of Buckingham's *Rehearsal* (1914), pp. 83 120.

[25] *Ibid.*, pp. 76-79 *et passim.*

[26] See above, pp. 186-187, 190.

[27] Aug. 7, 1667.

[28] *The Six Days Adventure*, 1671; *The Man of Newmarket*, 1678.

[29] A biographical notice is prefixed to C. N. Thurber's edition of *The Committee Univ. of Illinois St. in Lang. and Lit.*, VII, 1921.

[30] See above, pp. 84, 184.

[31] John Downes, *Roscius Anglicanus*, p. 22.

[32] *English Dramatick Poets*, p. 276.

[33] See above, p. 51.

[34] Dryden's note published with *The Indian Emperor.*

[35] Since the present study was completed, I have found reason to believe that *The Duke of Lerma* was adapted from a play by Ford. I shall publish my case shortly. Howard's *The Conquest of China by the Tartars*, which Dryden planned to revise (cf. A. W. Ward, *English Dramatic Literature*, III, 393), has not survived. In British Museum Add. MS. 28692, fol. 70 *seq.* exists one scene of the play contributed by Wilmot.

[36] Waged in *Epistle Dedicatory to The Rival Ladies*, 1664; *Preface to Four New Plays* (by Howard), 1665; *Essay of Dramatic Poesy*, 1668; *Preface to the Duke of Lerma*, 1668; *Defence of an Essay of Dramatic Poesy*, 1668. For Dryden-Howard problems see D. D. Arundell, *Dryden & Howard* (Camb. Univ. Press, 1929).

[37] *English Dramatic Literature*, III, 167.

[38] *DNB*, XLVI, 193.

[39] A partial exception to this rule is offered by the one who turned the shafts of ridicule upon the heroic tradition: the Duke of Buckingham had fought with the Cavaliers; he was fourteen, Charles II twelve, at the outbreak of the wars.

[40] See above, p. 85.

[41] Conjecturally assigned by A. Nicoll, *op. cit.*, p. 349.

[42] For these plays, and Flecknoe's, see above, pp. 220-221, 234.

[43] See above, pp. 85-87.

[44] See the publications of W. S. Clark, noted above, p. 70.

[45] W. S. Clark, *MLN*, XLII (1927), 16-20.

[46] See his prefatory remarks to *Annus Mirabilis, The Rival Ladies*, and the adapted *Tempest*, as well as his *Essay of Heroic Plays.*

[47] Upon *Sir Martin Mar-all*, see above, p. 89.

[48] At least temporarily; the persistence of the conventions of heroic valor and heroic love in drama well into the eighteenth century illustrates the depths of their roots.

[49] Preface to *Love's Kingdom.*

[50] Oct. 4, 1664.

CONCLUSION

IT is interesting to speculate upon what might have been in literary history, especially at points where a single critical event seems to have cut out a distinct channel of consequences. It is possible to imagine King Charles inspired with enough sense of conciliation to avert rebellion, and the task of limiting English monarchy fallen to a Parliament with a conservative faction strong enough to win small victories like keeping theatres open. Uninterrupted, then, what might have been the course of English dramatic history?

There is excellent reason to suppose that it would have been the course which we actually know. Five or ten years of delay might have been averted, and the developments we associate with the early 'sixties might have come in the early 'fifties, but this difference is not momentous. In view of the increasing constriction of the theatrical industry before 1642, and its increasing submission to court control, we can imagine the suppression by 1652 of all but two theatres—called, let us say, not the Duke's House and the Theatre Royal but Queen Henrietta's House and King Charles's House. And as for the royal monopolists in charge, what candidates could we suggest more likely than William Davenant and Thomas Killigrew? The former was already in the field and yearning to enter more deeply; the latter was a young courtier, energetic but unemployed, with an eye on the main chance and an active interest in theatricals. We can easily imagine Davenant putting into earlier effect the ideas for improving the theatre he had outlined in 1639, and Killigrew rising to meet the competition—with the result: a picture frame stage, movable scenery, women actors, increased musical embellishment, and all the rest.

The whole emphasis of this book has been upon the natural progression from dramatic types familiar before 1642 toward the two most conspicuous types of the Restoration—Drydenesque heroic tragedy and Etheregean social comedy; there is no need to cover the ground again. Such formal alterations of Cavalier dramatic romance as would convert it into heroic tragedy might have been wrought by Denham, or Waller, or more probably, by Davenant himself, with Dryden first pliantly following the lead and then perfecting the type. The new social comedy no doubt would have appeared somewhat later than heroic tragedy (as it did), for it would have had to wait upon gathering forces of reaction and upon the crystallization of a social ideal. But it would not have had to wait upon the example of Molière. We can imagine someone like Sir William Berkeley producing a play as advanced as *The Comical Revenge* at least by the time *The Hectors* was written; or perhaps the talents of Etherege himself would have ripened earlier under a less clouded theatrical sky. Before these types of drama had been formulated, Killigrew would have written his sequel to *The Parson's Wedding,* Newcastle would have engaged Shirley to "tie together" the scenes of some additional plays, and Dryden at Cambridge would have written a Bromean comedy or two in the manner of Cartwright and Mayne. In fact, a whole sheaf of Bromean comedies, and of dramas in the Cavalier mode, would have issued from hands unconstrained to forego the pen for the sword. These efforts-unborn the world has well been able to spare.

In a word, a dwelling with mid-seventeenth century drama enforces conviction of the continuity of literary development. This continuity is often obscured by the abruptness with which evolutionary trends produce their cumulative effect. Works like *Pamela* or *Lyrical Ballads* resemble the sports or mutations of biology; they are in the main line of development but do not always appear to be. If the advent of such works is preceded by some striking external phenomenon such as a political upheaval, their novel qualities, attributable only in some slight degree to this upheaval, are likely to be traced to it in their entirety. As a modern instance, certain brutalities in contemporary fiction seem to stem from the effects of the World War, yet one need only remember the pre-war novels of Somerset Maugham, Charles Norris, and other disciples of Zola to be troubled by doubt. The appearance of Restoration heroic tragedy and social comedy was preceded by a political upheaval, so that such plays as *The Siege of Rhodes* and *The Comical Revenge* are sometimes considered less as native mutations than as importations from abroad, or as the creations of special artistic fiats. These plays were no more unpredictable in their day, judged by the nature of earlier English drama, than *Tamburlaine, Philaster,* or *The Shepherd's Paradise* had been in *their* day.

Those influences called "French" were not properly foreign. France supplied to Restoration playwrights plot materials and technical instruction, but did not determine the modes of their drama nor its informing spirit. France did not, through her *romans de longue haleine* and her classical tragedy, engender in the English a taste for pseudo-heroic ideals and for rime. La Calprenède and Scudéry were themselves late-comers in a field. With their ten-tome tales they gave heroic romance its most spectacular expression, but none of its essential qualities; and to kindred literature in Restoration England, such as the heroic plays, their work stands in the relationship not of ancestry but of a collateral line. The preoccupation with sensational romance in England, as in France and the rest of the Continent, must be referred to something permeant in the temper of the times. France did not impregnate the court during its exile in Paris with ideals of wit, conduct, and the social graces, that resulted, with the assistance of Molière, in the creation of Restoration social comedy. Young Charles and Rochester would not have developed into solemn and industrious young men, eschewing wit, moral pecadillos, and the social graces, though there had been no exile and the English crown had descended in quiet and uninterrupted succession.

But there is nothing very novel in such conclusions, and our parting glance should be at Cavalier drama itself. It would be ludicrous to attempt to absolve it now on the basis of fancied artistic merits in view of all that has been admitted concerning its deficiences. Its charm as an antique, the suggestiveness of its age-mellowed stories, the glimpse it supplies into an older and more leisured world have no claim upon the affection of the busy general reader. But viewed in relation with the total dramatic output of the mid-seventeenth century as symptomatic of artistic, cultural, spiritual change, Cavalier drama is more interesting than some more estimable literature. We can perceive two antithetical but mutually explanatory strains. Romance had had its day, and the faith, the enthusiasm, the poetic vision which had nourished it had receded from its veins. Writers groping for something lost produced not romance but a travesty upon romance. The serious drama of the Cavaliers fell into schematized patterns, like the folds pictured in the vestments of the Byzantine saints. This drama, unpraiseworthy as art, is praiseworthy still as human endeavor for it reveals one impulse not purely negative: the impulse to experiment, and to exercise the intellect and sensibilities, however fruitlessly, in expressing an ideal and analyzing an ethical code. Then arising to complement these airy abstractions so singularly unnourished by contact with life, was the naturalistic strain in comedy—a strain eagerly intent upon contact with life. It is in the mid-seventeenth century, at the very time that the animated puppets of withering romance are in most violent agitation, that we perceive the beginnings of a reportorial art.

Comment upon the ebb of the poetic, imaginative inspiration of literature and upon the consequent flow of the scientific, factual inspirations seems like a long tail to attach to the little kite of Cavalier drama. Unlike Elizabethan drama, which expressed national impulses and aspirations and justifies generalizations, Cavalier drama was the expression of a clique, of a mere excrescence upon English society as a whole; and it seems presumptuous to discover large portents in the petty creations of a petty circle. But if we are forbidden to seek signs here, where else may we look? Is Milton's *Paradise Lost* a truer index of the impulses and aspirations of the times? Or, to grow truly spacious, let us suggest for analysis all the works and ways of that great national stratum which proved strong enough to wrest from the Cavaliers the government of England—a stratum which Milton and his epic do not fairly represent. Qualities in common may be found in the activities of the Cavaliers and their less artistically inclined opponents. Certainly there was something sensationally romantic about the theology of the Puritans, something ultra-realistic about their politics. They could at the same time erect pulpits for prophesying and organize an army of the New Model.

Since we have dealt so often upon the qualities in common in Cavalier and Restoration drama, we should add one last word about their qualities at variance. There was a difference, after all, between the two generations which produced them. The Cavaliers still believed in the gallantries of romance and were themselves capable of romantic follies—such as sacrificing their personal fortunes in their monarch's cause. This was one type of folly to which the next generation was disinclined; the gallantries of the heroic plays were for the young gentlemen of the Restoration as a thing apart. Artistically the new and impersonal attitude encouraged improvement; Dryden created brave spectacles, lavished attention upon technique, and lent æsthetic distance to material sorely in need of it. The Cavaliers were less inclined than the Restoration playwrights to view their plays as a visible index of their manners, which, like dress itself, was to be essentially correct; no doubt Carlell was more proud of his hunting, Newcastle of his horsemanship, Cartwright of his seraphical preaching.

The Cavaliers on the whole are more attractive to us than the generation they begat, not because they were less inclined to flaunt petty vices like an adornment, but because they were more ingenuous, less casehardened—and because they hugged about themselves the tattered garments of an outworn chivalry.

A LIST, CHRONOLOGICALLY ARRANGED, OF ALL PLAYS OF THE CAROLINE, COMMONWEALTH, AND EARLY RESTORATION PERIODS

EXPLANATION.—In the first column is the name of the author or authors of each play, followed by a question mark if the authorship rests upon conjecture. In the second column is a brief title of each play. An asterisk before the title indicates that the date of the play rests upon circumstantial evidence, and may be considered only as approximate. Unacted dramas are usually listed in the year of publication; others in the year of earliest performance. In the third column the type of play is indicated. The plays have been classified only according to major genera; most of the heroic plays, for instance, are listed as tragicomedies. In the fourth column is listed the name of the professional company first producing each play. When the play was left unacted, or produced otherwise than by professionals, the fact is indicated. In the fifth column is listed the date of earliest publication. Brackets enclosing an entire date indicate that the original title-page is undated. Brackets enclosing numerals following a particular date indicate that the original title-page was dated according to the year ending on March 25; the numerals enclosed, therefore, give the date according to our present system. Abbreviations, when used, are, I believe, self-explanatory with one exception: S. R. stands for *Stationers' Register*.

The facts included in the play-list have been checked with the most recent comment in periodicals and elsewhere, but derive chiefly from the following books: J. Q. Adams, *The Dramatic Records of Sir Henry Herbert* (Yale Univ. Press, 1917); W. W. Greg, *A List of English Plays* (London, 1900); W. W. Greg, *A List of English Masques, Pageants, &c.* (London, 1902); J. O. Halliwell, *A Dictionary of Old English Plays* (London, 1860); W. C. Hazlitt, *A Manual for the Collector and Amateur of Old English Plays* (London, 1892); F. G. Fleay, *A Biographical Chronicle of the English Drama*, 2 vols. (London, 1891); A. Nicoll, *A History of Restoration Drama* (Cambridge Univ. Press, 2 ed., 1928); F. E. Schelling, *Elizabethan Drama*, 2 vols. (Boston, 1908); G. M. Sibley, *The Lost Plays and Masques* (Cornell Univ. Press, 1933); M. S. Steele, *Plays and Masques at Court* (Yale Univ. Press, 1926).

1626

Davenport, R.	*King John and Matilda	Chronicle	Henrietta's	1655
Davenport, R.	*The Pirate	Unknown	Henrietta's ?	Lost
Fletcher, J., et al.	The Fair Maid of the Inn	Comedy	King's	1647
Fletcher, J., et al.	The Noble Gentleman	Comedy	King's	1647
Hawkins, Wm.	Apollo Shroving	Comedy	Hadleigh School	[1627]
Heywood, T. (?)	Dick of Devonshire	Tragicom.	Unknown	1883
May, T.	Cleopatra, Queen of Egypt	Tragedy	Unknown	1639
Massinger, P.	The Roman Actor	Tragedy	King's	1629
Middleton, T.	Health and Prosperity	Civ. Pag.	London	1626
Shirley, J.	The Brothers (Same as *Wedding* ?)	Tragicom. ?	Henrietta's ?	Lost ?
Shirley, J.	The Maid's Revenge	Tragedy	Henrietta's	1639
Shirley, J.	*The Wedding	Tragicom.	Henrietta's	1629

1627

Bellamy, H.	Iphis	Lat. Comedy	St. John's, Ox.?	MS
Crowther, Jos.	*"Cephalis et Procris"	Lat. Legend	St. John's, Ox.?	MS
Davenant, W.	The Cruel Brother	Tragedy	King's	1630
Ford, J.	*Love's Sacrifice	Tragedy	Henrietta's	1633
Ford, J.	*'Tis Pity She's a Whore	Tragedy	Henrietta's	1633
Massinger, P.	The Great Duke of Florence	Tragicom.	Henrietta's	1636
Massinger, P.	The Judge	Comedy	King's	Lost
May, T.	*Antigone, the Theban Princess	Tragedy	Unacted	1631
Newman, T.	Andria	Tr. Terence	Unacted ?	1627
Newman, T.	The Eunuch	Tr. Terence	Unacted ?	1627
Anonymous	A Welcome from the Isle of Ree	Entertainment	Unknown	MS

1628

Brome, R.	*The City Wit	Comedy	Unknown	1653
Brome, R.	*The New Academy	Comedy	Unknown	1659

Davenant, W.	*Albovine	Tragedy	Unacted	1629
Dekker, T.	Britannia's Honor	Civ. Pag.	London	1628
Ford, J.	The Lover's Melancholy	Tragicom.	King's	1629
Ford, J. (?)	*The Queen, or Excellency of Her Sex	Tragicom.	Unknown	1653
Gomersal, Lod.	*Lodowick Sforza	Tragedy	Unacted ?	1628
Hemming, W.	*The Jew's Tragedy	Tragedy	Unacted	1662
Massinger, P.	The Honor of Women	Comedy	Unknown	Lost
May, T.	Julia Agrippina	Tragedy	Unknown	1639
Reynolds, H.	Aminta	Tr. Tasso	Unacted	1628
Shirley, J.	The Witty Fair One	Comedy	Henrietta's	1633
Vincent, T.	Paria	Lat. Com.	Trin. C., Camb.	1648

1629

Brome, R.	The Lovesick Maid	Comedy	King's	Lost
Brome, R.	The Northern Lass	Comedy	King's	1632
Carlell, L.	*The Deserving Favorite	Tragicom.	King's	1629
Davenant, W.	The Just Italian	Comedy	King's	1630
Davenant, W.	The Siege	Tragicom.	King's ?	1673
Dekker, T.	London's Tempe	Civ. Pag.	London	[1629]
Ford, J.	*The Broken Heart	Tragedy	King's	1633
Jonson, B.	The New Inn	Comedy	King's	1631
Massinger, P.	Minerva's Sacrifice [or The Forced Lady (S. R.)]	Tragedy	King's	Lost
Massinger, P.	The Picture	Tragicom.	King's	1630
Randolph, T.	*Aristippus	Monologue	Trin. C., Camb.	1630
Randolph, T.	*The Conceited Pedlar	Monologue	Trin. C., Camb.	1630
Randolph, T. (?)	*Cornelianum Dolium	Lat. Com.	Trin. C., Camb. ?	1638
Randolph, T., augmented by "F. J."	*Hey for Honesty, Down with Knavery	Adapt. from Aristophanes	Trin. C., Camb. ?	1651
Shirley, J.	The Grateful Servant	Comedy	Henrietta's	1630

1630

Hemming, W.	*The Fatal Contract	Tragedy	Henrietta's	1653
Heywood, T.	*2 Fair Maid of the West	Comedy	Henrietta's	1631
Randolph, T.	Amyntas	Pastoral	K's Revels	1638
Randolph, T. (?)	*The Drinking Academy [The Prodigal Scholar (S. R.) ?]	Comedy	Trin. C., Camb. ?	1924
Randolph, T.	The Muses' Looking Glass	Comedy	K's Revels	1638
Sidnam, J.	*Filli di Sciro	Tr. Bonarelli	Unacted ?	1655
Sidnam, J.	*Il Pastor Fido	Tr. Guarini	Unacted ?	MS
Anonymous	*The Fairy Knight	Comedy	"Schoolboys"	MS
Anonymous	*Grobiana's Nuptials	Comedy	St. John's C., Ox. ?	MS
Anonymous	*The Spanish Tragedy	Tragedy	Rehearsed at Ox.	Lost

1631

Brome, R.	*The Queen's Exchange	Tragicom.	King's	1657
Hausted, P.	*Senile Odium	Lat. Com.	Queen's C., Camb.	1633
Heywood, T.	London's Jus Honorarium	Civ. Pag.	London	1631
Jonson, B.	Chloridia	Masque	Whitehall	1630[31]
Jonson, B.	Love's T. Through Callipolis	Masque	Whitehall	1630[31]
Knevet, R.	Rhodon and Iris	Pastoral	Florist's Feast, Norwich	1631
Mabbe, J.	Calisto and Melibœa	Tr. Rojas	Unacted	1631
Marmion, S.	Holland's Leaguer	Comedy	P. Charles's	1632
Massinger, P.	Believe as you List	Tragedy	King's	1849
Massinger, P.	The Emperor of the East	Tragicom.	King's	1632
Massinger, P.	The Unfortunate Piety [or The Italian Night-piece (S. R.)]	Tragedy ?	King's	Lost
Pestell, T., Sr.	Versipellis	Lat. Com.	Queen's C., Camb. ?	Lost
Shirley, J.	*Contention for Honor & Riches	Moral	Unacted ?	1633
Shirley, J.	The Humorous Courtier	Comedy	Henrietta's	1640
Shirley, J.	Love's Cruelty	Tragedy	Henrietta's	1640
Shirley, J.	The Traitor	Tragedy	Henrietta's	1635

Author	Title	Genre	Company/Place	Date
Simeon, J.	*Leo Armenus	Lat. Trag.	Camb. or Douay ?	1657
Simeon, J.	*Zeno	Lat. Trag.	Camb. or Douay ?	1648
Wilson, A.	The Swisser	Tragicom.	King's	1904
Zouche, R.	*The Sophister [Fallacy in MS]	Allegory	Oxford	1639
Anonymous	*The Costly Whore	Chronicle	K's Revels	1633
	1632			
Brome, R.	The Court Beggar	Comedy	King's ?	1653
Brome, R.	*The Novella	Comedy	King's	1653
Brome, R.	The Weeding of Covent Garden	Comedy	King's ?	1659
Hausted, P.	The Rival Friends	Tragicom.	Queen's C., Camb.	1632
Heywood, T.	Londini Artium et Scientium Scaturgio	Civ. Pag.	London	1632
Jonson, B.	*The Magnetic Lady	Comedy	King's	1640
Marmion, S.	*The Soldered Citizen	Comedy	Prince Charles's ?	MS
Massinger, P.	The City Madam	Comedy	King's	1658
Nabbes, T.	*Covent Garden	Comedy	Henrietta's	1638
Randolph, T.	The Jealous Lovers	Comedy	Trin. C., Camb.	1632
Shirley, J.	The Ball	Comedy	Henrietta's	1639
Shirley, J.	Changes	Comedy	K's Revels	1632
Shirley, J.	Hyde Park	Comedy	Henrietta's	1637
Tatham, J.	Love Crowns the End	Pastoral	Bingham School	1640
Townshend, A.	Albion's Triumph	Masque	Whitehall	1631[32]
Townshend, A.	Tempe Restored	Masque	Whitehall	1631[32]
Anonymous	*The Ring	Unknown	Unknown	Lost
	1633			
Blencowe, J.	*Mercurius sive Literarum Lucta	Lat. Com.	St. John's, Ox. ?	MS
Cokain, A.	*Trappolin Supposed a Prince	Comedy	Originally Unacted ?	1658
Cowley, A.	*Love's Riddle	Pastoral	Unacted	1638
Ford, J.	*Perkin Warbeck	Chronicle	Henrietta's	1634
Hemming, W.	The Coursing of the Hare	Comedy	K's Revels	Lost

Author	Title	Type	Place	Date
Heywood, T.	Londini Emporia	Civ. Pag.	London	1633
Heywood, T.	*A Maidenhead Well Lost	Comedy	Henrietta's	1634
Jonson, B.	Love's Welcome at Welbeck	Entertainment	Welbeck	1640
Marmion, S.	A Fine Companion	Comedy	Prince Charles's	1633
Massinger, P.	The Guardian	Comedy	King's	1655
Milton, J.	Arcades	Entertainment	Harefield	1645
Montague, W.	The Shepherd's Paradise	Pastoral	Whitehall	1629[59]
Mountfort, W.	The Launching of the Mary	Comedy	Unknown	1932
Nabbes, T.	*Tottenham Court	Comedy	Prince Charles's	1638
Rickets, J.	*Byrsa Basilica	Lat. Com.	Jesus C., Cam. ?	MS
Shirley, J.	The Bird in a Cage	Comedy	Henrietta's	1633
Shirley, J.	The Gamester	Comedy	Henrietta's	1637
Shirley, J.	The Young Admiral	Tragicom.	Henrietta's	1637
Wild, R.	*The Benefice	Comedy	Unknown	1689
Wilson, A.	The Corporal	Comedy	King's	MS frag.
Wilson, A.	The Inconstant Lady	Tragicom.	King's	1814
Anonymous	2 The City Shuffler	Comedy	K's Revels	Lost
Anonymous	Ent. of King Charles	Entertainment	Edinburgh	1633

1634

Author	Title	Type	Place	Date
Carew, T.	Coelum Britannicum	Masque	Whitehall	1638[34]
Carlell, L.	The Spartan Ladies	Tragicom.?	King's	Lost
Davenant, W.	Love and Honor	Tragicom.	King's	1649
Davenant, W.	The Wits	Comedy	King's	1636
Glapthorne, H.	*The Duchess of Fernandina	Tragedy	King's ?	Lost
Glapthorne, H.	*Albertus Wallenstein	Tragedy	King's	1639
Heyw. & Brome	The Late Lancashire Witches	Topical Play	King's	1634
Heyw. & Brome	*The Apprentice's Prize	Unknown	King's ?	Lost
Heyw. & Brome	*Sir Martin Skink	Comedy ?	King's ?	Lost
Heywood, T.	Love's Mistress	Myth. Play	Henrietta's	1636
Jonson, B.	Love's Welcome at Bolsover	Entertainment	Bolsover	1640

Le Grys, R.	*Nothing Impossible to Love	Unknown	Unknown	Lost
Lovelace, R.	The Scholar	Comedy	Glouc. Hall, Ox.	Lost
Massinger, P.	Cleander	Tragedy	King's	Lost
Massinger, P.	A Very Woman	Tragicom.	King's	1655
Milton, J.	Comus	Masque	Ludlow Castle	1637
Rutter, J.	*The Shepherds' Holiday	Past. Tragicom.	Henrietta's	1635
Shirley, J.	The Example	Comedy	Henrietta's	1637
Shirley, J.	The Opportunity	Comedy	Henrietta's	1640
Shirley, J.	The Triumph of Peace	Masque	Whitehall	1633[34]
Sparrowe, T.	*Confessor	Lat. Comedy	St. John's, Camb. ?	MS
Taylor, J.	Triumph of Fame and Honor	Civ. Pag.	London	1634
Anonymous	Ent. at Sir T. Middleton's	Entertainment	Chirke Castle	MS frag.
Anonymous	Love's Aftergame, or the Proxy	Comedy ?	K's Revels	Lost

1635

Atkinson, T.	*Homo	Lat. Trag.	St. John's, Ox. ?	MS
Bristow, F.	King Free Will	Tr. Bassano	Unacted ?	1635 (copy ext. ?)
Brome, R.	*The Queen and the Concubine	Tragicom.	K's Revels	1659
Brome, R.	The Sparagus Garden	Comedy	K's Revels	1640
Cartwright, W.	*The Ordinary	Comedy	Christ Ch., Ox. ?	1651
Davenant, W.	News from Plymouth	Comedy	King's	1673
Davenant, W.	The Platonic Lovers	Comedy	King's	1636
Davenant, W.	The Temple of Love	Masque	Whitehall	1634[35]
Digby, K.	*Amyntas & Pastor Fido	Tr. Tasso & Guarini	Unacted ?	Lost
Ford, J.	*The Fancies Chaste & Noble	Comedy	Henrietta's	1638
Glapthorne, H.	The Noble Trial [Same as following ?]	Unknown	Unknown	Lost ?
Glapthorne, H.	The Lady Mother	Tragicom.	K's Revels	1883
Heywood, T.	*A Challenge for Beauty	Tragicom.	King's	1636
Heywood, T.	Londini Sinus Salutis	Civ. Pag.	London	1635
Heywood, T.	*Pleasant Dialogues & Dramas	Dialogues	Unacted ?	1637
Jones, J.	Adrasta, or the Woman's Spleen	Tragicom.	Unacted	1635

Author	Title	Type	Venue	Date
Jonson, B.	*Fall of Mortimer	Chron. frag.	Unacted	1640
Jonson, B.	*The Sad Shepherd	Unfinished Past.	Unacted	1640
Killigrew, H.	*Pallantus and Eudora	Tragicom.	King's	1638
Killigrew, T.	The Prisoners	Tragicom.	Henrietta's	1641
Kirke, J.	*Seven Champions of Christendom	Tragicom.	Prince Charles's ?	1638
Marmion, S.	*The Antiquary	Comedy	Henrietta's	1641
Massinger, P.	The Orator [The Noble Choice ?]	Tragicom. ?	King's	Lost
Nabbes, T.	Hannibal and Scipio	Tragedy	Henrietta's	1637
Nabbes, T.	*Microcosmus	Moral Alleg.	K's Revels ?	1637
Rider, W.	*The Twins	Tragicom.	K's Revels ?	1655
Shirley, J.	A Lady of Pleasure	Comedy	Henrietta's	1637
Shirley, J.	The Coronation	Comedy	Henrietta's	1640
Wilde, G.	Eumorphus	Lat. Com.	St. John's C., Ox.	MS
Anonymous	Florimene	French Past.	Court	1635
Anonymous	Icon Ecclesiastici	Lat. Com.	Unknown	MS

1636

Author	Title	Type	Venue	Date
Brome, R.	*Mad Couple Well Matched	Comedy	Queen's ?	1653
Carlell, L.	1 Arviragus and Philicia	Tragicom.	King's	1639
Carlell, L.	2 Arviragus and Philicia	Tragicom.	King's	1639
Cartwright, W.	The Royal Slave	Tragicom.	Ch. Church, Ox.	1639
Cayworth, J.	Enchiridion Christiados	Religious Ent.	W. Paston's, Norfolk	MS
Davenant, W.	Triumphs of the Prince d'Amour	Masque	Middle Temple	1635[36]
Glapthorne, H.	The Hollander	Comedy	Henrietta's	1640
Hausted, P. (?)	*Senilis Amor	Lat. Com.	Queen's C., Camb. ?	MS
Killigrew, T.	*Claricilla	Tragicom.	Henrietta's	1641
Killigrew, T.	*The Princess	Tragicom.	Henrietta's	1664
Kynaston, F. (?)	Corona Minervæ	Masque	Museum Minervæ	1635[36]
Massinger, P.	The Bashful Lover	Tragicom.	King's	1655
May, T.	The Old Couple	Comedy	Unknown	1658
Rawlins, T.	*The Rebellion	Tragedy	K's Revels	1640

Sackville brothers, *et al.*	The King and Queen's Entertainment at Richmond	Comic show	Richmond	1636
Shirley, J.	The Duke's Mistress	Tragicom.	Henrietta's	1638
Speed, J.	Stonehenge	Pastoral	St. John's C., Ox.	Lost
Strode, W.	The Floating Island	Moral Alleg.	Ch. Church, Ox.	1655
Wilde, G.	*Hermorphus	Lat. Com.	St. John's C., Ox.	Lost
Wilde, G.	Love's Hospital	Comedy	St. John's C., Ox.	MS
Anonymous	*A Projector Lately Dead	Comedy ?	Unknown	Lost
Anonymous	Moore's Masque	Masque	"Near Eastgate, Ox."	MS ?
		1637		
Berkeley, W.	The Lost Lady	Tragicom.	King's	1638
Brome, R.	The English Moor	Comedy	Queen's	1659
Brome, R.	*Wit in a Madness	Comedy ?	Queen's ?	Lost
Carlell, L.	*The Fool would be a Favourite	Tragicom.	Queen's	1657
Carlell, L.	*Osmond, the Great Turk (revision ?)	Tragedy	Queen's	1657
Cartwright, W.	*The Lady Errant	Tragicom.	Ch. Church, Ox. ?	1651
Ford, J.	*Beauty in a Trance	Comedy	Unknown	Lost
Ford, J.	*The Royal Combat	Tragicom. ?	Unknown	Lost
Formido, C. (?)	The Governor	Tragedy	King's	Lost
Glapthorne, H.	*The Ladies Privilege	Tragicom.	K. and Q's	1640
Heywood, T.	Londoni Speculum	Civ. Pag.	London	1637
Mayne, J.	The City Match	Comedy	King's	1639
Nabbes, T.	*The Spring's Glory	Masque	Unknown	1638
Neale, T.	The Ward	Tragicom.	Unacted	MS
Richards, N.	*Messalina	Tragedy	K's Revels	1640
Rutter, J.	1 The Cid	Tr. Corneille	K. & Q's	1637
Shirley, J.	*St. Patrick for Ireland	Neo-Miracle	Dublin	1640
Suckling, J.	Aglaura	Tragedy	King's	1638
Suckling, J.	*The Sad One	Fragment of Tragicom.	Unacted	1659
Wilde, G.	The Converted Robber	Pastoral	St. John's, Ox.	MS
W., J.	*The Valiant Scot	Chronicle	Unacted ?	1637

1638

Author	Title	Genre	Place	Date
Berkeley, W. (?)	*Cornelia	Tragicom. ?	King's (in 1662)	Lost
Brome, Alex.	*The Cunning Lovers	Comedy	K. & Q's	1654
Brome, R.	*The Antipodes	Comedy	Queen's	1640
Brome, R.	*The Damoiselle	Comedy	K. & Q's ?	1653
Carlell, L.	1 The Passionate Lovers	Tragicom.	King's	1655
Carlell, L.	2 The Passionate Lovers	Tragicom.	King's	1655
Cartwright, W.	*The Siege	Tragicom.	Ch. Church, Ox. ?	1651
Davenant, W.	Britannia Triumphans	Masque	Whitehall	1637[38]
Davenant, W.	Luminalia	Masque	Whitehall	1637[38]
Davenant, W.	The Fair Favorite	Tragicom.	King's ?	1673
Davenant, W.	The Unfortunate Lovers	Tragedy	King's	1643
Ford, J.	The Lady's Trial	Comedy	K. & Q's	1639
Glapthorne, H.	*Argalus and Parthenia	Tragicom.	K. & Q's	1639
Heywood, T.	Porta Pietatis	Civ. Pag.	London	1638
Johnson, W.	Valetudinarium	Lat. Com.	Queen's C., Camb.	MS
Massinger, P.	The King and Subject	Tragedy	King's	Lost
Mayne, J.	*The Amorous War	Tragicom.	Ch. Church, Ox. ?	1648
Mead, R.	*The Combat of Love & Friendship	Tragicom.	Ch. Church, Ox. ?	1654
Nabbes, T.	The Bride	Comedy	K. & Q's	1639
Nabbes, T.	Presentation for the Prince	Entertainment	Court ?	1638
Riley, T. (?)	Cornelianum Dolium	Lat. Com.	Trinity C., Camb. ?	1638
Rutter, J.	*2 The Cid	Tr. Corneille	K. & Q's	1640
Shirley, J.	*The Constant Maid	Comedy	Dublin	1640
Shirley, J.	*The Royal Master	Comedy	Dublin ?; Queen's	1638
Shirley, J.	*St. Albans	Tragedy	Dublin ?	Lost
Suckling, J.	Aglaura (altered)	Tragicom.	King's	1638
Suckling, J.	*The Goblins	Comedy	King's	1646
Anonymous	*The Toy	Comedy ?	Dublin	Lost

1639

Author	Title	Type	Company	Date
Brome, R.	*Tom Hoyden o' Tanton Deane	Comedy	K. & Q's	Lost
Burnell, H.	*Landgartha	Chronicle	Dublin	1641
Cavendish, W.	*The Variety	Comedy	King's	1649
Cokain, A.	*The Obstinate Lady	Tragicom.	Unknown	1657
Cowley, A.	*Naufragium Joculare	Lat. Com.	Trinity C., Camb.	1638[39]
Davenant, W.	The Spanish Lovers	Comedy	King's ?	1673
Freeman, R.	Imperiale	Tragedy	Unacted	1639
Glapthorne, H.	Wit in a Constable	Comedy	K. & Q's	1640
Heywood, T.	Londini Status Pacatus	Civ. Pag.	London	1639
Lower, W.	The Phoenix in her Flames	Tragedy	Unacted ?	1639
Massinger, P.	Alexius, or the Chaste Gallant	Comedy ?	King's	Lost
Nabbes, T.	The Unfortunate Mother	Tragedy	Unacted	1639
Sadler, J.	Masquerade du Ciel	Masque	Unacted	1640
Sharpe, L.	*The Noble Stranger	Tragicom.	Queen's	1640
Shirley, J.	The Politician	Tragedy	Dublin ?; Queen's	1655
Shirley, J.	The Gentleman of Venice	Tragicom.	Dublin ?; Queen's	1655
Suckling, J.	Brennoralt	Tragedy	King's	[1640 ?]
Anonymous	The Whore New Vamped	Comedy	Prince Charles's	Lost
Anonymous	*The World	Unknown	K. & Q's	Lost
Anon. ("J. D.")	Knave in Grain	Comedy	Prince Charles's	1640

1640

Author	Title	Type	Company	Date
Brome, R.	*The Jewish Gentleman	Comedy ?	K. & Q's ?	Lost
Brome, R.	*Christianetta	Unknown	K. & Q's ?	Lost
Brome, R.	*The Lovesick Court	Tragicom.	K. & Q's ?	1659
Cavendish, W.	The Country Captain	Comedy	King's	1649
Chamberlain, R.	The Swaggering Damsel	Comedy	Unacted ?	1640
Cokain, A.	Masque at Bretby	Masque	Chesterfield's	1658
Davenant, W.	Salmacida Spolia	Masque	Whitehall	1639[40]
Fane, M.	Raguaillo D'Oceano	Masque	Apthorpe	MS

Author	Title	Genre	Theatre	Date
Glapthorne, H. (?)	*Revenge for Honor	Tragedy	Unknown	1654
Glapthorne, H.	*The Vestal	Unknown	Unknown	Lost
Gough, J.	The Strange Discovery	Tragicom.	Unacted	1640
Habington, W.	The Queen of Aragon	Tragicom.	King's	1640
Harding, S.	Sicily and Naples	Tragedy	Unacted ?	1640
Heywood, T.	*Love's Masterpiece	Comedy	Unknown	Lost
Jordan, T.	*Love Hath Found out his Eyes	Comedy	Unknown	Lost
Massinger, P.	Fair Anchoress of Pausilippo	Tragicom. ?	King's	Lost
Sandys, G.	Christ's Passion	Tr. de Groot	Unacted	1640
Shirley, J.	The Doubtful Heir	Tragicom.	Dublin ; & King's	1653
Shirley, J.	The Imposture	Tragicom.	King's	1653
"Shirley, J."	*Arcadia (old play falsely ascribed ?)	Tragicom.	Unknown	1640
Snelling, T.	Thibaldus	Lat. Trag.	Oxford	1640
Anonymous	*The Ghost	Comedy	Prince Charles's ?	1653

1641

Author	Title	Genre	Theatre	Date
Brathwaite, R.	Mercurius Britannicus	Political Satire	Unacted ?	1641
Brome, R.	A Jovial Crew	Comedy	K. & Q's	1652
Denham, J.	The Sophy	Tragedy	King's	1642
Fane, M.	Candy Restored	Polit. Alleg.	Apthorpe	MS
Jordan, T.	The Walks of Islington and Hogsdon	Comedy	Prince Charles's ?	1657
Killigrew, T.	*The Parson's Wedding	Comedy	K. & Q's ?	1664
Lovelace, R.	*The Soldier	Tragedy	King's ?	Lost
Quarles, F.	*The Virgin Widow	Tragicom.	Unknown	1649
Salisbury, T.	Masque at Knowsley	Masque	Lord Strange's	1926
Shirley, J.	The Brothers	Comedy	King's	1653
Shirley, J.	The Cardinal	Tragedy	King's	1653
Tatham, J. (?)	The Distracted State	Tragedy	Unknown	1651
Tatham, J. (?)	*The Whisperer	Unknown	Unknown	Lost
Taylor, J.	England's Comfort ...	Civ. Pag.	London	1641
Anonymous	Canterbury his Change of Diet	Pol. Satire	Unacted ?	1641

Author	Title	Genre	Location	Status
Anonymous	*England's First Happiness	Unknown	Unknown	Lost
Anonymous	*Parroiall [Pareil ?] of Princes	Unknown	Unknown	Lost
Anonymous	Read and Wonder	Pol. Satire	Unacted ?	1641
	1642			
Cowley, A.	The Guardian	Comedy	Trin. C., Camb.	1650
Fane, M.	The Change	Pol. Alleg.	Unacted ?	MS
Fane, M.	Time's Trick upon the Cards	Moral Alleg.	Apthorpe ?	MS
Jaques, F.	The Queen of Corsica	Tragedy	Unacted ?	MS
Kirke, J. (?)	The Irish Rebellion	Topical Play	Prince Charles's ?	Lost
Peaps, W.	*Love in its Ecstasy	Tragicom.	Unacted ?	1649
Shirley, J.	The Court Secret	Tragicom.	Unacted	1653
Shirley, J.	The Sisters	Comedy	King's	1653
S., J.	*Andromana	Tragedy	Unknown	1660
Anonymous	*Andronicus: Impiety's Long Success	Tragedy	Unacted	1661
Anonymous	*The Cyprian Conqueror	Comedy	Unacted ?	MS
	1643			
Bernard, S. (?)	*Andronicus: Impiety's Long Success	Tragedy	Oxford ?	1661
Fane, M. (?)	Time's Triumph	Moral Alleg.	Unacted ?	MS
Milton, J. (?)	Tyrannical Government Anatomized	Tr. Buchanan's Baptistes	Unacted	1643
Anonymous	The Cruel War (Extant?)	Tragedy	Unknown	1643 ?
Anonymous	*Fraus Pia	Lat. Com.	Unknown	MS
	1644			
Fane, M.	Virtue's Triumph	Moral Alleg.	Unacted ?	MS
Anonymous	Titus	Biblical Moral	Jesuit's College, Kilken..y	1644
	1645			
Burkhead, H.	Cola's Fury, or Lirenda's Misery	War Allegory	Unacted	1646
Cavendish, J. & Brackley, E.	*The Concealed Fancies	Comedy	Unacted ?	1931

Author	Title	Genre		Date
Cavendish, J. & Brackley, E.	*A Pastoral	Pastoral	Unacted ?	MS
Fane, M.	*Don Phoeba's Triumph	Masque	Unacted ?	MS
Shirley, J.	*Triumph of Beauty	Masque	Acted privately	1646
		1646		
Burroughs	*The Fatal Friendship	Tragedy	Unknown	Lost
Killigrew, T.	*The Pilgrim	Tragedy	English Co. in Paris ?	1664
		1647		
Baron, R.	Deorum Dona	Masque	Unacted	1647
Baron, R.	Gripus and Hegio	Pastoral	Unacted	1647
Fanshawe, R.	The Faithful Shepherd	Tr. Guarini	Unacted	1647
Mason, J.	The Combat of Caps	Academic Alleg.	Mason's School	1648
Nedham, M.	The Levelers Leveled	Pol. Satire	Unacted ?	1647
Sheppard, S.	The Committee Man Curried	Pol. Satire	Unacted ?	1647
Anonymous	News out of the West	Com. Interlude	Unknown	1647
Anonymous	Scottish Politic Presbyter	Pol. Satire	Unacted ?	1647
		1648		
Sherburne, E.	Medea	Tr. Seneca	Unacted	1648
Anonymous	Crafty Cromwell	Pol. Satire	Unacted ?	1648
Anonymous	Kentish Fair	Pol. Satire	Unacted ?	1648
Anonymous	Mistress Parliament	Pol. Satire	Unacted ?	1648
Anonymous	Cuckows Nest at Westminster	Pol. Satire	Unacted ?	1648
Anonymous	A Key to the Cabinet of Parliament	Pol. Satire	Unacted ?	1648
Anonymous	Women will have their Will	Pol. Satire	Unacted ?	1648
		1649		
Wase, C.	Electra	Tr. Sophocles	Unacted	1649
B, T.	The Rebellion of Naples	Tragedy	Unacted	1649
Anonymous	The Famous Tragedy of King Charles I	Chronicle	Unacted	1649

Author	Title	Type	Status	Date
Anonymous	A New Bull Baiting	Pol. Satire	Unacted ?	1649
Anonymous	A Bartholomew Fairing	Pol. Satire	Unacted ?	1649
Anonymous	The Disease of the House	Pol. Satire	Unacted ?	1649
Anonymous	New Market Fair	Pol. Satire	Unacted ?	1649
Anonymous	*Cyprian Conqueror	Comedy	Unacted ?	MS
				1650
Cartwright, G.	*The Heroic Lover	Tragicom.	Unacted ?	1661
Fane, M.	De Pugna Animi	Moral Alleg.	Unacted ?	MS
Flecknoe, R.	Love in its Infancy	Past. Tragicom.	Berseel	Lost
Garfield, B.	The Unfortunate Fortunate	Tragicom.	Unacted ?	Lost
Killigrew, T.	1 Cicilia and Clorinda	Tragicom.	Unacted	1664
Killigrew, T.	2 Cicilia and Clorinda	Tragicom.	Unacted	1664
Waterhouse, D.	Cleophilus	Lat. Com.	Unacted	1650
Anonymous	*Love's Changelings Change	Tragicom.	Unacted ?	MS
Anonymous	*Love's Victory	Pastoral	Unacted ?	1853
Anonymous	*The White Ethiopian	Tragicom.	Unacted ?	MS
				1651
Denny, W.	The Shepherd's Holiday	Pastoral	Unacted	1870
Prestwich, E.	Hippolytus	Tr. Seneca	Unacted	1651
Willan, L.	Astrea, or True Love's Mirror	Tragicom.	Unacted	1651
Anonymous	Marcus Tullius Cicero	Tragedy	Unacted	1651
Anonymous	Jovial Crew	Pol. Satire	Unacted ?	1651
Anonymous	Prince of Priggs Revels	Com. Interlude	Unacted ?	1651
				1652
Goldsmith, F.	Sophompaneas, or Joseph	Tr. Grotius	Unacted	1652
Killigrew, T.	1 Bellamira, her Dream	Tragicom.	Unacted	1664
Killigrew, T.	2 Bellamira, her Dream	Tragicom.	Unacted	1664

Author	Title	Type	Status	Date
Manuche, C.	The Just General	Tragicom.	Unacted	1652
Manuche, C.	The Loyal Lovers	Tragicom.	Unacted	1652
	The Feast	Comedy		
	Leontius, King of Cyprus	Tragedy		
Manuche, C. Plays composed circa 1652-64	The Captives	Tr. Plautus ?	Privately Acted ?	MS
	Marianni	Tragedy		
	Agamemnon	Trag. Frag.		
	The Mandrake	Com. Frag.		
	The Banished Shepherdess	Pastoral		
Manuche, C. (?)	The Bastard	Tragedy	Unacted ?	1652
Tatham, J.	Scot's Figaries	Comedy	Unacted	1652
Anonymous	Simo	Lat. Com.	Unacted	1652

1653

Author	Title	Type	Status	Date
Cox, R.	John Swabber	Droll	Acted at Red Bull	[1655]
Cox, R. Composed or adapted between 1653-55	Actaeon and Diana	Pastoral Interl.	Acted at Red Bull, etc.	[1655]
	Œnone	Pastoral Interl.		[1655]
	Singing Simpkin	Jig		[1655]
	Simpleton the Smith	Droll		1656
Possibly also presented by Cox during same period	The Black Man (a jig)			
	Diphilo and Granida	Drolls	Acted at Red Bull, etc. ?	1673
	King Ahasuerus			
	King Solomon's Wisdom			
	Philetis and Constantia			
	Venus and Adonis			

1654

Author	Title	Type	Status	Date
Shirley, J.	Cupid and Death	Moral Masque	Privately by Gentlemen	1653
Stapylton, R.	The Royal Choice	Tragicom. ?	Unknown	Lost
Fanshave, R.	To Love only for Love's Sake	Tr. Mendoza	Unacted	1670

Flecknoe, R.	Love's Dominion	Tragicom.	Unacted	1654
Howell, J.	Nuptials of Peleus and Thetis	Tr. French Entert.	Paris	1654
Jordan, T.	Cupid his Coronation	Masque	A girl's school	MS
Killigrew, T.	1 Thomaso, or The Wanderer	Comedy	Unacted	1664
Killigrew, T.	2 Thomaso, or The Wanderer	Comedy	Unacted	1664
R., T.	The Extravagant Shepherd	Tr. T. Corneille	Unacted	1664
Anonymous	*The Gossip's Brawl	Com. Interlude	Outside London	1651[55 ?]
Anonymous	The New Brawl	Com. Interlude	Unacted ?	1654
Anonymous	True Tragicom. [of Robert Carr]	Thesis Play	Unacted	MS

1655

Baron, R.	Mirza	Tragedy	Unacted	1655
Gayton, E.	Charity Triumphant	Civ. Pag.	London	1655
Lower, W.	Polyeuctus	Tr. Corneille	Unacted ?	1655
Lower, W.	*Scævoli	Unknown	Unknown	Lost
Stanley, T.	The Clouds	Tr. Aristophanes	Unacted	1655

1656

Davenant, W.	The First Day's Entertainment at Rutland H.	Declamations	"Opera" Co.	1657
Davenant, W.	*Satirical Declamations	Same as above ?	"Opera" Co. ?	Lost
Davenant, W.	*The Athenian's Reception of Phocian	Entertainment	"Opera" Co. ?	Lost
Davenant, W.	1 The Siege of Rhodes	Tragicom.	"Opera" Co.	1656
Holland, S.	*Cupid and Psyche	Burlesque Masque	Unacted	Lost
Holland, S.	*Enchanted Grove (2 parts)	Masque	Unknown	Lost
Holland, S.	Venus and Adonis	Burlesque Masque	Unacted	1656
Lower, W.	Horatius	Tr. Corneille	Unacted ?	1656
Prestwich, E.	The Hectors	Comedy	Unacted	1656
——, Samuel	The Governor	Tragicom.	Unacted ?	MS
B., J. (Bulteel?)	London's Triumph	Civ. Pag.	London	1656

Author	Title	Type	Acting	Date
Brewer, T.	A Knot of Fools	Droll	Unknown	1657
D'Ouvilley, G.	The False Favorite Disgraced	Tragicom.	Unacted	1657
Jordan, T.	Fancy's Festivals	Medley	Privated Acted	1657
Jordan, T.	*Money is an Ass	Comedy	Jordan's Men	1668
Lower, W.	Don Japhet of Armenia	Tr. Sarron	Unacted ?	MS
Lower, W.	*The Three Dorothies	Tr. Sarron	Unacted ?	MS
Meriton, T.	The Chaste Virgin	Tragicom. ?	Unacted	Lost
Meriton, T.	The Several Affairs	Comedy	Unacted	Lost
Talbot, G.	Filli di Sciro	Tr. Bonarelli	Unacted	MS
Tatham, J.	London's Triumph	Civ. Pag.	London	1657

1657

Author	Title	Type	Acting	Date
Cavendish, M. Composed between c. 1653 and 1662	The Apocryphal Ladies	Unique	Unacted	1662
	Bell in Campo			
	The Comical Hash			
	The Female Academy			
	The Lady Contemplation			
	Love's Adventures			
	The Matrimony Trouble			
	Nature's Three Daughters			
	The Public Wooing			
	The Religious			
	The Several Wits			
	The Unnatural Tragedy			
	The Wits' Cabal			
	Youth's Glory and Death's Banquet			
Anonymous	*The Comical Hist. of Don Quixote	Burlesque ?	Unacted ?	Lost

1658

Author	Title	Type	Acting	Date
Chamberlaine, W.	Love's Victory	Tragicom.	Unacted	1658
Davenant, W.	Cruelty of the Spaniards in Peru	Unique	"Opera" Co.	1658
Davenant, W.	*2 History of Sir F. Drake	(Same as above ?)	"Opera" Co.	Lost ?

Author	Title	Type	Acted	Date
Davenant, W.	*1 History of Sir F. Drake	Operatic Play	"Opera" Co.	1659
Fane, M.	*Ladrones, or the Robbers' Island	Unknown	Unknown	Lost
Fanshawe, R.	La Fida Pastora	Lat. Tr. Fletcher	Unacted	1658
Lower, W.	The Enchanted Lovers	Tragicom.	Unacted ?	1658
Meriton, T.	Love and War	Tragicom.	Acted Provately	1658
Meriton, T.	The Wandering Lover	Tragicom.	Acted Privately ?	1658
Shirley, J.	*Contention of Ajax & Ulysses	Entertainment	Acted Privately	1659
Swinhoe, G.	The Unhappy Fair Irene	Tragedy	Unacted ?	1658
Tatham, J.	London's Triumph	Civ. Pag.	London	1658
W[illan], L.	Orgula	Tragedy	Unacted	1658
	1659			
Burkhead, H. (?)	The Female Rebellion	Tragicom.	Unacted	1872
Davenant, W.	*2 The Siege of Rhodes	Tragicom.	"Opera" Co. ?	1663
Flecknoe, R.	Marriage of Oceanus and Britannia	Masque	Unknown	1659 ?
Kirkham, R. (?)	Alfred, or Right Reenthroned	Tragicom.	Unacted	MS
Lower, W.	The Noble Ingratitude	Tr. Quinault	Unacted ?	1659
Neville, H.	Shuffling, Cutting & Dealing	Pol. Satire	Unacted ?	1659
Tatham, J.	London's Triumph	Civ. Pag.	London	1659
B., H. H.	The World's Idol	Tr. Aristophanes	Unacted	1659
Anonymous	Lady Alimony	Comedy	Unacted	1659
Anonymous	*The London Chanticleers	Com. Interlude	Acted outside London	1659
Anonymous	The Florentine Ladies	Comedy	Acted Privately	Lost
	1660			
Dancer, J.	Aminta	Tr. Tasso	Unacted	1660
Forde, T.	Love's Labyrinth	Tragicom.	Unacted	1660
Howard, R.	The Blind Lady	Tragicom.	Unacted	1660
Jordan, T.	Bacchus Festival	Entertainment	Vintners' Hall	1660

Author	Title	Type	Place	Date
Jordan, T.	Speech to General Monk	Entertainments	Vintners' Hall	[1660]
	Speech to General Monk		Fishmongers' Hall	1660
	Speech to General Monk		Clothworkers' Hall	[1660]
	Speech to General Monk		Drapers' Hall	1660
	Speech to General Monk		Skinners' Hall	[1660]
	Speech to General Monk		Goldsmiths' Hall	1660
Lower, W.	The Amorous Fantasme	Tr. Quinault	Unacted ?	1660
Pordage, S.	Troades	Tr. Seneca	Unacted	1660
Sadler, A.	The Subject's Joy for the King's Restoration	Pol. Allegory	Unacted	1660
Tatham, J.	The Royal Oak	Civ. Pag.	London	1660
Tatham, J.	The Rump	Topical Play	At Dorset Court	1660
Thomson, T.	*The English Rogue	Comedy	Unknown	1668
R., W.	*The Christmas Ordinary	Comedy	Trinity C., Ox.	1683
Anonymous	Cromwell's Conspiracy	Pol. Satire	Unacted	1660
Anonymous	Life and Death of Mrs. Rump	Pol. Satire	Unacted	1660
Anonymous	A Phanatic Play	Pol. Satire	Unacted	1660
Anonymous	The Tragical Actors	Pol. Satire	Unacted	[1660]

1661

Author	Title	Type	Place	Date
Cowley, A.	Cutter of Coleman Street	Comedy	"Duke's"	1663
Flecknoe, R.	Erminia	Tragicom.	Unacted	1661
Fountain, J.	The Rewards of Virtue	Tragicom.	Unacted	1661
Jordan, J.	The New Medley (part of Bacchus Festival ?)	Jig	Unknown	1661
Kirkman, F. (?)	The Presbyterian Lash	Topical Play	Unacted	1661
Kirkman, F. (?)	Bottom the Weaver (from Midsummer Night's Dream)	Droll	Unacted ?	1661
Ogilby, J.	Relation of his Majesty's Entertainment	Des. of Coronation	London	1661
Tatham, J.	Neptune's Address	Coronation Ent.	London	1661
Tatham, J.	London's Triumphs	Civ. Pag.	London	1661
Thomson, T.	The Life of Mother Shipton	Comedy	Unknown	[1661]
"J., B."	Guy of Warwick	Redaction of old Chronicle ?	Unacted ?	1661

Author	Title	Type	Theatre	Year
Anonymous	Hewson Reduced	Pol. Satire	Unacted	1661
Anonymous	Hell's Higher Court of Justice	Pol. Satire	Unacted	1661
Anonymous	*The Liar	Comedy	King's	1661 ?
Anonymous	Love's Quarrel	Tragicom. ?	"Duke's"	Lost
Anonymous	Robinhood, and his Crew of Soldiers	Topical Play	Unacted ?	1661

1662

Author	Title	Type	Theatre	Year
Boyle, R.	The General [later Altemira]	Tragicom.	Dublin	1702
Codrington, Rob.	Ignoramus	Tr. Ruggles	Unacted	1662
Clerke, W.	Marciano	Tragicom.	Edinburgh	1663
Cokain, A.	The Tragedy of Ovid	Tragedy	Unacted	1662
Davenant, W.	Law Against Lovers	Ad. of Shakes.	Duke's	1673
Howard, R.	The Committee	Comedy	King's	1665
Howard, R.	The Surprisal	Tragicom.	King's	1665
Killigrew, W.	Selindra	Tragicom.	King's	1664

Kirkman, F. (?)

The Bouncing Knight (from S.'s 1 Hen. IV)
The Bubble (from Cooke's Green's Tu Quoque)
Bumpkin (from Cox's Actæon and Diana)
The Club-Men (from B. & F.'s Philaster)
Doctors of Dull-head College (from F.'s Mons. Thomas)
An Equal Match (from F.'s Rule a Wife)
The False Heir (from F.'s Scornful Lady)
Forced Valor (from F.'s Hum. Lieutenant)
The Grave-Makers (from S.'s Hamlet)
Hobbinol (from Cox's Œnone)
The Imperick (from J.'s Alchemist)
The Invisible Smirk (from Two Merry Milk-maids)
Jenkin's Love-Course (from Shirley's Love Tricks)

— Drolls, offered for acting — 1662 & 1673

Author	Title	Type	Theatre / Note	Date
Kirkman, F. (?)	The Lame Common-wealth (from F.'s Beggar's Bush)			
	The Landlady (from B. & F.'s Maid's Trag)			
	The Loyal Citizens (from F.'s Cupid's Rev.)	Drolls, offered for acting		1662 & 1673
	Monsieur Galliard (from Newcastle's Variety)			
	A Prince in Conceit (from Shirley's Opportunity)			
	The Sexton (from F.'s Spanish Curate)			
	The Stallion (from F.'s Custom of the Country)			
	The Surprise (from F.'s Maid in the Mill)			
	The Three Merry Boys (from F.'s Bloody Bro.)			
	The Cheater Cheated (from Marston's Dut. Court.)			
	Wiltshire Tom (from King and Q.'s Ent. at Rich.)			
Neville, R.	The Poor Scholar	Comedy	Unacted ?	1662
Parkhurst, F.	Ignoramus	Tr. Ruggles	Duke's	MS
Porter, T.	The Villain	Tragedy	Duke's	1663
Tatham, J.	Aqua Triumphalis	Water Pag.	Thames	1662
Tatham, J.	London's Triumph	Civ. Pag.	London	1662
Anonymous	The Faithful Virgins	Tragicom.	Duke's	MS
Anonymous	New Made Nobleman	Comedy	at Red Bull	Lost
Anonymous	The Renegado	Adapt. Massinger	Unknown	MS

1663

Author	Title	Type	Theatre / Note	Date
Davenant, W.	Macbeth	Ad. Shakespeare	Duke's	1674
Davenant, W.	Playhouse to be Let	Comic Medley	Duke's	1673
Digby, G.	*Elvira	Adapt. Calderón	Duke's	1667
Dryden, J.	The Wild Gallant	Comedy	King's	1669
Evelyn, J.	Thyrsander	Unknown	Unacted	Lost
Green, A.	The Politician Cheated	Comedy	Unacted	1663
Head, R.	Hic et Ubique	Comedy	Acted privately	1663

Author	Title	Type	Theatre	Date
Hoole, C.	The Eunuch	Tr. Terence	Unacted	1663
Howard, J.	The English Monsieur	Comedy	King's	1674
Jordan, I. (T.?)	A New Droll, or the Counter Scuffle (same as New Medley ?)	Droll	Unknown	1663
Killigrew, W.	*Ormasdes	Tragicom.	Unacted ?	1664
Killigrew, W.	*Pandora	Comedy	Duke's	1664
Phillips, C.	Pompey	Tr. Corneille	Dublin	1663
Porter, T.	A Witty Combat	Topical Play	Duke's ?	1663
Rhodes, R.	Flora's Vagaries	Comedy	King's	1670
Southland, T.	Love a la Mode	Comedy	Middlesex-House	1663
Stapylton, R.	The Slighted Maid	Tragicom.	Duke's	1663
Stapylton, R.	The Step-Mother	Tragicom.	Duke's	1664
Tatham, J.	Londinium Triumphans	Civ. Pag.	London	1663
Tuke, S.	The Adventures of Five Hours	Adapt. Cœllo	Duke's	1663
Wilson, J.	The Cheats	Comedy	King's	1664
Anonymous	The Exposure	Comedy ?	King's	Lost
Anonymous	Heraclius	Tr. Corneille	Duke's	Lost
Anonymous	School-Play	Academic Moral	A Middlesex Sch.	1664
Anonymous	The Unfortunate Usurper	Tragedy	Unacted	1663
Anonymous	Universal Motion	Entertainment	Lincoln's Inn	1662 [63]
Anonymous	The Wandering Whore's Complaint (Extant?)	Comedy	Unacted ?	1663 ?

1664

Author	Title	Type	Theatre	Date
Boyle, R.	History of Henry the Fifth	Tragicom.	Duke's	1668
Carlell, L.	Heraclius	Tr. Corneille	Unacted	1664
Cary, H.	The Marriage Night	Tragicom.	Duke's ?	1664
Davenant, W.	*The Rivals	Ad. Two Nob. Kin.	Duke's	1668
Digby, G.	*Worse and Worse	Adapt. Calderón	Duke's	Lost
Dryden, J.	The Rival Ladies	Tragicom.	King's	1664
Etherege, G.	The Comical Revenge	Comedy	Duke's	1664
Flecknoe, R.	Love's Kingdom	Tragicom.	Duke's	1664

Author	Title	Type	Theatre	Date
Holden, J. (?)	The German Princess	Comedy ?	Duke's	Lost
Howard, E.	The Usurper	Tragedy	King's	1668
Howard, J.	*Romeo and Juliet	Adapt. Shakes.	Duke's	Lost
Howard, R.	*The Vestal Virgin	Tragedy & Tragicom.	King's	1665
Howard, R. & Dryden	The Indian Queen	Tragicom.	King's	1665
Jordan, T.	The Cheaters Cheated	Jig	"For Sheriffs of London"	1664
Porter, T.	*The Carnival	Comedy	King's	1664
Southland, T. (?)	The Ungrateful Favorite	Tragedy	Unacted	1664
Tatham, J.	London's Triumphs	Civ. Pag.	London	1664
Waller, E., etc.	*Pompey the Great	Tr. Corneille	Duke's	1664
Waller, E.	*The Maid's Tragedy	Ad. Beau. & Flet.	Unknown	1690
Wilson, J.	Andronicus Comnenius	Tragedy	Unacted	1664
Anonymous	Irena	Tragedy	Unacted	1664
Anonymous	Knavery in all Trades	Comedy	By Apprentices	1664
Anonymous	The Labyrinth	Comedy	King's	Lost

1665

Author	Title	Type	Theatre	Date
Boyle, R.	The Widow	Comedy	Unknown	Lost
Boyle, R.	Mustapha	Tragedy	Duke's	1668
Brathwait, R.	Regicidium	Lat. Topical P.	Unacted	1665
Bulteel, J.	Amorous Orantus	Adapt. Corneille	Unknown	1665
Cavendish, M. Composed 1662-68	The Blazing World / The Bridals / The Convent of Pleasure / The Presence / The Sociable Companions	Unique	Unacted	1668
Cotton, C.	*Horace	Tr. Corneille	Unacted	1671
Digby, G.	*'Tis Better than it Was	Adapt. Calderón	Duke's ?	Lost
Dryden, J.	The Indian Emperor	Tragedy	King's	1667
Holden, J.	*The Ghosts	Comedy	Duke's	Lost
Killigrew, W.	*The Siege of Urbin	Tragicom.	Unacted ?	1666

Author	Title	Genre	Theatre	Year
Lacy, J.	*The Old Troop	Comedy	King's	1672
Stroud	*All Plot, or the Disguises	Comedy	Duke's	Lost
Wilson, J.	The Projectors	Comedy	Unacted ?	1665
	1666			
Carpenter, R.	*Pragmatical Jesuit new Leavened	Top. Satire	Unacted	[1666 ?]
Hoadley, S. (?)	The War of Grammar	School Alleg.	Cranebrook Sch.	MS
	1667			
Bailey, A.	The Spightful Sister	Comedy	Unacted ?	1667
Boyle, R.	The Black Prince	Tragicom.	King's	1669
Cavendish, W.	The Humorous Lovers	Comedy	Duke's	1677
(& Shadwell ?)				
Davenant, W. (?)	*Hamlet	Ad. Shakespeare	Duke's	1676
Davenant, W., & Dryden	The Tempest	Ad. Shakespeare	Duke's	1670
Denham, J.	Horace	Tr. Corneille	King's	1669
(completing Phillips, C.)				
Dover, J.	The Roman Generals	Tragedy	Unacted	1667
Dryden, J.	Secret Love	Tragicom.	King's	1668
Dryden, J.,	Sir Martin Mar-all	Comedy	Duke's	1668
& Cavendish, W.	Damoiselles a la Mode	Ad. Molière	Unacted ?	1667
Flecknoe, R.	*Physician against his Will	Ad. Molière	Unacted ?	Lost
Flecknoe, R.	The Change of Crowns	Tragicom.	King's	Lost
Howard, E.	*The London Gentleman	Comedy	King's ?	Lost
Howard, E.	All Mistaken	Tragicom.	King's	1672
Howard, J.	Sauny the Scot, or the Taming of the Shrew	Ad. Shakespeare	King's	1698
Lacy, J.	Tarugo's Wiles	Ad. Moréto y Cabana	Duke's	1668
St. Serfe, T.	The Chances	Ad. Fletcher	King's	1682
Villiers, G.	The Amazon Queen	Tragicom.	Unacted	1667
Weston, J.	St. Cicely or the Converted Twins	Ad. of old play ?	Unacted ?	1667
M. M. [Medbourne ?]				

1668

Author	Title	Type	Theatre	Date
Boyle, R.	Tryphon	Tragicom.	Duke's	1669
Davenant, W.	The Man's the Master	Tr. Scarron	Duke's	1669
Dryden, J.	An Evening's Love	Comedy	King's	1671
Etherege, G.	She Would if She Could	Comedy	Duke's	1668
Howard, R.	The Duke of Lerma	Tragicom.	King's	1668
Sedley, C.	The Mulberry-Garden	Comedy	King's	1668
Shadwell, T.	The Sullen Lovers	Comedy	Duke's	1668
Anonymous	Ladies a la Mode (identical with Flecknoe's Damoiselles a la Mode?)	Comedy	King's	1667 ?
Anonymous	The Feigned Astrologer	Ad. T. Corneille	Unacted ?	1668

1669

Author	Title	Type	Theatre	Date
Betterton, T. (?)	Appius and Virgina	Ad. Webster	Duke's	1670
Boothby, F.	Marcelia, or the Treacherous Friend	Tragicom.	King's	1670
Boyle, R.	Guzman	Comedy	Duke's	1693
Caryl, J.	Sir Salomon	Ad. Molière	Duke's	1671
Dryden, J.	Tyrannic Love	Tragedy	King's	1670
Howard, R. & Villiers, G.	The Country Gentleman	Comedy	"Forbidden"	Lost
Killigrew, W. (?)	The Imperial Tragedy	Tragedy	Barbican Nursery	1669
Lacy, J.	The Dumb Lady	Ad. Molière	King's	1672
Shadwell, T.	The Royal Shepherdess	Ad. Fountain	Duke's	1669
Stapyiton, R.	Hero and Leander	Tragedy	Unacted	1669
Taylor, S.	The Serenade, or Disappointment	Comedy ?	Unacted	Lost
Anonymous	The Generous Portugals	Ad. Fletcher	King's	1669
Anonymous	The Heiress	Comedy	King's	Lost
Anonymous	Pluto Furens & Vinctus	Satire	Unacted	1669

1626—1669

ADDENDA

SOME of the following manuscript plays may belong to the period covered by the above play-list: *The Disloyal Favorite* (Bodl., Rawl., D. 1361, ff. 285-306); *The Lover's Stratagem* (Bodl., MS. Rawl. Poet. 18); *Jugurtha, or the Faithless Cousin German* (Bodl., Rawl. Poet. 195); *Sisigambis, Queen of Syracuse* (Bodl., Rawl., Poet. 167); Titleless pastorals (B.M. Add. MS. 29, 496); Titleless Comedy (Brit. Mus. MS. Sloane 1828, ff. 1-45) Titleless Comedy (Bodl., Rawl., C. 923, ff. 24 *seq.*); Titleless Comedy (Bodl., Rawl., Poet. 93); Christmas Ent. (Bodl., Rawl. D. 1361, ff. 306-29); Titleless Play (B. M. Add. MS. 5001). To these may be added the titles of the following manuscript Latin plays, also of uncertain date: *Gallomyomachia* (B. M., Harl. 5664, Art. 5); *Sanctus Edwardus Confessor* (Magdalene Col., C, 2. 22); *Nottola* (Bodl., Douce 47); *Perfidius Hetruscus* (Bodl., Rawl. C 787); *Caracalla* (Bodl., Rawl. C 590).

Titles of certain non-extant pieces have been omitted from the above play-list because of the scanty data concerning them. In a book of airs (B. M. Add. MS. 10444) are many titles, some of which apparently belong to lost Caroline masques. Among the titles of the Warburton manuscripts, the following may pertain to mid-seventeenth century plays: *The Lovers of Ludgate, The Spanish Purchase* (Puecas?) *The Fairy Queen, Orpheus, Demetrius and Marina.* In Archer's play list of 1656 some of the following titles of lost plays probably belong to publications of the mid-century: *Patient Grissel, Impatient Grissel; Ortenus a Tragedy, Ortenus a Comedy, English Arcadia, Cleopatra, Bays, Mother Rumming.* In Rogers and Ley's list, 1656, is the additional title: *Play of the Netherlands.* Advertised between 1656 and 1661 were the following titles: *Chaste Woman Against her Will, The Tooth-drawer, King Lewis XI, The Fool Transformed, The Fair Spanish Captive, The French Schoolmaster.* A few additional titles of lost plays mentioned by Malone (*Plays and Poems of Shakespeare,* II, 438-439) may also have come from advertisements appended to seventeenth century books: *Love Yields to Honor, The Noble Friend, Titirus and Galatea, The Tragedy of Heildebrand.* The present author believes most of the following titles, entered in the Stationers' Register Nov. 29, 1653, belong to plays written during the decade preceding the closing of the theatres: *The Politic Bankrupt, The King's Mistress, The Countryman, The Noble Ravishers, The Florentine Friend, The Divorce, The Conceits, Castara or Cruelty without Lust, The Bondwoman, The Black Wedding, The Arraignment of Love, Pity the Maid, Salisbury Plain, The Supposed Inconstancy, The Woman's Law, the Woman's Masterpiece;* entered Sept. 9, 1653, were *The King's Mistress,* and *The Politic Bankrupt.* For the speculation on the various lost, anonymous plays, of uncertain date, enumerated above, see under titles in G. M. Sibley, *The Lost Plays and Masques,* (Cornell Univ. Press, 1933).

INDEX